ADMINISTERING THE SCHOOL LIBRARY MEDIA CENTER

ADMINISTERING THE SCHOOL LIBRARY MEDIA CENTER

John T. Gillespie
Diana L. Spirt

R. R. BOWKER COMPANY
NEW YORK AND LONDON, 1983

Published by R. R. Bowker Company,
a division of Reed Publishing (USA) Inc.
Copyright © 1983 by Reed Publishing (USA) Inc.
All rights reserved
Printed and bound in the United States of America

Library of Congress Cataloging in Publication Data

Gillespie, John Thomas, 1928–
    Administering the school library media center.

    Previous ed. published as: Creating a school media
program 1973.
    Bibliography: p.
    Includes index.
    1. Instructional materials centers.   I. Spirt,
Diana L.   II. Title.
Z675.S3G52   1983   027.8   83-2807
ISBN 0-8352-1514-8

CONTENTS

PREFACE   ix

1. SCHOOL LIBRARY TO MEDIA CENTER   1

   The Era of the School District Library/ The Genesis of
   the School Library/ The Age of Development/ The
   Emergence of the Media Center

2. FUNCTIONS OF THE SCHOOL LIBRARY
   MEDIA CENTER   19

   Services/ Functions Related to User Activities/
   Resources/ Converting a School Library into a Media
   Center/ For Further Reading

3. DEVELOPING A SCHOOL LIBRARY
   MEDIA CENTER PROGRAM   33

   The School Library Media Specialist and the Curriculum/
   The Instructional Program/ Publicizing the School Library
   Media Center/ Hours of Service and Attendance/ Public
   Relations/ Evaluating the Program/ For Further Reading

4. BUDGET   68

   Funding and Service/ Collecting Background Information/
   Budgeting Levels/ Cost-Allocation Methods/ Budgeting
   Systems/ For Further Reading

5. STAFF   100

Personnel Categories/ How Big a Staff?/ Representative
Center Tasks/ Job Descriptions/ Recruitment and Selection/
Supervision (Staff Evaluation)/ Manuals/ Future/
For Further Reading

6. FACILITIES   135

Planning/ Space/ Facilities for Major Functions/
Environmental Elements/ Furnishings/ Facilities for
Special Media Services/ For Further Reading

7. MEDIA SELECTION: POLICIES AND PROCEDURES   156

Background Knowledge/ Organizing the Media Selection
Program/ Writing a Media Selection Policy Statement/
Standards/ Selection Aids/ Practical Points to Aid
Selection/ Censorship and the School Library Media
Center/ For Further Reading

8. MEDIA SELECTION: CRITERIA AND
   SELECTION AIDS   182

General Criteria for Selecting Educational Materials/
Specific Criteria for Selecting Educational Materials/
General Criteria for Selecting Audiovisual Equipment/
Specific Criteria for Selecting Audiovisual Equipment/
Selection Aids for Educational Materials/ Selection
Aids for Equipment

9. COMPUTERS AND THE SCHOOL LIBRARY
   MEDIA CENTER   238

Computers and Their Operations/ Computer Use in
Schools/ Computer Use in the Center/ Information Utilities/
Basic Considerations in Setting up a Computer System/
Periodicals on Computers/ Directions for the Future/ For
Further Reading

10. ACQUISITION AND ORGANIZATION   266

Bidding/ Purchasing/ Order Processing/ Classification
and Cataloging/ Local Production of Materials/ Copyright
and the School Library Media Center/ For
Further Reading

11. MANAGERIAL CONCERNS   302

   Circulation/ Inventory and Weeding Procedures/
   Maintaining the Collection/ Records and Reports/
   Managing a Book Fair/ For Further Reading

12. NETWORKS AND NETWORKING   322

   Benefits/ Contributions/ Existing Networks and
   Functions/ Problems in Networking/ Evaluating a
   Network/ Implementing the Networking Concept/
   For Further Reading

13. BEYOND THE SINGLE SCHOOL LIBRARY
    MEDIA CENTER   333

   Associations/ Federal and State Agencies and Programs/
   School Library Media Specialist Reading Shelf/ For
   Further Reading

APPENDIX I Directory of State School Library Media
   Center Agencies   351

APPENDIX II Directory of Associations and Agencies   356

APPENDIX III Directory of Selected Library Furniture
   and Supply Houses   363

APPENDIX IV Key Documents   366

INDEX   377

PREFACE

When we began work on the revision of this book, originally published as *Creating a School Media Program* in 1973, we soon discovered that we were adding a great deal of new material but subtracting very little. Not that our prose was ageless, as indeed it was not, but we did find that most of the material written a decade earlier was still valid today. The additions were made primarily to accommodate two contradictory phenomena that we have seen emerge in the past few years. In some library media centers, because of declining financial support, professional personnel are now often asked to perform semiprofessional tasks, such as technical processes that previously may have been handled elsewhere. At the same time, these professionals are exploring and utilizing sophisticated areas in electronic communications. For those reasons, the chapter on acquisition and organization (10) and the chapter on managerial concerns (11) are almost double in size from the first edition, and there are entirely new chapters on computers (9) and networking (12). Additional coverage involves the new Copyright Act and censorship, plus a thorough updating of all material from the first edition.

The information on specific criteria for evaluating materials and equipment has been removed from the appendix, where it was in the first edition, and placed in a separate chapter (8), which now includes lists of basic selection aids. Another new chapter (13), "Beyond the Single School Library Media Center," includes data on key professional organizations, government agencies, lobbying, and important professional tools. All of the material in the four appendixes is new to this edition. Included are directories of state school library media center agencies, relevant associations, and library furniture and supply houses, plus a number of key documents of concern to the school library media specialist. Instead of a central bibliography, the updated reading list has been divided and placed after each chapter. In compiling these lists, emphasis was placed on accessibility of materials.

As in the first edition, background material on the history of the school library has been included, but the focus of the book is on practical considerations for establishing and operating a library media center within a single school. We have concentrated on recent developments in organizing and administering the center, and in so doing we hope to find an audience that includes both media personnel and library school students, as well as others.

Many people have helped in the preparation of this new edition. In particular, we would like to thank the Research Committee of the C. W. Post Center of Long Island University for their support, as well as the help of Ann Sector, Bette VanderWerf, and our understanding editor, Corinne Naden.

John T. Gillespie
Vice President for Academic Affairs

Diana L. Spirt
Professor, Palmer School of Library and Information Science
C. W. Post Center, Long Island University, New York

1

SCHOOL LIBRARY TO MEDIA CENTER

THE ERA OF THE SCHOOL DISTRICT LIBRARY

As early as 1740 Benjamin Franklin included a library in plans for his academy. However, the real beginning of the school library movement in the United States did not occur until almost a century later. New York State, under the leadership of Governor DeWitt Clinton, began the pioneer work. In 1835 the state legislature passed a law allowing school districts to use limited amounts of their tax monies to establish and maintain school libraries. When only a few districts decided to use their funds for this purpose, a second act was passed in 1839 to spur further action; it set aside a sum of $55,000 annually to be given on a matching-fund basis for the establishment of school district libraries. The effects were dramatic. During the school year 1841–1842, for example, more than 200,000 books were added to these collections. Several other states followed New York's leadership and passed similar legislation. In 1837, chiefly through the efforts of Horace Mann, Massachusetts enacted its first school district library law to enable school districts to raise funds for libraries. This law was liberalized in 1842 to give $15 per year from state funds to each school district that could supply a similar amount for library purposes. The Michigan law, also passed in 1837, stipulated that school districts that raised $10 maximum in taxes per year for libraries would be returned a proportion of the fines collected for breaches of the "disturbing the peace" laws! Connecticut followed with legislation in 1839, Rhode Island in 1840. By 1876, 19 states had passed some sort of law designed to promote public school libraries.

Yet the movement to build school district libraries during this period is generally considered a failure. The collections were usually

1

unattractive to children. They contained mainly textbooks or adult materials suitable only for a teacher's use. To capture this new book market, many unscrupulous publishers glutted the market with cheap, poorly written and produced texts, and without competently trained personnel to select library materials, many of these shoddy products found their way into collections. Facilities for housing these collections or the requisite abilities within each school district for organizing and administering them effectively were also insufficient. Consequently, the collections often became scattered; books disappeared and frequently were incorporated into the teacher's personal library. In time disillusionment set in concerning the value of this type of library service, and in many districts the money was diverted into other channels —supplies, equipment, and even teachers' salaries. One evidence of the decline of this movement is that New York State school district libraries in 1853 contained twice as many books as they did in 1890.

Perhaps a more important reason for the demise of the school district library is the growth of public libraries. Legislators as well as many educators began to support the development of a more broadly based agency that would be able to supply library service to more than a small segment of the community. In Massachusetts, for example, the 1837/1842 school library law was repealed in 1850 and replaced the following year by a law providing that tax monies be used to establish and develop public libraries. In time the public library superseded the school district library.

Although the school district library movement was perhaps premature—a phenomenon far in advance of existing social conditions—it is important historically for two reasons: the principle was established that a library facility in a school could have some educational value and a precedent was created for the use of public funds to support these libraries.

THE GENESIS OF THE SCHOOL LIBRARY

The year 1876 is considered the birth date of the modern American library movement. In that year the American Library Association (ALA) was created by librarians (led by Melvil Dewey) who were attending a series of meetings on national library development during the Centennial Exhibition in Philadelphia. The first issue of *Library Journal* also appeared that year, as well as an extensive report, *Public Libraries in the United States of America: Their History, Condition and Management*, issued by the United States Bureau of Education. The report's title is somewhat misleading because the publication also includes information on other types of libraries. According to the report, only 826 secondary school libraries were in existence in the United States (no elementary or grammar school libraries were reported) and their collections totaled only a million volumes.

Dismayed at the condition of school libraries in New York State and the seeming inability of local school districts to improve these conditions, Melvil Dewey, then secretary of the Board of Regents and director of the State Library, and Andrew S. Draper, Superintendent of Public Instruction, drafted a bill that the legislature passed in 1892. This law, a pioneering effort, allowed for the growth of school libraries in New York State and also served as a model for library legislation in other states. As in the 1839 school district library law, the new legislation provided that a single school district could receive monies on a matching-fund basis (no more than $500 per year) for the purchase of library books. In time other schemes were used to appropriate this money, and eventually a formula based on the size of the pupil population in the district became the yardstick. Only books approved by the Department of Public Instruction could be purchased with state funds. Lists of recommended titles were issued periodically, and they consisted of reference books, supplementary reading books, books related to the curriculum, and pedagogical books for use by teachers.

To prevent a reoccurrence of the disastrous ending of the school district library, these collections were intended to remain in the school at all times, but teachers, administrators, and pupils were allowed, on occasion, to borrow a single volume at a time for a period not to exceed two weeks.

A classroom teacher was to serve as school librarian, and by annual reports to the State Superintendent of Public Instruction, these "librarians" were made responsible for the care and upkeep of the collection. Given these rigid regulations, it is easy to see that many schools were discouraged from applying for state funds. That modifications were necessary soon became apparent, and in time they came. Gradually other states passed similar legislation.

In 1892 New York State also formed its School Libraries Division within the Department of Public Instruction. Annual reports from the department show an increased concern with the development of school libraries, and for the first time, in the report of 1900, a tentative standard was issued for libraries in elementary schools:

> A small library is becoming indispensable to the teacher and pupils of the grammar school. In order to give definiteness to this idea of a small library, suppose it to consist of five hundred to one thousand books, containing the best classic stories, poems, biographies, histories, travels, novels, and books of science suitable for the use of children below high school. . . . It is evident that a carefully selected library of the best books of this character should be found in every grammar school.

Other developments indicated an increasing interest in school library development. In 1896, the National Education Association (NEA) created its Library Section partly because of a petition requesting action circulated by John Cotton Dana, then president of ALA, and partly because of the impassioned speech on the importance of libraries in education delivered by Melvil Dewey at an NEA national convention in Buffalo. ALA created a committee to cooperate with NEA's Library Section. (In December 1914, ALA founded its own School Library Section.) In 1900 the first graduate of a library school in the United States to serve as a school librarian was employed at the Erasmus Hall High School in New York City. Several state teachers' associations began developing sections for school librarians. In 1910 New York State once more led the way, this time by creating the High School Library Section within the New York State Teachers Association. That no mention is made of elementary school librarians reflects the absence of any significant development in this area.

At this time the role of the librarian was considered primarily a clerical one, and in schools that hired professional librarians there developed a struggle for recognition of equal status in position and salary for librarians with teachers. New York was one of the first cities to recognize that librarians were essentially teachers rather than clerks. In 1914 its Board of Education adopted regulations that made salaries of qualified high school librarians comparable to those of teachers and also recommended that prospective librarians should be graduates of a one-year course in an approved library school.

Although library schools were often requested to add courses for school librarianship to their curricula, progress in this area was slow. What little professional training was available was supplied usually through courses taught in teacher training institutions and normal schools or by brief summer workshops and institutes usually sponsored by a state education department or a teachers' association.

The statistics for this period show a gradual and encouraging growth in size of school library collections. The actual sorry state of school libraries was revealed, however, in a *Library Journal* article of April 1913 entitled "Development of Secondary School Libraries," in which the author, E. D. Greenman, comments on the status of these collections:

> Most of them are small collections of reference and textbooks, poorly quartered, unclassified and neither cataloged nor readily accessible for constant use. Of the 10,000 public high school librarians in the country at the present time, not more than 250 possess collections containing 3000 volumes or over.

A further indication of how school libraries lagged behind development in other library areas is the national statistic, revealed by M. E. Hall in the *Library Journal* of September 1915, that only 50 trained librarians had been appointed to schools (all secondary) between 1905 and 1915. The sad conclusion is that, although some foundation had been laid during this period for the development of school libraries, most schools had either no libraries or ones that were inadequate in size, staff, and organization.

In addition to the school library operated as an integral part of the school organization, various other structural patterns for supplying library service to children emerged during this period. These often involved attempts to combine public and school library service. The four most important methods were: (1) In rural and remote areas without even public libraries, the state library agency provided traveling or "package" libraries to schools. (2) In urban areas, students used the public library resources exclusively, and liaison between the school and public library was maintained by such devices as visits to the school by professional librarians and placing loan collections in the schools. (3) A branch of the public library was created in the school to supply library service for both the children and adults in the community. In 1895, for example, a public library branch was established in Cleveland's Central High School, and four years later another was set up in a high school in Newark, New Jersey. Unfortunately, these book collections were usually more suited to adults, and often this division of interests resulted in neither population's being served adequately. (4) A system of joint control was established by which a public library branch to be used exclusively by students and teachers was placed in the school, but organized and administered by the staff of the public library. Once more problems arose involving the divided loyalties of the librarians and the inability of the library to respond immediately to changing curricular needs. More important, under this system of joint control the library was never an integral part of the school program, but was looked on as an outside agency.

Although some of these variant patterns of organization persisted into the middle of this century (and, indeed, in some areas are still in existence), they were gradually found unsuitable, and the prevailing pattern that emerged was an independent library in individual schools under the control of a board of education. Following this development several larger school districts formed central library agencies for supervision and guidance. In the interests of efficiency these agencies later expanded to provide such services as centralized processing, selection centers, and districtwide circulation of special collections.

THE AGE OF DEVELOPMENT

The rapid growth of school libraries following World War I parallels the similar general growth in public education. School population increased tremendously. In the 30-year span between 1900 and 1930, the elementary school population alone rose by 50 percent, and at the secondary level the growth was even more phenomenal.

A general population increase coupled with sustained faith in the importance of a general education were primary factors in producing this situation: less child labor was employed and there was a more stringent enforcement of school attendance regulations. Centralization of schools helped promote the development of larger units that now could afford what was sometimes regarded as the luxury of a library and the services of a qualified librarian.

Teaching systems also changed. The use of a single textbook and rote memorization were often supplanted by other teaching methods that stressed individualized instruction and a recognition of the differences among children. New curriculum structures, such as the Winnetka Plan (1920), the Dalton (Massachusetts) Plan (1920), and the many others that grew from the influence of John Dewey and his progressive education movement, underscored the need in schools for quantities of various kinds of educational materials. The logical source for this material was a well-stocked, well-administered school library.

The beginning of this period also saw the publication of the first national school library standards. In 1915, a nationwide survey on the teaching of English was conducted by the National Council of Teachers of English. Through this report the totally inadequate condition of school libraries in the United States came to light. This prompted NEA to appoint a committee of both librarians and educators under the chairmanship of Charles C. Certain to study secondary school libraries. The committee's final report was submitted to NEA in 1918 and was approved. ALA's Committee on Education also approved the report, and it was published by ALA in 1920. The report's official title is *Standard Library Organization and Equipment for Secondary Schools*, but it is commonly known as the "Certain report."[1]

The Certain report begins by painting a gloomy but truthful picture of the status of the post–World War I school library: "There are few well-planned high school libraries in the U.S. Sometimes there is a large study hall for the library—generally just one room with no workroom or conveniences of any kind for the staff."[2] Specific quantitative standards are given for secondary school libraries in schools of various sizes and grade levels. Included are liberal recommendations for physical facilities (the library should accommodate 5 to 10 percent

of the school population), qualifications of librarians (an undergraduate degree, one year of library science, and a minimum of one year of
library work with young adults), size of book collections (6–8 books per
student), as well as details on equipment, supplies, and budget.

The report is adamant on standards for the professional role of the
librarian: "Clerical work of the high school of the nature of office work
should not be demanded of the librarian." The standards are forward-
looking and even prophetic in their espousal of the media center concept long before the term came into existence:

> The Library should serve as the center and coordinating agency for all
> material used in the school for visual instruction, such as stereopticons,
> portable motion picture machines, stereopticon slides, moving picture
> films, pictures, maps, globes, bulletin board material, museum loans, etc.
> Such material should be regularly accessioned and cataloged, and its
> movements recorded, and directed from the library.[3]

The Certain high school standards (and their supplement of 1932)
had a beneficial effect on school library growth. They provided the
first yardstick to evaluate local libraries and also created a framework
from which other accrediting agencies—library departments, regional,
state, and local—could develop other sets of standards.

A second Certain report, *Elementary School Library Standards*, appeared in 1925 and received once more the endorsement of both NEA
and ALA. In these standards the integrated media approach was
restated:

> There is need, therefore, of a new department in the school whose func-
> tion it shall be to assemble and distribute the materials of instruc-
> tion. . . . In its first purpose, that of school library service, it may be
> thought of as the one agency in the school that makes possible a definite
> systematic manipulation and control of the materials of instruction. . . .
> [The collection should include] moving picture films, pictures for il-
> lustrative purposes, post cards, stereopticon slides, stereography, vic-
> trola records. This material shall be recorded by the librarian and
> distributed from the library.[4]

Once more these standards were exhaustive in the amount of specific
detail given. For example, included in the extensive supply lists are the
length of the ruler needed in the library office (18 inches), the brand of
paper clips to buy (Gem), the color of bookends to be purchased (olive
green). There is also appended a list of 212 basic books for the elementary school library. The twelve fiction titles include *Peter Pan*, *Heidi*,
and *Water Babies*. Because most elementary schools had no libraries
and the need for them was still generally unrecognized, the impact of
these standards was not as great as that of the 1920 standards.

In 1924 the North Central Association developed the "Score Card for School Libraries," a set of standards that began concentrating attention on programs or qualitative standards rather than on quantities of materials. In 1927 this association required each member high school to score its library.

That the Certain standards overemphasized the quantitative aspects of school library programs was criticized in other areas as well, and when the Cooperative Study of Secondary School Standards was formed in 1933, a new study was begun. This resulted in the publication of a numerical scoring technique to evaluate the secondary school (including the school library). Through numerous revisions, this publication has evolved into the *Evaluative Criteria*, an instrument still widely used by many accreditation associations and by schools for self-evaluation.

Other documents of the period focused attention on school libraries. In 1932, a national secondary school library survey was conducted by B. Lamar Johnson as part of the National Survey of Secondary Education sponsored by the U.S. Office of Education. The resultant publication, *The Secondary School Library*, supplied data on 390 libraries as well as special information on exemplary programs. Athough no specific recommendations are given, indirect guidance for library program development is suggested. The Department of Elementary School Principals of NEA entitled its twelfth annual yearbook *The Elementary School Library (1933)* and in 1943 the second part of the forty-second yearbook of the National Society for the Study of Education was called *The Library in General Education*. Many monographs also appeared that supplied, for the first time, guidance on how to establish and maintain a school library. Lucille F. Fargo wrote an ALA publication, *The Library in the School*, that had a publishing history of several editions and became the standard textbook on administering school library services. A detailed and sophisticated evaluation device for gathering data and measuring a school library's development appeared in 1951. The authors were Frances Henne, Ruth Ersted, and Alice Lohrer; the title, *A Planning Guide for the High School Library* (ALA). Other important administrative texts for various types of libraries and levels of professional competencies were written by Hannah Logasa, Azile Wofford, Mary Peacock Douglas, and Jewel Gardiner.

The second set of national school library standards, *School Libraries for Today and Tomorrow*, appeared in 1943. This was one of a series of documents on standards that was developed under the leadership of the ALA Committee on Post-War Planning. This publication represents the cooperative efforts of school library specialists then prominent in the field. The work is primarily descriptive. It contains separate chapters on the purposes of school libraries and the various services that can be offered through the school library. Quantitative standards are presented throughout the text and summarized in chart form in appendixes. The standards reflect a progressive and forward-looking view concerning the role of the school library in relation to the school's objectives and the equal importance of both elementary and secondary libraries. They are, however, less definite about the place of nonbook materials in the library than were the Certain standards. For example:

> The wide use of many books, periodicals, prints, maps, recordings, films and other audio-visual aids has made it imperative that information regarding all materials in the school be available from some central source. The school library appears to be the logical place for this information even when some of the materials are housed outside the library.[5]

Requirements for certification of school librarians improved and became more rigidly codified during this period. A U.S. Office of Education study conducted in 1940 showed that some provision for certifying school librarians existed in every state. Eight states provided this by specific state laws, 24 states allowed their education departments to provide their own certification requirements, and 16 states allowed local school boards to certify their librarians. The requirements varied considerably. For example, while one state required only two years of college and eight hours of library science, another required a bachelor's degree. New York State had the highest certification requirements, followed closely by California. By regulation effected in 1930, New York State required for permanent certification as a school librarian an undergraduate degree, 36 hours of library science (the maximum and minimum number of semester hours in each area of course work was specified), and 18 hours in education, including student teaching. In 1925, New York State mandated the appointment of a secondary school librarian (or, when necessary, a classroom teacher to serve in this capacity) for all but very small secondary schools in the state.

Although these certification requirements were written down, in many states, school districts often ignored them simply by not creating positions for school librarians. In most schools the library was still administered on a part-time basis by volunteer help or by classroom teachers who were given released time for this function.

The amount of statewide supervision of school librarians increased markedly during this period. In 1939 only 13 states employed full-time supervisors, but by 1960 more than half the states had developed these positions. Primarily because of increased federal spending for school libraries, virtually every state had some form of statewide supervision under qualified personnel by the end of the 1960s, and many had increased the number of the supervisors to four and five times more than there had been before World War II.

The question whether education for school librarianship should be based in library schools or in teacher training institutions continued to receive a great deal of attention. Many arguments favored the latter: teacher training institutions were more numerous and better situated geographically; library schools were primarily public- and academic-library oriented and unwilling to give courses in time slots (summers, for example) that were convenient to school personnel who wanted to be school librarians; certification requirements were generally so minimal that teacher training institutions could easily offer these basic courses; school administrators frequently wanted to hire only part-time librarians who were also qualified as subject specialists for classroom teaching.

During the 1950s a decided shift was noticeable from schools of education to library schools for courses in school librarianship. No single reason for this change can be given, but certain factors are apparent. Increased state standards for certification were adopted that often could be met only by attending a library school offering a complete program in library science. The proliferation of library schools during the period also helped. Some of them, ironically, developed from teacher training institutions. This tended to break the pattern of most library schools' being oriented mainly to adult services. As library schools and library school degrees become common, curricular programs and the number and variety of courses offered in library schools were expanded and became more specialized. Pressure also developed from within the library profession for library schools to extend into the school library area. For example, the 1951 standards for accrediting library schools and the interpretive document that accompanied them stressed the importance of developing multipurpose curricula that would not be confined solely to a single area of library service. The standards permitted only five-year programs to be eligible for accreditation, which weakened the drawing power of undergraduate programs offered within teachers' colleges.

In spite of these encouraging developments, national statistics continued to show the sorry state of school libraries in the United States. The Office of Education report *Public School Library Statistics for 1958–59* noted that about one-half of the nation's schools had no library and well over one-half did not have the services of a qualified librarian. Even in schools with libraries, collections averaged fewer than five books per student. The most seriously deprived area continued to be elementary schools, of which two-thirds were without a school library.

The decade of the 1960s is considered one of the greatest periods of school library growth. The period began with the publication, in 1960, of a new set of national standards developed by the American Association of School Librarians (AASL) of ALA with the cooperation of 19 other professional associations. In addition to their national impact, these standards influenced development and expansion of state and local standards. Although they deal primarily with various services offered by a functioning school library and make quantitative recommendations, these standards stress the responsibility of school boards, administrators, and various kinds of supervisory personnel in developing successful school library programs. The statement concerning school libraries as instructional materials centers, adopted by AASL in 1956, is reprinted in the standards, but there is no strong recommendation that the library and audiovisual collections be combined physically. Increased cooperation is suggested, however, where these collections are administered separately. Specific quantitative standards are included for audiovisual materials and equipment.

In the early 1960s, while school librarians were trying to implement their new standards, the NEA Department of Audiovisual Instruction (DAVI) had two committees working simultaneously on developing standards for audiovisual programs. The Committee on Professional Standards was working on quantitative standards and the Consultant Service Committee on the qualitative aspects. In June 1965 the quantitative standards were approved as the official guidelines for the organization.

In 1967, the Canadian School Library Association (CSLA) published the first set of standards geared to meeting the needs of Canadian school libraries. *The Standards of Library Service for Canadian Schools* (Ryerson Press) includes recommendations for types of media and also supplies detailed recommendations for services, personnel, and collections in various types of schools differentiated by size and location.

The greatest impetus for school library development in the 1960s came from increased financial aid from federal sources. The forerunner of this aid was the National Defense Education Act of 1958, which had as its aim the strengthening of teaching in the areas of science, foreign language, and mathematics through expenditures that could include purchases of equipment, library books, and other educational materials. Even more important was the passage of the Elementary and Secondary Education Act in 1965. Through Title II of this act, provision was made for millions of dollars to be spent developing school libraries. Other sections of the act supplied additional funds for providing library materials for disadvantaged students and for setting up model projects and demonstration libraries.

There was also an increased flow of money and support from private sources. Most notable was the Knapp School Libraries Project, which funded the establishment of several "ideal" school libraries across the country from 1963 through 1968. Thousands of educators visited these demonstration centers and thousands of others learned of them through written reports and other materials that were prepared to publicize the project. The Knapp Foundation later financed an intensive project to determine manpower needs in the area of school librarianship.

The effect of these new sources of support was phenomenal—hundreds of new libraries were founded, others were able to expand considerably their collections and services, and the demand for qualified librarians far exceeded the supply. Although federal support has subsequently varied considerably, the momentum for developing school libraries has continued.

THE EMERGENCE OF THE MEDIA CENTER

The aims of American education are usually expressed in terms of a dual responsibility to society and to the individual. The societal aims involve not only the preservation of those important values accumulated through time but also provisions to ensure growth and change in society. Education also attempts to equip the individual with knowledge to fit into the existing society and to contribute to that society's betterment.

When translating these aims into theories of learning, educators and psychologists become involved with the conditions of learning: how, where, why does learning take place? What outcomes can be expected after the learning experience? The examination of these questions has led to a number of schools of thought on the subject—of which many are in partial conflict and others seem to be based on irreconcilable dualisms. For example, the behaviorists and associationists, among them E. L. Thorndike and B. F. Skinner, believe learning is essentially a mechanistic response to external stimuli, or in short, a conditioning procedure. The Gestaltists and field theorists maintain that learning is a cognitive process involving personal perception in problem-solving situations. Practical applications of these theories—programmed texts and simulation games, for example—are increasingly present in today's schools.

Regardless of differences in theories, basic principles involving learning remain unchanged: (1) children learn as individuals; (2) children learn at various rates; (3) children learn according to different styles and patterns; and (4) education is a continuous process.

Their attempt to translate these principles into practice has led educators to pursue many new teaching strategies and organizational patterns that break with traditional modes. Among these have been the widespread adoption of unified media programs administered through a school library media center. Once more, professional associations helped lead the way. In 1969, the first joint standards cooperatively produced by DAVI and AASL were issued, *Standards for School Media Programs.* The development of these also involved 28 advisers from other professional associations. In addition to emphasizing the positive results that unified media programs can bring and supplying detailed quantitative guidelines, the media program standards also stress the necessity of fusing facilities and services if media personnel hope to meet the challenge of today's education.

The 1969 *Standards* recommended that a continuous review of these national standards be undertaken to ensure proper consideration of changes and developments particularly involving educational technology and learning techniques. It was also recommended that a new set of standards be published every two years. In response to these recommendations, two task forces were jointly appointed in 1971 by AASL and the Association for Educational Communications and Technology (AECT, the new name for DAVI), one to study media service standards for the single school and the other at the district level. (Since these areas were found to be inseparable, the two reports were later merged.) The collection of data for these standards involved use of questionnaires, literature searches, open forums at meetings of professional associations, and input from many educational specialists. The resulting document was published in 1975 as *Media Programs: District and School.* In addition to reaffirming the unified approaches to centralizing media and media services in schools, it stresses other concepts. Greater emphasis is placed on the media center's role in planning and executing the school's instructional program rather than being simply a passive support service. This stress on the media programs also includes an emphasis on user needs and educational growth as well as the necessity of participating in curriculum development by the library media staff.

In addition to furnishing specific goals and objectives for the media programs and their integration into the overall goals of the institution, these standards emphasize how sound managerial practices can help in achieving these goals.

But quantitative measurements are not ignored; for example,

specific square footage is given for various physical facilities and numerical amounts for both basic and advanced collections of various kinds of materials and equipment. These measurements, however, are made somewhat flexible to accommodate the uniqueness of each library media center program. The overall recommendation is that at least 10 percent of the national average per pupil operation cost (PPOC) be expended by local school boards for each student enrolled solely for the development of materials and equipment collections within the school district.

These standards allow for more specialization and differentiation in staffing patterns within the center by distinguishing among the media specialist (a professional who has broad preparation in both education and media), the media professional (a person with extensive preparation in a specific area of educational technology such as computer science), the media technician, media aide, and support personnel.

Renewed emphasis is placed on the importance of districtwide service and developing cooperative media programs with other agencies at the regional, state, and indeed national levels. This concept of networking of services and collections has subsequently become one of the salient characteristics of recent library development at all levels.

Media Programs and its 1969 predecessor are perhaps the most influential documents affecting the growth and development of school media programs during the 1970s and 1980s.

The concept of interdependence and the necessity of developing cooperative projects among school media centers and other information organizations have received additional support beyond the 1975 standards from such agencies as the National Commission on Libraries and Information Science (NCLIS). An independent federal agency in the executive branch, NCLIS has as its major task advising the president and Congress on the status of the nation's libraries. In its initial statement of priorities and policies in 1975, *Towards a National Program for Library and Information Services: Goals for Action*, it was stated that school library media centers must become part of a nationwide resource-sharing network "if we are to increase the opportunities for children and youth for independent study and add to their ability to become literate, well informed citizens capable of lifelong learning in a rapidly changing world."[6]

In January 1977, a task force consisting of representatives from existing network offices and other representatives from educational media associations and media personnel from local and state agencies was appointed to study the position of the library media center within the framework of a national cooperative network. The resulting document, *Report of the Task Force on the Role of the School Library*

Media Program in Networking, appeared late in 1978. It established an overriding rationale for including school media programs in a national network and identified five factors—psychological, political and legal, funding, communication, and planning—that inhibit this cooperation. In each case immediate and midrange recommendations are made to solve these problems. Only one long-range recommendation emerges—that within ten years "library networks in which school library media programs are full participating members be established and operating in every region, state, and area in the nation."[7] In 1979, NCLIS established another committee of key people in educational media, to identify priorities and work with NCLIS to implement the report's recommendation.

Another event that focused attention on the future of all the nation's libraries, including those in schools, was the first White House Conference on Library and Information Science, held in Washington November 15–19, 1979. The 826 delegates developed 64 recommendations that ranged from the passage of a national library act to the guarantee of adequate media services in each public school. The conference proceedings and recommendations are covered fully in its final report, *Information for the 80's.*[8]

The first meeting of the Ad Hoc Committee on Implementation of the White House Conference Resolutions met in September 1980 with the charge to establish priorities and policies concerning the implementation of these recommendations. Certainly solutions for solving the many problems facing school library media centers have been identified. Unfortunately, cutbacks in government spending in the 1980s have seriously delayed their implementation.

This more conservative national outlook, which emerged in the 1970s, is also reflected in the growing number of censorship cases involving school library media centers. A landmark Supreme Court decision handed down on June 25, 1982, ended a marathon court struggle that lasted six years involving a case of book banning. The lawsuit had been brought against a suburban New York State school district (Island Trees) by five students, led by Steven Pico, who claimed that their First Amendment rights had been violated by the school board's arbitrary removal of nine books from their high school library. The titles in question (for example, *The Fixer* by Bernard Malamud and *Slaughter House Five* by Kurt Vonnegut) had been chosen for inclusion in the school's collection by valid selection criteria, but had appeared on a list of objectionable titles circulated by a conservative parents' group.

In a 5–4 decision, the Court limited the power of public school officials to remove books simply because they found them objectionable, by ruling that school boards who remove books must defend their motives in court. The fact that there was such a division in the Court highlights the basic dualism involving the purposes of public education—that is, primarily to transmit the accepted values of the country or to use the classroom as a marketplace for ideas. The Supreme Court decision has been considered a victory for the latter concept. As Justice William Brennan stated in his opinion for the plurality: "Local school boards may not remove books from school library shelves simply because they dislike the ideas contained in those books and seek by their removal to prescribe what shall be orthodox in politics, nationalism, religion or other matters of opinion. Such purposes stand inseparably condemned by our precedents."

In general, looking back from the vantage point of the 1980s, the preceding decade showed continued expansion in the school media field. By the beginning of 1979, 84 percent of schools surveyed by the National Center for Educational Statistics showed that libraries and library media centers had holdings totaling 541 million volumes. The mean number of volumes per school was 7,719, or 13.4 books per student. Average seating capacity was 55. There were 81,759 full-time-equivalent certified staff members (3,400 more than in 1974–1975), of whom 71,605 were actually full time and 35,069 part time. (Slightly over 90 percent were women.) Overall educational statistics are also impressive. In school year 1981–1982, 57.6 million students were enrolled in schools and colleges (the record high was 61.3 million in 1975). Of these, 31 million were in high schools and 14.4 million in elementary schools. The overall cost of education in 1981–1982 was $198 billion, with $127 billion spent in elementary and high schools.

Although this high level of expenditure would appear to be more than adequate, actually many of the problems in the world of education in the 1980s, including those of school library media centers, have involved declining financial support. Some symptoms of this can be seen in budget cutting, elimination of staff, increased work loads assigned to personnel, unionization, job actions within the profession, increased competition for existing funds, and rising costs of educational materials. In many areas of the country, these fiscal problems are exacerbated by declining enrollments, school closings, and "excessing" of personnel. For school media personnel, further challenges in the 1980s have involved increased pressures by ultraconservatives to control collections, the emphasis from "back-to-basics" groups on the use of textbooks, and the necessity to absorb computer technology, library automation, and concepts of networking into library media center management.

In addition to the problems involving external pressures and changing financial support, there are also many challenges emerging from within the profession itself. Indeed, there are some who might question to what degree the term *professional* should be applied to the school library media specialist. Certainly many of the basic characteristics of professional status are there—for example, a knowledge base derived from theory and speculative thought; a set of procedures, methodologies, and skills based on this knowledge; a service orientation; and the awareness of choices available in decision making. Nevertheless, if this profession is to exist as a separate entity, there are problems that must be faced: the lack of uniform entrance standards to the profession; the diversity and uneven quality of programs that prepare candidates to become school library media specialists; the lack of monitoring standards within the profession, including a code of ethics that can be implemented; the need for more ongoing research; the identity crisis faced by library media personnel who feel torn between education and librarianship; and the division of allegiance within media personnel between the two major professional organizations—AECT of NEA and AASL of ALA.

On the other hand, there are many evidences in the professional literature and reports from the field that there is enough vigor and innovation to ensure progress throughout the 1980s. Library media specialists are becoming more aware of their role as educational consultant in the schools in both curriculum development and the ongoing educational program. As they assume greater leadership roles in the schools, they are also becoming more articulate about their mission, more aware of public relations techniques, and better able to carry their message to the school board and beyond. A healthy attitude toward change and flexibility has been demonstrated by which newer techniques and cooperative ventures have been adopted and assimilated. It is hoped that these developments will convince all persons and agencies involved in education that a sound library media program in the schools is a prerequisite for high quality education.

NOTES

1. Charles C. Certain Committee, *Standard Library Organization and Equipment for Secondary Schools* (Chicago: American Library Association, 1920).
2. Ibid., p. 2.
3. Ibid., p. 7.
4. Charles C. Certain Committee, *Elementary School Library Standards* (Chicago: American Library Association, 1925), p. 5.

5. Committee on Post-War Planning, *School Libraries for Today and Tomorrow* (Chicago: American Library Association, 1943), p. 11.
6. *Towards a National Program for Library and Information Services: Goals for Action* (Washington, D.C.: NCLIS, 1975), preface.
7. *Report of the Task Force on the Role of the School Library Media Program in Networking* (Washington, D.C.: NCLIS, 1978), p. 34.
8. *Information for the 80's* (Washington, D.C.: NCLIS, 1980).

2

FUNCTIONS OF THE SCHOOL LIBRARY MEDIA CENTER

Emphasis on the individual nature of learning continues to lead educators to question the methods that promote only teaching facts and rote learning, curricula that departmentalize knowledge into unrelated units, and organizational structures that produce artificial grade levels and perpetuate unrealistic expectations and rigid standards. Many organizational patterns have been developed: individualized instruction, team teaching, flexible and modular scheduling, large-group/small-group instruction, independent study programs, interdisciplinary studies, nongraded or multigraded classrooms, contract teaching, extra-school internships, and tutorial or directed study programs.

As before, the role of the school library media specialist today is one of organizer and guide, with a chief responsibility to provide a learning environment appropriate to the needs of the school community. The center staff functions to create this environment. Also needed is a variety of media at many levels of comprehension and interest, organized for easy accessibility, and a range of services and activities that involves the learner. The need for unification of media and services to promote learning through programs has led to the development of the school library media center.

This chapter on functions has a threefold aim: (1) to express briefly the nature of school library media programs by describing the functions of the media center at all levels, (2) to define and describe these functions as services and activities and to define resources as well as guidelines that are helpful in planning, establishing, and maintaining these collections, and (3) to formulate a plan for inaugurating or strengthening a school library media center in an individual school.

19

SERVICES

The school library media center's program should provide a range of learning opportunities for both large and small groups and for individuals. The focus is on facilitating and improving the learning process, with emphasis on intellectual content, inquiry, and the learner. Because people do not react in the same way to the same medium, learners are encouraged to read, view, listen, construct, and create to learn in their own way. The center program is a cooperative venture in which school library media specialists, teachers, and administrators work together to provide opportunities for the social, cultural, and educational growth of the student. It is a coordinated effort in which activities take place in the school library media center, laboratory, classroom, and throughout the school.

There are several ways to describe school library media center programs. One is to outline the services performed by the staff. A list of 195 services (exclusive of providing materials and equipment) in secondary school libraries has been compiled by Mary V. Gaver in *Services of Secondary School Media Centers, Evaluation and Development* (ALA 1971). Sixty-eight typical elementary school media services are outlined in the NEA pamphlet *Elementary School Media Programs: An Approach to Individualized Instruction* (1970).

The Gaver list is comprehensive and identifies exemplary secondary school library media centers as well as indicating services that should be considered in developing a program on that level. Many of the services, such as posting information about television and radio programs, also apply at the elementary school level.

Some of the staff functions that are basic to providing minimal services in any school library media center are:

1. Budgeting balanced media programs.
2. Selecting materials and equipment.
3. Acquiring and processing (where not centrally done) all media and equipment.
4. Organizing collections of media and equipment for easy access.
5. Circulating media and equipment.
6. Arranging schedules that provide accessibility.
7. Handling repair procedures.
8. Preparing operational handbooks for the center.
9. Promoting the center.
10. Instructing in the location and use of media and equipment.
11. Offering reading, viewing, and listening guidance.

Another way to describe school library media center programs is through activities that take place in the center and in the school as a result of the services. Activities among centers vary by type and also by combination. Nevertheless, some of the same activities or services appear in all dynamic centers: students or teachers, individually or in groups, listen to tapes and cassettes, make transparencies and other visuals, view films and slides, conduct media searches for projects, prepare multimedia presentations, or use computers for projects. Programs across the country reveal numerous activities and the underlying functions that support them. A collection of these activities is presented in the following section. With a little imagination, the majority of these activities can be redesigned for use in other school library media centers.

Although the examples described below can apply in many instances to any of the three major audiences of a school library media program—students, teachers and administrators, plus the community—they are grouped under the audiences with which they will be used most often. By comparing a function or service and the resulting activity, it becomes obvious that measurement of the objectives as they result in audience activity will give a more accurate evaluation of educational progress than will the work measures of staff.

FUNCTIONS RELATED TO USER ACTIVITIES

All the examples[1] are arranged to show the relationship between staff function and the activities of school library media center user. The school library media center staff functions so that students, teachers, administrators, or community members can participate in an activity resulting in a learning experience.

Services to Students

Reading, Viewing, and Listening

Organize media and equipment; preview, evaluate, and weed ⟶ Participate as members of a review committee to evaluate media.

Compile "mediagraphies" ⟶ Learn to use an annotated list that includes books, cassettes, films, and games about a theme or topic.

Give presentations using school library media ⟶ Learn importance of using a variety of media, for example, books, realia, computers, maps, sound recordings, and microfiche to illustrate a discussion of "courage."

Assist in developing school library media presentation skills ➡ Present programs to groups of friends or to younger students. An eleventh-grade varsity ballplayer could highlight a talk on sports novels for eighth-graders by using transparencies to illustrate game techniques; an older student might help a younger one select school library media to present to a home economics class.

Provide for local production of media ➡ Use locally produced media in a variety of ways, for example, preparing transparencies, laminating pictures and clippings, videotaping and filming school reports.

Reference Work

Provide accessible reference materials ➡ Locate a variety of school library media by using mediagraphies to establish a school library media reference collection for a third-grade unit on nature (provision of computer searches for advanced senior high).

Use of newer school library media to develop study skills (A videotape unit on this part of reference work might be shown to individuals and to classes) ➡ Recognize the need to compare and evaluate sources.

Correlate collections for classroom or subject area use ➡ Learn to use out-of-print books and periodicals on microfilm or online for an individualized American studies project.

Establish liaison with public, university, and special libraries ➡ Use interlibrary loans, for example, a student might request a scientific monograph from a cooperating research library for an advanced placement chemistry class.

Instruction

Teach reference skills and equipment use ➡ Learn the skills for competent school library media and equipment use so that a third-grade class can practice alphabetizing by working with the catalog, or a seventh-grade English class can undertake a television production of excerpts from *The Great Gilly Hopkins*.

Give orientation tours and workshops ➡ Learn the organization and administration of a library, for example, each grade level might participate in a series of workshops.

Teach use of special reference materials ➡ Learn to use essential print reference materials, for example, fifth-graders choose a suitable encyclopedia and atlas to complete an oral report on a country.

Help develop and teach a standard mediagraphic form ⟶ Learn the school's mediagraphic rules by using a programmed learning workbook manually or on a computer.

Develop ideas for using school library media ⟶ Learn about other community resources by presenting a print, recording, or film project about the local pet shop's dog-care course.

Clubs and Social and Vocational Programs

Develop assistantship programs ⟶ Learn school library media center work as a volunteer, as a part-time paid employee, or as part of course work in a vocational course.

Assist in extra class activities ⟶ Participate in social and educational activities such as trips to local libraries, theaters, and museums; plan a school library media club trip to a museum film festival.

Sponsor paperback book fairs, film festivals ⟶ Learn to share the experience and work of sponsoring exhibits. Examples: fourth-to-sixth-grade students help to run a paperback book fair; seventh-to-ninth-grade students assist in planning a film festival of novels that have been made into feature or television films.

Plan school library media center publicity ⟶ Help to promote school library media center resources and services, for example, high school journalism classes and radio clubs prepare and disseminate publicity.

Suggest school library media use ideas for assemblies, Parent-Teacher Association programs, classroom projects, and plays ⟶ Assist in recording school meetings, speeches, and special programs, for example, videotape special school programs for community use.

Services to Teachers and Administrators

Curriculum Development

Teach use of school library media through the role model of teacher-librarian ⟶ Develop cooperatively a unit to be taught by a school library media specialist and teacher team, for example, a unit on myths for the fifth or sixth grade.

Attend grade-level or subject-area departmental meetings ⟶ Participate in designing courses incorporating new uses of media, for example, a ninth-grade survey of careers that uses resource people, films, government pamphlets, and so forth.

Help to design instructional systems ➡ Study existing curriculum to develop new instructional approaches; school library media specialist can recommend appropriate school library media for a second-grade reading program using trade books, readers, kits, enrichment films, interactive computers, and so forth.

Learn teachers' instructional methods and school library media needs through individual conferences ➡ Plan to use school library media support for basic and enrichment programs, for example, easy-reading materials, filmstrips, and films on anthropology for third-graders.

Plan school library media programs for teachers' professional and recreational needs ➡ Attend exhibits of new professional materials, screenings of noteworthy films or videocassettes, and demonstrations and displays of the newest equipment.

Assisting in the Use of Materials

Help teachers become familiar with the school library media center ➡ Participate in videotaping a school library media center orientation program to use throughout the school.

Teach use of a school library media center for research ➡ Develop with a group a local-history project that can be used as a demonstration of how to use the school library media center's research resources.

Organize routines for convenient use of materials and equipment; make self-instruction programs available ➡ Develop simple programmed-instruction booklets to teach youngsters some fundamental school library media center skills such as classification.

Encourage local production of materials ➡ Teachers and administrators can develop their own "tailor-made" materials.

Establish departmental or auxiliary resource centers ➡ Develop cooperatively a place for storing equipment and specialized materials within floor levels, grade levels, or departments so that they receive maximum use.

Services to the Community

Give talks to parents and community groups ➡ Groups of parents of preschool children discuss reading aloud to youngsters with school library media staff at evening meetings; take home selective lists of read-aloud books.

Observe national media-related events ⟶ Participate in special programs to highlight the National Book Awards, the American Film Festival, the Right-to-Read Program, and so forth.

Publicize school library media center activities ⟶ Local radio might produce spot announcements with school library media staff help; newspapers run information about school library media center programs.

Engage community business and professional persons to speak to school and school library media center groups ⟶ Local persons serve as resource specialists, for example, a florist might participate in a school library media center home economics program on flower arranging.

RESOURCES

The school provides in each building a collection of materials and the equipment needed to use it that fits in variety and scope both the curricula of the school and the interests and abilities of the users.

Collection Size and Variety

The range of the collection can be broad, from books and jigsaw puzzles or videocassette tapes to community resource files and computers or microfiche. The collection should include some material in every available medium.

The following suggestions are based on the state of Maryland's recommendations. Basic initial collections should be available in every school. Each school, regardless of enrollment, should have a fully cataloged and processed print and nonprint collection. The quantity of material in a basic collection will depend on enrollment, range of grades, variety of subjects taught, and special needs of the school population. The funds needed for initial collections should be included in capital-outlay budgets. The acquisition of a new collection is time-consuming because selection, acquisition, and technical processing must be done before the collection is ready and the school library media program can be initiated. The building of a collection ideally should begin when a new or remodeled school library media center is first planned. Some duplication should be anticipated if decentralized resource centers by subject area or grade level are to be housed in the same building.

The size of the collection in a school library media center can be established based on enrollment for different levels of schools. This approach to collection building reinforces the unified concept of a school library media center. Following are guidelines for quantities of items that are necessary to carry on a basic media program:

Elementary schools (K–6)	Twenty items for each pupil (8,000 for 400 students)
Junior high or middle schools (6–9)	Twenty items for each pupil (10,000 for 500 students)
Junior or senior high schools (9–12)	Thirty items for each pupil (36,000 for 1,200 students)

No one way of assigning print and nonprint materials according to a predetermined percentage scale is necessarily the best for each school. Instead, a primary consideration should be that the subject matter— instructional or recreational—is represented in as many formats and to the same degree that it is needed by the faculty and students of the school.

Equipment

Recommendations for quantities of equipment follow the same pattern as those for the collection because the equipment is so closely tied to the material with which it is used. There is no maximum or minimum quantity; the amount depends on the school's program. However, careful consideration must be given to equipment purchasing because obsolescence is an integral part of technology. This fact should not, however, prevent the school library media specialist from incorporating into the program new developments in equipment. It should caution the media specialist that complete information about each type of equipment should be gathered and attention given to current technological developments.

Ideally a unified program will provide a plan for using the equipment throughout the school as well as in the media center itself. The list of equipment shown in Table 2–1 suggests quantities for both of these service areas.

Quality of the Program

The quality of the program cannot be measured solely by the size of the collection. However, when only a minimal quantity of media is provided, educational opportunities for students are limited. Although it is difficult to prove that a given quantity of materials and equipment will ensure that a child will learn, the knowledge gathered from experience and research is that young people are more likely to show educational gains within an environment that includes a variety of media.

TABLE 2-1 EQUIPMENT COLLECTION FOR A BASIC MEDIA PROGRAM[a]

Equipment	Number in Center	Number per Teaching Station (per grade level)	
Record player with earphones	5	1	(K-6)
		1/5	(6-12)
Tape recorders, reel-to-reel	5	1/5	—[b]
Cassette player-recorders			
Classroom size	10	1/3	(K-6)
		1/5	(6-12)
Portable	6	1/3	(K-6)
		1	(6-12)
Listening stations with 6-10 headsets	2	1	(K-6)
		1/10	(6-12)
Basic stereo sound system with quadraphonic capability, amplifier, turntable, reel-to-reel and cassette recorders, speakers, cart	1[c]	—	—[b]
Projectors			
16mm sound	3	1/4	
8mm silent	5	1/10	
8mm sound	6	1/4	
2x2 slide	3	1/5	
filmstrip			
sound	2	1/4	
overhead	2	1	
opaque	1	1[c]	
microprojector	1	—	
Previewers			
filmstrip	5	1/2	
2x2 slide	5	1/2	
Microreaders	1	1/10	(6-12)
Microreader-printer	2	—	(6-12)
Microfiche reader	2	1/2	(6-12)
Microfiche printer	2	—	(6-12)
Accessories			
projection carts	—[d]	—[d]	
screens			
wall or ceiling	1	1	
portable	1	1/5	
rear	1	1/2	
typewriters for student use	3-6	—	
lecterns			
standing	—	1	
table	1	1	
Duplicating equipment			
ditto or stencil	1	1/20	
electrostatic or thermal	1	1/20	
Local production equipment	—[e]		
Dry-mount press and tacking iron, paper cutters, Thermo and Diazo transparency production equipment, Super 8mm camera;			

TABLE 2–1 (cont.)

Equipment	Number in Center	Number per Teaching Station (per grade level)
rapid-process camera, equipment for dark-room, spirit duplicator, primary typewriter, copy camera and stand, light box, 35mm still camera, film rewind, film splicer (8 and 16mm), slide reproducer, mechanical lettering devices		
Video, TV, and radio equipment		
portable videotape recorder		
camera and monitor	1	1/5
playback unit	1	1/15
videocassette recorder	1	—
TV receivers	1	1/15
closed-circuit television	1	1/5
AM-FM radio receiver	1	1/5

[a] Based on 600 pupil enrollment.
[b] Where grade level is not indicated quantities are the same for elementary and secondary levels.
[c] For building use.
[d] One for each 16mm and overhead projector in media center and in building.
[e] Quantities depend on the development of the production program in the individual school.

National standards and state and local organization recommendations can serve as guidelines in the development of collections for both materials and equipment. Many national associations provide helpful guides that school library media specialists can use. One of the more important is *Media Programs: District and School.*[2] Although these guidelines were published in 1975, the Standards Program and Implementation Committee of AASL, which "plan[s] and coordinate[s] activities and programs of development, revision, and implementation concerning school library media standards," endorses them today. The Association for Educational Communications and Technology (AECT) issued *An Instrument for Self-Evaluating an Educational Media Program in School Systems* in 1979 as one of its "nonperiodic" publications. Both will be helpful.

Many state education departments also issue recommendations, sometimes in phases or developmental stages, that can be used by the media specialist. (See Appendix 1 for the appropriate state address.) Depending on the particular state and the structure in the education department, either the department that handles the combined school library media business or the departments that treat the school library and media concerns should be contacted. In addition, state organizations that represent the school library media field may issue guidelines, for example, the New York Library Association. Regional or local organizations in the field sometimes recommend guidelines, for example, the Long Island School Media Association (LISMA), which combines the former School Library and Educational Technology organizations for Long Island, New York. Other organizations are listed in Appendix 2.

CONVERTING A SCHOOL LIBRARY INTO A MEDIA CENTER

Many things should be explored before the task of converting a traditional school library into a school library media center is begun. Perhaps the most important concern should be whether the person who is to run the center fully accepts the concept of multimedia centers as dissemination points for ideas and information regardless of the medium in which they appear. To embrace this concept also requires acceptance of the equipment that some media require for the transmission of the ideas or information. Once a wholehearted commitment to this philosophy is made, the specialist is ready to take some immediate steps toward developing a school library media center and to plan for some long-range steps.

The school library media specialist should assume leadership throughout the entire conversion process. This leadership is vital and one of the key factors for the eventual success of a program. But a word of caution is necessary. Experience has shown that when presenting a new program, it is best not to attempt to introduce a great number of new services in the initial stages, but to concentrate on developing a total program by adding a few services to those that have proved successful. By no means should one try to build a school library media center solely by adding new or different media; this is a denial of the basic philosophy of such a center. Instead, integrate media into the grade-level unit or course of study that is widely used in the school.

Immediate Steps

1. Identify a curriculum or recreational area around which to build the school library media concept.
2. Contact one or two teachers who are interested in working cooperatively to build a balanced media collection in the one area.
3. Encourage students to use the media in the developing collection for individual satisfaction as well as for classroom work. Simple production of transparencies, laminating pictures, and the use of microcomputers with their software are three possibilities.

4. As soon as the program activity is completed, evaluate the school library media services that have been added according to the teacher's educational objectives and student responses. The evaluations can serve as a basis on which to make future changes and also to urge the administration to institute the unified media concept in the school.

5. Encourage other teachers and students to participate to the extent that staff and funds are available. If necessary, postpone organizational details, such as an integrated catalog, in favor of creating interest in the use of media and eventually persuading the principal to provide additional support.

6. Enlist the support of the principal and administration for instituting an increasing role for multimedia in the school library media center.

Long-Range Steps

1. Use the educational philosophy of the district and individual school together with the specific objectives for each area in the overall curricula to formulate evaluative criteria for measuring the success of the school library media program.

2. Seek a consultant's help if possible; visit other centers.

3. Evaluate present services, resources, facilities, and so forth (see the School Library Media Program Self-Evaluation Form in Chapter 3, Exhibit 3-4).

4. Focus on a total school library media center program that is uniquely suited to the school and set the priorities within multiyear phases in which the services, newer resources, and remodeled facilities will be inaugurated.

5. Establish effective communication with the principal by building on the successful operation of some past program services. Ensure a clear organizational pattern as well as acceptance that only one person will head the school library media center operation in the school, including the distribution or, more likely, decentralization of equipment for classroom use.

6. Continue to enlist the support of teachers and students by providing services they need, but about which they may be unaware.

7. Revise plans as necessary, guided by the evaluation of the program against the evaluation criteria set up in the first of the long-range conversion steps.

8. Explore the possibility of developing a unified school library media program on a district level.

NOTES

1. Examples of several of the programs on which the lists are based are highlighted with brief descriptions in Chapter 4, *Creating a School Media Program*, by the authors (New York: R. R. Bowker, 1973).
2. *Media Programs: District and School* (Chicago: American Library Association, 1975).

FOR FURTHER READING

Aaron, Shirley L. *A Study of Combined School-Public Libraries*. Chicago: American Library Association, 1980.

Adams, Charles W. "The School Media Program: A Position Statement." *School Media Quarterly*, Winter 1974, 127–143.

Bagan, Beverley, et al. *The Role of the Librarian in Media*. New York: Random House/Miller Brody, 1975. Sound filmstrips.

Broderick, Dorothy M. *Library Work with Children*. New York: H. W. Wilson, 1977.

Clark, Geraldine. "Echoes of '60s Advocacy in the School Media Center of the '80s." *American Libraries*, June 1979, pp. 369–372.

Elementary School Media Programs: An Approach to Individualized Instruction. Washington, D.C.: NEA, 1970.

Frontiers of Library Service for Youth: Essays Honoring Frances E. Henne. New York: Columbia University Press, 1979.

Galvin, Thomas J., et al., eds. *Excellence in School Library Media Programs: Essays Honoring Elizabeth T. Fast*. Chicago: American Library Association, 1980.

Gaver, Mary V. *Services of Secondary School Media Centers, Evaluation and Development*. Chicago: American Library Association, 1971.

Luskay, Jack R. "The White House Conference on Library and Information Services, November 15–19, 1979: A Report." *School Media Quarterly*, Spring 1980, pp. 137–152.

Media Programs: District and School. Chicago: American Library Association, 1975.

Nadler, Myra. *How to Start an Audiovisual Collection*. Metuchen, N.J.: Scarecrow, 1978.

Peterson, Gary T. *The Learning Center: A Sphere for Nontraditional Approaches to Education*. Linnet Books, 1975.

School Libraries for All. Kalamazoo: IASL (Wales), Western Michigan University, 1981.

"School Media Services and Automation." *School Media Quarterly*, Summer 1979, pp. 257–268+.

Shapiro, Lillian L. *Serving Youth: Communication and Commitment in the High School Library*. New York: R. R. Bowker, 1975.

Shera, Jesse. *Introduction to Library Science*. Littleton, Colo.: Libraries Unlimited, 1976.

Springer, Lonnie. "Put Media at the Core of the Curriculum." *Instructional Innovator*, November 1981, pp. 24–25.

Thomas, James L. *Turning Kids on to Print Using Nonprint*. Littleton, Colo.: Libraries Unlimited, 1978.

——, and Loring, Ruth M., eds. *Motivating Children and Young Adults to Read*. Phoenix, Ariz.: Oryx, 1979.

U.S. National Commission on Libraries and Information Science. *Toward a National Program for Library and Information Services: Goals for Action*. Washington, D.C.: Government Printing Office, 1975.

White House Conference on Library and Information Services, 1979. *Information for the 1980's*. Washington, D.C.: Government Printing Office, 1980.

Woolard, Wilma Lee Broughton. *Combined School/Public Libraries: A Survey with Conclusions and Recommendations*. Metuchen, N.J.: Scarecrow, 1980.

3

DEVELOPING A SCHOOL LIBRARY MEDIA CENTER PROGRAM

This chapter discusses three functions that can help the school library media specialist to make a school library media program more effective: (1) conducting the instructional program, (2) utilizing public relations methods to acquaint the school community with the center's resources and services, and (3) evaluating the school library media center program. The measurable results of these functions provide a means to assess the success or failure of the program. Also described are the importance of the curriculum; reading, viewing, and listening guidance; in-service programs; and cooperation with the public library and other library media agencies.

THE SCHOOL LIBRARY MEDIA SPECIALIST AND THE CURRICULUM

The school library media center's program for helping students in the use of materials depends largely on the curriculum. Regardless of how the particular school assigns responsibility for teaching various study skills, the school library media specialist has a unique advantage for observing, helping, and evaluating student competence in this area. Where individualized learning or independent inquiry takes place, careful planning for these students is a fundamental factor in the success of a program. This principle is vital to the development of any successful school library media center program of instruction. It involves the curriculum, both instructional and recreational, or the curricula of the school community in its entirety. The school library media specialist's role in the program dealing with methods of inquiry and study skills is that of the specialist in giving reading, viewing, and listening guidance and in giving instruction in school library media skills as a teacher. This strongly suggests that the specialist is basically a teacher, as declared in the certification in many states. Understanding current and future teaching methods is important for each professional person on the staff; experience will add to this.

School library media programs of instruction are fundamental in a modern, growing curriculum. These programs flow directly from the classroom. Two consequential results of such programs are increased student competence and student appreciation in satisfying emerging interests. There is a trend for state departments of education to produce curriculum guides for school library media centers. Awareness of new sources of information and various formats mandates that more will be done. The curriculum will continue to be the basis for developing students' locational skills and improving media use for learning in school and throughout life.

THE INSTRUCTIONAL PROGRAM

Students

There are differing opinions about the amount of media skills teaching that should take place in the center. Those in favor of an extensive teaching program maintain that mastery of skills is necessary to produce independent, resourceful users of media. Opponents argue that although learning how to locate materials may be necessary, too much valuable time is spent on details such as explaining the catalog card or the Dewey decimal system when the most important aspect of reference and research work is actually using the materials. Whatever policies are adopted, the instructional program should not be conducted in a vacuum unrelated to students' actual needs. Skills teaching should be functional and should be integrated with the students' other educational activities.

The instructional program is conducted on two levels: informal and formal.

Informal Instruction

The teaching that takes place spontaneously when answering an individual student's request is an example of informal instruction. This might include supplying directions and help in locating material in reference books or giving a brief, impromptu book talk to answer the question: "Could you recommend a good book to read?"

Informal instruction is certainly valuable because it directly satisfies a student's individual needs. The obvious drawbacks are that it is time-consuming and repetitious for the staff and that it depends on student willingness or ability to ask questions. To help match instruction to immediate needs, some school library media centers produce short teaching tapes for cassette playbacks. Each tape deals concisely with a particular topic, for example, the arrangement of the material on shelves, instructions for operating a particular piece of equipment, or the use of materials such as the *Reader's Guide*. The cassette equipment is placed close to the material described on the tape. Some centers use specially prepared or commercially produced charts and posters and short, programmed instruction booklets to acquaint students with the media center's resources. Others have developed self-instruction laboratories where students can use tapes, filmstrips, and other materials to teach themselves media skills.

Formal Instruction

This involves presenting preplanned lessons before a group of students. The presentations should adhere to established guidelines of teaching that include a statement of goals expressed in concrete behavioral terms, an introduction that catches students' attention and explains the purpose of the lesson, an effective presentation of the material to be learned, and an opportunity for feedback and evaluation. The lessons should be scheduled in school library media center classrooms where materials are accessible, but where disruptions to other patrons can be avoided. Many commercially prepared aids for teaching media center skills are available: packaged kits, films, filmstrips, workbooks, computer software, and the like. Some can be modified when necessary to fit specific needs.

The practice of scheduling groups or classes into the center on an informal, as-need-demands basis is now widely accepted. Not only does this promote cooperative planning between teachers and the center's staff, but it also helps achieve the goal of making school library media center instruction an integrated, cohesive part of the school curriculum. Nevertheless there are, unfortunately, many schools where rigid scheduling of classes into the school library media center is still practiced. Usually the reason for adhering to this traditional and outmoded procedure is more administrative than educational and often is in the interest of freeing teachers for preparation periods. Rigid scheduling can throw both content and timing of lessons off balance, causing eventual harm to the entire instructional program.

One fear sometimes expressed about free or open scheduling is that, depending on the teacher, some classes will not visit the school library media center often enough or that certain skills will not be taught. In practice this fear has proved groundless. Any such danger can be avoided in a well-run program where there is constant communication with teachers and where realistic, flexible instructional programs have been adopted.

Open scheduling does not mean that teaching media skills should be placed on a catch-as-catch-can, unstructured basis. Every school district should adopt a sequential instructional plan that indicates the skills to be mastered at various grade levels. However, apart from a basic orientation to the school library media center, the teaching of these skills should be integrated with subject-matter courses and student activities. (Exhibits 3-1, 3-2, and 3-3 should aid the specialist in formulating teaching objectives.)

The Department of Educational Media and Technology of Montgomery County Public Schools in Maryland initiated its Media Skills Project in 1971 to determine a continuum of instructional objectives for school library media study skills in Maryland County schools. A committee of ten teachers and school library media specialists developed the tentative schedule shown in Exhibit 3-1. Although constantly changing, the plan as outlined is thorough and practical, and can serve as a workable model in districts where schedules have not been adopted. The Bureau of School Library Media Programs of the State Education Department, University of the State of New York, produced a library media skills curriculum in 1980 for grades K–6. More than 20 teachers and school library media specialists field-tested the plan; see as a sample the study skill lesson for grade 3 in Exhibit 3-2.

Although formal and informal instruction are the principal ways of informing students about the resources of the school library media center, there are other approaches as well. Some media centers prepare and distribute student handbooks. These publications vary considerably in size and depth of coverage. A handbook should provide the following basic information: (1) a floor plan of the center, (2) general information on the size and nature of the collection, (3) a list of center personnel and the services available to students, (4) a brief description of major locating devices used in the center (card catalog, Dewey decimal classification, periodical indexes), and (5) statements on the center's policies regarding hours of service, collection, and attendance. More elaborate handbooks also include annotations for major reference sources, longer descriptions of locating devices, and instructions on how to use various items of equipment. To decide how extensive the handbook should be, the school library media specialist should measure its projected value and expected use against the time and money that must be spent for production.

(text continues on page 46)

EXHIBIT 3-1   INSTRUCTIONAL OBJECTIVES
FOR MEDIA RESEARCH SKILLS*

The objectives described at each level are sequential. If a student is not performing at the suggested level, remedial instruction should be provided.

I. MEDIA CENTER ORIENTATION

GRADE LEVELS	OBJECTIVES
K-1	1. Name library personnel.
	2. Observe library rules.
	3. Handle books properly.
	4. Check out materials properly.
	5. Identify kinds of media (at ability level).
2-12	6. Check out material properly without assistance.

II. ORGANIZATION OF RESOURCES

GRADE LEVELS	OBJECTIVES
K-1	1. Locate "easy materials" (picture books).
	2. Find materials correctly in "easy reader" section.
2	3. Locate fiction and nonfiction collection and magazines.
	4. Locate card catalog, book catalogs.
	5. Locate filmstrips.
	6. Locate tapes and cassettes.
	7. Locate film loop projector.
	8. Locate records.
	9. Locate encyclopedias.
3	10. Find materials correctly in the fiction collection.
	11. Locate filmstrip projectors, film projectors, overhead, opaque, and slide projectors.
4	12. Find different categories of books according to the Dewey Decimal system.
	13. Locate the vertical file.
5-6	14. Identify correct placement of books using Dewey Decimal system.
	15. Locate indexes, atlases, almanacs, newspapers, and other reference materials.
	16. Locate guide to children's magazines.
7-8	17. Locate reference materials related to specific subject areas or courses (assessment tasks for this level should be geared to locating such works as *Current Biography, Reader's Guide, World Almanac*, etc.).

*Adapted from Montgomery County (Maryland) Dept. of Educational Media and Technology Media Skills Project.

EXHIBIT 3-1 (cont.)

II. ORGANIZATION OF RESOURCES (cont.)

GRADE LEVELS	OBJECTIVES
9–10	*Note*: Assessment tasks for this level should be geared to locating:
	1. Additional works such as *Statesman's Yearbook*, *Bartlett's Familiar Quotations*, *Dictionary of American Biography*, *Encyclopedia of American History*, etc.
	2. Newspaper indexes.
	3. Microfilm viewer, videotape recorder, video cartridge.
	4. Public library *adult catalog*.
11–12	*Note*: Assessment tasks for this level should be geared to locating:
	1. Additional works such as *Encyclopedia of European History*, Cambridge *History of English Literature*, Oxford *Companion to American Literature*, math dictionaries, Chemical Rubber Co. *Mathematics Handbook*, etc.

III. SELECTION OF RESOURCES

GRADE LEVELS	OBJECTIVES
K–1	1. Select materials for personal interest.
2	2. Select materials appropriate to student's reading level.
3	3. Choose a dictionary to find the meaning of a word.
	4. Distinguish between the content of a fiction and a nonfiction book.
	5. Distinguish between the use of filmstrip, film, overhead, opaque, and slide projectors.
4	6. Distinguish between content of a dictionary and of an encyclopedia.
	7. Select correct volume (using alphabetical order of encyclopedia) to find specific information.
5–6	8. Select correct materials for a specified topic.
	9. Select correct index for a specified purpose.
7–8	10. Select suitable source for information on a living person.
	11. Select source for quick summaries of facts.
	12. Select source for short, factual articles.
	13. Select source for identification of poetry and quotations.

EXHIBIT 3-1 (cont.)

III. SELECTION OF RESOURCES (cont.)

GRADE LEVELS	OBJECTIVES
9–12	14. Identify proper sources for information on specified subjects.
	15. Select suitable books and AV materials for a specified subject.
	16. Select readings that are authoritative, current, useful, etc.

IV. UTILIZATION OF RESOURCES

GRADE LEVELS	OBJECTIVES
K–1	1. Use a record and cassette player.
	2. Identify a book's illustrator, title, author.
2	3. Identify a book's front, back, spine.
	4. Use an 8mm film loop projector.
	5. Operate a filmstrip and slide previewer.
3	6. Alphabetize to second letter of author's last name.
	7. Identify a book's index.
	8. Use filmstrip, overhead, opaque, and slide projectors (optional).
4	9. Alphabetize to third letter of author's name, titles, etc.
	10. Identify a book's title page and table of contents.
	11. Identify copyright date and publisher.
	12. Use card and book catalogs to find call numbers.
	13. Use film projectors (optional).
	14. Use vertical files to obtain pamphlets, pictures, etc.
5–6	15. Alphabetize titles to the end of words.
	16. Distinguish between word-by-word and letter-by-letter alphabetizing.
	17. Identify a book's appendix or glossary.
	18. Use call numbers to find resources.
	19. Use tape recorder.
	20. Identify and state the purpose of the basic information on a catalog card.
7–8	21. Use cross references in card catalog.
	22. Use general reference works.
	23. Use reference works related to specific subject areas.
	24. Identify the sections of a newspaper and describe each one.

Note: Assessment tasks should be geared to student use of general works related to specific subjects such as those cited for grade level 7–8, section II.

EXHIBIT 3-1 (cont.)

IV. UTILIZATION OF RESOURCES (cont.)

GRADE LEVELS	OBJECTIVES
9–10	25. Use all necessary sources available to collect information for a specified subject. 26. Use microfilm viewer, videotape recorder (optional). 27. Obtain and use materials for local public libraries.
11–12	*Note*: Assessment tasks for this level should be geared to use of general and reference works related to specific subject areas such as those cited for grade level 9–10, section II.

V. COMPREHENSION AND STUDY SKILLS

GRADE LEVELS	OBJECTIVES
K–2	1. Use picture clues to aid in understanding material. 2. Identify main idea. 3. Identify a sequence of events.
3	4. Find specific information by using pictures and filmstrips. 5. Interpret simple pictorial maps and graphs. 6. Skim to find a word, name, date, phrase, sentence, idea, or answer to a question.
4	7. Use a book's table of contents to locate information. 8. Use a specified book to locate a specific fact. 9. Summarize simple information. 10. Use a book's index to locate information. 11. Find words in a dictionary. 12. Identify key words and key phrases in a reference work. 13. Use guide words.
5–6	14. Use encyclopedias, atlases, almanacs, telephone directories. 15. Find words in *Roget's Thesaurus*. 16. Write a simple outline. 17. Compile a simple bibliography. 18. Take notes using simple procedures.
7–8	19. Paraphrase or summarize information. 20. Use bibliographies to aid in locating information. 21. Skim to get an overview of material. 22. Compile a bibliography following a specified style. 23. Organize to show sequence. 24. Take notes using prescribed procedures. 25. Outline information in a topic or sentence outline.

EXHIBIT 3-1 (cont.)

V. COMPREHENSION AND STUDY SKILLS (cont.)

GRADE LEVELS	OBJECTIVES
	26. Identify topic sentence.
	27. Infer facts and ideas in a reading.
9–12	28. Compare figures in maps, graphs, statistical tables, to make generalizations, to infer, and to draw conclusions.
	29. Use specialized reference materials to develop and support research and select data bearing on a problem.
	30. Use preface, chapter headings, indexes, and cross references as research aids.
	31. Evaluate material for accuracy and appropriateness.
	32. Recognize digressions from the main idea of a subject.
	33. Select relevant information for a given purpose from within content of material.
	34. Skim to find material relevant to a topic.
	35. Distinguish between factual and emotional writing.
	36. Distinguish between fact and opinion.
	37. Use formal outline to organize information from reading selections and to aid in recall.
	38. Identify unsubstantiated statements.

VI. PRODUCTION (optional)

GRADE LEVELS	OBJECTIVES
K–2	1. Construct a picture based upon ideas in a story.
3	2. Construct a picture or series of pictures to illustrate a story.
4	3. Construct a model story book with a title, author, front, back, spine, table of contents, copyright date, publisher.
	4. Construct a "handmade" transparency.
5–6	5. Make a tape recording.
	6. Make a "machine-made" transparency.
7–8	7. Make a map floor plan of the media center.
	8. Make a color-lift.
	9. Make slides.
	10. Make filmstrips.
9–12	11. Make a videotape.
	12. Make a film or film loop.
	13. Prepare a detailed report using audiovisual aids.

EXHIBIT 3-2   GRADE THREE: LANGUAGE ARTS—
LITERARY COMPREHENSION, A SPRINGBOARD
TO CREATIVE WRITING*

Skills of Inquiry and Investigation
Literary Understanding and Appreciation
Use of Resources

RATIONALE

Children are led to examine the components of a story; they can by third grade recognize character, setting, and plot, and to a lesser degree, mood and theme. More importantly, children are led to react orally to what they read and hear.

This unit encourages teachers and library media specialists to read aloud to students every day in preparation for the culminating writing experience.... Objectives drawn from strands in *English Language Arts: Composition* and *Literature*, and *Composition K-6: A Packet for Teachers*, New York State Education Department, stress the sequential development of these skills.

APPROACH

The librarian, classroom teacher, and art teacher plan the unit together, setting up the roles that each will play and the schedule of activities. A picture book that will be used as a springboard for unit activities is selected.... For purposes of illustration, the motivational questions for part of this unit were based on *Where the Wild Things Are* by Maurice Sendak....

The saturation of exposure to literature through hearing and reading books is the initial stage of the unit....

The finished writing may be utilized in many ways depending on the interests, abilities of the class, and the time, interest, and ability of the librarian and teacher....

OBJECTIVES

I. Library Media Skills of Location and Use
   Using library resources, students will:
      Identify the following parts of a book: spine, etc. ...
      Find the title page and identify the author, etc. ...
      Participate in the construction of a model book. ...

II. Skills of Inquiry and Investigation
    Vocabulary Development
       Using beginning dictionaries, students will:
          Extract an appropriate definition.

---

*Adapted from University of the State of New York, State Education Department, *The Elementary Library Media Skills Curriculum, Grades K-6* (Albany, N.Y.: Bureau of School Library Media Programs, September 1980), pp. 43–48. ED 205199.

EXHIBIT 3-2 (cont.)

Using a thesaurus, students will:
Identify synonyms for an idea.
Identify associated words for an idea.
Identify shades of meaning in synonyms.

III. Literary Understanding and Appreciation
Using picture books, students will:
Grasp the main idea for a story.
Identify the main character in the story.
Describe the main character in the story.
Follow the pictures and retell the story.
Give oral reaction to vicarious experience.
Using traditional folktales, students will:
Draw conclusions from given facts.
Increase vocabulary to include ethnic idioms.
Take turns as storyteller, retelling parts of an entire story with increased detail.
Using fantasy, students will:
Develop greater imagination.
Hear models of standard spoken English.

IV. Language Arts Skills
Literature
The child learns what a character is like from: what he says, what he does, what the author says about him, how the illustrator portrays him.
The child learns that the outcome or conclusion of a story results logically from the actions of the character.
The child learns to recognize that the setting can influence the actions of the characters.
The child learns to identify the speaker in a selection.
The child learns to identify comparisons involving "like" or "as."
The child learns to recognize that each selection has an idea, which is called its theme.
Composition
The Sentence
The child learns to:
Understand and use basic sentence patterns.
Understand the relationship of order to meaning.
Use words and phrases to expand sentence patterns.
Develop a sense of word choice.
Organization and Development
The child learns to:
Understand unity and coherence.
Understand and organize by time order.
Recognize tone.

EXHIBIT 3-2 (cont.)

ACTIVITIES

Much of the practice of oral reading to give children broad exposure to good writing occurs outside the 6–8 week time frame of this unit. . . .

Librarian or teacher reads a picture book to the class and elicits from them identification of the components under objectives.

a. Pivotal questions
   1. Who is the most important person in the story?
   2. What words would you use to describe him/her/it?
   3. Who else is in the story? Describe them.
   4. Are there any characters in the story who are all bad or all good? Why do you think so?
   5. Does Max have a problem? What do you think?
   . . .
   13. Do you ever have Max's problem?

b. Resource
   A picture book selected for its excellent literary qualities and illustrations, [one] in which a theme common to children's experiences has been treated in an imaginative way. . . .

   Let children write descriptive sentences of what caused the sound in the story. . . .
   Have music teacher discuss with children the way in which music evokes moods.
   If a learning center approach is a familiar one for the students, a creative writing corner can be set up in the library media center or classroom. . . .

Developmental

   Students retell favorite story from stories heard or read. They prepare one picture cut from magazines or drawn to go with the story. These stories are taped.
   Show illustrations from several versions of the same folktales. Children explain whether the illustration is based on the beginning, middle, or end. They then arrange the illustrations in sequential order. . . .
   Using pictures of sports, games, or performances cut out from old magazines or posters, let students describe orally the most exciting moments in their favorite sports, games, or performances. . . .
   Ask students to bring pictures that describe sports, animals, television shows, personalities they like. They tell what they like about these. Students build their word banks to include more descriptive language. They use the thesaurus to find degrees of meaning of synonyms. . . .
   Building on skill in using similes and metaphors from language arts program, have students watch for new similes and metaphors. . . .

EXHIBIT 3-2 (cont.)

... Let children show examples of their favorite art work from picture books on display....

... Develop a series of mad-glad episodes and corresponding illustrations with the group.

Have students take turns telling familiar stories from the point of view of another character, e.g., "The 3 Pigs" from the point of view of the wolf....

Provide students with the beginning of a story. Then they add their own ending.

Let students practice telling their own stories first....

Show filmstrips *The Island of the Skog* and *How a Picture Book Is Made.* Have students list the steps in writing a book and getting it published. Have students find parts of the book using several titles.

Show 16mm film *Pagoo* or *Story of a Book,* 2nd ed. Have students discuss where an author gets the ideas for writing....

Share: Mathis, *The Hundred Penny Box,* Miles, *Annie and the Old One,* and Tazwell, *Littlest Angel* with the class. Let children describe orally one of their precious possessions. Write one or two of the "stories" on chart paper....

Use the recording of "These Are a Few of My Favorite Things" as background for sharing session with first graders as students tell their stories and show the objects....

Culminating

Have children go back to some of their favorite books to tell why they liked them. Encourage the use of terms—characterization, setting, plot, mood, theme.

... selections from ETV *Spinning Stories* (Maryland State Department of Education) 1977....

Discuss:
"That's Me"
"Do Something"
"My Feelings"
"Making Moods"
"Bubbles and Beanstalks"
"It's My Own"

... The overhead or large experience chart should be used to help show revisions of student work.

Review with the class shorter writing or taped assignments prepared earlier in the unit. Have class critique these and decide which ones they'd like to add to or hear more about....

Find patterned stories that children feel at home with; e.g., cumulative folktale, traditional folktale, etc.... Discuss these. Let each child tell (while teacher writes) or write his/her own patterned story. Have students critique these....

EXHIBIT 3-2 (cont.)

Prepare ways of sharing the writing done in this unit—displays, drama, puppetry, storytelling, original books, original filmstrips. . . .

Numerous suggestions for sharing children's writing are noted in *Composition K-6: A Packet for Teachers* (New York State Education Department, 1978).

Schools usually have stated goals in general terms, for example, to become a better citizen or to understand the beauty of language. Worthy as such aims may be, they remain abstract and difficult, if not impossible, to measure. Simple, overt student behavior is most easily cast in behavioral or instructional objectives, for example, a pupil will be able to locate the word *dinosaur* in a dictionary in three minutes. However, since learning is based on a multitude of fundamental previous learnings (the alphabet, in the above example), it is not a good idea to start with such a basic exercise either. The important thing is not to confine objective writing to the lowest level of cognitive, affective, or psychomotor learning. The guidelines in Exhibit 3-3 will help the school library media specialist to write objectives more skillfully.

Four specific points should be used in formulating instructional objectives:

1.   Identify by name the behavior you expect. Specify the kind of behavior that will be accepted as evidence that the learner has achieved the objective.

Ask: What should the pupil be able to do at the end of the activity that he or she cannot do now?

2.   Define the desired behavior further by describing the conditions under which the behavior will be expected to occur.

Ask: Under what limitations of time, place, and so on will the student be expected to show the desired outcome?

3.   Specify the criteria of acceptable performance by describing how well the student must perform.

Ask: Exactly how well must the student perform to be acceptable?

4.   Identify a suitable measure by which to judge the relative degree of success or failure of the activity.

Ask: How can the teacher measure what the student can do?

Following are general principles in regard to formulating objectives: (1) use an active verb that describes a visible activity or one that can

EXHIBIT 3-3   WRITING INSTRUCTIONAL OBJECTIVES

1. Behavioral task: What do you want the student to do? _____

_____

2. Curriculum area _____ 3. Estimated time _____

4. What intellectual process is involved? The student will have to:
   Learn definitions_____
   Remember principles_____
   Apply concepts_____
   Follow rules_____
   Change or paraphrase information from one form to another_____

   _____
   Look for relationships between ideas_____
   Apply principles, rules, or information to unfamiliar problems or situations__

   _____
   Analyze something by breaking it down into its parts_____

   _____
   Produce original solutions_____
   Evaluate information, object, or solutions against specific criteria_____

   _____

5. What will you provide for the student?
   Information_____Print and nonprint materials_____
   Equipment_____Other_____

6. How will the student be observed performing the task?
   Alone ____   Speaking _____ In groups _____ Reading _____
   Writing _____ Listening _____ Other _____

7. How will you judge the success of the performance?_____

   _____

_____

be measured or tested in some way, (2) leave only one interpretation possible; if the behavior is inconclusive, the testing will be also, (3) as a final check to test the validity of the objectives, ask the following four questions: What do I want the student to do? Under what conditions do I expect the student to do it? How will the student do it? How will I know when the student has done it?

Putting all these elements together in a hypothetical educational objective frame in behavioral terms, the following might result: Within 20 minutes, the sixth-grader will list on paper the location, author, and title of five media—including book and nonbook—about computers (or any appropriate subject) with all the above information exactly as it appears on the catalog card. The form shown in Exhibit 3-3 will be useful in preparing instructional objectives.

PUBLICIZING THE SCHOOL LIBRARY MEDIA CENTER

Orientation

The school library media center staff should be active in developing in-service training for the faculty. The training can be informal, during joint planning sessions with teachers, classroom visits, or at grade-level or departmental meetings. More structured presentations can be conducted at faculty meetings or during workshop sessions.

Part of the orientation program for new teachers should be a tour of the center conducted by the staff, supplying a general introduction to the collection and the services available to the faculty. Some centers also prepare a special handbook for teachers or a section for the general faculty handbook used in the school. The section on publicizing the center later in this chapter gives other useful techniques for working with teachers.

Orientation periods and close supervision during initial work sessions are two useful methods of introducing new members of the clerical staff or volunteer workers to the procedures and routines of the school library media center. Staff manuals are another helpful training tool.

Before the beginning of the school year, some school districts conduct special in-service courses of one or two weeks' duration for new clerical assistants. Basic topics that should be covered in these sessions are:

1. General orientation
   a. Recent developments in education and their relation to the school library media center concept.
   b. The program of the school library media center in individual schools.
   c. Media center services available outside the school (district-wide centralized services, services supplied by other libraries and information agencies).
   d. The administrative structure of the school district.
   e. The role of the clerical assistant.
2. Ordering and receiving procedures
   a. Forms used in the district.
   b. Ordering procedures for books, texts, other instructional materials, bindary items, equipment, furniture, professional materials, supplies, and rentals.
   c. Accounting and business practices.
3. Processing of material (If there is a centralized processing agency, coverage of this topic will be brief.)

4. Arrangement of material
   a. Dewey decimal classification system.
   b. Catalog (e.g., card, book, computer).
   c. Shelf list.
   d. Arrangement of cards, and so forth (filing rules and procedures).
   e. Practice in card filing.
5. Operation and maintenance of equipment
   a. Demonstration and practice with various types of equipment.
   b. Simple repairs required on equipment.
6. Local production of materials
   a. Demonstration and practice, for example, in duplicating materials and in making transparencies.
   b. Techniques used, for example, in mounting materials.
7. Care of materials
   a. Instruction and practice in performing simple repairs on printed materials.
   b. Care of nonprint materials.

In-service courses will have to be supplemented in two ways: (1) with districtwide sessions during the school year to update personnel on new developments or to serve as refresher courses, and (2) at the local level, with additional in-service work to acquaint new personnel with the routines and procedures peculiar to the individual school.

HOURS OF SERVICE AND ATTENDANCE

School library media centers usually open for service at the time the first students and teachers arrive (about half an hour before classes begin), are open during the entire school day, and remain open for an hour or an hour and a half after the school day ends, or as long as students are present in sufficient numbers to warrant keeping the center open. The number of afterschool hours depends on several factors: transportation available to students who remain after school hours, other library resources available in the district and their accessibility, the number of afterschool activities that make use of the collection, and the flexibility of the center's circulation policies. Some school library media centers have experienced varying degrees of success with extending hours into the evenings and weekends, thus supplying students and other members of the community additional opportunities to use the collection. Special summer school library media programs are also held where there are both need and funds.

The objective of attendance policies is to get as many students into the center as often as they wish. Ideally, therefore, any student who wishes to use the center should have free and open access to it. In some secondary schools that have adopted flexible schedules, students in the upper grades are given some choice concerning where they will spend their free time. They may visit the school library media center, a study hall, or the student lounge. In more rigidly structured situations, students often must obtain passes before they are allowed to go to the center from study halls. A pass system frequently admits students to the center from classrooms. Sometimes students have the option of attending a study hall or checking into the center.

Restrictive policies sometimes have to be adopted to prevent overcrowding in the school library media center. They are also methods of keeping an account of students during the school day. Since each school situation is unique to some degree, the merits and deficiencies of various plans should be studied to find the one that best promotes good use of the school library media center and at the same time allows students suitable access to the collection.

Whenever possible, teachers should schedule classes or small groups into the school library media center at least a few days in advance of the visit. In this way center staff members can allocate their time and provide the necessary physical space, prepare lessons, collect needed material, and check with the teacher on such preparations before the class is due. The center should maintain "sign-up sheets" that give the time and purpose of the visit. On a daily or weekly basis, a master schedule should be distributed to teachers and administrators to inform them when the staff is free for conferences or last-minute scheduling.

The days of the "shushing" librarian have drawn to a close and "Silence Please" signs are no longer found in library supply house catalogs. It is natural and normal for students to talk quietly in the school library media center and the staff should not try to prevent a healthy level of conversation. Students increasingly become accustomed to background noises and seem able to block them out easily. Certain areas in the school library media center should therefore be designated for quiet conversation. Spaces around the periodical collection, lounge areas, and specified tables set aside for small-group work are suitable for this purpose. On the other hand, some sections of the center, such as areas where there are individual study carrels, should be designated for quiet study where there are no distracting interruptions.

Of course, the center staff will have to cope with discipline problems at times. A staff member should try to deal with the individual responsible for the disruption in a personal conference rather than before the group. It is important for the staff to understand any underlying basic problems of the student so that the real cause and not just a symptom may be treated, although the episode must be handled immediately. Perhaps the best advice for school library media specialists in these situations is not to interpret such occurrences as personal affronts but instead to maintain a balanced view and a sense of humor.

PUBLIC RELATIONS

Good public relations requires conscious and continuous effort; such a program cannot be turned on or off at will. Every time a patron has any contact with the school library media center—directly or indirectly—an impression is created that will either enhance or damage the center's image. Any and every aspect of the center and its program affects public relations.

Of initial importance in public relations concerning the school library media center is the atmosphere. The center should be a friendly, cheery place. This feeling may be produced partly by the physical surroundings—they should be inviting and pleasant and convey warmth and a feeling of hospitality. Center personnel should constantly reassess the facilities from the standpoint of users who are entering for the first time. Is the general impression favorable? Is the furniture comfortable? Is it attractively arranged? Are browsing and lounge areas provided that are conducive to relaxation and enjoyment? Are all the various parts of the collection clearly marked for easy identification? Are all display areas well used?

Bulletin boards and display cases attract potential users to the school library media center, publicize its services, and familiarize students with the collection. Although displays are important inside the center, display facilities in corridors and classrooms should also advertise and promote it. Displays can be fitted into a number of places. Conventional bulletin boards and table- or window-type display cases are most frequently used, but any unused wall space can accommodate a corkboard or pegboard hooked onto the space, suspended by wires from the ceiling, or displayed on a simple easel setup on the floor. Easels can also be used for direct display of posters or other informational resources. Bare walls can serve as a display area for continuous multimedia shows, and corners of a school library media center area can be used to exhibit life-size displays of resources and activities.

Following are some steps for preparing a display:

1. Decide on the subject; a specific, concrete subject is usually better than a general one.
2. Select a caption; make it short, interest-catching, and large

enough to be seen at a distance. Where appropriate, present it with a light touch—perhaps with a play on words or some similar device (e.g., "Take me to your reader").

3. Make a rough sketch showing both placement and color of material and backdrop; arrange the parts so that they have a logical form and the eye travels naturally and easily from one section to another. One of the most common devices is to arrange the parts so that they lead the eye to the center of the display.

4. Produce an interesting balance and keep the display uncluttered.

5. Keep it neat. Lettering is not everyone's forte; if this is the case, use commercially manufactured letters.

6. Maintain a file of materials and ideas.

Materials for displays can be easily improvised. Attractive backgrounds can be created with wallpaper, poster paper, burlap, metallic paper, or foil. A variety of simple materials can be used for a three-dimensional effect. Mailing tubes can become large pencils or rocket ships; paper plates can become frames; and cotton batting or steel wool can serve as clouds or hair. Coat hangers make an excellent framework for mobiles.

Some other pointers: Change the display often—in order not to run the risk of losing the audience—and integrate student projects and community resources with the school library media center's materials. Copies of the material on display should also be available for circulation in the center. This will mean using articles for which there are duplicate copies in the center or, in the case of books or filmstrips, using dust jackets or promotional material obtained from publishers or producers. With a bit of imagination and ingenuity, the center staff can easily produce attractive, eye-catching displays, but if ideas are slow in coming or time is too tight to allow for original planning, consult the many guide books and articles written about producing displays. The card catalog is a good place to start.

The well-being of patrons is a responsibility of every worker in the center—from volunteer students and parents to the school library media center's full-time staff. It is important that each person be given instructions in how to act toward patrons and how to give proper assistance. In some cases, simply referring the patron to a professional staff member might fulfill the person's responsibility. This simple operation, as all others, should be handled with tact and concern for the patron. All helpers should be aware not only of the established regulations governing the center's program, but also of the reasons why these regulations have been adopted. In this way simple explanations can be given to patrons when particular policies are questioned.

The center staff should also periodically review adopted policies to determine whether they actually promote and facilitate the program or simply act as roadblocks between the patron and the services that are needed.

In wholesome public relations promoting school library media center services, center personnel will work with several different groups inside the school—students, teachers, administrators, and in the community—parents, community groups, local news media, public and other library agencies. Successful communication with one group certainly can affect and influence the others. In spite of this interrelationship, it is helpful to isolate and study the development of good relations with each.

Students

There are many special ways to promote the school library media center and its services with students. The staff should try to relate the general activities of the school and the current interests and experiences of the students to the center. For example, a student play or assembly program or an important sport event can form the basis of a display, mediography, or some special library program. Also usable are popular television programs, current movies, community activities, world events, or social issues.

All available channels of information should be used to disseminate news about the school library media center. The school newspaper and public address system are two such channels. Some centers publish their own bulletins containing such items as new acquisitions; student reviews; lists of titles that reflect reading, listening, and viewing preferences of different classes or teachers; news on school library media center events; and mediographies of current popular subjects. In addition to the book talks and story hours offered in the center, visits can be arranged to classrooms or to club meetings to introduce appropriate material to students and teachers.

Student reading, listening, and viewing experiences can help to promote the school library media center. Informal sharing periods are popular with students, during which they talk about titles they have enjoyed. A separate file drawer of cards containing titles recommended by students (and arranged by students' last names) is often used. Bulletin board displays or printed booklets containing brief reviews written by students can also draw attention to student preferences.

The promotion of such special events as National Book Week and Children's Book Week, as well as media center–sponsored assembly

programs, book fairs, and bookstores, not only furnish valuable services but also help publicize and promote the total program. Many
school library media centers sponsor group activities, such as reading
clubs and film forums, play-reading groups, career programs, or discussion groups on topics of interest to students.

Planners of group activities should remember to schedule meetings
on a regular basis and to allow sufficient time before each event to
publicize it thoroughly. It is advisable to form a planning group or club
council composed chiefly of students to assure potential interest in the
program. A prepared agenda should be drawn up before each meeting.
Resource persons and materials for programs may often be found
within the community and backup material from the school library
media center can be utilized. When appropriate, mention may be made
during the meeting of other media center material related to the topic
under discussion. Specially prepared mediagraphies might be distributed to teachers.

Teachers

Many of the techniques used with students can help to develop good
public relations with teachers. For example, using school library media
center materials in joint displays in the classroom and the center is an
excellent way to gain the support of teachers and at the same time promote the center's collection. Some school library media centers, particularly in very large schools where direct communication between
the center and its users is difficult, have organized advisory committees composed of teachers, students, and representatives from both
the central administration and the media center staff. These committees gather information on user needs, supply advice on policymaking, and, in turn, publicize and interpret those policies to the
general public.

The development of special services involving the professional collection is another useful technique. These services could include
routing pertinent articles from professional journals, announcing the
arrival of new material, and preparing mediagraphies on educational
topics of current interest to the faculty. The active participation of the
school library media center's staff on teacher committees and in professional organizations and the use of the staff as resource personnel
for these groups will help build a liaison between the media center and
the faculty.

Perhaps the best way to reach teachers is by giving them the personalized attention and professional concern that will aid them in
preparing, organizing, and presenting instructional programs—in

short, providing the support that will help them to become better teachers. School library media center specialists sometimes assign individual staff members to act as advisers to specific grade levels, academic departments, or teaching teams. Staff time is often set aside for conferences with teachers in the center. Other specialists arrange discussions with teachers in the classroom setting. In any case, faculty members should be encouraged to spend part of their classroom preparation periods consulting with the center staff, preferably in the school library media center, and becoming acquainted with the center's resources that are appropriate to their classroom needs.

Administrators

The same techniques used with students and teachers (displays, newsletters, and the like) will also make the administration aware of the various facets of the school library media center's resources and programs. The school administration should always be consulted in developing media center policies, and members should be invited to participate in any special events held in the center.

The resources of the school library media center should be made available for those activities that grow out of the administrative function. For example, the media center staff might prepare visuals to aid in a budget presentation or to illustrate and interpret a new teaching program before a parent group. The staff should also be available to provide any backup reference service required by the administration. This might be in supplying specific information, locating material, preparing mediographies, or routing professional materials. Specifically, the center staff should keep the administration abreast of the latest developments in media and school library media centers. In addition to furnishing material on these subjects, center personnel should be encouraged to invite administrators to local conferences, workshops, or exhibits where educational media and their uses are presented.

Community

Although one of the most important links in a good public relations program is informing the community about the services of the school library media center, this is probably the area given the least attention. Many parents and school board officials are still not aware of the concept of the school library media center, let alone the specific activities and programs connected with it. Yet the support that the center receives from a community helps to determine its success. This support may be directly related to school budgets or indirectly related to forwarding the school's philosophy. It is therefore essential that the media center's professional staff members devote some of their time to explaining and interpreting their program to persons who may not use their services, but who nevertheless sustain the program through financial and moral support.

These are a few techniques to help reach this "hidden" public:

1. Prepare a simple slide/tape presentation that illustrates the services given to students by the school library media center and present it (followed by a discussion period) to parent and community groups.
2. Utilize local news media to publicize the activities of the center.
3. Schedule a once-a-year School Library Media Night for parent groups to acquaint them with the latest developments at the center.
4. Plan special programs for those occasions—a Back-to-School Night, for example—when parents visit the school.
5. Encourage parents, school board members, and community leaders to visit the center while school is in session.
6. Utilize community resources for displays and speaking engagements.
7. Make school library media center resources available for use by school-based parent groups.
8. Attend and participate in community functions.
9. Utilize parents' help for such special functions as book fairs.
10. Prepare and distribute to parents mediographies, recommended lists, and guides to reference books and information sources.

Cooperation with Agencies

Building good relations between the school library media center and other library agencies in the community not only helps to promote and publicize the center's program, but, more importantly, can result in better service and more effective use of material by students. An initial step is for the staffs to become acquainted with each other and familiar with the resources and regulations of each other's services. In many school districts, an interlibrary council has been established to discuss mutual problems and concerns in order to develop procedures to help solve or eliminate them. The school library media center staff can also serve as a clearinghouse of information about other libraries by publicizing their programs, having their colleagues—especially public librarians—visit the school to talk before students and teachers, and arranging class visits to other libraries.

The school library media center staff should keep in touch with other libraries on a regular basis and notify them of school assignments, recent curriculum changes, new acquisitions, and other developments within the school that might affect the students' use of a given library's collection. This line of communication should be maintained particularly with the public library, and in turn the public library can promote special events and services offered by the school library media center. To avoid duplication and wasted time and effort, some activities, such as film forums or summer reading programs, might be jointly planned and sponsored by several media centers, together with the public library.

It is necessary for the school library media center's staff to look outside itself and reach all groups affected by the center. Each situation is unique in some respects and, therefore, will require different solutions. Many of the suggestions in this chapter might not be applicable or feasible, others might have to be modified, and in some cases totally new approaches may have to be devised. Professionalism, imagination, and an honest desire to supply maximum service with the materials available are keynotes in utilizing and promoting the resources of the school library media center.

EVALUATING THE PROGRAM

Evaluating a program for effectiveness and direction for future improvement is becoming increasingly important, as well as complex. There are a number of studies concerning the evaluation of school library media programs, such as:

Bantley, Harold. *The Media Program Profile: An Assessment Technique.* Framingham, Mass.: New England Development Council, 1978.

Committee on Evaluation of Media Programs. *Evaluating Media Programs: District & School.* Washington, D.C.: AECT, 1980.

Liesner, Joseph. *Instruments for Planning and Evaluating Library Media Programs,* rev. ed. College Park, Md.: University of Maryland Library Service, 1980.

Loertscher, David V., and Janet G. Stroud. *PSES: Purdue Self-Evaluation System for School Media Centers—Elementary Catalog.* Fayetteville, Ark.: Hi Willow, 1976.

———. *PSES: Purdue Self-Evaluation System for School Media Centers—Jr. Sr. High Catalog.* Fayetteville, Ark.: Hi Willow, 1976.

School Library Manpower Project. *Evaluation of Alternative Curricula:*

Approaches to School Library Media Education. Chicago: American Library Association, 1975.

Woolls, Blanche, et al. *Evaluation Techniques for School Library/Media Programs: A Work Shop Outline.* Pittsburgh, Pa.: Graduate School of Library and Information Sciences, University of Pittsburgh, 1977.

All of these studies can be examined, but a good way to begin is to use the self-evaluation forms shown in Exhibits 3-4 and 3-5, which suggest the vital areas in the program that may be measured and that will give a quantitative and qualitative picture of the existing program. For example, ascertaining the numerical range of people served in each of the audiences will allow the school library media specialist to view the program realistically and consequently to reorder priorities and institute other services to give a better balance to the program in the individual school. Each school library media specialist may also wish to develop a special measure that relates more closely to the local school library media program.

The process of program evaluation is continuous and includes the steps shown in the illustration.

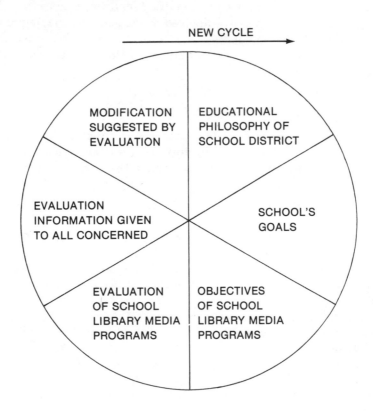

EXHIBIT 3-4
SCHOOL LIBRARY MEDIA PROGRAM SELF-EVALUATION FORM

Grades____ to____   No. of students_____   No. of teachers_____

High school curriculum: ____% college bound   ____% vocational
                        ____% handicapped

Elementary curriculum: ____% exceptional   ____% slow learner
                       ____% handicapped

Attrition rate ____% Average class size ____

Services to Students	Total school	½ or more	¼ or more	less than ¼
Guidance in reading, viewing, listening	_____	_____	_____	_____
Reference				
Assistance	_____	_____	_____	_____
Queries answered	_____	_____	_____	_____
Library media orientation				
Once a year	_____	_____	_____	_____
Periodically	_____	_____	_____	_____
Library media instruction				
Regularly	_____	_____	_____	_____
Infrequently	_____	_____	_____	_____
Local production	_____	_____	_____	_____
Vocational guidance				
Clubs	_____	_____	_____	_____
Presentations	_____	_____	_____	_____
Special programs				
Computers	_____	_____	_____	_____
Film	_____	_____	_____	_____
Other	_____	_____	_____	_____

Services to Teachers	Total faculty	½ or more	¼ or more	less than ¼
Media examination & selection	_____	_____	_____	_____
Local production facilities	_____	_____	_____	_____
Provision of media for developing students' independent study skills	_____	_____	_____	_____
Coordination of materials with instructional program	_____	_____	_____	_____
Assistance in planning & presenting instructional skills lessons	_____	_____	_____	_____

EXHIBIT 3-4 (cont.)

Services to Teachers	Total faculty	½ or more	¼ or more	less than ¼
Participation in teaching re-source units	_____	_____	_____	_____
Media for personal needs	_____	_____	_____	_____
In-service courses	_____	_____	_____	_____

Services to Administrators	All info. needed	½ or more	¼ or more	none
Serve as clearinghouse for information on: professional courses, workshops, meetings; community resources	_____	_____	_____	_____
Media for school programs	_____	_____	_____	_____
Media for personal needs	_____	_____	_____	_____
Local production	_____	_____	_____	_____

Services to Community & Community Groups

Media for group programs	_____	_____	_____	_____
Media for personal needs	_____	_____	_____	_____
Other	_____	_____	_____	_____

Accountability Measurements

Instructional Objectives
  Performance level achieved   _____ program 1   _____ program 2
Instruction
  Reference   _____ students   _____ teachers
  Information services   _____ students   _____ teachers
  Team teaching   _____ courses   _____ hours
Daily circulation
  Materials   _____ school   _____ home
  Equipment   _____ school   _____ home
Attendance
  Regular hours   _____ daily   _____ annually
  Extended hours   _____ daily   _____ annually

EXHIBIT 3-5   SUPPORT SERVICES SELF-EVALUATION FORM

BUDGET INFORMATION

Item	Quantity needed	Average cost per item	Total
Books	_____	_____	_____
Periodicals	_____	_____	_____
Pamphlets, etc.	_____	_____	_____
		Print total _____	
Films, purchase	_____	_____	_____
Films, rental	_____	_____	_____
Filmstrips	_____	_____	_____
Slides	_____	_____	_____
Records	_____	_____	_____
Computer software	_____	_____	_____
Tapes	_____	_____	_____
Cassettes, audio	_____	_____	_____
Cassettes, video	_____	_____	_____
Flat pictures	_____	_____	_____
Microfilm or fiche	_____	_____	_____
		Nonprint total _____	
Supplies	_____	_____	_____
Equipment	_____	_____	_____
Repairs	_____	_____	_____
Other	_____	_____	_____
		Total expenses _____	

STAFF INFORMATION

Job Category	Number	Years in position	Years in district	Salaries
Professional	_____	_____	_____	_____
Paraprofessional	_____	_____	_____	_____
Nonprofessional	_____	_____	_____	_____
Clerks	_____	_____	_____	_____
Technicians	_____	_____	_____	_____
Volunteers	_____	_____	_____	_____
Students	_____	_____	_____	_____
Parents	_____	_____	_____	_____

EXHIBIT 3-5 (cont.)

FACILITIES INFORMATION

Activities Areas	Size (sq. ft.)	Seating capacity
Reading, viewing, listening	_____	_____
Teachers' library media prep. room	_____	_____
Conference room	_____	_____
Typing room	_____	_____
Office	_____	_____
Library media classroom	_____	_____
Workrooms	_____	_____
Production	_____	_____
Radio & TV studios	_____	_____

Storage	Size (sq. ft.)	Location
Print	_____	_____
Nonprint	_____	_____
Equipment	_____	_____
Magazines	_____	_____
Darkroom	_____	_____

Environmental Elements	Type	Number
Acoustics	_____	_____
Lighting control	_____	_____
Electrical outlets	_____	_____
Cables for TV, computers, etc.	_____	_____
Temperature control	_____	_____
Furniture (wood, metal, etc.)	_____	_____
Card, book, or computer catalog	_____	_____
Circulation desk	_____	_____
Tables, chairs	_____	_____
Study carrels, nonelectronic	_____	_____
Study carrels, electronic	_____	_____
Pamphlet files	_____	_____
Displays	_____	_____
Bulletin boards	_____	_____

EXHIBIT 3-5 (cont.)

ACQUISITIONS & ORGANIZATION INFORMATION

Activity	Centralized	Decentralized
Purchasing	_____	_____
Processing	_____	_____
Organization	_____	_____

POLICIES

Public Relations
   Students _____ Teachers _____ Administrators _____
   Parents _____ Community _____ Public library _____
   Other agencies _____
Hours open
   Before school _____ After school _____ Evenings _____
   Saturday _____ Summer _____
Communications
   Telephone service _____ Delivery service _____
Circulation
   System _____ Records _____ Fines _____
Records and Reports
   Financial _____ Inventory _____ Organization manual _____

FOR FURTHER READING

"All Day Workshop in Library Services for Disabled Persons." Proceedings of workshop held on March 30, 1981, Queens College Graduate School of Library and Information Studies, New York City.

American Association of School Librarians, Evaluation of School Media Programs Committee. *Evaluating the School Library Media Program: A Working Bibliography for the Building-Level Media Specialist.* Chicago: AASL, 1981.

Angoff, Alan. *Public Relations for Libraries.* Westport, Conn.: Greenwood, 1973.

Association for Educational Communications and Technology, Committee on Evaluation of Media Programs. *Evaluating Media Programs: District and School, A Method and an Instrument.* Washington, D.C.: AECT, 1976.

Baker, D. Philip. "School and Public Library Programs and Information Dissemination." *School Media Quarterly*, Winter 1977, pp. 119–127.

——, and Bender, David. *Library Media Programs and the Special Learner.* Hamden, Conn.: Library Professional Publications, 1981.

Barron, David. "Role of the School Media Program and Specialist in Community Education." *School Media Quarterly*, Fall 1978, pp. 12–18.

Baskin, Barbara Holland, and Harris, Karen H. *The Special Child in the Library*. Chicago: American Library Association, 1976.

Bell, Irene Wood. *Basic Media Skills through Games*. Littleton, Colo.: Libraries Unlimited, 1979.

Blostein, Fay. *Invitations, Celebrations: A Handbook of Ideas and Techniques for Promoting Reading in Junior and Senior High Schools*. Toronto: Ontario Library Association, 1980.

Bowers, Melvyn K. *Easy Bulletin Boards—Number 2*. Metuchen, N.J.: Scarecrow, 1974.

Branscombe, F. R., and Newsom, H. *Resource Services for Canadian Schools*. New York: McGraw-Hill Ryerson, 1977.

Caparelli, F. A. *A Practical Approach to Programming*. Chicago: American Library Association/Reference and Adult Services Division, 1982.

Case, Robert N., and Lowrey, Anna Mary. *Curriculum Alternatives*. Chicago: American Library Association, 1974.

———. *Evaluation of Alternate Curricula*. Chicago: American Library Association, 1975.

Clendening, Corinne, and Davies, Ruth Ann. *Creating Programs for the Gifted*. New York: R. R. Bowker, 1980.

Commissioner's Committee on State Library Development. Albany: University of the State of New York, 1981.

Conference on Library Orientation. *Improving Library Instruction*. Ann Arbor, Mich.: Pierian Press, 1979.

Coplan, Kate. *Effective Library Exhibits*, rev. 2nd ed. Dobbs Ferry, N.Y.: Oceana, 1974.

"Curriculum-Integrated Library Instruction." *Liberal Education*, Winter 1980, pp. 402–409.

Davies, Ruth Ann. *The School Library Media Program: Instructional Force for Excellence,* 3rd ed. New York: R. R. Bowker, 1979.

Delaney, Jack J. *The Media Program in the Elementary and Middle Schools*. Hamden, Conn.: Linnett Books, 1976.

Dequin, Henry C., and Smith, Jane. "Learning Disabled Students Can Be Tutors in Library Media Skills." *Top of the News*, Summer 1980, pp. 352–356.

Dick, Walter, and Carey, Lou. *The Systematic Design of Instruction*. Glenview, Ill.: Scott Foresman, 1978.

Dyer, Esther. *Cooperation in Library Service to Children*. Metuchen, N.J.: Scarecrow, 1978.

Edsall, Marian S. *Library Promotion Handbook*. Phoenix, Ariz.: Oryx, 1981.

———. Library Public Relations Audio Tapes. Phoenix, Ariz.: Oryx, 1982.

Ehrhardt, Margaret W., and Griffin, Mary Frances. *Media Programs: An Evaluation Guide. Techniques for Improving Media Services (K–12)*. Columbia: South Carolina State Department of Education, 1978.

Evaluative Checklist: An Instrument for Self-Evaluating an Educational Media Program in School Systems. Washington, D.C.: AECT, 1979.

Franklin, Linda C. *Library Display Ideas.* Jefferson, N.C.: McFarland & Co., 1980.

Garvey, Mona. *Library Public Relations.* Bronx, N.Y.: H. W. Wilson, 1980.

Gaver, Mary. *Services of Secondary School Media Centers: Evaluation and Development.* Chicago: American Library Association, 1971.

Gillespie, John T. *A Model School District Media Program: Montgomery County as a Case Study.* Chicago: American Library Association, 1977.

Grazier, Margaret Hayes. "A Role for Media Specialists in the Curriculum Development Process." *School Media Quarterly,* Spring 1976, pp. 199-204.

Guidelines for California Library Media Programs. Burlingame: California Media and Libraries Educators Association, 1977.

Hart, Thomas L., ed. *Instruction in School Media Center Use.* Chicago: American Library Association, 1978.

Herring, James. *School Librarianship.* Hamden, Conn.: Shoe String, 1982.

Hirsch, Ruth, and Lewinger, Miriam. "Oral History: The Family Is the Curriculum," *Teacher,* November 1975, pp. 60-62.

Hoffman, Elizabeth P. "The Art of Public Relations." *School Media Quarterly,* Fall 1980, pp. 31-35.

Hopkins, Lee Bennett. *The Best of Book Bonanza.* New York: Holt, 1980.

"How to Prepare a Presentation." Washington, D.C.: National School Public Relations Association. Sound filmstrip.

"Instructional Development in Schools: A Proposed Model." *School Media Quarterly,* Summer 1981, pp. 256-260+.

Instructional Media Programs in the State Library Network. Madison: Wisconsin State Department of Public Instruction, 1980.

Jay, Ellen. *Library Media Programs for the Gifted.* Hamden, Conn.: Shoe String, 1982.

Jonassen, David H. *Non-Book Media, A Self-Paced Instruction Handbook.* Hamden, Conn.: Shoe String, 1982.

Karnes, Frances A., and Collins, Emily C. *Handbook of Instructional Resources and References for Teaching the Gifted.* Boston: Allyn & Bacon, 1980.

Kies, Cosette, *Projecting a Positive Image through Public Relations.* Chicago: American Library Association, 1979.

Kirkendall, Carolyn B. *Improving Library Instruction.* Ann Arbor, Mich.: Pierian Press, 1979.

Kohn, Rita, and Tepper, Krysta A. *Have You Got What They Want? Public Relations Strategies for the School Librarian/Media Specialist.* Metuchen, N.J.: Scarecrow, 1982.

——. *You Can Do It: A PR Skills Manual for Librarians.* Metuchen, N.J.: Scarecrow, 1981.

Kroth, Roger, and Brown, Gweneth Blacklock. "Welcome in the Parent." *School Media Quarterly*, Summer 1978, pp. 246–252.

Leerburger, B. A. *Marketing the Library*. White Plains, N.Y.: Knowledge Industry, 1981.

Levitan, Karen. "The School Library as an Instructional Information System." *School Media Quarterly*, Spring 1975, pp. 194–203.

Liesener, James W. *A Systematic Process for Planning Media Programs*. Chicago: American Library Association, 1976.

Martin, Betty, and Sargent, L. *The Teacher's Handbook on the School Library Media Center*. Hamden, Conn.: Shoe String, 1980.

Nordling, Jo Anne. *Dear Faculty: A Discovery Method Guidebook to the High School Library*. Westwood, Mass.: Faxon, 1976.

Ohio Educational Library/Media Association. Public Relations Committee. *Practical Public Relations: Effective PR Techniques for School Library/ Media Specialists*. Columbus, Ohio: OELMA, 1981.

Pillon, Nancy B. "Media Specialist, An Active Member of the Teaching Team." *Indiana Media Journal*, Summer 1980, pp. 27–28.

Polette, Nancy, and Hamlin, Marjorie. *Reading Guidance in a Media Age*. Metuchen, N.J.: Scarecrow, 1975.

The Report on Library Cooperation, 4th ed. Washington, D.C.: Government Printing Office, 1982.

Robotham, John S., and LaFleur, Lydia. *Library Programs: How to Select, Plan and Produce Them*. Metuchen, N.J.: Scarecrow, 1981.

Schipper, William. "Overview of the Legislation—P.L. 94-142." *School Media Quarterly*, Fall 1979, pp. 17–21.

Shapiro, Lillian L. *Teaching Yourself in Libraries: A Guide to the High School Media Center and Other Libraries*. Bronx, N.Y.: H. W. Wilson, 1978.

Sherman, Steve. *ABC's of Library Promotion*, 2nd ed. Metuchen, N.J.: Scarecrow, 1980.

Silverman, Eleanor. *101 Media Center Ideas*. Metuchen, N.J.: Scarecrow, 1980.

"Some Libraries Do Everything Well! An Example of School/Public Library Cooperation." *Top of the News*, Summer 1980, pp. 357–362.

Spirt, Diana L. *Library/Media Manual*. Bronx, N.Y.: H. W. Wilson, 1979.

Thomas, Carol H., and Thomas, James L. *Meeting the Needs of the Handicapped: A Resource for Teachers and Librarians*. Phoenix, Ariz.: Oryx, 1980.

Thomas, James L. *Turning Kids on to Print Using Non-Print*. Littleton, Colo.: Libraries Unlimited, 1978.

Thomason, Nevada Wallis. *The Library Media Specialist in Curriculum Development*. Metuchen, N.J.: Scarecrow, 1981.

"Understanding Educational Technology." Washington, D.C.: AECT, 1977. Sound filmstrip.

"Using the Library and Media Center." Jamaica, N.Y.: Eye-Gate Media, 1976. Sound filmstrip.

Vandergrift, Kay E. *The Teaching Role of the School Media Specialist.* Chicago: American Library Association, 1979.

Velleman, Ruth. *Serving Physically Disabled People.* New York: R. R. Bowker, 1980.

Walker, H. Thomas. "Media Services for Gifted Learners." *School Media Quarterly,* Summer 1978, pp. 253–254+.

Walker, H. Thomas, and Montgomery, Paula Kay. *Teaching Media Skills: An Instructional Program for Elementary and Middle School Students.* Littleton, Colo.: Libraries Unlimited, 1977.

Wasserman, Paul, and Rizzo, J. R. "Course in Administration for Managers of Information Services: Design, Implementation and Topical Outline." *Information: Reports and Bibliographies,* 1977, pp. 2–28.

Wehmeyer, Lillian Biermann. *The School Librarian as Educator.* Littleton, Colo.: Libraries Unlimited, 1976.

Weisburg, Hilda, and Toor, Ruth. *Elementary School Librarians Almanac: A Complete Media Program for Every Month of the School Year.* West Nyack, N.Y.: Center for Applied Research in Education, 1979.

Wisconsin School Library Media Association. *The Wisconsin Library Media Skills Guide.* Madison: Wisconsin Library Association, 1980.

Wise, Bernice Kemler. *Teaching Materials for the Learning Disabled: A Selected List for Grades 6–12.* Chicago: American Library Association, 1980.

Yungmeyer, Elinor. "District Media Program" in *Frontiers of Library Service for Youth.* New York: School of Library Science, Columbia University Press, 1979.

Zettel, Jeffrey J., and Abeson, Alan. "Litigation, Law & the Handicapped." *School Media Quarterly,* Summer 1978, pp. 234–245.

4

BUDGET

The budget has become increasingly important to all parts of the school and to the community since the 1960s. Because accounting principles and needs have also changed, it is imperative for the school library media specialist to pay close attention to the center's budget. Over the years schools have developed newer approaches to teaching and have refined those that are timeless. They have also adopted some form of unified media program based on societal changes, especially those that are responses to electrically powered equipment. Schools, as always, remain a microcosm of society. Because of these complex factors, the budget for the school library media center is vital. It determines whether the specialist can afford to present ideas to students in any of the mechanical, electrical, or electronic means available. This requires a center program with a unity of purpose that will strengthen the educational potential of a school. In its largest sense, the center program is the sum of all the activities in which students, teachers, administrators, and others in an educational setting use materials and equipment to facilitate communication and promote learning.

The school library media center is an arena filled with varied programs in which many types of collections and services exist in arrangements to facilitate rather than restrict use and that encourages progress toward present and future educational goals. It is a center of purposeful activity, the vortex of action in a school where individuals learn.

An understanding of budgetary practice and record keeping is essential for all media specialists and becomes more important as monies become more difficult to obtain. Such a center has the responsibility to provide leadership in developing good budgetary practices and record-keeping routines. Accountability is not new to education. Ever since the first sign-in sheet appeared in the principal's office, school personnel have been held accountable for the hours they work. The emphasis on program accountability has increased as available funds have decreased. Traditionally the budget has been a device for financial accounting, but the emphasis has shifted to include accountability for program results. The complexities of accountability in this sense require an increased understanding of the budgeting process. In a broad sense, a budget is a chart for a future course of action. It records the outcome of an essentially political process in which alternative plans are examined, preferences are indicated, and decisions are made. In its final form, the budget is a statement of policy on which expenditures are based. As every administrator knows, it contains the assigned priorities that are the outcome of bargaining over conflicting goals.

A school library media center budget is only one part of a school district's total executive budget, which includes the operating budget for each school. The media center portion of the overall school budget is sometimes given only minor consideration due to the lack of recognition of the importance of media in instruction and the absence of a well-prepared budget prepared by a media specialist. Reflecting educational change, however, the media center budget, which represents the direction the program will take in the immediate future, assumes greater importance. The budget is essentially the philosophy of the center stated in quantitative terms, in the same way that a school district budget expresses the educational philosophy of a community.

The aim of this chapter is to (1) describe the levels of funding, (2) present various types of budgets, and (3) list categories of record keeping. Although Planning Programming Budgeting System (PPBS) has not been widely adopted in education, it is included here in outline because parts of it are used. The sophistication of the PPBS method and skepticism in the attitudes of users[1] have resulted in the more prevalent use of the expenditure type of budget in schools.

FUNDING AND SERVICE

Funding on federal, state, regional, and district levels supports school library media center programs in the individual school. Although federal and state programs offer less direct help to the individual program, they should not be overlooked. With the decrease in federal funds for education,[2] increasing importance has been placed on state funds. State and local funds for education are presently about the same and are projected to be so for most of the 1980s.[3] Although the federal Department of Education is the pinnacle of the hierarchical structure of education, there are 50 state education or public instruction departments and thousands of school districts. Since the 1950s, many educators have endorsed a unified media program and some have restructured formerly separate library bureaus. Regardless of departmental composition, however, the state level assumes an increasing importance as a source of guidance and funding.

Federal

On the federal level, the Department of Education, created in 1979 as a cabinet-level bureau, establishes policy and administers federal assistance to education. *American Education*, available from the Superintendent of Documents, is the official journal of the department. Included in the jurisdiction of the Assistant Secretary for Elementary and Secondary Education is the program of grants to state educational agencies.

Within this structure, which has traditionally administered library programs in the public and college library areas, some programs directly related to public education are also handled. One of the main purposes is to develop ways of delivering all kinds of instructional services to the American educational community. The intent is to provide leadership for continuous improvement in the nation's educational system by maintaining an information clearinghouse at the federal level. Federal funds are to go to the states as block grants, except for a few special programs. The federal-level status can be monitored retrospectively through the latest annual edition of the *U.S. Government Manual*, while the current status can be obtained by using *Facts on File* or conducting a computerized bibliographic search of the *New York Times* or *National Newspaper Index* databases.

Federal funds presently available for use by school library media specialists can be determined most readily from information at the business office of the school district and the state department of education (see Appendix 1). Federal financial support is there for those who are willing to seek it. (See also Chapter 13.)

State

Within each state department of education, it is common to find that the responsibility for the development of media programs, with the exception of such highly specialized elements of instruction as instructional television, rests in a library bureau under a division devoted to instructional services. Each bureau generally includes a staff professionally trained in educational technology and library science that can serve as liaison with the federal level, other divisions within the state education department, and the schools in the state.

The state bureaus also act as agents in linking school library media centers with already existing large public libraries and regional resource centers in order to form statewide media networks. The ultimate goal is to provide access to any material needed in the schools. Some state bureaus have initiated research projects to identify specific staff and student needs, as well as to issue guidelines for instructions in library media skills, particularly in the elementary grades. Some have also established criteria for forming and evaluating programs that will be suitable for use with the appropriate budgeting system. In view of the continuing emphasis on accountability for program results, the budgeting system suggested by the state generally includes a statement of descriptive justification for each coded expenditure. As the role of the state in the distribution of funds for education increases, it is important for the media specialist to learn about the state department's suggestions for financial assistance and budgetary practices. Appropriate state education department addresses are listed in Appendix 1 to enable media specialists to get in touch with their state bureau to obtain valuable information and documents.

Regional

A level of media services similar in many ways to that obtainable under the largest school district operation is the regional network that unites school library media centers with resource centers in an effort to broaden and enrich the programs of the individual school centers. In the past, generally with seed money from federal funds, some public libraries have been trend setters in this type of organization. Although school library media centers have not been able to initiate comparable school network systems (primarily because of restrictions in local funding), they have in some instances joined cooperative regional networks. This type of plan assumes that efficiency, economy, and better service will result from shared resources and services. Regional plans, whether for instructional television, films, cataloging, computerized information sources, or expensive and infrequently used materials, have proved most valuable when the contract services supply resources that are too costly for small school districts. Such networks have also been operative for in-service courses. Regional cooperation for media services and resources can be beneficial among schools in districts that are not large enough to support a centralized resource center and employ a director of media. However, it is desirable for a district with a minimum of six school buildings to use a centralized method of organization in addition to regional cooperation. Larger school systems have found that centralized district media services for large operations, such as film and professional libraries or centralized media acquisitions and preparation, have been and remain important first steps toward excellence in media center program operation. Inquiries to the existing regional networks is the place to start (see Chapter 12 for further information on networks).

School District Programs

A school library media center program at the district level functions both as a centralized resource for the district and as support for the program in individual schools. The resources and services that form a base of operations at the district level can provide the services needed by many of the schools. Each school can retain its individuality by its own selection and use of resources, as well as by its unique use of the district services. No system with fewer with 40,000 students can sustain all centralized media center services.

The district school library media program includes several internal district responsibilities: (1) preparation of annual budgets; (2) interpretation of the total media program (central and individual schools) to the public, to the board of education, and to the staff; (3) applications for funds from federal, state, and foundation sources; (4) administration of the funds for special projects; and (5) formulation of reports (to the district board of education, the state department of education, foundations, and so on).

Two of the major tasks of the school district media program are planning and evaluating the foundation for media services on the system and individual school-building levels. Planning is generally based on the knowledge of (1) the educational philosophy of the school system and the objectives of the instructional program, (2) staffing patterns, (3) curricula, (4) various methods of instruction, (5) availability and utilization of technology, (6) awareness of new technology. Evaluation is a continuous process of measuring the quality and effectiveness of the programs available to the users, that is, the administration, teachers, students and community, in order to make decisions about program modification and changes. The results of this regular evaluation are essential for use in the planning and construction of the budget.

On a district level, media services under the direction of a coordinator who is knowledgeable both in the library field and in educational technology and who exhibits leadership capabilities will ensure greater development of media programs at the school-building level. To provide these services on a system level requires appropriate staffing, funding, and facilities. The district professional staff also should have general competence in the library, information science, and audiovisual fields and some degree of specialization in both media and subject areas.

Seven percent of the school district's instructional budget is recommended to support a district media program. Any mix of media that is appropriate to the district's educational plan is permissible. One that is commonly suggested for schools with a beginning district media program is 25 percent for textbooks, 25 percent traditional media (books, films, recordings), and 50 percent newer media and equipment (videotapes, audiovisual equipment, computers).

Individual School Programs

A school library media center in an individual school building is actually a multiplicity of activities and services that together are sometimes called the program. The operation of the center provides the base for the other activities or programs. The center operation may itself be considered a fundamental program. Often, because of limitations in monetary support, staff, and facilities, it has been the only program. These factors have slowly changed with the increasing recognition that the use of media in schools is important in the teaching-learning process, and as a result the media center has developed other programs for its school audiences, such as local production of film and tape presentations and the provision of items such as computers and microfiche readers for individual use. These programs expand the educational potential of the center and make it an exciting and vital part of education.

COLLECTING BACKGROUND INFORMATION

A prerequisite for budget preparation is collecting background information in several important areas: sources of financial support, standards in the field, inventory of existing collections, community needs, curricula in the schools, and the budget system and accounting code in use in a particular district. Some of these areas are discussed in relation to the media selection process in Chapter 8. In this chapter they are explained specifically as they relate to the budget.

Sources of Funding

Monies for education come mainly from local and state taxes. These funds are often the only ones that can be relied on for budget purposes, and sometimes even these sources are undependable. Nevertheless, the possibility of receiving funds from sources outside the city and state should be investigated.

In 1958, the federal government started to provide supplementary education monies through the various titles of the National Defense Education Act (NDEA) and later the Elementary and Secondary Education Act (ESEA). There has been a decrease in the amounts and suggested restructuring in the organization of these funds since 1980; at present, however, they are still available. Future developments should be monitored.

In some states, special-purpose grants have been made. Each state department has used and will continue to use federal and state funds in its own unique way to develop and strengthen both programs in school library media centers in individual schools and county and regional agencies that help to support the development of such programs in schools. A solid foundation has been laid with these many selective and innovative efforts. Just as the bulk of the funds behind these programs has been awarded to the centers whose specialists kept up with the status of educational legislation, so too will state funds (and regional, special, and local funds) be allocated to those who keep abreast of the federal and state structure regarding funding. For example, contractual arrangements with regional groups for large and expensive services, such as instructional television (ITV), are common throughout the country.

Local financial support outside the tax levies for educational purposes is encouraged; it may be more readily available than is commonly realized. There may well be increasing reliance on this source of funding for media center special projects. School representatives who are willing to do the necessary public relations work may find community groups and businesses willing to donate money. In addition, special grants are available from professional organizations and foundations, for example, the American Association of School Librarians/ American Library Association, National Endowment for the Humanities, and the Knapp Foundation. What was true in the past is even truer today in a constricted economy: The media specialist must be willing to investigate and try to use many kinds of sources for funding extra projects. Meantime, both local and state funding sources should provide the bedrock on which to build, given good planning, evaluation, and budgetary practices.

Standards in the Field

After possible sources of extra revenue have been explored—and this in itself may prove a continuing project—long-range goals for the school library media center should be established. Because standards undergo continuous revision, it is important to keep abreast of recent changes. It is also important to realize that national standards are ultimate goals for the majority of schools in the nation—the pinnacle toward which schools should strive. There is an increasing tendency to stress the service goals of the school library media center.

Many states have issued suggested standards. Usually these are less ambitious than the national standards because the state hopes the school will achieve them sooner. A state's suggested standards should always be considered along with those of the national professional organizations and of local or regional associations or government units that issue standards.

Many school officials are likely to be influenced in their decisions about media programs and funding by local standards, that is, how the schools in the local area compare. Therefore, a survey of a few neighboring school districts taken by the media specialist or a recent survey issued to members by a regional professional library or media organization may become a basic consideration in budgeting.

Inventory of Existing Collections

A quantitative inventory of the existing school library media center holdings of materials, equipment, and services charted together with the recommendations of national, state, and local standards and projected for multiyear budgeting will give a comprehensive picture of the present status of the media collection and indicate future directions for growth. Exhibit 4-1, Materials Inventory/Standards Checklist, shows how the quantity of materials available in the center can be compared with recommended standards in order to plan the budget in an orderly way for a period of time. The same form may be used as an Equipment Inventory/Standards Checklist by substituting a list of equipment in the left column.

The form shown in Exhibit 4-1 can also be used for measuring available services and equipment against national, state, or local standards. Some of the items that would be listed on a Services Inventory/Standards Checklist are:

Printing	Transparency reproduction
Duplicating	Computerized services
Tape duplication	Equipment servicing
Graphic production	Central cataloging
Photographic production	Cross-reference cataloging

Personnel training	Technical
Personnel	Clerical
Professional	Student

Media specialists in individual schools can adapt the inventory/standards form for their use by dropping the last two columns, Schools and District Center Collection. A director in a multischool situation would use all the columns. A one- to ten-year projection of the needed units of materials, equipment, and services can then be examined, along with other preliminary information, and translated finally into dollar figures in the budget.

Community Needs

An educational budget should reflect the needs of both the target school population and the local community. This is a difficult task. Legally it is the responsibility of the board of education, but in practice it is often delegated to the school superintendent. A school library media specialist, along with other school staff, can help in this process by recognizing and understanding local needs. Defining community priorities is properly a cooperative task and requires a study group, ideally headed by the superintendent and with representatives from among educators as well as various community groups, business, religious, fraternal, social. The study group should include a mixture of the ethnic, racial, religious, and economic makeup of the community. A socioeconomic community study sponsored by the chamber of commerce, local Rotary club, or other group would be a practical first step.

Both teachers and media specialists are needed to relate the community and societal needs to the curriculum and media collections. The public librarian should also be included so that the total spectrum of library and media service is presented to the community. One long-term result of the study group's survey of community educational needs would be information useful in budgeting. However, a school library media center budget can be framed realistically over a shorter period of time with a fair knowledge of the community supplemented by census information from the district office.

Curricula in the Schools

The vitality of a school's curriculum depends on continuous revision and updating to align it with societal and community needs. Taken together with classroom instruction, a school library media program designed to enrich the curriculum is perhaps the most important ele-

EXHIBIT 4-1 MATERIALS INVENTORY/STANDARDS CHECKLIST

Materials	Total Inventory	Standards (in units)			Units Needed				Schools (in units)			District Center Collection (in units)
		Local	State	Natl.	Now	3 yr.	5 yr.	10 yr.	Bldg. A	Bldg. B	Bldg. C	
Books												
Paperbacks												
Filmstrips												
Maps												
Charts												
Moving pictures												
16mm												
8mm												
8mm super												
Pamphlets												
Periodicals												
Newspapers												
Microfilm/fiche												
Books												
Magazines												
Newspapers												
Slides												
Recordings												
Disc												
Tape												
Cassette												
Video												
Computers												
Flat pictures												
Transparencies												
Kits												
Programmed material												
ETV												

ment in the education process. Media specialists have the paradoxical obligation to follow and to lead in the formulation of the curriculum. They must also stay closely in touch with national curricular trends, especially in periods of great change and uncertainty in society.

By relating community needs to curriculum, as shown in Table 4-1, the range of key educational concerns, especially programs, can be seen so that administrators will have a better basis on which to make monetary decisions. The capability of a computer to rearrange and retrieve coded data rapidly is responsible for enlarging the ways in which schooling can be viewed. For example, an administrator can

TABLE 4-1   COMMUNITY NEEDS RELATED TO
CURRICULUM AND MEDIA PROGRAMS

Community Needs	Curriculum	Media Support Program
Clearinghouse on local summer jobs for youth	9–12 special social studies short program	1. Variety of special reading, viewing, listening collections 2. Locally produced film and slide/tape presentations 3. Brochures and printed materials from local sources 4. Speakers from local organizations and businesses

Sex education to fight high VD rate	Units in:
	    Physical education
	    Health
	    Biology
	    Home economics
	    Social studies
		Pamphlets, charts, study prints, models, 16mm and 8mm films, filmstrips, magazines, books

Vocational programs for physically handicapped students	Specialized courses:
	    Tailoring
	    Dressmaking
	    Data processing
	    Paramedical positions
		Pamphlets, filmstrips, books, equipment, special demonstrations

Special program for the gifted	Programs in English/Social Studies, 6–8, in addition to units in regular courses	1. Computerized bibliographic searches 2. College-level print materials: books, GPO brochures, magazines, video software, local production services, microfiche

determine exactly how much money is being spent for improving reading, viewing, and listening and where in a school or district it is being spent—for an entire school, for the total district, for any one grade level. The 1973 revision of *Financial Accounting ... for Local and State School Systems* differs from earlier editions in its use of three sets of account codes instead of the traditional one code for expenditures.[4] Expenses, revenues, and balances are kept under separate codes for greater fiscal integrity. This multicoding also provides for an in-depth analysis showing the program the money was spent for, the department that spent it, when it was spent, and why it was spent. Keeping the accounting record by the programs that the schools decide to budget is stressed.

The school library media specialist will be able to plan center support programs that eventually can be translated into quantitative terms in the budget document. This practice should be carried out regardless of the budget system used.

Accounting Code in District Use

Many of the current state and local guides for school districts are based on the federal handbook.[5] The financial accounting system suggested in the 1973 revision of the 1957 edition encourages a more sophisticated managerial approach by providing control over a wider area.

In *Financial Accounting ... for Local and State School Systems*, a federal model is proposed for each local education agency (LEA). It is suggested that each LEA state its financial transactions in a minimum of the first seven dimensions that are explained: (1) fund, (2) object, (3) function, (4) operational unit, (5) program, (6) source of

TABLE 4-2   BUDGET DESCRIPTION

Fund	Object	Function	Operational Unit	Program	Source	Fiscal Year
	Salaries					
General fund	Supplies and materials	Instruction	(*name of school*)	Goals	Federal	
	Capital outlay	Regular programs		Subjects	State	
				Pupils level	Intermediate (regional)	
				age	Local	
				type		

funds, and (7) fiscal year (see Table 4-2). Each dimension has an alphanumeric code that varies state by state.

Each state has the right and privilege to adapt the model to conform to its plans and needs. Therefore, it is advisable that the media specialist obtain and digest the appropriate alphanumeric codes and their descriptions as provided by the state department of education. For example, the State of New York published a handbook that is extremely useful to local LEA administrators in understanding the requisition account coding that is used. The codes in this chapter are taken from that handbook.[6] See sample code below.

Sample account code: A2610.11
A = Fund—general
2610 = Functional unit—school library and AV
.11 = Object—library supplies

Since the advent of electronic data processing, a computer code system converts raw information into usable form. Table 4-3 illustrates the account codes for a partial media center budget extracted from a total school district budget. Table 4-4 gives a more detailed presentation of the audiovisual supplies part of a center budget.

TABLE 4-3   SCHOOL LIBRARY MEDIA BUDGET ACCOUNT CODES

Code	Description	Cost	Total
A2610.110-200	Furniture and equipment, purchase		
	microfiche reader	$ 250.00	
	magazine rack	325.00	$ 575.00
.110-501	Library supplies		1,635.00
.110-511	Library books, 800 @ $12 av.	9,600.00	
	pamphlets (including GPO)	2,400.00	
	100 books for English basic skills	1,200.00	13,200.00
A2610.110-512	Magazines 350 @ $14		
	Current issue, 250	3,500.00	
	Retrospective issues, 50	700.00	
	100 for English basic skills	1,400.00	5,600.00
.150-20	Librarian, 4 hrs. wkly after school		
	× 40 wks. × $14		2,240.00
.402 (supply #)	ALA and state conference and travel (including local visits)		800.00
.433 (supply #)	Photocopy machine, rental		1,500.00
A2615.110-200	Audiovisual equipment		
	16mm projector	750.00	
	screen, 70 × 70 tripod	100.00	
	microcomputer	1,750.00	

TABLE 4-3 (cont.)

Code	Description	Cost	Total
	VTR with VHS camera, portable	1,700.00	
	Lights, studio with barn doors	500.00	4,800.00
.110-501	Audiovisual supplies, e.g., film developer		2,000.00
.110-510	Audiovisual materials		
	Regular support	4,200.00	
	Items for English basic skills	1,200.00	5,400.00
.417 (supply #)	Films, rental		4,000.00
.426 (supply #)	Postage, film return		600.00
.435 (supply #)	Repair, AV equipment		1,500.00
A2620.110-200	Educational television, maintenance		2,200.00
.110-501	ETV supplies		1,500.00
.110-510	ETV, commercial program purchase		500.00
.110-518	ETV, program subscriptions		350.00
.435 (supply #)	Repair, ETV equipment		1,000.00
	Total	$29,575.00	$49,400.00

TABLE 4-4 A26 15.110-501 AUDIOVISUAL SUPPLIES (A Detail)

Quantity	Description	Unit Price	Total
1	Film cleaner, perma wash 1 gal.	5.35	5.35
4	Film developer, b/w, 1 gal.	2.35	9.40
10	Fixer	2.03	20.30
4	Film developer, color kit	11.45	45.80
1	Cord, grounded electric, 25 ft.	8.95	8.95
10	Batteries, C-type	1.45	14.50
4	Lamps, 16mm projection	14.70	58.80
30	Mounts, cardboard, 2 × 2 slides (50/pkg)	6.45	193.50
1	Paper, photographic (250 sheets/pkg)	76.25	76.25
1	Laminating paper, 18-inch	25.65	25.65

A final step in gathering information prior to preparing the school library media center budget is finding out what accounting code the district uses. This information is usually available from the assistant superintendent in charge of business. School monies, both revenue and expense, have long been categorized under numerical or alphanumerical account codes that permit the business office to keep expenditures for like items together. Coding has assumed even greater importance in accounting because of the infinite variety of information that can be made readily available through computers.

Some states have a pastiche of cumbersome financial regulations; for example, some may stipulate that unspent funds must be returned to a general account to be used to defray local taxes. Other states have changed this regulation to permit balances to be spent in a new school year. Another ambiguous area is the definition of the term *capital outlay*. Generally, this covers items that have a useful school life of two or more years and an initial cost per unit of at least $100. Videorecorders, video cameras, and computers, for example, would be considered capital outlay expenditures.

The general responsibility for budget preparation rests on (1) the board of education, (2) the chief school administrator, (3) the administrative staff, (4) principals, (5) other staff members, (6) students, and (7) community representatives. In actual procedure, however, the "other staff members," usually the heads of the departments and teachers, prepare the previously coded requisition sheets for the building principal, whose office compiles the building budget that goes into the overall or executive budget at the superintendent's office.

Requisition forms generally come to the individual building principal from the chief school administrator's office. The media specialist can generally expect or request forms for the following categories: (1) textbooks and supplementary instructional material, (2) supplies, (3) nonstandard supplies to be used within a year, (4) repairs and replacements of equipment, (5) furniture replacements and alterations to area, and (6) new equipment that will last more than one year.

Suggestions for Budget Preparation

Plan the budget based on a representative educational plan.

Extend the plan for at least 3–5 years for good direction.

Keep people, for example, staff and community, informed and request items needed.

Work cooperatively with the principal and other administrators.

Be aware of state educational legalities as they affect the budget.

Keep abreast of district income and problems and practices.

Use budgetary practices such as transference of funds; do not "pad."

Practice continuous and smooth budgetary control by using an encumbrance system and/or regular reports on unexpended funds.

Establish and maintain an effective public relations arm for media center budgetary concerns.

Budget Calendar

The public school fiscal year varies according to state law. In many states it runs from July 1 to June 30, and in these cases a school library media center budget is generally developed in the fall, discussed and integrated into the school executive budget in the winter, and adopted in spring or early summer. Budgeting is increasingly a continuous or year-round task, the more complex it becomes.

Although there are different administrative patterns among various states and school districts, a budget calendar is usually used in a district. It is imperative for the school library media specialist to obtain the budget calendar from the principal or assistant superintendent for business office (see the sample school budget calendar in Table 4-5).

TABLE 4-5   SCHOOL BUDGET CALENDAR (JULY-JUNE FISCAL YEAR)

Rework budget calendar and request forms	June	July	
Future explanations for next year	June	July	August
Establish new budget folders	June	July	August
Gather preliminary estimates for major repairs	June	July	August
Gather preliminary estimates for questions regarding transportation		July	August
Questions for district or school curriculum committees	June	July	August
Preliminary informational needs based on school census			August
Evaluation process of advisory committees	October		
Curriculum and evaluation committee reports	January		
Furniture and equipment requests	January		
Requests for library and media books and supplies	February		
Requests for instructional supplies	February		
Requests for new positions	February		

TABLE 4-5 (cont.)

Final salary decisions	February
Preliminary compilation of budget	March
Preliminary draft of budget	March
Final budget compiled and distributed	April May June
Budget adoption	May (prior to June 30)
Public notification	Generally within 10 days of vote

It is apparent from the sample budget calendar that the compilation of the budget is a continuing task. However, the analysis and coding on the requisition forms obviously are completed before February for school districts that are on a July–June fiscal year. These three tasks of planning, continuous budgeting, and close attention to the district's requisition dates from its official calendar are vital in budget preparation.

BUDGETING LEVELS

Before exploring the major budgeting systems in current use, it is helpful to make a preliminary determination of the level or levels on which the budget is to be constructed and to look at costs and methods of allocating them.

The simplest level of budgeting and the easiest to work with is commonly called the maintenance or continuity budget. If a program is well established and productive, if the educational goals remain the same, and if no unusual expansion is planned, the same level of expenditures will be maintained and the program will be continued as before. Of course, the budget should provide for small increases or decreases in student or faculty numbers as well as replacement and inflationary costs in goods and labor. Maintenance-level budgeting is common in an established school library media center; it can, however, lead to complacency if the person who is planning neither recognizes nor cares about strengthening programs or reflecting changes.

If there are external and internal changes, such as large increases or decreases in the number of students and staff or a desire to improve or bring a basic program up to standards goals, this can be reflected in an incremental budget. It is common in incremental-level budgeting for the cost of the larger increases to be distributed over a 3–5-year period.

However, if major reorganization or important developments are anticipated in the immediate future, a third type, the expansion budget, is preferred. For example, creative budgeting of this type would be used for initiating programs and in the initial planning for the opening of a new school library media center, and it would involve expending capital outlay funds. Because capital outlay money represents reserve funds from which interest revenue may be anticipated, it is generally tapped with understandable reluctance. Therefore, extensive preparation must go into expansion-level budgeting; needs must be clearly identified and directly related to the additional funds being sought.

A realistic rule of thumb for a school library media specialist is to determine how much spending is likely to be acceptable to the administration and community and then to frame the budget to reflect that expectation. The most important factor, however, is obtaining and maintaining the support and confidence of the media center audience: students, teachers, administrators, and the community.

COST-ALLOCATION METHODS

How costs are reported will depend on the budgeting system used, but no matter what system the media specialist employs, costs must be established and direct expenses noted for the materials, equipment, salaries, and services that together constitute the operation and program of a school library media center.

Direct Expenses

Each direct expense must be allocated to center use and maintenance, media center activity, or specific program. Direct costs in each category may be determined by multiplying the average price of the physical unit (book, cassette, supplies, and so on) by the number of units needed. The list price is usually used for items in the capital-outlay category. If items are bid or let out to state contract, the quoted unit or bid price is used in the budget. Some useful annual and current sources of price information are the *Bowker Annual* (New York: R. R. Bowker), *Booklist, Instructional Innovator*, and publisher, distributor, and supply-house catalogs.

Indirect Expenses

Most schools report only the direct expenses for running a school library. However, if a district adopts the PPBS system, indirect expenses have to be added so that at the district level the budget data can be summarized by program area, for example, instruction, community service, and so forth. The total combined direct and indirect expenses represent the real cost of the program.

BUDGETING SYSTEMS

The common and sometimes confusing synonyms for the major budgeting systems reflect the development and changes in the rationale of the budgeting process within this century. Although budgeting on a national level began officially in 1921 with the establishment of an executive budgeting system from the Bureau of the Budget, it already had a long history in local government. A major trend in budgeting systems has been a shifting emphasis from solely fiscal accountability to accountability for program results as well. The major budgeting systems are described below in the chronological order in which they were developed, with an emphasis on the object-of-expenditure budget because it is the most widely used. For a more complete explanation of PPBS, see the authors' first edition of this book, *Creating a School Media Program* (New York: R. R. Bowker, 1973).

Lump-sum Budget

Although it was once widely used, this system provides little, if any, accountability and is used today only where costs are not clearly known. Nevertheless, there may be some media center programs in schools without specialists where a principal or department representative may put a lump-sum figure for the media center program in his or her executive budget. This, of course, represents peripheral interest in a center's program and in effect removes the center from serious consideration as a force in education. Defensible uses of lump-sum budgeting are to obtain emergency funds and/or to estimate initial costs.

Line-item Budget

This early type of budget can be extremely detailed and cumbersome, depending on the nature and size of the agency or institution that uses it. It is simply a list that includes items and services, with each notation appearing on a successive line just as it does in a personal checking account. It permits no flexibility and controls only those direct expenses that are funneled into an operation. Programs, however, do not enter into the accounting process. Where a school library media center operates with either a lump-sum or line-item budget, there is no possibility for program accountability, that is, for determining if a program has achieved its stated objectives. Because of newer and better accounting practices, line-item budgeting is rarely used.

Object-of-Expenditure Budget

In this popular type of budget, related expenditures are grouped in categories. Tables 4-6 to 4-14 show simplified school library media center budget requisitions in which the items and services that are the foundation of a program are listed by category under the designated account codes (see Table 4-3 for identification of codes) and are given a purchase price. A budget constructed in this way can provide careful fiscal management. As shown in the tables, each category lists related items. Tables 4-6 through 4-9 are concerned with code 2610. In Table 4-6, grouped under account 110-200, are the quantity and total cost figures for initial purchase of library furniture and equipment (a microfiche reader and a magazine rack); under code 110-501/11/12 (Table 4-7) are costs for library supplies; library books purchased, with the unit price (average) for each book, and a lump sum added for pam-

(text continues on pg. 90)

TABLE 4-6   SCHOOL DISTRICT BUDGET REQUISITION—CODE 2610

SCHEDULE 2 (equipment)

Function code: 2610 (school library and AV)

School: Note: *(instructions to business office)*

School year:

Object Code	Quantity	Description	Current Inventory	Budgeted Last Yr.	Proposed Budget	Total
110-200	1	Microfiche reader	1	$225	$250	
110-200	1	Magazine rack double face	1	0	325	$575

Justification

The microfiche reader will facilitate the student's search for information both in the term papers in regular classes and in the program projected for basic skills in English.

The addition of a display unit for magazines is necessitated by the tremendous increase in their use in instruction over the last few years.

TABLE 4-7   SCHOOL DISTRICT BUDGET REQUISITION—
CODE 2610 (cont.)

SCHEDULE 3 (supplies and materials)

Function Code: 2610

School: Note: (*instructions to business office*)

School year:

Object Code	Quan-tity	Description	Current Inven-tory	Bud-geted Last Yr.	Pro-posed Budget	Total
110-501		Library supplies		$1,500		$ 1,635
110-511		Library Books				
		800 @ $12 av.		9,600		
		100 English basic skills		1,200		
		Pamphlets (inc. GPO)		2,400		13,200
110-512		Magazines, 350 @ $14				
		Current issues, 250		3,500		
		Retrospective, 50		700		
		100 for English basic skills		1,400		5,600

Justification

Items necessary for the daily maintenance and operation of the media center, for example, book jacket covers, spine tape, repair tape.

As discussed with the teachers and principal, the school library media center will add 800 books to keep the collection useful.

Also, 100 books will be obtained to supplement and aid the basic skills program in English. The provision of magazines specifically for the basic skills program in English will help the students in this program.

Since much of the informational and recreational material is available in pamphlet format, the media center staff, along with the teachers and the principal, wishes to add to this vital collection on a regular basis.

The presence of current magazines is necessary because of their important place in young people's interest.

The retrospective magazine issues on microfiche are mandated by the school's need to provide information sources for the student.

TABLE 4-8   SCHOOL DISTRICT BUDGET REQUISITION—
CODE 2610 (cont.)

SCHEDULE 1 (non-instructional personnel)

Function code: 2610

School: Note: *(instructions to business office)*

School year:

Object Code	Quantity	Description	Current Inventory	Budgeted Last Yr.	Proposed Budget	Total
150-20		Librarian, after school 4 hrs. × 40 wks. × $14				$2,240

Justification
A librarian is needed to keep the media center open from 3:00 to 5:00 P.M. two afternoons a week when the school is extremely active. This development, as discussed, will allow at a minimum students to exchange materials and solve informational problems.

TABLE 4-9   SCHOOL DISTRICT BUDGET REQUISITION—
CODE 2610 (cont.)

SCHEDULE 4 (contractual expenses)

Function code: 2610

School: Note: *(instructions to business office)*

School year:

Object Code	Quantity	Description	Current Inventory	Budgeted Last Yr.	Proposed Budget	Total
402		Conference and travel				$ 800
433		Photocopy machine, rental				1,500

Justification
The funds are for local visitation travel and attendance at ALA and state conventions.

In discussion with representative members of the school community, it is deemed advisable to rent a suitable coin-operated machine. The present rental model is several generations away from the faster models on today's market; replacement would diminish the long lines of people needing to use this service for instructional purposes.

A2610 Total (Tables 4-6 to 4-9)   **$25,550.00**

(text continued from pg. 87)

phlets and other printed material; and magazine costs. Tables 4-8 and 4-9 cover personnel and contractual expenses. At the bottom of Table 4-9 is a total figure for all expenses under code 2610 (Tables 4-6 through 4-9).

Tables 4-10 through 4-12 cover code 2615 (see Table 4-3 for identification of codes), with a total figure for expenses in this category at the bottom of Table 4-12. Tables 4-13 and 4-14 are concerned with code 2620, with total expenses in this category at the bottom of Table 4-14.

Because there is no provision for determining how well the money that is spent on items and services is meeting the educational objectives of the school, the person responsible for this justifies the costs by appending a written statement briefly describing the way these items will support general objectives (see Justification at the bottom of Tables 4-6 through 4-14). The number of books and other media to be

(text continues on pg. 93)

TABLE 4-10   SCHOOL DISTRICT BUDGET REQUISITION—CODE 2615

SCHEDULE 2 (equipment)

Function code: 2615

School: Note: *(instructions to business office)*

School year:

Object Code	Quantity	Description	Current Inventory	Budgeted Last Yr.	Proposed Budget	Total
110-200	1	16mm projector	4	$ 0.00	$ 750.00	
	1	screen, 70 × 70	2	0.00	100.00	
	2	microcomputers	4	1,500.00	1,750.00	
	1	VTR with camera	1	0.00	1,700.00	
	1	studio lights	1	500.00	500.00	$4,800.00

Justification

A replacement of one of the school library media center's projectors is necessary. It has become uneconomical to repair the machine purchased 10 years ago.

A larger screen is required for viewing in the media center and for community events. It will prove most helpful to the board of education and parents' council meetings also.

More computers are needed in the center because of their increased use by pupils for the informational needs emphasized in the classroom.

This VTR unit will enable the center to enhance its own programs and cover existing school and community events on a schedule.

The lights will aid our students in photography and add a necessary ingredient to the staging and taping of ETV programs.

TABLE 4-11   SCHOOL DISTRICT BUDGET REQUISITION—
CODE 2615 (cont.)

SCHEDULE

Function code: 2615

School: Note: *(instructions to business office)*

School year:

Object Code	Quantity	Description	Current Inventory	Budgeted Last Yr.	Proposed Budget	Total
110-501		Audiovisual supplies			$1,750.00	$2,000.00
110-510		Audiovisual materials				
		Regular		$2,750.00	4,200.00	
		English basic skills		0.00	1,200.00	5,400.00

Justification

These AV supply items are to be used by students (e.g., in producing computer programs) and by teachers in preparing AV instructional materials (e.g., splicing tape, cords, transparency sheets, etc.).

The AV materials are not expendable and include instructional media that meet curricular needs, for example, cassettes, filmstrips, slides, kits, videotapes, and so forth. The items for English basic skills are designed and recommended especially for aid in this area.

TABLE 4-12   SCHOOL DISTRICT BUDGET REQUISITION—
CODE 2615 (cont.)

SCHEDULE (AV services)

Function code: 2615

School: Note: *(instructions to business office)*

School year:

Object Code	Quantity	Description	Current Inventory	Budgeted Last Yr.	Proposed Budget	Total
417 (supply #)		Films, rental		$3,500		$4,000
426 (supply #)		Postage, film return		400		600
435 (supply #)		Repair, AV equipment		1,250		1,500

TABLE 4-12 (cont.)

Justification

Based on past experience with the use of film for instruction, as well as on consultation with the school community, the above figures are required for this service.

An annual survey of equipment status and condition indicates that the above amount will be needed to keep our audiovisual equipment serviceable for use by the school population.

2615 Total (Tables 4-10 to 4-12):	**$18,300.00**

TABLE 4-13   SCHOOL DISTRICT BUDGET REQUISITION—CODE 2620

SCHEDULE (television)

Function code: 2620

School: Note: *(instructions to business office)*

School year:

Object Code	Quantity	Description	Current Inventory	Budgeted Last Yr.	Proposed Budget	Total
A2620.110-200		ETV, maintenance		$2,000		$2,200
.110-501		ETV supplies		750		1,500
.110-510		ETV, programs purchase			0	500
.110-518		ETV, programs subscriptions		150		350

Justification

The increase in ETV supplies is warranted because of the expressed interest of teachers and students in ETV use in the classroom.

The school library media center would for the above reason start to add another component to this program. This rationale also extends to the subscriptions.

TABLE 4-14   SCHOOL DISTRICT BUDGET REQUISITION— CODE 2620 (cont.)

SCHEDULE (television services)

Function code: 2620

School: Note: *(instructions to business office)*

School year:

TABLE 4-14 (cont.)

Object Code	Quantity	Description	Current Inventory	Budgeted Last Yr.	Proposed Budget	Total
A2620.435 (supply #)		Repair, ETV equip- ment		$750.00		$1,000.00

Justification
Because the media center has new ETV equipment, it is anticipated that this amount will cover inevitable small problems this year (providing "Murphy's Law" does not become all-encompassing).

		A2620 Total:	**$5,550.00**

(text continued from pg. 90)
purchased can be indicated, but this type of budget cannot describe how they will be used unless the justification statements and evaluation are made.

This type of budget is easy to prepare and understand; it is also effective in fiscal management. The previous year's financial base is readily visible and handy in adjusting and projecting the new base. Object-of-expenditure budgeting is based on an assumption common to all budgeting systems prior to the emphasis on program seen in PPBS and zero-base budgeting; that is, certain responses are needed to perform certain functions, based on the belief that certain activities always produce certain results. Needless to say, this may or may not happen, depending on other factors; the assumption is poor unless there is an intent to monitor the descriptive justifications and see that programs are essential to the school library media center.

Performance Budget

Performance budgeting had its origin and greatest use to date in public libraries. It developed from the desire to relate the achievement of objectives to the resources that were required to carry out a library program. For the first time the results were deemed as important for analysis and control as were the resources themselves. It is sometimes called "program" budgeting, unfortunately confusing it with PPBS, from which it differs.

In the performance budget, library activities such as cataloging, preparation of materials, and information services are grouped together as functions. After these activities are identified, they are broken down into basic units of work so that a unit cost or work measurement can be applied to the total number of units needed for each activity. Therefore, the number of units required and the unit cost become the dual focus for both formulating and analyzing the budget (see Table 4-15).

TABLE 4-15   PERFORMANCE BUDGET

Activity	Unit	Number of Units	Unit Cost	Total
Acquisition of materials	Book	3,000	$12.00	$ 36,000.00
Cataloging and preparation of materials	Book	3,000	6.00	18,000.00
Lending services	Book	25,000	1.00	25,000.00
Information services	Inquiry	30,000	10.00	300,000.00
Building maintenance	Sq. ft.	3,000	3.00	9,000.00
Group services	Client contact	400	20.00	8,000.00
Special programs	Event	10	95.00	950.00

Although it is a major budgeting system, the performance budget has been infrequently used in school library media centers because the initial preparation of unit costs and the auditing process are complex, particularly for small, multipurpose centers where there often is overlapping of activities and functions. Performance budgeting can be related to the traditional object-of-expenditure budgeting if the media specialist wishes to relate the budget figures to the functions and amount of work that is being carried out in the center. To do this, the various object-code category items are distributed by percent of time, dollar figures, or other appropriate measure among the activities or functions in which they belong (see Table 4-16). By looking at an object-performance ladder, it is simple to see which and how much of the expenditures are used in each of the center's functions. This process, however, does not provide information about how well the center is meeting educational objectives in terms of student growth and development.

PLANNING, PROGRAMMING, BUDGETING, EVALUATING SYSTEM

This type of budgeting is usually referred to as PPBS. Although the letter E is dropped from the acronym, evaluating is nevertheless an essential part of the system. PPBS is a complex and detailed refinement of the performance-budgeting concept, but with the emphasis on human change rather than on the materials and costs needed to bring

TABLE 4-16 OBJECT-PERFORMANCE LADDER*

Accounts	Acquisition	Cataloging	Lending Services	Information Services	Bldg. Maintenance	Group Services	Special Programs
A2610.150-20 Salaries specialist paraprofessional clerk	*(percentage of time needed for each function converted to dollar salary figures)*						
A2610.110-200 Initial library furniture and equipment	*(dollar figures)*						
A2610.110-501 Instructional supplies (including AV)	*(dollar figures)*						
A2610.110-511 Books Pamphlets Supplies							

*Relates account code to library function; see Table 4-3 for account codes.

change about. It differs from earlier kinds of budget preparation because it measures the educational products (for example, how well a child who is given materials can study independently) rather than school characteristics (for example, how many books should be bought per child or how many projectors should be purchased per teaching station). It is a management technique that seeks to obtain the greatest value for the money spent in terms of satisfying human needs, based on the economic assumption that there are unlimited human needs and limited resources.

PPBS tends to focus community and administrative support for programs on the performance of the pupils rather than on the resources or instructional staff and facilities. Although all of these factors are implicit, the programs are measured finally by how well the pupils attain the stated objectives, distributing more equitable shares of responsibility for pupil growth and learning throughout a community. In this way, a community may be asked to scrutinize its expectations more closely in relation to its willingness to give support to its schools.

The following characteristics are unique to PPBS:

1. Establishment of educational objectives for at least five years.
2. Development of alternative programs that will attempt to reach the same objectives.
3. Identification of activities that can be used to implement the programs.
4. Discovery of the visible and covert factors that may interfere with the success of each program.
5. Analysis and comparison of the alternative programs in relation to both costs and constraints.
6. Decision as to program(s) that will be most likely to accomplish the goals at the lowest cost with the least constraints.
7. Provision of continuous evaluation of the program based on the objectives.

CONCLUSION

The budget practices that are discussed in this chapter and various practices in preceding chapter point out the differences between the school library of the past and today's school library media center. The conventional school library was adequate when information was transmitted in traditional ways. Increasingly, however, our electronic environment makes it imperative that educators utilize new sources of information and teach the skills necessary to understand and interpret them.

Although the school library media center described in this book might seem difficult to attain, there are many schools that have instituted programs similar to those described here. Institutional change is often a slow and gradual process, but with imagination and perseverance a beginning can be made in even the most limited situation. Whatever may be the future of public education, school library media centers are destined to play an increasingly important role.

NOTES

1. James Haden, University of the State of New York, State Education Department, Management Services, Division of Education, telephone conversation, April 1, 1981.
2. National Center for Educational Statistics, *The Condition of Education* (Washington, D.C.: Government Printing Office, 1982).
3. Allan Odden and John Augenblick, with the assistance of Kent McGuire, *School Finance Reform in the States*, Report No. F80-1 (Denver, Col.: Education Commission of the States, Education Finance Center, 1980).
4. Charles T. Roberts and Allan R. Lichtenberger, eds., *Financial Accounting: Classifications and Standard Terminology for Local and State School Systems* (Washington, D.C.: U.S. National Center for Educational Statistics, 1973), 197 pp. ED081103. (Available in your nearest government depository library.)
5. Ibid.
6. Edward V. Regan, *Uniform System of Accounts for School Districts* (Albany, N.Y.: Dept. of Audit and Control, Division of Municipal Affairs, Municipal Accounting Systems, 1965, rev. 1979, suppl. 1973 Program Budgeting).

FOR FURTHER READING

Alley, Brian, and Cargill, Jennifer. *Keeping Track of What You Spend.* Phoenix, Ariz.: Oryx, 1981.

Ashford, R. "Pennywise: A Summary of Budgeting Procedures." *School Library Journal*, October 1981, pp. 100–103.

Babunakis, Michael. *Budgets: An Analysis and Procedure Handbook for Government and Nonprofit Organizations.* Westport, Conn.: Greenwood, 1976.

Baker & Taylor Company. *Winning the Money Game: A Guide to Community-Based Library Fundraising.* New York: Baker & Taylor, 1979.

Bens, C. "Library Budgets: Hard Sell for a Soft Service." *Ontario Library Review*, June 1981, pp. 88–100.

Blazek, Ron, ed. *Achieving Accountability: Readings on the Evaluation of Media Centers.* Chicago: American Library Association, 1981.

Boss, Richard W. *Grant Money and How to Get It: A Handbook for Librarians.* New York: R. R. Bowker, 1980.

Breivik, Patricia S., and Gibson, E. *Funding Alternatives for Libraries.* Chicago: American Library Association, 1979.

Bruemmer, Alice, ed. *Library Management in Review.* New York: Special Libraries Association, 1982.

"Cancellation Decisions: Evaluating Standing Orders." *Library Resources and Technical Services,* Fall 1978, pp. 368-379.

Chen, Ching-chih. *Zero-Base Budgeting in Library Management.* Phoenix, Ariz.: Oryx, 1980.

Drott, Carl M. "Budgeting for School Media Centers." *Drexel Library Quarterly,* July 1978, pp. 78-94.

Evans, G. T. "Cost of Information about Library Acquisition Budgets." *Collection Management,* Spring 1978, pp. 3-23.

Heintze, Robert A., and Hodes, Lance. *Statistics of Public School Libraries/Media Centers.* Washington, D.C.: Government Printing Office, 1981.

McCauley, Elfrieda. "Budgeting for School Media Services." *School Media Quarterly,* Winter 1976, pp. 126-134.

Oster, G. "Local Business May Have Money for the Asking." *American Libraries,* June 1980, pp. 373-377.

Pattie, Kenton. "How to Get Money for AV." *Media and Methods,* January 1980, pp. 32-33.

"Planning and Budgeting for School Media Programs." *Journal of the American Society for Information Science,* January 1979, pp. 41-50.

Ramer, B. "Dr. Ramer's Rx for Fighting Fiscal Fever." *NYLA Bulletin,* January 1979, pp. 1+.

"Random Thoughts on School Library Media Management and the Budget Process." *Catholic Library World,* November 1979, pp. 154-157.

Raub, S. "Developing and Promoting School District Budgets." *Journal of the New York State School Boards Association,* March 1980, p. 7.

Riggs, James R. "Intimacy with Your Budget Can Make You a Wise Leader." *American School Board Journal,* October 1980, pp. 23-25.

Rizzo, John R. *Management for Librarians: Fundamentals and Issues.* Westport, Conn.: Greenwood, 1980.

Ross, V. J. "How to Let the Community Help You Make the Tough Decisions on Budget Cuts." *American School Board Journal,* June 1981, pp. 29-30.

Roth, Robert A. "Educational Retrenchment: A State Perspective." *Action in Teacher Education,* Summer/Fall 1981, pp. 43-48.

Simpson, I. S. *Basic Statistics for Librarians,* 2nd ed. Hamden, Conn.: Shoe String, 1982.

Sine, Mary Robinson. "Budget Considerations and Media Selection: Getting the Most for the Dollar." *Catholic Library World,* September 1978, pp. 65-67.

Triviero, Louis E. "Control and Master Your Budget." *American School Board Journal*, November 1981, pp. 31–33.

Williams, Dianne McAfee. "Funding Sources—Selected Emphasis on School Media Programs." *Wisconsin Library Bulletin*, March/April 1980, pp. 57–59.

Wilson, William K., and Wilson, Betty, eds. *Directory of Research Grants*. Phoenix, Ariz.: Oryx, 1982.

5
STAFF

The staff is the foundation of a dynamic and effective center and the mainstay of a school library media program. The persons who create and develop the activities are directly responsible for the overall success of the program in each school. Each staff member usually functions in a dual capacity: individually as a specialist and cooperatively as a member of the media program team. A school library media center staff should include personnel with a broad range of experience and skills. To promote good personal relationships and ensure a well-functioning program, school administrators should encourage media specialists to participate in the selection of staff.

There are common areas of concern when dealing with human beings—self-worth, pride, and security. Any constructive criticism and positive motivation should take these fundamental factors into account; for example, the security of having job descriptions and participatory evaluations will aid each staff member and supervisor.

This chapter takes a look at some supervisory practices as concerning the school library media center. Supervision is a difficult task, but good supervision ensures good staff relations, good program results, and firm educational goals. The main purpose of this chapter is to help those who have a responsibility to select staff for a school library media center in a single school building. It describes the principal categories of personnel and an overview of certification for specialists, emphasizing staff requirements and certification. It also treats other staffing concerns, for example, recruitment, selection, and evaluation, that confront the school library media specialist.

PERSONNEL CATEGORIES

Although there are many ways to define staff roles, studies of human resources in school library media centers indicate three broad categories under which the majority of media center personnel may be listed: professional, paraprofessional, and nonprofessional.[1]

Professionals

Persons educated and certified as school library media specialists, librarians, or audiovisual specialists by a state or other accrediting agency are considered professionals, regardless of their primary responsibility. Media center directors, assistant librarians, and audiovisual specialists with competency in a specialty within some communication technology—for example, television and radio—generally meet these requirements. It is their responsibility to assume leadership in planning, developing, and evaluating a program that meets the needs of faculty, students, and community. They must be interested and knowledgeable in media and the components of media, instructional materials, and communications technology, including computerization. Knowledge of materials in different formats, appreciation of service as resource personnel, ability to operate equipment and aid in the production of materials are their primary responsibilities. They should also be proficient in the principles of teaching and learning and knowledgeable about the media program of the school and the characteristics of the students with whom they work. Because the school library media program involves students, teachers, and administrators, each staff member, especially in a single-school situation, must be able to work well with people of all ages. The center is so integral a part of the total school program that it is difficult to say where the school stops and the center begins.

A school library media center is usually located in the building that houses all its potential users. The media specialist must work shoulder to shoulder with classroom teachers in helping students make full use of the media. In fact, the media specialist is a teacher operating through the center rather than in a classroom. In the doubt-provoking 1980s, as in the expansive 1960s and 1970s, the media specialist continues to find this challenging role exciting and intrinsically rewarding.

Coordinators

The school library media center coordinator or director usually has training in library and information science and the traditional audiovisual services, and, in addition, should have demonstrable leadership qualities. Certified persons should have the primary responsibility for administrating the school library media center at both the elementary and secondary levels. When two or more professionals are employed in the same center, only one should be in charge of and responsible for the program. The coordinator in the school that is establishing a unified program should have professional-level competency in all media; in addition to administration, the coordinator shares a common responsibility with other center staff personnel for general services, or all phases of program work. The coordinator is also in charge of developing in other staff members the necessary knowledge, skill, and competence to perform their jobs well. As the program expands, the coordinator sees to the employment of additional staff who have complementary preparation and subject specialization. In new and developing programs with a small-size staff, where the coordinator must spend much time in administration, program planning and implementation, and evaluation and media selection, some of these tasks are redistributed.

School Library Media Specialists

Generally the specialist has been educated in both the traditional field of librarianship and information science and in audiovisual service, with an emphasis on instructional materials. However, both by interest and training, media specialists may work with the equipment or with any part of the instructional technology of the program. This is especially true on a small-size staff that has neither an audiovisual specialist nor a technician.

The main functions of the school library media specialist cluster around general services and services to students and teachers. Functions commonly associated with the specialist are labeled *M* on the list of representative tasks (see later in this chapter). Specifically these are the tasks that contribute to the center's organization and to its circulation, instruction, and selection services. In addition, the specialist helps to develop the program by implementing many of the center's activities. A subject or grade-level specialization, together with some facility in cataloging nonprint materials, is useful. If the media specialist is the only professional on the staff, he or she assumes as much of the coordinator and specialist roles as possible, assigning priority to the most important and immediate demands. The program will grow in direct ratio to the size, qualifications, and imagination of the staff.

Audiovisual Specialists

The audiovisual specialist is certified as a professional in instructional or communications technology by education, by experience, or both. Some education in librarianship is becoming part of the audiovisual specialist's training. The positions of media specialist and audiovisual specialist may overlap in many instances, the basic or traditional difference being that the media specialist generally concentrates on the materials services and the audiovisual specialist's concern is the equipment. Audiovisual specialists are also increasingly concerned with media instructional applications. Although this has been the typical division for staff positions, an interesting variation, particularly on larger staffs, is the newer role where competencies exist in both materials and equipment or technology, and the person combines them into a subject or grade-level approach that permits the specialist to become part of a team of teachers. This increases the specialist's usefulness to both students and teachers and fits in with the idea of differentiated staffing where educational personnel assume responsibilities based on carefully defined educational functions. For this arrangement to work well, the newer type of specialist must assume the broad tasks of the media and audiovisual specialists and refine them by curriculum and grade level.

The primary responsibilities of the past, more traditional audiovisual specialist role were nonprint materials and equipment services, which at their least sophisticated level are still often performed by paraprofessionals or technicians. Audiovisual specialists also continue to take part in the development of the program, selection of media—particularly equipment, and production. The role of the audiovisual specialist in a school library media program, still in a state of transition, is largely determined by the size of the staff. In a single school with only two or three staff members, one popular, economical pattern uses a professional media specialist, a technician, and clerical support. The duties most commonly associated with the audiovisual specialist are labeled *A* on the representative tasks list (see later in this chapter).

Paraprofessionals

A person qualified in a special area of media work, for example, photography, graphics, or electronics, but who does not hold a bachelor's degree generally is classified as a paraprofessional. Usually identified as a technical assistant, this person is an important staff member in any large school library media center program and, given the wide range of the technical assistant's competencies, a worthwhile member of a small staff. Technical assistants are often recruited from industry, community colleges, and the like, and their duties are mainly in production, preparation, maintenance, and special services to faculty and students, with whom they often work directly. Some of the technical assistant's specific tasks are noted under Paraprofessional

Staff in the representative tasks list (see later in this chapter). If the post of technical assistant does not exist in the center program, the duties of this position are assumed by school library media specialists and supportive personnel such as clerks.

Nonprofessionals

Technicians and clerks form the regular nonprofessional staff of the school library media center program. They may be salaried personnel or unpaid volunteer aides, and they work under the direction of a professional. Their schooling and experience may range from a grade-school diploma to training in a technical or clerical institute to graduate study. Preparation for their work in the center is acquired by specialized training or practical experience, but they are rarely certified as media specialists. In a center with only one nonprofessional, the tasks are combined with those of the professional and paraprofessional staffs.

Technicians

Technicians usually are highly specialized in some aspect of the media program, with a special emphasis on the equipment and production tasks, for example, operating and distributing equipment and producing transparencies or tapes. On a large staff, specialized areas such as computerized services, display techniques, and television broadcasting usually require technicians to help the professionals. Technicians are often recruited directly from high school or technical training institutions.

Clerks

Clerks usually have the clerical and secretarial training and experience that make them especially useful in carrying out the routine business operations of a school library media center program under the supervision of a professional. Their tasks fall into the areas of acquisition, organization, preparation, and circulation of material, along with some production of materials. In recent years, skill in word processing has been added to a clerk's possible list of assets.

Volunteers

Volunteers can be a valuable community liaison. They are usually parents from the school community, students, or both, and are often unpaid. In some cases, student assistants receive course credit for their work in the center; the work may be associated with vocational programs for high school technical and business students. The volunteers' work should be creative and rewarding and exploitation of the volunteer aide can be avoided if the volunteer assistant program is formulated and managed with the individual's development as a primary objective. This can be accomplished by:

Assigning tedious, boring tasks, such as shelving books, infrequently.

Regularly rotating the more desirable jobs, such as circulation desk work.

Training in more complex library work, such as helping students locate materials.

Continuing instruction and job evaluation.

Appropriate incentives and rewards for successful job performance.

Opportunities for social and educational activities, such as theater and museum trips.

A newer category of volunteer is the professional center retiree or other professional personnel who may offer some time to the center. Another variation, one that is controversial, is part-time staffing both by retirees and professional school library media specialists. Each situation must be judged objectively, using the purpose and goals of the center as a final arbiter.

HOW BIG A STAFF?

The size of the media staff depends on several factors: the school enrollment and the diversity of student needs, the number of grades, the nature of the program and instructional pattern, the existence of district level media services, and community support. Many sources have recommendations on staff size, among them the national and individual state standards.[2]

REPRESENTATIVE CENTER TASKS

The Task Analysis Survey Instrument in *School Library Personnel Task Analysis Survey* (Special Report of the Research Division, NEA) identifies more than 300 tasks for a school library media center staff. Well-developed centers with adequate staff will carry out most of the tasks; at least one-third of the tasks are essential in the operation of even the smallest program with the least amount of staff.

The following 100 representative tasks are excerpted from the NEA survey. The list is divided among the three main categories of media center personnel: professional, paraprofessional, and nonprofessional. Tasks may be interchangeable among the staff, depending on the local situation. As a general rule, however, even with only two or three staff persons, all tasks will be covered, some minimally. As the staff size increases in response to an effective program, that is, when an audiovisual specialist, media specialist, or clerk is added, the coordinator will increasingly assume the tasks that are starred (*), the media specialist will assume those designated *M*, and the audiovisual specialist, and in certain cases a technician, will take on those designated *A*. The remaining tasks are chiefly clerical and, as has also been plainly stated in the national standards, are assumed by a clerk or technician on a large staff. There is no one way in which these tasks and the many other service-related functions can be specified; the pattern ultimately depends on the nature of the program and the competencies and interests of the staff. However, tasks for each category are given in the next section; each school library media center should use them as samples in constructing workable ones for the specific situation.

100 Tasks

The asterisk and letter symbols for the professional staff in the following list indicate tasks that will be increasingly assumed by certain persons as staff size increases in response to an effective program:

    * = coordinator
    M = school library media specialist
    A = audiovisual specialist, and in some cases a technician

Professional Staff

   * Determine educational objectives of school library media center policies.
   * Plan programs and center operations and maintenance.
   * Help determine overall school library media center policies.
   * Assist in selecting center staff.
   * Prepare work schedules for center staff.
   * Supervise work of professional and nonprofessional staff.
   * Work with and submit reports to administration.
   * Determine records and statistics needed.
   * Enlist faculty in writing a materials selection policy.
   * Establish cataloging and classification policies.

* Plan for reorganization and relocation of collections.
* Formulate policies and procedures for circulating materials and equipment.
* Assume responsibility for decisions concerning disciplinary actions.
* Develop handbook for teachers and students.
* Work with teachers to establish procedures for group or individual assignments.
* Inform faculty of available in-service courses, workshops, professional meetings, and the community's educational resources.
* Promote use of professional library.
* Plan and participate in community relations activities.
* Visit other schools and participate in professional meetings.
* Determine policy for accepting gifts.

M/A Schedule use of facilities.

M/A Conduct in-service work.

M/A Participate in curriculum development and review.

M/A Train student aides and volunteers.

M/A Initiate projects and activities relating to media resources.

M/A Originate and conduct special activities for interest groups.

M/A Maintain in the media center schedules of class activities.

M/A Orient students to center.

M/A Plan sequential programs of instruction in research techniques.

M/A Inform teachers of new services.

M/A Introduce teachers to bibliographic tools in subject and grade-level areas.

M/A Outline publicity; write articles, promotional materials, and notices for school and local papers.

M/A Work with teachers and students in reading, viewing, and listening activities.

M/A Plan with faculty members to coordinate materials and media activities.

M/A Observe classroom work to coordinate with media center program.

M/A Participate in team teaching.

M/A Enlist faculty participation and recommendations in evaluating or selecting materials.

M/A Develop evaluation forms.

M/A Read books, magazines, professional journals, review services, and local publications for information on selecting materials and equipment.

M/A Evaluate and select materials and equipment.

M/A Organize and maintain reserve and special media collections.

M/A Plan the system for scheduling and delivering materials and equipment.

M/A Compile media lists.

M/A Administer interlibrary loan services.

M/A Perform general reference services.

Paraprofessional Staff

Develop new uses for materials and equipment.

Work with teachers to design innovations in instruction.

Help to determine space for equipment to be purchased.

Develop evaluation forms.

Adapt commercial materials and equipment to meet special needs.

Design publicity materials in all media.

Make simple display devices for use in instruction.

Operate lettering and drawing devices.

Microfilm materials.

Produce specialized materials for school needs (tapes, record programs, etc.).

Handle photography and film course and recreation-related media center work.

Maintain dial-access and computer equipment and programs.

Provide for preparation of materials (laminating, making transparencies, etc.).

Make major repairs of equipment if not under service contract.

Evaluate students' special school library media center projects.

Assist with independent study.

Assist teachers and students in locating and selecting materials and equipment.

Assist teachers and students in using equipment and materials.

Assist teachers and students with taping services.

Assist teachers and students with production techniques.

Answer simple reference questions.

Plan and prepare displays.

Plan and supervise media fairs.

Develop forms for operation of the center in area of specialization.

Maintain materials and equipment evaluation file.

Perform routine print-shop activities.

Schedule use of and deliver materials and equipment.

Maintain cumulative records of condition of and maintenance work on equipment.

Nonprofessional Staff

Determine need for, control, order, inventory, and maintain supplies.

Handle clerical and secretarial work of correspondence (filing, typing, mailing, etc.).

Type notices, requisitions, bulletins, mediagraphies, and so forth.

Assist in sale of paperback books.

Perform messenger service.

Maintain selection aids for finding new materials.

Check shelf list and other aids to prepare bibliographic data for ordering and duplicating materials.

Transact clerical business operations: file orders and invoices; receive credit memoranda and invoices and transmit them to appropriate office; verify total purchase costs; follow up outstanding orders.

Unpack and check new materials and equipment received, and verify invoices with shipment and order.

Post receipt of periodical and newspaper issues and take care of missing items.

Prepare items received for use.

Stamp ownership mark on all materials.

Place subject headings on vertical file folders.

Adapt commercial catalog cards for local use.

Prepare and file shelf-list and catalog cards.

Sort and place materials on shelves or in containers and keep them in reasonable order.

Process records for materials and equipment withdrawn from collection.

Compile and revise media book catalogs.

Compile review files for materials and equipment.

Maintain media inventory records and assist in inventory.

Set up and operate audiovisual equipment, such as projectors and video readers.

Inspect and make necessary repairs to print and nonprint materials and equipment.

JOB DESCRIPTIONS

The sample job descriptions that follow are for positions that most often exist in the school library media center in an individual building. They agree with the tasks that have been described earlier. They also identify some of the major specific duties that are generally universal. The use of job descriptions is recommended both for the applicant or employee and the supervisor. Each job description can be designed specifically for a particular position by using these samples as guidelines. Of necessity, the job description that evolves will contain the tasks specific to the position.

Position:	District School Library Media Director (coordinator, supervisor, etc.)
Supervisor:	District administrative authority, e.g., assistant superintendent
Supervises:	District school library media center School library media heads
Education:	Advanced course work in a specialization or a doctorate (additional competencies beyond those for a school library media head)
Nature:	Leadership in district's school library media center development
Responsibilities:	Serve as liaison with the superintendent, state and federal levels.
	Determine educational objectives of school library media center policies.
	Establish cooperatively overall school library media center policy.

Determine statistics needed.

Work with and submit reports to district administration.

Recruit and select cooperatively center staff.

Prepare cooperatively job descriptions for directly reporting staff.

Supervise work of staff.

Oversee adoption by board of education and use of selection policy by district.

Establish policies for all categories, e.g., cataloging and classification, circulating materials and equipment, maintenance of media, etc.

Supervise instructional development in centers.

Plan for reorganizations and relocations.

Supervise promotional work, e.g., local history projects.

Establish center for encouragement of staff development, e.g., announcement of courses, conferences, etc.

Maintain a professional collection.

Provide interdistrict and regional sharing of resources.

Explore current developments in field and relate them to school library media center personnel.

Position:	School Library Media Head
Supervisor:	District school library media director
	Administrative head of school (principal)
Supervises:	School library media center staff (other specialists, technicians, clerks, etc.)
Education:	Additional competencies beyond those expected of a school library media specialist, e.g., administration, information science
Nature:	Responsibility to administer the school library media center to help accomplish the educational goals of the school district (if there is no district director, also to plan and develop cooperatively the school library media center policy)
Responsibilities:	Assume the duties, as able, of the district school library media director when there is none.

Serve as liaison with principal and school library media district director.

Implement center policies.

Submit reports to district director and principal.

Help to recruit and select staff.

Participate in preparing job descriptions.

Supervise staff; develop evaluation forms.

Plan systems for maintenance, scheduling, and delivery of materials and equipment.

Enlist faculty participation in evaluating and selecting.

Serve as curriculum consultant and also review curriculum.

Observe classroom work to coordinate school library media center programs.

Prepare instructional programs cooperatively and conduct in-service courses.

Plan orientation programs for students, faculty, administrators, and the community.

Develop and implement plans for reorganizations and relocations.

Initiate promotional work related to media, such as publications.

Promote use of professional collections.

Investigate resource sharing.

Explore current developments in the field.

Position:	School Library Media Specialist
Supervisor:	School library media head
Supervises:	Technicians (paraprofessionals)
	Clerks (nonprofessionals)
	Student assistants
	Volunteers
Education:	Professional degree; the first level of professional responsibility as a fully prepared specialist
Nature:	Knowledge and ability in media and related equipment; participation as a specialist in their effective use in all categories of the curriculum
Responsibilities:	Help to plan scheduling and delivery systems.

Schedule use of facilities.

Participate in curriculum development committees.

Help to coordinate classroom work with school library media programs.

Introduce teachers to media aids in their subjects or grade levels.

Work with students and teachers in reading, viewing, and listening.

Inform teachers of new services.

Compile media lists.

Read widely for information on selecting materials and equipment.

Help to evaluate and select media.

Organize and reserve special collections.

Perform general reference services.

Administer interlibrary loan and resource sharing.

Plan and conduct programs of instruction in research techniques.

Conduct in-service courses.

Orient students to school library media center(s).

Train student assistants and volunteers.

Initiate projects and activities relating to media resources.

Originate and conduct programs for special-interest groups.

Outline and conduct public relations, e.g., write articles, maintain schedules of class activities.

Position:	School Library Media Technician
Supervisor:	School library media head
	School library media specialist
Education:	Generally two years of higher education, including specialized training and/or experience
Nature:	Competency as a team member of the staff to provide technical services and specialized operations for school library media centers
Responsibilities:	Help to schedule use and delivery of media.

Produce specialized materials for school needs, e.g., tapes.

Provide for preparation of materials, e.g., transparencies.

Make simple display devices for instruction.

Operate lettering and drawing devices, microfilm, etc.

Handle photography and film courses for recreational related work.

Maintain computer equipment and help with programs.

Adapt commercial materials and equipment to meet special needs.

Evaluate student's special school library media center projects.

Assist with independent study.

Help students and teachers using equipment and materials.

Assist teachers and students in locating and selecting media.

Involve and help students and teachers with production techniques.

Work with teachers to design innovations in instruction.

Develop new uses for materials and equipment.

Help to develop evaluation forms for equipment.

Maintain cumulative records of repair and condition of equipment.

Make repairs on equipment and investigate contract method for major repairs.

Plan and prepare displays for public relations, e.g., school library media center fair.

Perform routine and simple print shop activities.

Position:	School Library Media Secretary (aide, etc.)
Supervisor:	School library media head, specialist, technician, or other specified head.
Supervises:	Student assistants/volunteers
Education:	Secretarial training/experience, including typing ability
Nature:	Fulfill the routine operations of a school library media center, under direction of a professional
Responsibilities:	Transact clerical business operations.

Handle secretarial work of correspondence, etc.

Control ordering, inventory, and maintenance of supplies.

Check shelf list and other aids for ordering and duplicating.

Prepare and file catalog cards for media, e.g., microforms.

Help to adapt commercial catalog cards, if used, for local use.

Maintain selection aids for finding new materials.

Compile and revise media catalogs, whether book, computerized, etc.

Maintain review files for media.

Type notices, requisitions, bulletins, mediagraphies, etc.

Post receipt of periodicals, newspapers, etc.

Place subject headings on vertical file folders.

Process records for media withdrawn from the collection.

Maintain media inventory records.

Assist in the inventory.

Position:	Student Assistant/Volunteer
Supervisor:	School library media head or school library media specialist, technician, media aide or secretary, or other specified authority
Education:	Training on the job, generally

Nature:	Assistance to the staff
Responsibilities:	Assist at the circulation desk.

Unpack and check new materials and equipment and verify invoices.

Place ownership and identification mark on each item.

Ready items received for use.

Sort and place items in proper locations, maintaining proper order.

Perform messenger service.

Set up and operate equipment for teachers and students.

Assist in public relations work, e.g., bulletin boards.

Certification

The publication *Standards for School Library Programs*[3] represented the first national recognition of the need for unified media services in the school; the standards published in the 1975 *Media Programs . . .*[4] confirmed it. Although economic uncertainty has slowed and in some cases stopped the implementation of this stage of the developmental process, most in the field are now aware of this long-developing movement. The American Association of School Librarians (AASL), the American Library Association (ALA), and the Association for Educational Communications and Technology (AECT) fostered the development of the school library media specialist as a professional with training and experience in library science and instructional technology.

The preparation of professionals in school library media work increasingly follows this pattern, as reflected particularly in state requirements for media coordinators. For example, in Michigan, there is no school library media specialist certification; in New York there is. Both states, however, require that each media specialist or person filling that position be certified as a teacher.[5] Preparation as a classroom teacher is generally stipulated. Although previously issued certificates are honored, as they are in most states under a grandfather clause, more balanced course work appears more and more frequently in the preparation of the media specialist.

A common pattern in certification in the increasingly complex school library media field generally includes training in five areas: administration and supervision, organization, selection and utilization, production, and communications theory and systems, plus supporting courses that increasingly include information science. Many state plans for certification on the level of administration and supervision of media favor the newer combination of fields while remaining flexible enough to permit specialization, particularly in such areas as television or data processing.

Audiovisual Specialist (Instructional Technologist)

Just as the traditional certification as a school librarian with emphasis solely on print materials continues to exist in a few states, so does its counterpart, certification as an audiovisual specialist and/or instructional technologist with emphasis on nonprint materials and equipment. Because of the changes and revisions in audiovisual course titles and descriptions, including name changes, it is difficult to determine the certification requirements for the traditional type of audiovisual work in schools. Nevertheless, there are some states that still have this type of certification. Some continue revising certification to agree with the trend; others have plans, some indefinite, to work on it. The states with dual certification have no plans to change.

In spite of the mixture of certification standards, some generalizations about the audiovisual certificate, where it exists, are possible. The minimum requirements are a baccalaureate degree, a teaching certificate, and some classroom or directed teaching experience; from 12 to 15 hours of graduate credit in audiovisual courses are usually required. Many states attach these requirements as a rider to regular teaching certificates. AECT has also been considering acting as a certification agency.[6]

School Library Media Specialist

Certification for school library media specialists exists in most states. The title of the certificate varies from teacher-librarian, instructional developer, media manager, to media specialist and even media generalist. This confusion in titles reflects clearly the lack of standardization among the states in terminology, grades of certificates, number of required hours, distribution of subjects, and method of certifying. Some general observations are nevertheless possible; for example, some states issue more than one grade of certificate with a different number of hours required for each. The number of hours necessary for certification varies from a low of 6 (teacher-librarian, New Hampshire) to a high of 60 above the baccalaureate (coordinator, Florida and Indiana). There are only a few states in either of these extreme categories; the majority mandate 18, 24, or 30 hours. The master's degree and teaching experience are increasingly a part of the requirements, although the undergraduate degree is also accepted by some states, for example, Michigan. The conflicts among state requirements are generally related to the different grades of certificates, the variety of the certificate labels, and the diversity of course descriptions.

The distribution of course content needed by a media specialist varies among the states. Comparatively few states require a full range of production and audiovisual courses, although some do require the latter. Seven areas of competency are identified: (1) relation of media to instructional systems, (2) administration of media programs, (3) selection of media, (4) utilization of media, (5) production of media, (6) certification and evaluation of staff, and (7) leadership and professionalism. A model[7] was published in 1976 by ALA to encourage the states and other accrediting agencies to establish and upgrade certification standards. Although not a startling reaction, there has been a small improvement in certification standards for school library media specialists among the states and other accrediting agencies.

There are several ways of granting certification. A state board of education, a national or regional accrediting body such as ALA, or both are the chief agents. Certification can be given directly on examination of the applicant's records or indirectly by automatic certification on completion of an ALA or state-approved (or both) library school program. The teacher certification board in a state education department evaluates an applicant's record and responds to inquiries about the state's certification requirements. School system superintendents are also able in many instances to obtain temporary certification for their employees. However, a school library media specialist who wants to work in a state other than the one in which the course work was completed needs to check into the requirements, since there is no national system of reciprocity in accreditation.

Another method of certification is currently being explored by some of the states. Basic endorsement is given based on an applicant's demonstrated proficiency in such areas as cataloging, materials selection, utilization and production of media, and administration. For professional media endorsement, Utah, for example, requires demonstrated ability in the following areas: human relations, leadership, supervision, and communications theory.

Aside from this practical examination procedure, a portfolio method of examination has also been proposed. An unsettled economic climate has contributed to slow acceptance of any of these methods. Nevertheless the movement, however slow, indicates that the trend will continue to bring the print, nonprint, and technological component of school media service into a more balanced certification position.

RECRUITMENT AND SELECTION

The selection of staff is a creative task that is both difficult and rewarding. The process is usually divided into recruitment and selection. Recruitment methods generally include:

1. Advertisements in appropriate media, for example, newspapers.
2. Listings with professional organizations, such as ALA, AECT, including state and local associations.
3. Notification of college and university clearinghouses.
4. Announcements to state and regional agencies.
5. Recommendations of local staff.

Sometimes all of these methods are used; however, the informal "word of mouth" procedure is often the most popular and influential. Nevertheless, depending on various factors, such as geographical location, each of the above methods can be effective in recruitment. It is important that the media specialist make the principal and higher administration aware of these methods. It is also advisable for the specialist to provide them with a current list of newspapers, magazines, associations, and agencies that might be of help.

The selection of personnel is a complicated and demanding responsibility. It is advisable to emphasize objective factors, while recognizing that the ability of the person to get along well with the individuals already on staff is significant. Once an applicant has been identified and an application received, an interview is usually scheduled. The application should contain at least the following: (1) name, address, and phone number, (2) educational background, (3) work experience, (4) memberships and honors, (5) interests and hobbies, and (6) other, for example, status and availability. The administrator generally verifies the educational background through the transcripts that the applicant has sent and through appropriate telephone calls or letters, for example, the persons listed for recommendations, who can substantiate facts on the resume. These facts are checked either before or after the interview depending on the pattern of the administrator and the pressure of time. The administrator and the applicant can have the luxury of accomplishing these transactions during the spring if it is known that the position will be available. However, it is not uncommon for a position to be filled at the last minute in August. Since the same procedure must be followed, the pressure on both individuals is greater.

The principal or assistant superintendent usually conducts the first interview. At this time, an objective/subjective determination is made about the applicant's abilities and personality. The former determination will be checked and the latter judged by the interviewer and others who may be added to the subsequent interviews, for example, other faculty and staff. When the selection process reaches this point, a "short list" (depending on the number of applicants or predetermined number of finalists) is generally made. These applicants can be called back for another interview with a larger group or the superintendent alone. Where time is pressing, this process is condensed. Finally, a recommendation is made to the board of education. Generally approved, the applicant then receives an official letter stipulating the already expressed working dates and salary.

An increasingly prevalent practice is for the administrator doing the hiring to include the school library media specialist early in the selection process. In the past few years, it has also been the policy of administration to include more staff and school faculty in the interview process, rather than in simple orientation tours. This step is based on the knowledge that such participatory action promotes good human relations.

In the majority of situations, the applicant for a professional position will receive tenure in a stipulated period of time or, in rare instances, at once. This depends on various conditions, such as need, qualifications, hiring policies. It is advisable for the applicant to determine this before or certainly during an interview. There is always the possibility, especially in times of economic hardship, that economizing will be attempted by hiring and then recommending dismissal before tenure has to be granted by policy. Fortunately, such action is not prevalent. It is advisable, however, for professionals to be aware of this concern and to determine the attitude of the employer early in the selection process. If all else is well, including the evaluations that are usually required at least annually, the board of education, based on the superintendent's recommendation, votes positively on the approval for tenure.

SUPERVISION (STAFF EVALUATION)

One of the more significant factors in assessment is supervision or staff evaluation. Qualities of leadership and the knowledge of a few fundamental principles form the capstone of competent supervision. The following paragraphs describe some of the most important principles and practices of school library media center supervision on all levels, emphasizing the role of the school library media specialist as supervisor of the program in the individual school.

The term *coordinator* is used interchangeably with such other descriptive titles as supervisor, director, consultant, or chairperson, since the goals and functions of the positions so described and of the coordinator are the same. Supervision stresses leadership, coordination, cooperation, creativity, self-direction, and effective public relations. The school library media coordinator, as one of the instructional specialists in a school system, regional board of education, or state or federal department of public instruction, shares the responsibility for the overall educational program.

The school library media coordinator should be the leader of the program. This person should have training as a teacher and as a media specialist. Regardless of title, the position should be equal in rank and authority to that of other administrative instructional specialists in the system. This administrative unit is the keystone for well-planned, economically sound school library media service. School media supervision exists at all levels, from federal to local.

Federal Level

The U.S. Department of Education includes a supervisory position to guide and improve school library media service throughout the nation. Two of the purposes of this position are: (1) to serve as an informational clearinghouse, and (2) to act as liaison between the federal, state, and local educational agencies.

State Level

In many states, the state supervisor plans and administers the overall school library media services. The state supervisor provides leadership and supervisory services to local school authorities. As a part of a state's accreditation of library schools, the appropriate bureau or division fosters the concept of the school library media center as a unified program throughout the school. The state bureau reinforces the federal supervisory functions by adapting them to the state level of service. In addition, the state supervisors provide services appropriate to their unique position. These services can be classified under the categories listed below.

Guidelines

Develop all regular qualitative and quantitative standards for school library media centers.

Appraise and plan the remodeling of and consult on library media quarters in new school buildings.

Supervision

Design a long-range plan for school library media development in the state.

Evaluate school library media programs in the state.

Guide the development of programs of library and information science education in the state.

Encourage the development of demonstration school library media centers throughout the state.

Distribution of Information

Interpret the role and importance of media to the legislature, boards of education, school personnel, and other groups.

Advise on and interpret state and federal legislation and regulations regarding school library media centers.

Supply information and publications on school library media programs to administrators, teachers, and media specialists.

Prepare annual reports, special reports, and articles.

Statistics and Research

Collect, analyze, and disseminate statistical data on media service in schools.

Initiate and promote research on school library media programs.

Secure government and private grants to further the development of school library media centers within the state.

Certification

Serve as resource centers and advisers on professional qualifications for school library media specialists.

Aid in the recruitment of school library media specialists.

Cooperation

Work closely with the chief state school officer.

Coordinate the school library media program with other programs within the state education department.

Participate in national, state, regional, and local education and library organizations.

Serve as consultants on school library media centers and as resource persons with other groups.

Arrange cooperative programs and projects with other professional groups.

Cooperate with government agencies, such as state libraries and regional boards.

Cooperate with nongovernmental organizations, such as teachers' associations, PTAs, and so forth.

System, City, and District Levels

While each system network or regional cooperative service has its own services and activities that are available to the school district, some basic services and activities are offered by most of them, as follows:

1. Establishing a union catalog based on the collections of the cooperating schools' libraries.
2. Forming depository collections to supplement the regular school collections.
3. Assigning areas of subject or media specialization to member schools.
4. Sharing operating and maintenance costs of expensive facilities, such as television studios.
5. Computerizing such routines as ordering, preparing, circulating, and inventorying media.
6. Providing central facilities and consultants for large-group meetings and instruction.
7. Coordinating in-service workshops with other groups.

Many cities and districts employ school library media coordinators to utilize federal and state supervisory services and provide effective management of the local program. A school system with five or more school buildings should establish the position. The formation of school library media centers into a separate administrative unit has proved to be educationally efficient and economically sound. In addition to directing the school district's media program, the coordinator can effect economies by assigning nonprofessional library routines to paraprofessional and nonprofessional staff. Although administering these technical services is important, the primary responsibility of the school library media coordinator lies in working with media specialists, teachers, and administrators. In essence, school library media supervision involves the development and supervision of a satisfactory school system media program designed to aid teachers in solving their instructional problems, students in participating fully in the learning process, and the community in supporting the program.

A city, county, or large-school media center system usually provides a majority of the following services to its individual schools, either directly or by contractual arrangement with another district or regional agency:

1. Establishing central purchasing, cataloging, and preparation of media.
2. Maintaining additional materials for smaller schools that cannot adequately meet the variety of student and teacher needs.
3. Developing an examination system for the selection of materials and equipment.
4. Producing specialized forms of materials, such as slides, audiotapes, videotapes, and so forth.
5. Maintaining equipment.
6. Establishing printing services.
7. Developing in-service programs for training the entire district faculty (e.g., on the evaluation and use of newer media).
8. Assisting in recruiting and selecting media staff for the district.
9. Coordinating professional collections for teachers and administrators.
10. Initiating the borrowing or renting of costly or infrequently used materials.
11. Establishing a central source for consumable supplies.
12. Developing television services that may include the following types: open circuit, closed circuit, or community antenna.
13. Developing computer services for technical services, information retrieval, and instruction assistance.

Although each local district will have unique problems, the basic functions of district school library media program supervision are similar. The major responsibilities are:

1. Advising local school administrators on the role and management of school library media centers.
2. Interpreting school library media functions to the board of education, legislature, PTA, citizen groups, and other public bodies.
3. Working with other coordinators and department heads to improve media service.
4. Implementing school library media standards.
5. Promoting a media concept in the school by incorporating media services in the center and including media in bibliographies.
6. Assisting in selecting and organizing the media, including equipment.

7. Coordinating the work of all media centers in the school system, including purchasing and technical services.

8. Providing for local production and distribution of instructional aids and materials.

9. Evaluating school library media services.

10. Serving on curriculum committees and as a resource person for other specialists.

11. Initiating and directing in-service programs on school library media center materials and services, for example, providing instruction in newer media.

12. Recruiting and directing a qualified staff.

13. Preparing a budget, annual and specific reports, and articles.

14. Participating in professional organizations and conferences.

15. Providing a center where educational media can be examined and evaluated.

16. Exploring the use of new technology, such as optical scanners.

17. Fostering research and experimentation with instructional uses of media and media services arrangements and applying the results of research to the program.

Supervision in the Individual School

In a school library media center that has a small staff and lacks a coordinator on the district level, the school library media specialist assumes the supervisory role and carries out as many as possible of the districtwide functions that have been enumerated. The specialists in individual schools may consult directly with state and federal school library media departments. Other agencies, such as public and college library consortia, will also give advice and aid to the school library media specialist.

In addition to the important policymaking and program-coordinating functions, another basic task for the coordinator is staff evaluation. The sample evaluation checklist that follows can be used by both the individual who is being evaluated and by the evaluator. Both parties should independently fill out the checklist and then discuss the two perceptions. The evaluative checklist should include in priority the expected responsibilities. Therefore, it is desirable that each evaluation form correspond closely to the pertinent lists of duties and the announced and understood expectations of the designated authority.

EXHIBIT 5-1   EVALUATION CHECKLIST
(1 = Excellent; 2 = Good; 3 = Satisfactory; 4 = Poor; 5 = Inadequate)

How do you rate in . . . ?	1	2	3	4	5
Helping to plan scheduling and delivery systems?	___	___	___	___	___
Do the systems agree with the district educational policy? Are the teachers and students satisfied?					
Scheduling the use of facilities?	___	___	___	___	___
Do attendance policies encourage students to come for instructional and recreational purposes? Do the teachers think so?					
Participation with curriculum committees?	___	___	___	___	___
Do you participate in any? How many would a school library media specialist be able to work with?					
Coordinating classroom work with media center programs?	___	___	___	___	___
Do you attend or investigate ongoing classroom work regularly?					
Introducing teachers to media aids?	___	___	___	___	___
Do you use a regular system for keeping the teachers aware?					
Informing teachers of new services?	___	___	___	___	___
Do you use a regular system for keeping the teachers aware?					
Working with students in reading, viewing, and listening?	___	___	___	___	___
Are the students aware and satisfied with your group/individual help? Are you?					
Compiling Media Lists?	___	___	___	___	___
Do you do this on a regular basis, as needed, etc.?					
Keeping abreast of selection information?	___	___	___	___	___
How many media do you regularly look at specifically for this? Do you do this as part of your work or on home time?					

EXHIBIT 5-1 (cont.)

How do you rate in . . . ?	1	2	3	4	5
Helping to evaluate and select media?	___	___	___	___	___
Do you participate in this task as much as you can?					
Organizing and reserving special collections?	___	___	___	___	___
Do you actively encourage the development of this?					
Performing general reference services?	___	___	___	___	___
Are you generally able to solve most requests?					
Administering resource sharing and interlibrary loan?	___	___	___	___	___
Do you actively encourage and accomplish obtaining media?					
Instructing students in research techniques?	___	___	___	___	___
Do the students produce sound mediagraphies after the instruction?					
Conducting in-service courses?	___	___	___	___	___
Do you have a good background in or desire to teach such courses for the teachers?					
Orienting students?	___	___	___	___	___
Do you have a regular plan for conducting orientation? Is it satisfactory to the students, teachers, and you?					
Training student assistants and volunteers?	___	___	___	___	___
How many do you train annually?					
Initiating projects and activities?	___	___	___	___	___
Can you highlight one or more that you have planned and carried out in the past year?					
Conducting programs for special-interest groups?	___	___	___	___	___
Can you also highlight programs					

EXHIBIT 5-1 (cont.)

How do you rate in ... ?	1	2	3	4	5
you originated and conducted for this, as distinct from the above?					
Outlining and conducting public relations?	___	___	___	___	___
Within the past year, what are the things, e.g., writing articles for the school or local newspaper, for which you were responsible in public relations for the school library media center?					
Continuing growth in education?	___	___	___	___	___
Have you done anything within the past year that would show this growth?					
Attitude toward students?	___	___	___	___	___
Do you agree with and maintain the official district policy of discipline?					
Performing any administrative procedures, such as processing of materials that has not been mentioned?	___	___	___	___	___
Do you follow the procedures that have been developed to the satisfaction of everyone?					
The production of materials?	___	___	___	___	___
Do you use your skills in this work for student and teacher satisfaction?					
Helping to evaluate the media center programs?	___	___	___	___	___
Is evaluation an automatic part of your assessment procedure for any program of which you are a part?					
Human relations among the students staff teachers administration in the building other administration community?	___	___	___	___	___

MANUALS

Guides and manuals are another important aspect of staff development in school library media centers. They help to give efficient and more consistent service. Interested personnel can find manuals in a few reliable places that will enable them to follow established patterns that have produced beneficial results. Aside from neighboring media centers, which may have developed some manuals, and nearby library and information science colleges, which may have examples in their libraries, the ALA headquarters library has a listing of about 30 staff manuals and guides, available on request. Also, the ALA headquarters library asks for a copy of any staff manual for distribution.

Manuals provide a rationale and a handy guide to the operation of the school library media center for various groups. Some of the most common types are for staff, student assistants and volunteers, and the community. Although each school library media center is different and needs to develop its own personalized guides, there are a few common concerns central to all manuals. The first is the district educational philosophy, which should be followed by the school library media center educational rationale, which flows from the district's. The harmony of these statements and the further agreement of every procedure or rule that appears with this basic philosophy is vital. No loop-hole should exist due to lack of logic. Another consideration is the commonsense principle that the manual or guide should enable its readers to accomplish the purpose for which it is composed, for example, the student assistants should be able to do the task described and the community should be able to tell at least the educational philosophy, hours, rules, services, and any special community services. The latter will, of course, be highlighted in manuals for community use.

Manuals and guides are generally of three types: policy, operations (or a combination), and public relations. A policy manual contains a statement explaining the basic position for each category, for example, for production and for selection. In an operations manual, the procedure required by each task is described. One method of constructing this type of staff manual is to outline the typical work procedure for each responsibility listed on the job description (see Exhibit 5-3, Sample Staff Manual [Student Assistants]). The policy and operations manuals can be combined if desired. The manual for public relations should tell the reader, at a minimum, the location, hours, rules, public services, educational philosophy, and special community programs in clear terms. (Three sample contents pages from manuals follow.)

EXHIBIT 5-2   SAMPLE STAFF MANUAL (POLICY)

Full Identification (Address)
District educational philosophy

School Library Media Center rationale

Roles of school library media specialists (Means of reaching staff)

Budget and reports
  example

The collection (Selection objectives, procedures, procedures for handling challenged materials)

Maintenance

Access (Regulations, including eligibility and identification means)

Circulation

Arrangement

The learning environment

Services (Loan, interlibrary loan, reference, manual and online, etc.)
  students
  teachers
  administrators
  community

Local production

Days and hours of service

Description of major holdings
    Date

EXHIBIT 5-3   SAMPLE STAFF MANUAL (STUDENT ASSISTANTS)

Message

Important papers (e.g., School Library Bill of Rights, ALA)

Policies and responsibilities (Condensed)

Arrangement
  Classification

Circulation and other school library media center procedures (e.g., processing)

Access (Regulations)

Rules for filing catalog cards

List and location of supplies

Procedures for inventory

Displays and bulletin board procedures

EXHIBIT 5-3   (cont.)

School library media clubs

Services

Housekeeping chores

   Date

EXHIBIT 5-4   SAMPLE PUBLIC RELATIONS COMMUNITY GUIDE

Identification (Address and location in building)

Hours

Regulations

Messages

Local official names of sponsoring group

Scenario of public services

Educational philosophy

Community resources

Special community programs

The collection
   selection policy, procedures for all materials, procedures for handling challenged materials

Reading, viewing and listening references

A note about new things in the center (e.g., computers)

Notes (for the recipient)

Logos

   Date

FUTURE

Although the immediate future of the school library media center may be threatened by declining numbers of students, the economic reality of lowered budgets, the continuing disparate attitudes among media specialists, and the unsettled political position in education, the history of the media center movement indicates that there is a cyclical and developing nature to this important part of American education. The decade of the 1980s calls for redoubled efforts and long-range optimism. An increase in the birthrate points to an increase in the student population. Both budget problems and national political attitudes toward American education must continue to be addressed realistically and constructively. These factors, however, should not be used as a rationale for doing less than a superlative job. The object, as always, is to have the best staff possible.

There are many encouraging signs for the future; one is the leadership shown by many states. For example, a commissioner's committee was appointed in New York to report on statewide library development. In 1981, the published report, *Meeting Information Needs Of the 80's*, stated clearly for school libraries that they should be strengthened by: (1) a revision of regulations, (2) development of resource-sharing programs, (3) upgrading and raising state standards and improving compliance, (4) including the cost of school library media programs in the contingency budget in the event of a community budget defeat, and (5) employing the necessary staff and having adequate resources for each school district's educational goals.[8]

This type of state recognition foretells library direction and development providing that the field continues to provoke constructive action. Although activity to improve the status of school library media centers varies widely among the states, it is still true that those who are in the forefront regarding acceptance and recognition cause constructive ferment among those who may be lagging. An equally encouraging sign for the future of school library media centers appeared in the mention of school libraries and school media programs in the report of the National Commission on Libraries and Information Science,[9] which served to place centers squarely on the national scene. Internationally, the Canadian School Library Association, representing a practicing group of professionals, presented its view on the education of school library and information science professionals.[10] Although the views are many and wide, the field improves slowly from the mix and modifications continue, giving it vitality and direction.

NOTES

1. *Media Programs, District and School.* . . . Chicago: ALA/AECT, 1975, ch. 4, pp. 21–35.
2. See Ibid, pp. 33–35.
3. *Standards for School Library Programs.* Chicago: ALA/NEA, 1969.
4. *Media Programs.*
5. Kenneth E. Vance, "Certification and Library Education," *Media Spectrum* 7, no. 1 (1980); 3–4.
6. Ronald K. Bass and Marvin Duncan, "Certification," *Florida Media Quarterly* 5, no. 1 (Fall 1979): 22.
7. ALA/AASL Certification of School Media Specialists Committee, Chicago: ALA, 1976.

8. University of the State of New York, Report of the Commissioner on Statewide Library Development, *Meeting Information Needs of the 80's* (Albany: State Education Department, 1981), pp. 5-6.

9. U.S. National Commission on Libraries and Information Science, *Toward a National Program for Library and Information Services-Goals for Action* (Washington, D.C.: Government Printing Office, 1975), pp. 15-16.

10. "CLSA Policy Statement: A Recommended Curriculum for Education for School Librarianship—1981," *School Libraries in Canada* 1, no. 4 (Summer 1981): 3-10ff.

FOR FURTHER READING

Aaron, Shirley L., and Mann, Elizabeth B. "The Media Supervisor as an Agent of Change." *Drexel Library Quarterly*, April 1977, pp. 36-47.

American Association of School Librarians, Certification of School Media Specialists Committee. *Certification Model for Professional School Media Personnel.* Chicago: American Library Association, 1976.

Asheim, Lester. "Librarians as Professionals." *Library Trends*, Winter 1979, pp. 225-257.

Association for Educational Communications and Technology, *Guidelines for Certification of Media Specialists.* Washington, D.C.: AECT, 1977.

Carter, Jane Robbins. "Practical Research for Practicing Librarians." *Top of the News*, Winter 1981, pp. 128-137.

Casciero, Albert J., and Roney, Raymond G. *Introduction to AV for Technical Assistants.* Littleton, Colo.: Libraries Unlimited, 1980.

Case, Robert N., and Lowrey, Anna Mary. *Behavioral Requirements Analysis Checklist: A Compilation of Competency-Based Job Functions and Task Statements for School Library Media Personnel.* Chicago: American Library Association, 1973.

Chernick, Barbara E. *Introduction to Library Service for Library Technicians.* Littleton, Colo.: Libraries Unlimited, 1982.

Chirgwin, F. J., and Oldfield, P. *The Library Assistant's Manual.* Hamden, Conn.: Shoe String, 1978.

"Consulting in Union-Management Relations." *Library Trends*, Winter 1980, pp. 411-424.

Creth, Sheila, and Duda, Fred. *Personnel Administration in Libraries.* New York: Neal-Schuman, 1981.

"The Curriculum Consultant Role of the School Library Media Specialist." *Library Trends*, Fall 1979, pp. 263-279.

Fitzgibbons, Shirley A. "Professionalism and Ethical Behavior: Relationship to School Library Media Personnel." *School Media Quarterly*, Winter 1980, pp. 82-100.

Florida Association for Media in Education. "Suggested Model for School Media Specialists." *Florida Media Quarterly*, Summer 1980, pp. 10-11.

"The Instructional Role of the School Library Media Specialist: What Research Says to Us Now." *School Media Quarterly*, Summer 1981, pp. 281–285.

"The Involvement of the Librarian in the Total Educational Process." *Library Trends*, Summer 1980, pp. 127–138.

Kearney, Carol A. "Organizing for School Library Service: The District Library Supervisor." *Bookmark*, Winter 1980, pp. 292–296.

McCauley, Elfrieda. "Beyond Canisters, Cartridges and Reel Cans." *School Media Quarterly*, Winter 1977, pp. 105–108.

McClaren, M. Bruce. "District Media Management." *Media Spectrum*, 1979, p. 2.

Manatt, Richard P., and Brown, Steven Michael. "How to Rate a Media Specialist's Performance." *AV Instruction*, November 1978, pp. 44–45.

Media Programs, District and School. . . . Chicago: ALA/AECT, 1975.

"The Media Supervisor and the Selection Process." *Drexel Library* Quarterly, July 1978, pp. 45–64.

Mohajerin, Kathryn S., and Smith, Earl P. "Perceptions of the Role of the School Media Specialist." *School Media Quarterly*, Spring 1981, pp. 152–163.

Morris, J. G. "School Media Specialists Plan for Successful Volunteer Programs." *Indiana Media Journal*, Fall 1980, pp. 7–8.

Mugnier, Charlotte. *The Paraprofessional and the Professional Job Structure.* Chicago: American Library Association, 1980.

"Personnel in Libraries." *Library Journal* Special Report, 1979.

Pillon, Nancy B. "Media Specialist: An Active Member of the Teaching Team." *Indiana Media Journal*, Summer 1980, pp. 27–28.

Polette, Nancy. *In-Service: School Library/Media Workshops and Conferences.* Metuchen, N.J.: Scarecrow, 1973.

"A Practical Look at Media Supervision and Curriculum." *School Media Quarterly*, Spring 1979, pp. 204–211.

Rainforth, John. *Perceptions of the High School Librarian.* Dallas: Dallas University/Libraries and School of Library Service, 1981.

Rawles, Beverly A. *Human Resource Management in Small Libraries.* Hamden, Conn.: Shoe String, 1982.

Reeves, William Joseph. *Librarians as Professionals: The Occupation's Management for Librarians: Fundamentals and Issues.* Westport, Conn.: Greenwood, 1980.

"Research: The How and Why of It." *Top of the News*, Winter 1981, pp. 127–156.

"Role and Responsibility of the Media Specialist." *Peabody Journal of Education*, April 1978, pp. 172–177.

School Library Personnel Task Analysis Survey. Washington, D.C.: NEA, 1969.

"Some Reflections on Participative Management." *College & Research Libraries*, July 1978, pp. 253–262.

Standards for School Library Programs. Chicago: ALA/NEA, 1969.

"Staff Planning in a Time of Recession." *Canadian Library Journal*, December 1979, pp. 335–337.

Staples, E. Susan. "60 Competency Ratings for School Media Specialists." *Instructional Innovator*, November 1981, pp. 19–21.

Stevens, Rolland E., ed. *Supervision of Employees in Libraries.* Urbana: Graduate School of Library Science, University of Illinois, 1979.

"Supervision of Instructional Media Services." *Drexel Library Quarterly*, Part I, April 1977; Part II, July 1978.

"Supervisory Interface: Reality and Action." *Drexel Library Quarterly*, July 1978, pp. 65–77.

Thaxter, Schuyler. "When You're the One and Only." *Instructional Innovator*, May 1980, p. 30.

Thomason, Nevada Wallis. *The Library Media Specialist in Curriculum Development.* Metuchen, N.J.: Scarecrow, 1981.

"Toward a Work-Force Analysis of the School Library Media Professional." *School Media Quarterly*, Summer 1981, pp. 235–249.

Turner, Philip M. *Handbook for School Media Personnel*, 2nd ed. Littleton, Colo.: Libraries Unlimited, 1980.

Van Zant, Nancy, ed. *Personnel Policies in Libraries.* New York: Neal-Schuman, 1980.

Wehmeyer, Lillian B. *The School Library Volunteer.* Littleton, Colo.: Libraries Unlimited, 1975.

6

FACILITIES

School library media center facilities share a common purpose: to provide the physical surroundings in which the media needs of the school can be met. They may, however, vary considerably in size, shape, and age of building or renovation. In a society characterized by change, the maxim of an earlier and more stable era, "form follows function," is now more realistically phrased as "form permits function." A school library media program, therefore, is shaped to some extent by the size, shape, and age of its facilities. Well-designed spaces add an important dimension to the program and enrich the school community.

This chapter covers the major points that a school library media specialist should consider in designing or remodeling a facility. Preplanning and planning with various individuals and groups are treated first, followed by a discussion of space requirements for the four major kinds of activities that take place in a center. Suggestions are given for such elements as lighting, the thermal environment, electrical power, acoustics, color, and furnishings. A short list of companies widely known for their school library media furnishings is included. Also treated briefly are facilities for expensive media services, for example, television, that would normally be handled through a central source. Although the guidelines in this chapter can be used for designing a center in a new school building, the focus is on renovating school library media quarters. Specialists are advised to consult other technical sources, and some suggestions for further reading are listed at the end of the chapter.

PLANNING

The expression "form permits function" has direct application in planning school library media centers, whether the goal is designing a new facility with an architect or initiating a simple remodeling project with the help of a principal. In either case, the chief school administrator has the prime responsibility and his or her approval is needed. To plan a functional facility, a knowledgeable school library media specialist and consultant must work together with the administrator and architect in carefully assessing the desired outcomes of the program. Additional help can come from studying plans of other schools and visiting operating school library media centers. Many districts have found it helpful to use special consultants to advise on various matters concerning facilities. Staff, faculty, students, and other persons who will use the center should also be involved in the planning. Experience has shown that it is vital to have the cooperation of all groups in the school setting, from the administrator to the community users. Designs have failed because there was little or no consultation, especially at the planning stage, with those who would be using the center facilities for work, study, or recreation.

Some important factors to investigate in the introductory planning phase are the nature of the curriculum and the teaching methods in the school, the clientele of the center, what routines and services must be accommodated, and the type and quantity of the materials and equipment to be housed. Future projections of the number of students, new services, and the size of collections should also be considered. National and state standards will supply guidelines.

Other factors that influence planning are the overall design of the school building, the accessibility of community resources, and the number of departmental or decentralized collections available elsewhere in the school or district. The importance of this initial study by the school library media specialist cannot be stressed enough. If the program is examined carefully and written down before any blueprints are drawn, it will be possible to tell the administrator and architect exactly what is needed and why.

Each school library media program takes on the characteristics of its facility. No one design can be singled out as the best; each center has a character of its own. The conventional rectangle filled with cafeteria-style tables and chairs is a model that has not been considered adequate for a long time. The design of today's school library media centers stresses openness and flexibility in dividing space and providing for individual and group use with the inclusion of areas for reading, viewing, and listening.

SPACE

Space requirements of the school library media center depend on the organizational pattern of the instructional program, the commitment to media services in that program, and the funds available for either new construction or remodeling. When a new or remodeled media center is planned, the first step is usually to consider location. The center should be central and accessible to all who will participate in the instructional program. Avoid proximity to such noise-producing areas as bus-loading zones or band-practice rooms. The quarters should be placed where access to the rest of the building can be restricted if necessary. This will facilitate use of the center in the evenings, on Saturdays, or during the summer months when the rest of the school might be closed.

If the original facility was located with future remodeling in mind, it will be away from stairwells, lavatories, or expensive permanent facilities that require great structural change. It will be near relatively open spaces, such as classrooms, so that walls can be removed and extensive remodeling accomplished if necessary. Expansion is also made easier if there is at least one exterior wall that faces an unused space or an interior court.

An important second step in planning space needs is awareness of the needs of the physically disabled as they relate to the school library media center.

A third step in the allocation of space is consideration of size. The school library media center is often designed as an activity area that students, teachers, and other persons go to not only for media but also for the experience of learning. The variety of spaces throughout the facility should accommodate all activities that are helpful in developing and encouraging imagination and inquisitiveness about learning among the school community.

Exact figures for the recommended size of a school library media center can serve only as guidelines for individual situations. Such variables as enrollment, size and nature of collections, and services to be offered are important in determining space needs. The national guidelines for school library media centers published by the American Library Association, which give square footage figures or footage figures by percentage of pupils enrolled for functional areas, are helpful in establishing footage requirements.

A recent survey conducted by the authors indicates that many state education departments also suggest footage requirements, for example, Kentucky, Missouri, North Carolina, and Tennessee. Some use stages of recommended footage for developing school library media centers, for example, Michigan; others, such as Indiana, list the figures in a single stage. A few states, for example, Idaho, present detailed explanations together with the square footage for each area. The Maryland State Department of Education continues to recommend that the total media services area should have: (1) no less than 7–10 square feet per student, (2) accommodation for approximately 25 percent of the enrollment, and (3) not more than 100 seats in any one area.

Examine both the national guidelines and the figures that your state recommends. Each functional area receives separate treatment. To illustrate, a comparison is given in Table 6-1, Space Allocation for School Library Media Centers, between Maryland's current criteria and those of the national guidelines (in a shortened version) for space allocation in school library media centers.

Schools that produce their own television and radio programs and have a computerized learning laboratory will also need the following: (1) soundproof 40 × 40-foot television studio and control room with 15-foot ceiling and 14 × 12-foot doors, storage space for television properties, visuals, and so on—800 square feet minimum, (2) office with work space, placed back-to-back with television studio—1,200 square feet minimum, (3) 12 × 12-foot audio studio and control space, which may be near the television studio, (4) computerized learning laboratory—minimum 900 square feet.

FACILITIES FOR MAJOR FUNCTIONS

In general, areas for four major groups of functions should be worked into a plan for any school library media center: (1) reading, listening, and viewing, (2) distributing, organizing, and storing the collections, (3) producing instructional materials, and (4) maintaining and repairing equipment.

Reading, Listening and Viewing Areas

To reflect the emphasis on instruction in the school, reading, listening, and viewing areas should be usable by large and small groups and by individuals—teachers as well as students. To accommodate these activities, a main study area and adjoining rooms of various sizes are necessary. The combined area should be large enough to seat at least 20–30 percent of the school population.

In the main area, approximately 10–30 square feet is generally recommended as comfortable space for each user; it will provide adequate room for furniture, aisles, and so on. Not more than 80–100 seats should be located in any one area, with experience suggesting the lesser figure as the maximum. If the reading area is to have a larger seating capacity, it should be arranged in a variety of combinations of space within space; students and teachers often dislike one big room because it tends to be too noisy and too open. Flexibility for individual as well as group needs can be accommodated in the space-within-space design concept.

In school library media center planning, and especially in open or semiopen centers, the entire area should be visualized in sound zones in order to separate somewhat noisy group activities from quiet individual ones. For example, flexible folding walls can create an area for large-group film viewing; a furniture arrangement can build a "quiet corner" for persons who need to concentrate.

Seminar rooms or instructional areas are useful for many school activities, including small-group work, previewing videotapes, and listening to cassettes. If separate rooms are used, as for computers, they should be next to or at least near the main area. Flexibility in accommodating groups of varying sizes in a main area is one of the elements of good planning and design. In this type of arrangement, modular lighting and ventilation units are a necessity. Ideally each separate room should be soundproof, contain darkening facilities, and be approximately 120–150 square feet in size. Sufficient electrical outlets are absolutely essential. Furnishings may include retractable ceiling or wall screens, tables and chairs, shelving, and display stands. A soundproof typing room is sometimes provided for student use and is often incorporated into the production area.

A separate classroom is frequently planned, especially in renovations. Here, library-related instruction may be given to an entire class, reference work supervised, or other activities carried on. Furniture may include student desks, teacher's desk, tables, computer and microfiche stands, carrels, bulletin boards, chalkboards, permanent screen, book truck, shelving, and any furnishings appropriate to the many purposes of the room. Darkening facilities and numerous electrical outlets are also necessary.

A teachers' seminar room or area is often provided for preparation and professional work as well as for teachers' meetings. This area is generally combined with or placed next to the school library media center facility for the production of material.

Distributing, Organizing, and Storing Collections

Space for distributing, organizing, and storing collections is usually provided in several places: the main area, workroom, office, and storage sites. In the main area the circulation desk should be large

TABLE 6-1 SPACE ALLOCATION FOR SCHOOL LIBRARY MEDIA CENTERS

Maryland Criteria[a]				National Guidelines[b]		
Needs	600 or less enrollment	600– 900	900– 1,200	Areas	Relationships and Special Considerations	Suggested Space Allocations
Space for circulation	500 sq. ft.	600 sq. ft.	750 sq. ft.	Circulation, etc.	Near main entrance Copying, etc.	800 sq. ft. 200 sq. ft.
Space for reading, viewing	3,000 sq. ft.	4,500 sq. ft.	6,000 sq. ft.	Reading	Reference area Instructional programs	15 to 30% of enrollment Min. 9 sq. ft.
Several activity rooms	300 sq. ft.	400 sq. ft.	600 sq. ft.	Small-group	Listening and viewing	Min. 150 sq. ft.
				Conference	Quiet area	150 sq. ft. (3 rooms)
				Computerized learning lab.	Adjacent to instruction area	Depends on computer use
Large-group room	400 sq. ft.	600 sq. ft.	900 sq. ft.	Group projects	Adjacent to reference	900–1,200 sq. ft.
Office space	200 sq. ft.	250 sq. ft.	300 sq. ft.	Administration	Office for media specialist Other desk space	150 sq. ft. per media professional

Space for local production	300 sq. ft.	400 sq. ft.	600 sq. ft.	Work space Media production lab.	Distribution Adjacent to equipment storage Provide housing	300–400 sq. ft. Min. 800 sq. ft. Additional space
Darkroom	100 sq. ft.	150 sq. ft.	150 sq. ft.	Darkroom	Darkroom adjacent to production	150–200 sq. ft.
Storage space	350 sq. ft.	650 sq. ft.	800 sq. ft.	Equipment storage Stacks	Near corridor Near reserve area	Min. 400 sq. ft. Min. 400 sq. ft., additional space for textbooks
				Magazine and newspaper	Space needed for microform readers	Min. 400 sq. ft.
Videotaping	500 sq. ft.	500 sq. ft.	1,000 sq. ft.	—	—	—

[a]Table adapted from *Criteria for Modern School Library Media Programs*, rev. ed. (Maryland State Department of Education, 1978). For an enrollment over 1,200, 5 sq. ft. per student suggested.
[b]Figures compiled from *Media Programs: District and School* (Washington, D.C.: ALA, 1975), pp. 95–103.

enough to handle all distribution procedures for the media collections. A slot and depressible bin for the return of materials are worthwhile additions to a functional circulation desk. If possible, shelving for temporary housing of materials should be provided in or close to the main desk. The catalog, card, Computer Output Microform (COM), and other indexes should also be located near the circulation desk.

The nature and quantity of materials housed in the main area depends on the amount of storage space available elsewhere. Increasingly the application of computerization will help the ever-present problem of lack of space. Extremely bulky and infrequently used materials are often housed nearby, but outside the main area. The main collections of media and the current issues of periodicals and newspapers, as well as the retrospective fiche collections, are generally kept in the main area, although they may also be decentralized in departments or at grade-level resource sites.

Workroom areas for many support functions should be provided, including places for materials production (described in the next section) and for materials preparation where incoming items are received and checked and whatever technical services that are unavailable centrally or commercially are performed. Sometimes these two areas are combined. Since workroom access to the library and to an outside corridor is important for receipt of materials and equipment, adequate entrances should be provided. Workroom size will vary with each school, but 150–400 square feet is suggested. Counter space with sink and running water should be included, with storage cabinets, shelving, worktables, chairs, typewriter, and several strategically placed electrical outlets.

The school library media specialist will, of course, spend the major portion of the work day involved with the center's audiences in various activities. Nevertheless, an office for the specialist, separate from the workroom areas, is essential. Here the specialist may conduct private conferences with teachers and students and deal with the administrative details of the center. The office should be 150–300 square feet in size and convenient to both the workrooms and the main area. Its equipment should include a desk and several chairs, at least one legal-size vertical file, shelving, a telephone for outside school communication, and sufficient electrical outlets.

Storage areas should also be included in the plan. Three different types of media are sometimes stored close to but outside the main area: (1) print materials, (2) nonprint materials, and (3) instructional equipment. Back issues of periodicals (although increasingly this material is handled on microfilm and microfiche), supplementary library books, and sets of additional texts are common examples of print materials that are often stored. The storage area should contain an adequate amount of shelving as well as a working surface, chair or stools, and machine or equipment stands.

The types of nonprint materials in storage areas will depend on what is housed in the main area. No absolute rules are possible; each media specialist will make these decisions based on variable criteria, with accessibility the final criterion. Storage space for bulky nonprint materials, such as 16mm films, videotapes, models, large posters, and maps, is often provided outside the main area.

Because instructional equipment tends to be cumbersome and is often mounted on rolling carts, the storage area for such equipment must be large. Much of the equipment for classroom use may be successfully decentralized throughout the school by department or floor level. Special storage bins can also be constructed in the central area to hold additional film, slide, and filmstrip projectors, overhead projectors, tape recorders, screens, television sets, computer display terminals and keyboards, microfiche readers-printers, and cassette players for ready accessibility and use in the center.

Producing Instructional Materials

The size of the area for producing noncommercial materials and modifying commercial products for local curriculum use will depend on the nature of the school's program. A basic list of activities includes: (1) preparation of graphics, such as posters, slides, transparencies, charts, and computerized graphics, and (2) duplication of materials for teacher and student use. Equipment includes duplicating machines, computer and computer printers, photocopier, drymount press, large-typeface typewriter, worktables and chairs, paper cutter, and suitable supplies. Some centers have extended the capabilities of the production area to include photographic darkrooms as well as taping and recording studios. Students are increasingly involved in the production processes through their recreational as well as curricular interests.

In addition to the workroom areas, the center often provides a separate teachers' study room where the professional library can be housed and teachers can pursue individual projects and hold small-group meetings. Equipping the room with appropriate shelving and comfortable seating similar to that in the main area will encourage teacher use of the study facility. Sometimes the larger production area is set up to accommodate teachers' needs for space to accomplish their varied instruction-related activities. (For more information on the local production of instructional materials, see Chapter 10.)

Maintaining and Repairing Equipment

An area that can be used for the repair and maintenance of instructional equipment is sometimes provided, especially if a technician is on the staff or available in the school. A workbench and chairs plus adequate outlets and tools should be available. In small schools, media specialists frequently rely on a contract with an audiovisual repair service to keep the equipment in good operating condition. If a work area for equipment maintenance is not required, repair space may be combined with the production workroom area or equipment storage areas.

As trends in constructing and remodeling school library media centers continue to develop, the process of using space for changing needs becomes more creative. Many schools built both before and after World War II limit the use of newer instructional strategies because of the predominance of self-contained classrooms and double-loaded corridor construction. The main problem in modernizing school library media center facilities is basically one of improving the use of existing space in order to take care of variable groupings of persons pursuing different learning experiences.

Flexibility is the word most commonly used to describe the overall attempt to solve this problem, and open planning is one of the newer approaches. In this concept, the degree and variety of flexibility as well as its purposes have to be clearly stated in planning the facilities. Flexibility can be incorporated in a design in a permanent way with additions, structural changes, and spaces for different-size groups; it can be accomplished in a temporary way with movable partitions or furnishings that can be arranged as spaces within space. Program planning must precede any creative designing of the facility in order to integrate center activities with the total educational program in the school.

ENVIRONMENTAL ELEMENTS

Although the possibility for continuing change is vital in dynamic remodeling and designing, some environmental elements are basic. They are: lighting, thermal environment, electrical power, acoustics, and color.

Lighting

A functional school library media center environment requires optimal lighting conditions for the eye comfort of its users, an adequate level of lighting for the whole area, and local lighting for particular activities. Lighting should be tailored to the specific need in each space and even for task areas within the space. Thirty lumens per square foot plus a 2 percent daylight factor for overall desk work is often recommended. Another measurement is 35 to 70 footcandles for regular viewing tasks, or 100 to 200 footcandles for special work that requires more illumination. Energy conservation and the physiological requirements of human beings live in a delicate balance. Although extensive use of natural light is generally not recommended because of the difficulty in controlling both brightness and heat, some degree of natural light relieves the uniformity of artificial light, makes an interior appear livelier, and enriches the environment. And a glance at a distant view through a window is a refresher for tired eyes.

Light sources, especially for independent study areas, should exhibit some imaginative possibilities, while adhering to the following general principles of lighting:

1. The angle at which the light strikes the work surface is probably more important than the amount of light.
2. The height of lighting levels should depend on the age group served.
3. The type of light source should be adapted to the purpose for the space.
4. The type of light fixture should reflect area and height needs.
5. There should be capability for dimming and darkening lights.

It is advisable to avoid highly polished surfaces in a school library media center. Warm white fluorescent lamps with diffusers, as well as the mercury vapor-type illumination, are suggested light sources. Grid fixtures that move horizontally or vertically along poles or beams, fixtures attached to permanent strips, and portable floor or desk fixtures can be used creatively to suit area and height needs. Special polarized lamps that direct the light downward at an angle are available. Certainly important in a school library media center is some provision for darkening areas for projection, with some means of retaining a minimum illumination in case of equipment failure and other problems.

Thermal Environment

Heating, cooling, and ventilating are three interdependent major considerations when deciding on the media center's thermal environment. Techniques for controlling these elements are, of course, available to planners. Solutions should take into consideration such external factors as the outside climate and yearly use of the facility and such internal factors as the location of the center's main area, such as near a boiler room.

No one thermal factor can be evaluated separately or judged without reference to all others. A comfortable thermal environment is a matter of deciding on a proper balance. Appropriate heating, cooling, and ventilating techniques can then be used.

Minimum standards for thermal requirements are generally written into official building codes. In almost all cases, however, school library media specialists must see that the requirements are not only reached but exceeded, because any extreme temperature or inadequate air exchange will generally impair both physical and mental efficiency. Air conditioning is the best solution to the ventilation problem in a facility where people work in a warm, humid climate. There is need for heat control in cold climates. However, in many of the less extreme weather belts, a media specialist may have to emphasize the need for a balance of heating, cooling, and ventilation, especially with energy conservation such an important consideration.

There are several points to watch for in overseeing a thermal environment. Ventilation and heating outlets should be located where they will not reduce shelf space or interfere with furniture arrangements. The rooms that house mechanical equipment and compressors should be isolated from the center so that any noise or vibration will not intrude.

The use of outside glass will affect the thermal environment and is not recommended because of energy conservation needs. Sufficient insulation should be used to ensure that the appropriate environment will be maintained. A form of ventilation should be installed that will keep an even temperature between 65 and 68 degrees and a humidity reading of approximately 40 percent. Air conditioning is apparently the most efficient and, in the long run, most economical method of ventilation. As with lighting, temperature control facilities should allow for flexibility in space division.

Electrical Power

With the increasing use of computers, projectors, recorders, and other types of electrically operated teaching and learning equipment, electrical outlets must be provided in sufficient number and in a variety of locations to allow flexibility in use. Electrical outlets should be placed where they will best serve the center's future as well as immediate needs, on the floor, ceiling, walls, or all three surface areas. A minimum of four 15-ampere outlets is suggested for each small area for traditional audiovisual equipment.

A most important factor in dealing with electrical power is safety, especially when students and volunteers use electrically operated equipment. Attention should be given to conduits for future internal coaxial cables, a master antenna array, and the electrical power system throughout the school for a number of receivers. The following steps can help to evaluate present and future electrical power requirements for the school library media center:

1. Try to determine your school's needs in relation to such activities as television that may be carried out in the center at some future time.

2. Draw up a present and future plan for needed electrical power based on step 1.

3. Gather information from the following associations on the newer kinds of equipment that require electrical power: Electronic Industries Association (EIA), Joint Council on Educational Telecommunications (JCET), American Society for Information Science (ASIS). (See Appendix 2.)

Because the costs of rewiring are often prohibitive, media specialists should assume that centers in the future will utilize more electrical equipment than present needs call for.

Acoustics

Any library media center that is a focal point for learning activity in a school must deal effectively with problems of sound. Controlling the sounds made by people and machines is an important part of designing or remodeling centers. With the emergence of open-plan schools and centers, a new attitude toward acceptance of background noise is developing as well as a better understanding of the noise that is naturally produced by young people at different ages.

Sound is highly directional; unrelated sounds of different types and intensities combine to make noise. It requires more energy for a listener or speaker to hear or be heard under poor sound conditions; therefore, a good environment controls both the sounds that originate within an area and the distracting sounds from outside that combine to produce intolerable noise levels.

There are many ways to deal with the problems of sound, such as room shape, use of acoustical materials and sound systems, and improved space dividers. Research suggests that an equal proportion of depth and width in a room provides the best sound environment. Another way to reduce sound that reflects from barriers, especially hard surfaces, is to set the walls and ceilings on slightly irregular planes, rather than in the traditional parallel pattern.

Materials to be used for sound conditioning should be tested under in-use conditions similar to those being planned. Any soft, absorbent material, such as heat insulation fibers, will muffle sound, but will allow it to be transmitted in some form to adjacent areas. Materials that impede the transmission of sound have a high density. Baffles placed in air ventilation ducts will also retard the transmission of sound from one area to another.

As noted in the section on thermal environment, the location of the school library media center is important. Vibrations from heavy school equipment, such as printing presses in a vocational education department or natural but distracting sounds from a cafeteria or gymnasium, for example, can rarely be overcome and are best avoided.

Electronic amplification systems are used in many school library media centers, and the sounds they produce, in both speaking and hearing with the aid of this equipment, must be reckoned with. Also, the trend toward open-space centers and areas makes the construction and design of space dividers an important consideration. For example, folding plywood partitions easily change the area arrangement, but they generally permit an unwanted level of seepage noise. Research suggests that woven fabrics with appropriate density and decreased porosity due to the use of special materials and weaving techniques may be one answer to noise problems in an area.

In some media center areas, such as conference rooms, a certain level of sound from conversation is expected. However, in a main study area, noise and motion can be kept to a minimum in two ways: (1) by using sound-reducing materials in construction and (2) by the arrangement of the facilities. An acoustically treated ceiling will help reduce sound, as will carpeting on the floor and on wall surfaces. Studies indicate that excessive use of acoustical-tile ceilings is unnecessary, however, and may even add sound problems. For best results, at least one-third of the area to be covered should be given acoustical treatment.

Before deciding on the proper acoustical treatment for a floor surface, the underlying floor construction, the heating system, and the scope of activities intended for the facility must be determined. The floor should be draft-free and warm enough in winter. If the audience for the center is from prekindergarten children to ninth-graders, the floor plan and construction should provide for both play and work activities. Acoustic flooring may be satisfactory for specific purposes in some areas. Although higher in initial cost, carpeting equals out in cost to other flooring material over a period of time, chiefly because of savings on maintenance. Industrial carpeting, such as that used in offices and restaurants, may be satisfactory. It is attractive, comfortable, and generally long-wearing.

In planning the facilities, one should break up large areas by furnishings to avoid an uninterrupted traveling path for sound. Noise-producing activities should be isolated from sections where quiet is needed. Shelving should be located away from study areas, as should the circulation desk, entrances, and exits. Avoid arrangements that force students to walk through the main area to get to the shelves or catalog. A preliminary study of traffic patterns will help determine the appropriate placement of areas and furnishings to control sound.

Color

A color scheme that provides both variety and harmony can help to make the school library media center a pleasant place to work in and visit. Planning for color in the environment is important because people are negatively or positively influenced by color. There is color in everything in a school library media center environment: in structural materials, walls, woodwork, furnishings, materials, equipment, in the views out-of-doors. Care should be taken to coordinate this variety of visual experiences into a cohesive, if continuously varying, and harmonious environment.

Two general rules on color can aid the school library media specialist who must operate without the benefit of a color consultant:

1. Study scientific recommendations on the use of color as it relates to reflectivity and contrast, such as the fact that white enamel surfaces reflect light so effectively that they appear much larger in size than a similar object painted a dull black, which absorbs light. Each color shade and tone obeys similar rules of reflectivity and contrast and has a complicated relationship of harmony value to the shade and tone of other colors.

2. Use these recommendations cautiously, knowing that the students who are surrounded by color will be affected differently depending on age. Young children benefit from the stimulation of cheerful, bright areas of color; students in the middle grades or junior high school need less color stimulation; a more sophisticated blend of color is appropriate in the high school.

Oversaturation—too many colors or color clashes—can be disturbing to many users. Remember that the materials, equipment, and people in a school library media center generally provide much color, and a plain background color scheme is often needed in contrast. Carpeting or flooring should be in a plain, unbroken pattern, and preferably a light color. Furniture and walls may vary from pastels to subdued shades of some of the stronger colors, depending on the age of the patrons. With imaginative use of good design, attractive furniture, and inviting colors, the center can be an interesting, aesthetically appealing area in which to work and study.

FURNISHINGS

The traditional furnishings in schools and library media centers are being replaced today by modular, easy-to-move, compact, multi-purpose furniture that answers the need for flexibility that is brought about by changing instructional techniques and various sizes of instructional groups. The trend in furniture, shelving, display cases, wall hangings, and floor coverings continues to be toward comfort and toward the aesthetic appeal that can be found by imaginative combination of standard and eclectic designs with objects of little or no commercial value. For example, large electrical cable spools can be painted and used as low tables, heavy shipping crates can be arranged and fixed into a multilevel carpeted reading area, and an old wall unit juke box can be wired with headsets for listening. Sometimes "free methods of furnishing" can be discovered. They can be exciting and valuable educationally because they match the young people's developmental needs.

Regardless of the type of furniture in the center, some specific selection criteria should apply. The school library media specialist should try to see that all furnishings are (1) simple and safe, (2) rugged and durable, (3) useful and comfortable, (4) eye-pleasing and compact. Not every piece of furnishing can fit all these criteria, but each piece should at least be safe and comfortable.

Carrels, Tables, and Chairs

Students like movable, versatile furniture with a potential for privacy. They prefer table surfaces to desks in a group situation and carrels to tables for individual study. Carrels provide private places where students may work undisturbed by others or by program activities going on in the center. There are no hard-and-fast rules for locating and placing carrels. Generally, only a few should be distributed among the collections and the rest placed as spatial dividers, singly or in small groups. Large groupings give less privacy to the student and an institutional appearance to any area.

The table surface in a carrel should be not less than 3 feet wide by 2 feet deep. It should also have 18- to 20-inch partitions on three sides, some shelf or storage space, electrical power outlets, and lighting where necessary.

Although many different types of carrels are available commercially, the simplest and least expensive type can be set up by using any conventional library table. Movable panel dividers made of acoustical material, such as cork or acoustic fabric–covered fiberboard, can transform a library table into study carrels. Shelves and electrical inputs from a plug strip can be added so that portable equipment can be used in each carrel. A more sophisticated variation uses the same construction principle with the addition of permanent electrical wiring to permit the installation of fixed equipment.

Along with carrels, some tables and chairs should be in each area. Two important considerations for choosing the correct mix of carrels and tables are the nature and size of the instructional groups in the school, and an appropriate mixture of different seating and working arrangements. A combination of round, octagonal, rectangular, and trapezoidal tables presents an attractive variety in a large main area.

Tables and chairs, like carrels, should not be placed in regimented ways. They should be distributed judiciously within areas to help provide an atmosphere that is conducive to study. Sturdy chairs should be provided. It is suggested that they have legs that extend at an angle from under the seat. A beneficial extra is the convenient underseat shelf or basket for student books and papers.

Some comfortable casual chairs and low tables are also recommended in the center. A large variety of items that can be used for sitting should be investigated. The age of the student and the purpose of the seating should be important considerations. Bricks or concrete blocks and boards can make inexpensive and attractive low tables or benches. Inflatable cushions can also be used. Almost any large and sturdy cylindrical commercial "throwaway" can be adapted for casual seating. Chimney flues (on their sides), discarded computer or round film storage cans (taped together), and foam-filled fabric-covered shapes can also be used creatively as furnishings. Informal lounge furniture is often placed close to magazine and newspaper racks to encourage recreational and informational reading. Microfilm, microfiche, and other types of copying equipment may also be located in the main area.

Other standard furniture items include a circulation desk, separate containers for shelf lists, units for catalogs, filing cabinets, book and equipment trucks. The circulation desk should be large enough to handle the flow of multimedia and small equipment for home use; cabinets and tables for a catalog and shelf list should each have enough space. The filing cabinets, some of which should accommodate legal or larger size materials, are important for pamphlets, transparencies, clippings, and small pictures. Filing cabinets are available with three or four drawers or open-faced to be used with hanging file folders. A large drawerlike cabinet or bin may also be needed for large pictures and maps. Mobile book and equipment trucks are available from commercial suppliers (see Appendix 3). The prime requisites are ease of movement, which is determined by the size of the wheels, and sturdiness.

Shelving

Books and other materials are generally made accessible to the user on standard adjustable library shelves. There are various types of shelving: steel bracket, freestanding sliding shelves; wood cases with metal strips and clips for supporting shelves; sloping wood or metal shelves; stack columns that hold boxes, lockers, and reading tables. They generally come in three-foot unit lengths with end panels. The use of freestanding double-faced shelving is preferable to wall shelving. The stacks should be close to the circulation area for ease of use and supervision. When arranged, the shelves should not be longer than 15 feet with 4½-foot rows between them and a 5-foot clearance between the shelves and adjacent furniture.

From five to six shelves per section are useful in high school, but fewer fit the elementary school needs better. One good use for counter-height shelving is to define areas within a room. Rows of shelves grouped in blocks facilitate accessibility. Generally, the greater percentage of the shelves should be 8 inches wide, the remainder 10–14 inches wide, for oversize material. Reference books and nonprint items, such as films, may require different types of shelving. Shelving to house a minimum of 15 items (books, slide sets, computer software, and other materials) per student is the rule in planning for shelving needs.

Other Storage and Display Furnishings

Other types of furniture in the center should include bins to store phonograph records, racks to display current magazines and newspapers, and cabinets for filmstrips, slides, and film loops, if these are not intershelved. Special multimedia shelving to interfile print and nonprint materials in the same way they appear in a catalog has found an audience among some school library media specialists and is worth investigating. This type of accessibility can be explored initially by using specially constructed or locally produced multimedia shelving for a curriculum unit within one area of the Dewey decimal classification system. Legal-size filing cabinets can be provided for difficult-to-shelve pamphlets, pictures, and clippings. Rolling trucks for print and nonprint and combination or separate atlas-dictionary stands are also useful.

Display shelving for magazines, with sloping shelves that are generally 36 inches wide and 16 inches deep, lends itself to the use of imaginative as well as standard ideas. The primary purpose of any display is to make the front cover as visible as possible. This can be achieved by the creative use of a clothesline or metal rod strung across one or more areas with colorful clothespins or magnetic clamps to secure the magazines.

Other display facilities, such as bulletin boards and pegboards, exhibit cases, and various display stands, that may be used in the ways outlined in the promotion and public relations section in Chapter 3 should be available in the main study area as well as directly outside the main entrance.

The emergence of videocassettes expands the usefulness of closed-circuit television (CCTV) in schools by permitting the taping of broadcast or "off-air" television programs within copyright permission laws and replaying them on CCTV receivers in any part of a school. Some state departments of public instruction, for example, the New York State Bureau of Mass Communications, have a duplication service of videocassettes from a master print of special programs. The usefulness to school library media centers and schools of videotaping, both alone and with CCTV, is important enough for small schools to explore this development.

FACILITIES FOR SPECIAL MEDIA SERVICES

Film, radio, and television services in most schools are still too costly for the individual school to maintain. The materials and services in each are generally handled on a network basis at either a system, regional, or state level. Films in a school are generally selected, previewed, and rented by the school library media specialist in consultation with the teachers, administrators, and, in many instances, students. If the school system is large enough, it may support a centralized facility that maintains a film library. For an individual school that wishes to start a film library, videocassettes offer some of the same potential as 16mm film. Although not all 16mm films are available in videocassettes, many classic and newer releases are.

Radio and television are media that require special facilities. Although radio was once briefly popular in education, it has generally been superseded by television, except in very rural or wilderness areas. The use of television in education continues to grow in many different directions. Presently available for educators are several types of television that differ in technical ways. Only the larger school systems or the more forward-looking smaller ones have tried to incorporate this medium and they have generally done so from a district or regional level.

FOR FURTHER READING

American Association of School Librarians and Iowa Department of Public Instruction. *A Yardstick for Planning School Library Media Centers.* Washington, D.C.: American Association of School Librarians, 1981.

Cheatham, Bertha M. "A School Becomes a Library: An Interior Designer Tells How." *School Library Journal*, November 1981, pp. 33–37.

Cleaver, Betty. "A Media Facility Makeover." *Instructional Innovator*, March 1981, pp. 20–23.

Cohen, Aaron, and Cohen, Elaine. *Designing and Space Planning For Libraries: A Behavioral Guide.* New York: R. R. Bowker, 1978.

——. "Remodeling the Library." *School Library Journal*, February 1978, pp. 30–33.

Draper, James, and Brooks, James. *Interior Designs for Libraries.* Chicago: American Library Association, 1979.

Ely, Donald P. "Some Prior Questions." *School Media Quarterly*, Summer 1976, pp. 317–322.

Guide for the Conversion of School Libraries into Media Centers. New York: UNESCO (Unipub), 1977.

Hannigan, Jane A., and Estes, Glenn. *Media Center Facilities Design.* Chicago: American Library Association, 1978.

"Integrated Shelving: Three Case Studies." *School Media Quarterly*, Fall 1976, pp. 25–30.

Jaworski, Ferdinand. "12 Common Mistakes in Library Interior Planning." *American School and University*, January 1973, pp. 16–20.

Library Administration and Management Association/American Library Association. *Running Out of Space: What Are the Alternatives?* Chicago: American Library Association, 1978.

Lushington, Nolan. *Libraries Designed for Users: A Planning Handbook.* Syracuse, N.Y.: Gaylord, 1979.

Mason, Ellsworth. *Mason on Library Buildings.* Metuchen, N.J.: Scarecrow, 1980.

"Remodeling: A Lot More Than a Library." *National Schools and Colleges*, April 1975, pp. 18–20.

Silverman, Eleanor. *Trash into Treasure: Recycling Ideas for Library/Media Centers.* Metuchen, N.J.: Scarecrow, 1982.

Sullivan, Janet. "Nine Design Factors for Better Learning." *Instructional Innovator*, March 1981, pp. 14-16.

Sullivan, Peggy, comp. *Planning School Library Media Center Facilities.* Chicago: ALA/LAMA, 1977.

7

MEDIA SELECTION: POLICIES AND PROCEDURES

The library media center collection is in many ways like a living organism—it grows and develops; it is dynamic and ever-changing, expanding in some areas while contracting in others. To supervise this growth and to regulate these changes is exciting, taxing, and ultimately one of the most professional tasks performed by the library media specialist.

To build a collection wisely and well, the school library media specialist should develop judgment and good taste along with a thorough knowledge of all the variables that influence selection, like the needs of the community and the nature of the curriculum. The library media specialist must be alert to changes and trends, show impartiality and objectivity, be imaginative, curious, and resourceful, and be dedicated to the public and the schools being served.

This chapter discusses the background body of knowledge necessary for the creation of the selection process as well as information on how to organize it. Other areas treated are the development of a selection policy, selection aids, and practical points on selection.

Media selection must be considered an ongoing process; although orders for media are placed only a few times each year, selection occurs daily. The machinery of selection should swing into action each time a reference question raised at the center cannot be answered with the available material on a subject—for example, when a hitherto ignored part of the world suddenly becomes newsworthy or a different fad hits a school population. The arrival of a new issue of a reviewing periodical should also signal the selection process to start.

No two library media centers contain—or should contain—the same collection. Each center's collection should reflect the specific needs of the school it serves. Yet while each media center is thus unique, all centers share three basic aims: (1) to help satisfy the needs of students for curriculum-related materials, (2) to fulfill students' wishes concerning materials for recreational purposes, and (3) to provide teachers with professional information. In good school programs, as in good educational materials, the first two aims often become intermingled and indistinguishable.

BACKGROUND KNOWLEDGE

Before beginning the selection process, the school library media specialist must learn something about the community; the students, faculty, and curriculum; media; bibliographic and reviewing tools; the existing collection; and budgeting.

Knowledge of the Community

Every community has many aspects that must be considered by the library media specialist. To learn the characteristics of the population, the specialist must investigate inhabitants' ethnic and religious backgrounds, age groupings, occupations, general economic status, cultural and recreational interests, and educational levels. Each of these factors will be reflected in the young people attending the schools. The nature of residential buildings, the kinds of businesses, and even transportation routes provide clues helpful in understanding the community. The media specialist should also become familiar with the community's other libraries and cultural resources as well as its recreational resources. Does the average child come from a home where there is at least a basic reference collection? How numerous and accessible are other public and private collections of educational materials? How adequate are these collections? Are there art galleries or other cultural institutions nearby? What provisions are there for recreational facilities, athletic fields, meeting rooms for clubs and hobby groups? One device to use in studying a community is to draw a simple map of the community and locate on it the various community resources and the school and public bus routes as well as other modes of transportation.

Knowledge of Students

In addition to knowing the general age and grade levels in the school, the media specialist should probe deeper into the activities and interests of the students. He or she should determine the range of abilities and the degree of concentration of these abilities at various levels—for the whole school as well as for each class. Reading ability must be determined and test scores used to help verify range and concentration. Becoming familiar with the interests and activities of each age group—their hobbies, favorite sports and social interests, popular TV shows, part-time jobs, and size of allowances—will provide the specialist with valuable insights. What are the general social and emotional maturity levels of the students? How sophisticated, independent, and experienced are they at handling social adjustments, emotional problems, concerns about physical growth and maturation, relations with other members of the family, school assignments, and contemporary affairs? Both general and specific reading interests must be analyzed. By general reading interests is meant the common interests of a specific age group. For example, junior high school boys generally enjoy science fiction and stories of true adventure. However, within these general-interest categories, and in addition to them, there are specific differentiations and subtleties of taste that are characteristic of the individual school. A study of circulation records and comparisons with the experience of others working with the same age group will help bring some of these differences into focus. Although it may seem an impossible task, in order to know more than just names and faces the school library media specialist should try to collect this mass of information not only for the student body as a whole but also for each actual and potential user of the center.

Knowledge of the Faculty

The interests, backgrounds, strengths, and weaknesses of the faculty are reflected in their teaching assignments, their classroom use of media, and the ways in which they and their students use the media center. The media specialist should be aware of the teaching methods employed, the nature of media center use by specific departments and at various grade levels, and areas where in-service work in media use seems needed. Each term he or she should find out the courses being taken by teachers for continuing education so that additions may be made to the professional collection to assist them.

Knowledge of the Curriculum

Knowing about the school's curriculum involves more than just a knowledge of what subjects are taught and when. It also means knowing the objectives of the school and how the library media center relates to them. It involves attending curriculum meetings, conferring with teachers about classroom assignments before they are given, becoming thoroughly familiar with the classroom textbooks used, and, when possible, visiting classrooms to observe presentation techniques and use of media.

Knowledge of Media

The media specialist must become familiar with the various forms of educational materials, their characteristics, strengths, and limitations, and their potential for use in various situations. Similar information should be obtained for the accompanying equipment. There is no substitute for firsthand knowledge. Library media specialists, at every opportunity, should be reading books, viewing films, using equipment, and engaging in other activities that will continually augment their knowledge of media centers and their contents. This body of knowledge should be applied when considering future acquisitions.

Knowledge of Bibliographic and Reviewing Tools

Not all material can or should be appraised locally. Opinions of experts outside the immediate school district should be consulted. There are literally hundreds of bibliographies, media lists, and reviewing journals that can help the media specialist in selection. They are issued by professional associations, commercial publishers of reviewing media, government library agencies (federal, state, and local), producers and publishers of educational media, and many library systems. Details on the types of selection aids and criteria for their evaluation are given in Chapter 8.

Knowledge of the Existing Collection

If a library media center has been in existence for some time, the media specialist must determine the size, nature, strengths and weaknesses, age and general physical condition, and basic usefulness of its contents before undertaking new selection. Several methods can be used to gain this knowledge. First, the shelf list and equipment inventory may be examined to determine which areas have been stressed or slighted, the amount of duplication, and the recency of titles and equipment. Another method is to "read" the shelves, glancing particularly at unfamiliar titles. Another is to check the collection against standard bibliographies to determine what proportion of these basic titles is present. The school library media specialist can also become acquainted with the media center's holdings by repeated use of the card catalog. In evaluating an existing collection it is important to check outside the media center to find out what the school's holdings are, for example, in textbooks, classroom collections, study centers, and departmental libraries.

Knowledge of the Budget

Before beginning to select media, the library media specialist should have at hand the budget allotments for the current year and, if at all possible, for the coming year or years. The selector of media must inquire about the share of additional funds that might be available through federal, state, or local funding programs. Long-range planning, particularly for expensive book sets, motion pictures, and audiovisual equipment, is necessary. Unfortunately, less expensive substitutes will sometimes have to be found or the purchase of a desired item postponed to ensure balance and equity in distribution of budgetary funds.

ORGANIZING THE MEDIA SELECTION PROGRAM

The number and extent of selection services provided by the single school will depend largely on how many related services are available at the district level. The keynote is the development of a systematized process in which each supplements the other without unnecessary duplication of effort. Certain services, such as maintaining a book examination center or exhibiting samples of media center furniture, are best handled in a centralized, districtwide agency, but routing of bibliographies to individual faculty members, for example, should logically be administered at the individual-school level. Patterns of organization will therefore differ considerably from one situation to another, depending on local conditions. However, one trend is becoming apparent: school district personnel now realize that it is impossible to have firsthand evaluations of all media before purchase recommendations are given. Nor is this necessary. The reviewing sources that are available for many materials (for example, library books) are of sufficient quantity and quality that to ignore these sources in favor of local reviewing not only wastes time and duplicates effort but also fails to utilize the expertise of the knowledgeable critics and subject specialists who review in these publications.

In areas where the reviewing media are inadequate or where the items under consideration are either very costly or highly specialized, some form of local reviewing will take place. The cost of an initial investment, for example, the purchase price of videocassettes or 16mm films, will often mandate previewing sessions for evaluation. In general, one of two methods, or a combination of both, is used to systematize local reviewing. The first is to organize reviewing committees composed chiefly of teachers, with representation from administration and the media center and, when possible, from the student body. At the district level these committees should represent a cross section of the district school personnel and should be organized according to the participants' subject specialties and general grade-level interests. In individual schools the committees may be organized according to academic departments or specific grade levels. In a single-school situation there are also many opportunities to arrange for individual teachers or groups representing many curricular interests to review specific materials.

The second method is to have a teacher or teachers use the material in question in a classroom situation similar to that for which the item to be purchased is intended and thus gain an on-the-spot evaluation.

Regardless of the method or methods used, some type of formal reporting of local evaluations should be made. Many schools have developed standardized forms to ensure conformity in these reports. Because each media format has distinct characteristics, it is difficult, if not impossible, to produce a single form that can be useful with all types of materials. However, to avoid developing a multitude of reporting forms, materials can be grouped into logical divisions. For example, the same form can be used for films, filmstrips, slides, and transparencies and another for textbooks and other book materials. A rating scale is often used for each criterion on the form—this could be a numerical scale ranging from 5 for excellent to 1 for poor. Spaces should be supplied for name of the person requesting a review, dates of the request and of the review, kind of material and its subject area and general grade level, an overall priority rating (basic or supplementary), and a space for the evaluator's comments. Other items generally covered in these forms include: (1) bibliographic information, for example, title, author, producer, vendor, publisher, (2) format or technical aspects, for example, quality of sound, color, picture, binding, (3) content, for example, scope of work, limitations of coverage, up-to-dateness, objectivity, (4) organization and presentation, for example, suitability of length, logic, clarity of presentation, interest, pacing, amount of review, and repetition, (5) suitability, for example, appropriateness to the medium as well as to subject and grade levels, special uses, (6) teachers' aids, for example, manuals, workbooks, other correlated materials. Similar forms may be devised for equipment evaluation. The evaluative criteria found in Chapter 8 may also be used.

As stated earlier, responsibilities for selection are assigned in various patterns at the district and single-school levels. The single school will share some of the duties with the district center, for example, workshops on media evaluation. However, the following selection-related activities should be initiated at the single-school level:

1. Organize and administer the reviewing procedures within the school.
2. Obtain, either through the school library media center or the district office, preview copies of material requested by teachers.
3. Maintain liaison with the central selection agency and jointly coordinate activities.
4. Involve as many people in the school as possible in the selection process.
5. Route bibliographies and other selection aids, asking for purchase suggestions.
6. Attend faculty meetings as well as departmental or grade-level meetings to become acquainted with curriculum changes and to discuss future acquisition plans.
7. Conduct interest inventories with students to determine what topics interest them most and least. These inventories may be arranged alphabetically in checklist form—from "airplanes" to "zoos."
8. Maintain a file of locally reviewed educational materials and basic commercially produced selection aids.

The following list gives some selection activities that seem best suited to be performed at the district level; some might be shared with individual schools or where centralized selection services are nonexistent, initiated within the schools:

1. Organize and administer a districtwide reviewing network for materials for which standard reviewing sources are inadequate or that need supplementary local appraisal.
2. Print, disseminate, and maintain a permanent file of reviews of the locally reviewed items.
3. Schedule and make provisions for individual and group faculty visits to the examination center on a regular basis.
4. Arrange for preview privileges for material when examination copies are unavailable for extended loan.
5. Maintain liaison with other central administrative and curricular agencies or departments to ensure coordination of efforts.

6. Establish and develop cooperative acquisition projects between individual schools in the district and with other libraries in the area—public, academic, and special.

7. Act as liaison between public schools and manufacturers' representatives; maintain a file of current commercial catalogs of materials and equipment.

8. Maintain a cataloged permanent collection of basic titles that can be used as a guide in establishing new collections or reevaluating established collections.

9. Provide an exhibit collection of current books and other print and nonprint media representing at least the current and immediate past publishing seasons. Clip reviews from standard selection aids and insert them in the material on exhibit.

10. Organize a sample collection of audiovisual equipment and center furniture.

11. Assemble special multimedia displays or media fairs on specific subjects and, when possible, route these to individual schools.

12. Be a clearinghouse for new bibliographies and selection aids that should be brought to the attention of other media personnel and a dissemination point for the lists produced in individual schools.

13. Purchase and make available expensive or specialized reviewing sources that normally would not be purchased or made available by individual schools.

14. Conduct workshops for teachers and media specialists on the evaluation of media.

Whatever administrative patterns evolve in the selection process, two considerations are paramount: organization and participation. If these can be achieved within a congenial atmosphere conducive to free expression and the development of professional attitudes, a successful program should result.

WRITING A MEDIA SELECTION POLICY STATEMENT

Considering the amount of published material on the necessity for a written media-selection policy, it is amazing how many school districts have not adopted such a document. Yet in reality it should be the cornerstone of a media program, giving both shape and direction to the development of that program. A written selection policy can serve several purposes. It can supply a blueprint for future growth and refinement and prevent haphazard collection development. It can also help prevent extended and unnecessary disputes involving controversial material. Besides supplying criteria and selection procedures for the center's staff, it can help clarify these matters for the rest of the school personnel and the community.

Before developing a policy statement, the media specialist should become familiar with the basic documents concerning intellectual freedom. The American Library Association's (ALA) "Freedom to Read Statement" and "The School Library Bill of Rights" from the American Association of School Librarians are two such documents (see Appendix IV, Key Documents). One or more of these documents is often incorporated into the selection policy. Additional policies and hints on developing them may be found in the books listed in the bibliography at the end of this chapter. Other useful material, including the *Intellectual Freedom Newsletter*, is available from ALA's Office of Intellectual Freedom.

The selection policy should not be constructed in a vacuum. It certainly should include broad universal principles, but as well must reflect local conditions. All groups affected by the policy should participate in its formation. This includes representatives from the library media center staff, faculty, administration, students, and the community. The policy should be officially accepted by all of these groups, including the district school board. After adoption, it should be disseminated widely. No policy statement, however, should be considered permanent; instead it should reflect a dynamic stage of growth and be capable of easy amendment or revision when conditions warrant a change. It should also be broad enough to cover many contingencies, but precise enough to prevent ambiguity. Material selection policies often contain the following elements:

1. A statement of the school district and individual school philosophy, particularly in relation to educational materials and intellectual freedom.

2. A similar statement summarizing the aims and objectives of the library media center in relation to this overall philosophy.

3. A list of those who participate in selection and of the specific objectives of the selection function.

4. An indication of delegated as well as final responsibility for selection including a definition of the position of the media center personnel in this operation.

5. A list of the types of media found in the center and of the criteria applied to the selection of each.

6. An enumeration of the selection aids most frequently consulted.

7. A description of the procedures, forms, and practices used in selection.

8. An indication of areas of the collection that will be either stressed or deemphasized.

9. Additional or modifying criteria for the various clientele served. For example, a different set of standards might apply when buying professional materials for teachers than for purchasing high-interest material for slow or reluctant readers.

10. Statements concerning the media center's policies toward gifts, sponsored material, weeding, duplication, and replacement.

11. Information concerning any cooperative acquisition projects in which the center is involved with other schools and libraries.

12. A description of the procedures for handling complaints and a copy of any forms used when a request is made to reevaluate a particular piece of material.

STANDARDS

A variety of published standards specify norms for the quantities of materials in a school library media center collection and, in some cases, the quality of the center's collection. The historical background on these standards is discussed in Chapter 1.

Standards can fulfill several beneficial functions. They can become a blueprint for future growth for both new and established media centers and serve as a method of evaluating existing collections. They should be seen primarily as a method that can help schools to implement their educational goals. It is often very difficult to state objective standards in certain areas, particularly where the quality of a program is to be measured. Even when quantities of material are specified, standards are hard to formulate because of frequent changes in educational techniques and teaching practices. For these reasons, standards should be under constant review and revised when needed.

In applying standards it is necessary to relate each recommendation to the whole set of standards. A single standard regarding recommended numbers of particular media should be related to other parts of the existing collection, and on a larger scale, the size of the entire collection, actual or recommended, should be seen in terms of the school's educational philosophy and objectives. It must also be noted that quantities of materials do not in themselves indicate a quality program—they merely supply one of the conditions on which a fine program can be built.

Standards are of two types, *comparative* and *projective*. Comparative standards are usually short range and are based on existing, not optimum, conditions. For example, a school district with a superior materials collection in one school might attempt to bring the collections in other schools up to this level by using the size of the single collection as a standard for the other schools. Projective standards are long range and deal more abstractly with ultimate goals. Most published well-developed standards are projective. Often these standards are stated in terms of phases that represent various stages of growth. There are usually three phases: *basic* (or minimum), *good*, and *advanced* (or excellent). This breakdown can be utilized as a rating scale and can serve also as a guideline for developing short-term or immediate goals. Many state standards are expressed in these terms.

Several agencies have issued standards. The principal ones are at the federal and state levels, although school districts, too, often develop and adopt local standards. The district standards are usually closely associated with short-term goals and are often comparative in nature and based on an exemplary program either within the district or in a neighboring district. The district standards are easily modified or enlarged to meet changing local conditions. Flexibility is one of the chief advantages of this type of goal.

Individuals have also developed standards for library media centers that have appeared in monographs dealing with schools and educational materials. For example, Ralph Ellsworth in his *The School Library* (New York: Educational Facilities Laboratories, 1963) states that every school library should have a basic collection of 50,000 books. However, he suggests that if a school's population has access to a strong public or college library, this figure could be adjusted downward to 30,000 volumes.

The school library media specialist should become familiar with as many as possible of the various sets of standards, particularly those at the national, state, and local levels that bear directly on the school's media program. It is also the responsibility of the media center staff to make other interested groups—administrators, faculties, parents, school boards—aware of these standards and their implications for expansion of existing facilities and programs.

SELECTION AIDS

Like the serious researcher, the media specialist in the process of selection has available both primary and secondary sources. Primary source means that the material or equipment is itself examined before purchase. Media specialists have many opportunities to do this.

Visiting exhibits at professional conventions is an excellent way. Such displays as the Combined Book Exhibit are usually part of the national and state library association conferences. Opportunities to see demonstrations of equipment and materials and make on-the-spot comparisons and evaluations are possible at these conferences as well as chances to browse through a publisher's stock of new books. At the local level, previewing prints or on-approval copies can often be secured. Many jobbers and wholesalers allow media personnel to visit and preview the stock. There are, of course, many functioning media examination centers scattered about the country, some operating at the school district or citywide level, others at the multidistrict or state level. Many public library systems also have examination centers. Other examination centers, for example, the one operated by the Children's Book Council in New York City, exist through private funding. There is also a very accessible resource that media personnel apparently seldom use—the collections of their colleagues in other media centers and libraries.

With the explosion of information in all media and with the age of specialization upon us, however, prior examination of all material is neither possible nor practical. Media personnel must depend on the opinions and advice of professional specialists, which are often found in various reviewing media. Commonly called selection aids, these are bibliographies, catalogs, indexes, review periodicals, and "basic" or "best" lists. The proper interpretation, evaluation, and understanding of these aids is one of the essentials of effective selection.

The two major kinds of selection aids are the *retrospective* and the *current*. Retrospective aids list materials that are time-tested and generally recommended for specific needs. They are helpful in building the initial collection and can be used with existing collections to indicate material that has been missed but is still useful and important. Examples of retrospective aids are *Books for Elementary School Libraries* (Chicago: ALA), *Senior High School Library Catalog* (New York: H. W. Wilson), and *Best Books for Children* (New York: R. R. Bowker).

Current aids, such as *Booklist* (ALA) or *School Library Journal* (R. R. Bowker), are primarily intended to report on new material. Many current selection aids must be used to obtain a range of critical opinion. Selecting material on the basis of its recommendation in only one source is extremely unwise. Because less than 50 percent of all material that might be useful in the school is reviewed in the standard tools of the trade, the librarian must also consult reviews in such specialized professional journals as *English Journal* (from National Council of Teachers of English). Selection aids are further subdivided according to the type of media reviewed: general or special subject, single format or multimedia, and so on. Regardless of how the aid is classified, the would-be user must explore it thoroughly and become familiar with its contents before it can be utilized effectively. There are many bibliographies that list recommended selection aids. Some examples are:

Association for Library Services to Children and Young Adult Services Division. *Selecting Materials for Children and Young Adults: A Bibliography of Bibliographies and Review Sources.* Chicago: American Library Association, 1980.

Buckingham, Betty Jo. *Selection Bibliography: A Bibliography of Selection Services for School Library Media Centers,* 4th ed. 1979. ED 185965.

Cawthon, June B. *Tools of the Trade: Sources and Aids for Media Selection.* Athens: University of Georgia, 1981.

Hart, Thomas L., et al. *Multi-media Indexes, Lists, and Review Sources.* New York: Marcel Dekker, 1975.

Mirwis, Allan. *Guides to Educational Media Software.* New York: Educational Media Information Service, Inc., 1977.

Rufsvold, Margaret I. *Guides to Educational Media,* 4th ed. Chicago: American Library Association, 1977.

Simmons, Beatrice T., and Carter, Yvonne B. *Aids to Media Selection for Students and Teachers.* Indianola, Iowa: National Association of State Educational Media Professionals, 1982.

Sive, Mary R. *The Complete Media Monitor: Guide to Learning Resources.* Metuchen, N.J.: Scarecrow, 1981.

———. *Selecting Instructional Media: A Guide to Audio-visual and Other Instructional Media Lists.* Littleton, Colo.: Libraries Unlimited, 1982.

Taggart, Dorothy T. *A Guide to Services in Educational Media and Technology.* Metuchen, N.J.: Scarecrow, 1975.

Woodbury, Marda L. *A Guide to Sources of Educational Information.* Arlington, Va.: Information Resources Press, 1976.

———. *Selecting Materials for Instruction: Media and the Curriculum.* Littleton, Colo.: Libraries Unlimited, 1980.

———. *Selecting Materials for Instruction: Subject Areas and Implementation.* Littleton, Colo.: Libraries Unlimited, 1980.

Individual selection aids are listed in Chapter 8 following the criteria for selecting educational material or equipment.

Criteria for Choosing Selection Aids

The media selector should be aware of the strengths and weaknesses of a bibliography before using it for selection purposes. When there is an understanding of the general nature as well as the specific limitations, shortcomings, and possible areas of utilization of selection tools, the possibility of using each wisely and effectively increases. The criteria for selecting media and equipment (presented in Chapter 8) should be applied, after which the following specific questions should be asked to make certain that all pertinent information has been collected.

Authority

Who are the reviewers and editors and what are their qualifications?
Do the reviewers represent a particular point of view?
Are the reviews signed?

Scope

Is this a selective (such as the "best of" type) or an all-inclusive bibliography?
What types of material are listed? Are there limitations on inclusion, including format (classes of material), subject, time period, age group, language, and place of origin?
Are adequate directions on how to use the aid provided?
What is the intended audience?
How often does the bibliography appear?
How up-to-date are the reviews?
In general, how much bibliographic data is included?

Arrangement

Is it arranged alphabetically, by classification or subject, chronologically, by format, or by a combination of these?
Is there an index?
Is the index cumulated? How often?

Annotations or Reviews

What is their average length?
Are they descriptive, critical or both?
Is each piece of material reviewed separately?
Does the review include comparisons with other similar material, or with the producer's or author's other works?

Is there some indication, perhaps through a coding system, as to whether the material is basic or supplemental?

Are the reviews generally consistent in length, point of view, scope, and treatment?

Do the reviews indicate comprehension, suitability, and interest levels and make suggestions for possible use?

Has the reviewer objectively tested the accuracy, reliability and up-to-dateness of the material?

Special Features

Does the aid include any special material, such as directories of publishers, professional organizations, manufacturers, distributors, selection centers, rental libraries, or depositories?

Are the reviews indexed or excerpted in another publication, such as *Book Review Digest*?

PRACTICAL POINTS TO AID SELECTION

The following is a list of practical hints and guidelines that should be followed to ensure the development of useful, well-rounded collections. Some are offshoots and extensions of the general principles stated earlier in the chapter; others introduce new factors into the selection process.

Participation in the Selection Process

As many of the school's population as possible should be involved in selecting materials for the media center. Reviewing periodicals and preview copies of materials may be routed to the faculty for comments and suggestions. School personnel should be invited to special previewing sessions. Students should also become involved. The Canton (Ohio) Public Schools, for example, have successfully used children as book reviewers. Students in elementary schools read and comment on from 25 to 50 new books per school year. The nature of their reactions is an important factor in deciding whether the book is recommended for purchase. Involving others in the selection process not only adds new dimensions to the collection, but provides better insight into users' tastes and interests, and new avenues of communication are opened between the center and its patrons. Media specialists also find that participation of this sort results in increased interest in the general welfare of the center.

Diversity in Material

Although satisfying the needs of the center's patrons is the major guiding principle behind selection, when building the basic or core collection, the maxim should be: "Get something on everything." This means that the center's collection should contain information in each of the important divisions of human knowledge. In a high school, for example, Greek philosophy may not be a topic of great popularity, yet most certainly the library media center should have some material on it.

Diversity in Students

Within classes in any heterogeneously organized classroom there are three basic achievement levels of students: above-average, average, and below-average. Translated specifically into terms of reading ability, there will be those reading above grade level, those reading at the expected level, and those reading below it. When buying material on a given topic, the media specialist must therefore bear in mind the various ability levels of the students who will be investigating this topic and try to obtain a sufficiently wide range of materials at each of these levels.

Purchasing for Nonusers

One selection trap that must be avoided is purchasing solely for the teachers and students in the school who use the library media center regularly. If the taste and interests of the nonusers are not represented in the collection, appropriate material is not at hand when the opportunity occurs to convert them into center users. Thus a second maxim might be: "There should be something for everybody."

Input from the School Library Media Specialist

Throughout this chapter stress has been placed on the involvement of a number of people in the selection process. This does not in any way mean that the media specialist abdicates responsibility in this area. Unlike many college libraries that buy material only on specific request from faculty members, library media center professional personnel should initiate some orders, act as representatives for those who are not involved in selection, and have the final word in approving items for purchase.

Selection, Not Censorship

Selection is a positive process, and in evaluating the contents of materials remember that the aim is neither to shock nor to protect. Overprotection can be as harmful as overexposure. Certain guidelines and limitations will be adopted for purchasing center material solely because of the maturity of the center's audience, but emphasis must not be on what "shouldn't" but what "should" be purchased. It should be remembered that, through mass media, young people are much more knowledgeable about social issues and once taboo subjects than their counterparts were a generation ago.

In trying to avoid controversial subjects or shunning basic realities, the media center collection can become so safe that it is deadly dull and out of touch with the students. Where an item is purchased that is a particularly potent target for the censor, a special file should be kept noting reviews or discussions involving it in other censorship battles. ALA's *Intellectual Freedom Newsletter* is a good source of information for this file.

Subjectivity vs. Objectivity

The temptation is always present to buy from the standpoint of one's own interests. If, for example, a burning interest in Greek drama is not shared by members of the faculty and student body, or is not part of the curriculum, purchases in this area will be minimal. On the other hand, the subject of automobiles may appear to be quite dull, but it is usually one of the primary interests of teenage boys. Purchases should be made from the user's point of view—not only what the student *should* be reading or using, but what students want, need, and are capable of using.

Media and Messages

When selecting materials, match the message with appropriate media. The question that should be asked is: Is this medium the most appropriate and best suited to convey the contents of the material? As an example, a motion picture that shows how seeds travel would probably be better than a filmstrip, because the idea of movement is such an integral part of this learning experience.

Duplication

User demand is the yardstick that should determine the extent to which duplication of materials takes place. Yet some library media specialists associate duplication of titles with wastefulness; they think that buying a second copy uses funds that could be spent on a different title, thus increasing the general scope of the collection. Obviously, however, it is better to have five copies of a book that is constantly in circulation than five different titles, four of which stay unread on the shelves. With books, paperbacks afford an easy and inexpensive way to supply additional copies of a popular title.

Selection and Space Limitations

If space limitations are interfering with new purchasing, explore more efficient storage systems so that new material can still be added to the collection. Two obvious ways are to "retire" infrequently used items to other parts of the school and to rotate collections of recreational reading materials to various classrooms.

Technical Services and Selection

Library media centers that are responsible for their own processing should try to prepare an item for circulation as quickly as possible. This applies particularly to topical materials and materials that have been specifically requested. If rapid processing is not possible, the material should be allowed to circulate for a time uncataloged. The rapidity with which users' requests are answered will be directly reflected in their interest in future acquisitions.

Use of Multiple Selection Aids

Using only one or two selection aids is restrictive; using many aids will help assure wiser decisions in purchasing materials that add greater depth and more points of view to the collection.

Review of Selection Aids

Tastes and needs are constantly changing; a book considered unsuitable one school year may be useful the following year. Therefore, a system of continuous review of selection aids should be organized. The basic retrospective one should be checked at least once a year.

Cooperative Acquisitions

There are many cooperative acquisition projects presently operating at the university and public library levels. One of the earliest was the Farmington Plan, involving purchase of foreign-language materials. Schools within a particular area can also band together to form mini-

Farmington Plans, whereby each school at a particular level is assigned a particular subject specialty or area of concentration (these could be arrived at by thorough examination of curriculum requirements). This method could also be used to ensure that at least one cooperating school has a copy of expensive items like a well-reviewed set of sound filmstrips or a new edition of a multivolume reference work. (See Chapter 12 on networking.)

Out-of-Print Materials

An out-of-print notice from a jobber, publisher, or producer should not be interpreted as meaning complete unavailability. With print materials, if their acquisition is extremely important, check with out-of-print dealers, catalogs of facsimile-edition companies, or the book production services of University Microfilms in Ann Arbor, Michigan. These routes are particularly valuable in building up local history collections.

Publishers' and Manufacturers' Catalogs

Extreme care must be exercised in using publishers' or manufacturers' catalogs in the selection process. They should be considered only as descriptive announcements of what is available, not an indication of quality. Buying on the basis of the blurbs found in these catalogs is dangerous. Quotes from dependable reviewing sources published in these annotations are often misleading; excerpting can turn a panning into what appears to be a rave. An exception should be pointed out: Several jobbers and wholesalers have hired reputable media personnel to compile lists of recommended materials, basic book lists, and the like. If the authority that compiled the work is noncommercial and reliable, the list may be considered a valid selection aid.

Series and Comics

Even the most prestigious of series may vary in quality from one title to the next, and regardless of the standards of quality within a series, in all likelihood not all titles will be suitable for a collection. Each item should be treated as an individual entity that must be evaluated on its own merits. Educators in general are scornful of such "pulp" series as the Hardy Boys and Nancy Drew. Certainly the literary quality of these books is practically nonexistent. But if this is the only level on which students are reading, inclusion of some of these series books and similar titles should be seriously considered. Here, at least, is a beginning on which the media center staff can perhaps build through proper reading guidance.

The same policy should apply to comics. Here the question of quality is not quite as important because there are a number of comics of acceptable quality now in paperback format that could easily be included in a school library media center collection. Some examples are *Peanuts, Mad,* and Ripley's *Believe It or Not.*

Book Clubs

Through use of petty cash or similar contingency funds, many library media centers join book clubs. They are generally of two main types: those that distribute hardcover editions (for example, the Junior Literary Guild, for ages 3–16, and the adult clubs, Book-of-the-Month and Literary Guild of America) and the paperback clubs (for example, the various Scholastic Book Services clubs).* While both types of clubs offer carefully selected, appealing titles, the hardcover clubs give subscribers the advantage of getting new books quickly and at a fair discount over publishers' prices (although sometimes not as much as a book jobber might give) and paperback clubs offer very inexpensive reprints of well-received hardcover editions and in some cases original titles that are available only through the clubs.

Gifts and Free Materials

Media centers should welcome gifts as possible additions to the collection. In developing a policy for receiving gifts two points should be stressed: (1) only items appropriate to the collection will be kept, and (2) the center may dispose of the remaining material any way it wishes.

A wealth of free material commonly referred to as "sponsored material" is available from various industries, manufacturers, transportation companies, and so on. Before accepting items of sponsored material for the collection, check to see if there is excessive advertising or proselytizing, distortion of facts to promote products or points of view, or material about one company's wares stated in a way that would prejudice the reader or viewer against a competitor's products. Some school districts have adopted specific regulations concerning the presence of advertising in the schools. Inquiries should be made on the matter before final selections are made.

---

*Junior Literary Guild, 245 Park Ave., New York, NY 10017; Book-of-the-Month Club, 485 Lexington Ave., New York, NY 10017; Literary Guild of America, 245 Park Ave., New York, NY 10017; Scholastic Book Services, 50 W. 44th St., New York, NY 10036.

The Professional Library

Faculty members should have available to them a collection of up-to-date, well-selected professional literature. At the single-school level, the size and nature of this collection will depend on budgetary limitations and the resources available at the district level or from other agencies. Because the faculty should be largely responsible for selecting the contents of this special collection, a committee made up of teachers and a representative from the media center should be charged with developing acquisition and administrative procedures.

In addition to basic and current books, periodicals, and pamphlets on education, the professional library should contain such items as sample textbooks, workbooks, curriculum guides, indexes to periodicals, media catalogs, and local, state, and federal documents related to education. To ensure access to other collections of related materials, the media specialists will have to organize or become part of a network that facilitates borrowing from the district library, other school systems, neighboring colleges and universities, or perhaps the state's central library agency. *The Teacher's Library* (NEA), although now somewhat dated, is a useful booklet that contains pointers on selection as well as a basic bibliography of books and periodicals in the field of education.

Local-History Collections

Each school library media center should build up a collection on local history and community affairs, whether or not these topics are considered a formal part of the curriculum. The material can be used in a variety of ways: at election time, for background information on community projects, for debating clubs, when classroom discussions turn to topics on public affairs with local implications. In addition to regular printed and pictorial sources, including pertinent community directories, a special file should be maintained of clippings from local newspapers and available material on community industries, clubs, and church and professional organizations. A separate card file should also be maintained on local resources—field trips, speakers, collections of materials, and so on—that are available to the school. Many schools have instituted photography projects and have supplemented the media center collections on local topics with photographs of key installations, historical landmarks, and persons of local importance. Others have developed oral history collections by taping interviews with prominent residents and storing the tapes in the media center. Particularly important interviews may be transcribed and used in print form.

Reevaluation of the collection

Like Topsy, collections often just grow. Media selectors should bear in mind that with each new addition or deletion new balances and relationships are created. Continuous reevaluation of the collection is necessary to determine what areas are showing greatest growth, whether the greatest-growth areas are commensurate with users' needs, and that all types of media are being added in proper balance. This kind of watchdog activity can keep the collection balanced, vital, and in line with the school's needs.

Long-range planning

To ensure continuity, perspective, and orderly progression in collection development, future goals and the steps by which they will be reached should be carefully outlined by the media center personnel in cooperation with faculty and administration. Priorities must be stated and timetables organized that specify the sequential stages for achieving desired growth. This kind of planning is particularly important in respect to major expenditures, such as investing in new equipment or retiring and replacing machines in the existing collection. If possible, a three- to five-year plan should be developed. To ensure the long-range plan's flexibility and use under various circumstances, it should state for each year alternative courses of action that take various levels of funding into consideration. Other aspects of the interrelationship between the selection process and the school library media center budget are discussed in Chapter 4.

CENSORSHIP AND THE SCHOOL LIBRARY MEDIA CENTER

Complaints concerning the appropriateness of some of the materials housed in the school library media center fall into two categories. The first could be considered the routine, often in-house request to reevaluate specific material, perhaps because it is now out of date or is no longer suited to the curriculum. These are usually generated by teachers within the school and are often settled quickly and without rancor. The second, arising from citizens' complaints, are usually more complex and less easily solved. The subject areas in which most challenges occur are sex, race, religion, profanity, drugs, and sex-role stereotypes. Unfortunately, some people tend to evaluate books and other educational materials not on intrinsic merits but on sets of personal values and prejudices; however, as stated in the "Students' Right to Read Statement" (Urbana, Ill.: National Council of Teachers of English, 1962), "censorship of books can leave American students with an inadequate grasp of the values and ideals of their culture" and "what the teacher sees as his responsibility is to lead his students to understand all aspects of their culture and society—the good and the bad." There has been increased activity in book banning in schools recently and in spite of the Island Trees decision (see Chapter 1), schools had best make advance preparation.

A preliminary step to prevent or forestall censorship of educational materials in a community has already been mentioned: the preparation and adoption of a sound, detailed selection policy. As well, the community should be informed of this policy and have an opportunity to discuss it; it can be reaffirmed by various interest community groups including the local Parent-Teacher Association (PTA). Some superintendents of school districts also ask the PTA to form a committee specifically charged to hear such complaints. One such committee in existence consists of one teacher, one library media specialist, one central administrator, five members of the community, and when the material questioned is at the junior high school level or above, three high school students. In the case of highly controversial subjects, permission from parents is sought before eliciting responses from students. In other districts these committees are composed entirely of educational personnel and are appointed in an ad hoc fashion to hear a particular case. One such committee consists of a library media specialist, a classroom teacher, a subject specialist, and a principal. If possible, members of the committee should not be staff members of the school where the complaint originated.

In addition to setting up the mechanics to handle complaints, the school district should adopt or develop a Citizen's Request Form for Reevaluation of Learning Resource Center Materials (see Appendix IV, Key Documents, for a sample). These forms should identify the complainant, any group or organization that he or she represents, the particular work in question, and the strengths and weaknesses of this work. Further information sought includes the suitability level, the statement that the complainant has read or seen the entire work, a determination that critical reviews of the item have been consulted, and a recommendation concerning the eventual disposition of this material (for example, restrict its use or eliminate it entirely). Each form should also be signed by the complainant.

After these advance preparations, the steps used in complaint handling are as follows. When the presence of a particular piece of material in the library media center has been challenged on unsound grounds, an explanation should be given to the complainant of the selection procedures or policies in effect (perhaps even supplying a copy of the selection policy will help), the criteria used, and the qualifications of the selector. The library media specialist should make sure all the salient facts about the complaint have been made known. An offer to supply the complainant with suitable documentary evidence (such as reviews and recommendations) could also be made if necessary.

If the principal and/or the library media specialist is not able to convince the complainant of the necessity of retaining the material, the complainant should file the full complaint form. The material in question should not be removed from the shelves during the reevaluation process, as this will be interpreted as an admission of error.

The next step is to refer the matter to the reevaluation committee along with copies of the material in question and pertinent data, including reviews. Usually the date of the first committee meeting is made public so that anyone in the district may have the opportunity to submit evidence. The decision of the committee is often sent to the superintendent for review. It is eventually given to the complainant. Some sort of regulation should be enforced that prohibits a further reevaluation of that material for a given period, usually three years. Although this process will usually end with the superintendent's notification, some of these complaints will eventually be decided in court. Certainly, two elements are necessary if the library is to prevail in these cases: (1) a detailed, explicit, and widely distributed set of policies and procedures, and (2) the support and loyalty of the school board and administrators at all levels. Unfortunately, censors are rarely convinced that their causes are not just and proper and in spite of a defeat will often seek out new materials to challenge.

FOR FURTHER READING

American Association of School Librarians. *Policies and Procedures for Selection of Instructional Materials.* Chicago: AASL, 1976.

American Association of School Librarians. *Selecting Materials for School Media Centers: Guidelines and Selection Sources to Insure Quality Collections.* Chicago: AASL, 1978.

American Library Association, Office of Intellectual Freedom. *Intellectual Freedom Manual.* Chicago: American Library Association, 1975.

Audiovisual Instruction. *Selecting Materials for Learning.* Washington, D.C.: AECT, 1974.

Ballard, Jan. *If YA Is the Answer, What Is the Question?* Phoenix, Ariz.: Oryx, 1979.

Belland, John. "Factors Influencing Selection of Materials." *School Media Quarterly* (Winter 1978), pp. 112–119.

Boyer, Calvin J., and Eaton, Nancy L. *Book Selection Policies in American Libraries.* Austin, Tex.: Armadillo Press, 1971.

Broadus, Robert N. *Selecting Materials for Libraries.* New York: H. W. Wilson, 1981.

Carter, Mary Duncan, Bonk, Wallace John, and Magrill, Rose Mary. *Building Library Collections.* Metuchen, N.J.: Scarecrow, 1974.

Council on Interracial Books for Children. *Human (and Anti-Human) Values in Children's Books: A Contest Rating Instrument for Educators and Concerned Parents.* New York: C.I.B.C., 1976.

Davis, James E. *Dealing with Censorship.* Urbana, Ill.: National Council of Teachers of English, 1979.

Educational Product Information Exchange Institute. *Improving Materials Selection Procedures: A Basic "How to Handbook."* Stony Brook, N.Y.: EPIE.

Egoff, Sheila. *The Republic of Childhood: A Critical Guide of Canadian Children's Literature in English,* 2nd ed. New York: Oxford University Press, 1975.

———. *Thursday's Child: Trends and Patterns in Contemporary Children's Literature.* Chicago: American Library Association, 1981.

"Evaluating Materials for Children and Young Adults." *Canadian Library Journal* (December 1978).

Evans, Arthur. "An Evaluation Form That Makes Sense." *Instructional Innovator* (March 1981): 32–33.

Harris, Karen H. "Selecting Library Materials for Exceptional Children." *School Media Quarterly,* 8, no. 1 (Fall 1979): 22–28.

Hearne, Betsy. *Choosing Books for Children: A Commonsense Guide.* New York: Delacorte, 1981.

Issues in Children's Book Selection, articles reprinted from *School Library Journal,* 1973.

Jenkinson, Edward B. *Censors in the Classroom: The Mind Benders.* Edwardsville: Southern Illinois University Press, 1980.

Jonassen, David H. *Nonbook Media: A Self-Paced Instructional Handbook for Teachers and Library Media Personnel.* Hamden, Conn.: Shoe String, 1982.

Katz, William. *Collection Development: Selection of Materials for Libraries.* New York: Holt, 1979.

Klein, M. Frances. *About Learning Materials.* Washington, D.C.: Association for Supervision and Curriculum Development, 1978.

Miller, Marilyn L. "Collection Development in School Library Media Centers: National Recommendation and Reality." *Collection Development,* 1 (1978): 25–28.

National Council of Teachers of English. *The Student's Right to Read.* Urbana, Ill.: NCTE, 1972.

National Education Association. *The Teachers' Library: How to Organize It and What to Include.* Washington, D.C.: NEA, 1968.

Nelson, Jack, and Roberts, Gene, Jr. *The Censors and the Schools.* Boston: Little, Brown, 1963.

Perkins, David L. *Guidelines for Collection Development.* Chicago: American Library Association, 1979.

Right to Read Committee, American Association of School Librarians, Children's Service Division, and the Public Library Association. *The Right to Read and the Nation's Libraries.* Chicago: American Library Association, 1974.

Selecting Media for Learning. Washington, D.C.: Association for Educational Communications Technology, 1976.

Stannek, Lou Willett. *Censorship: A Guide for Teachers, Librarians, and Others Concerned with Intellectual Freedom.* New York: Dell, 1976.

Teaque, Fred A. "A Form for All Reasons." *Audiovisual Instruction* (November 1978), pp. 40–41.

Van Orden, Phyllis. *The Collection Program in Elementary and Middle Schools: Concepts, Practices, and Information Sources.* Littleton, Colo.: Libraries Unlimited, 1982.

——. "Promotion, Review and Examination of Materials." *School Media Quarterly* (Winter 1978), pp. 120–122, 127–132.

—— and Phillips, Edith B. *Background Readings in Building Library Collections*, 2nd ed. Metuchen, N.J.: Scarecrow, 1979.

Vandergrift, Kay E. "Selection: Reexamination and Reassessment." *School Media Quarterly*, 6, no. 2 (Winter 1978): 103–11.

Webster, William. *Evaluation of Instructional Materials.* Washington, D.C.: Association for Educational Communications & Technology, 1978.

Witucke, Virginia. "A Comparative Analysis of Juvenile Book Review Media." *School Media Quarterly*, 8, no. 3 (Spring 1980): 153–160.

Woodbury, Marda. *Selecting Materials for Instruction: Issues and Policies.* Littleton, Colo.: Libraries Unlimited, 1979.

Woods, L. B. *A Decade of Censorship in America: The Threat to Classrooms and Libraries 1966-1975.* Metuchen, N.J.: Scarecrow, 1979.

8

MEDIA SELECTION: CRITERIA AND SELECTION AIDS

The use of criteria helps to make objective an otherwise subjective operation. Two levels of criteria are necessary: criteria that apply to all materials, and more specific criteria that apply only to a particular genre such as films, books, or filmstrips. This same distinction applies to criteria for purchasing equipment. In this chapter, general and specific criteria are given for educational materials and equipment selection, followed by a list of appropriate selection aids.

GENERAL CRITERIA FOR SELECTING EDUCATIONAL MATERIALS

Authority

This refers to the qualifications of the people responsible for creating the material (the author, the producer or publisher) and how capable and prepared they are to have undertaken the project in question. Information on their background, education, experience, reputation, and previous works will supply useful clues. Also, a determination of the nature and repute of research sources used is useful. If the item under consideration is an adaptation or revision of another work, the extent and nature of the differences should be determined; often these are so slight that a media center that owns the old work may not wish to purchase the revision.

Scope

Essentially, this refers to the overall purpose and coverage of the material. When the breadth and limitation of scope are determined, the

182

work should be compared with others on the same subject to see if it presents a fresh viewpoint or if it displaces, amplifies, or simply repeats existing material in the collection.

Format and Technical Quality

The physical makeup of the material should be appropriate to its content. It should meet acceptable production standards and be of sufficient quality to help promote use. Each form of educational material has distinctive physical characteristics.

Authenticity

The contents should be checked for validity, reliability, and completeness, as well as for the degree of bias or objectivity. Recency is also important. The copyright date and imprint date should relate favorably; sometimes they are valid guides to the up-to-dateness of the material. However, the contents will usually have to be examined to make a final and accurate determination of currency.

Treatment and Arrangement

The material should be clearly presented in a well-organized fashion. This involves a logical development; the sequence of the content should flow naturally and easily from one section into another. The material should be well balanced and place particular stress on the elements of greatest importance. The arrangement should bear a direct relationship to use of the material and be judged by the degree to which it facilitates that use. The style of presentation, the general comprehension level, and the nature of the concepts being developed must be appropriate, both to the intended audience and to the nature and depth of coverage intended. The material should be developed in light of sound educational principles and make provision for such elements as review and reinforcement. Finally, the work should catch and hold the user's interest and provide stimulation for further learning.

Aesthetic Considerations

The item must be acceptable artistically, with separate elements combining to form an aesthetically pleasing whole. The material should appeal to the imagination, to the senses, and to the intellect, so that the user's taste and sense of artistic appreciation will be developed.

Price

The acquisition of any piece of material, and particularly expensive items, must be seen in relation to existing budget limitations. It might be necessary to find out if a satisfactory substitute at a lower price is available. Certainly the initial cost will be weighed against the amount of intended use.

Special Features

The media specialist should try to ascertain the characteristics, if any, that make the item under consideration distinctive among others of the same type and on the same subject. These might be, for example, an unusual approach to a subject matter, the presence of usage guides, sets of questions and answers, or a list of suggested follow-up activities.

General Suitability

Having evaluated the material in the preceding general terms, the media specialist now must view the material in light of the school's existing collection. The appropriateness of the material to the school's educational objectives and curriculum is an important factor. Such questions as: Is there sufficient need for the item? How many will use it? Is it suited to the particular needs and abilities of those who will use it? must be answered.

SPECIFIC CRITERIA FOR SELECTING EDUCATIONAL MATERIALS

Books

Regardless of how varied the materials are in the school's media center, books will remain one of the mainstays of the collection. Each center will strike different balances concerning the number of titles found in various subject areas; such factors as differences in curricula and student abilities mandate that such variations in collections should exist from school to school. Table 8-1 gives a general indication of the average size of various parts of book collections at the elementary and secondary levels. These figures are given to indicate relative sizes, not to be used as hard-and-fast buying guides or as a tool to evaluate existing collections, because, as has been stated, these figures will and should vary from one media center to another. The figures are arranged, as are the collections they represent, by Dewey decimal numbers.

TABLE 8-1   PERCENT OF BOOK COLLECTION
PER DEWEY CLASSIFICATION

		Percent of Collection	
	Dewey Classification	K–6	7–12
000–099	General Works and Reference	2–5 %	6–8 %
100–199	Philosophy, Psychology	.5	1–2
200–299	Religion and Mythology	1–2	1–2
300–399	Social Sciences, Folklore	5–10	10–15
400–499	Language	.5	2–5
500–599	Pure Science	10	5–10
600–699	Applied Science	10	5–10
700–799	Fine Arts, Recreation	5	5–10
800–899	Literature	5	5–10
900–999	History, Geography, Biography	20	20
F	Fiction	20	20–25
E	Easy Books, Picture Books	20–25	

In addition to the general criteria for selection, criteria related to format are also important. The book's size should be appropriate to its audience. The paper should be of good quality and sufficiently opaque to prevent seeing through to the next page. Besides being clear and easy to read, the typeface should be suitable for the intended user. Adequate spacing between words and the leading between lines are important. The binding must show the necessary durability and strength related to the type of use the book will receive. Interesting page layouts, pleasing use of color, and an eye-catching cover help make the book physically attractive. Hardcover books should lie flat when open.

Furthermore, specific types of books require specific criteria.

Fiction

Whenever possible fiction titles should reach acceptable literary standards, although in providing stories for reluctant and slow readers, these standards might have to be modified or altered in some way. Good fiction generally has the characteristics described below:

Characterization. The characters should be believable and constant. Changes in character should arise naturally and convincingly from the plot. Stereotypes should be avoided. The author should use imaginative but suitable ways to reveal characterization through combinations of direct exposition, dialogue, thought, and action.

Plot. This is probably the most important element for young readers. It should be logical and well constructed, move at an active rate, and appropriately reflect the central theme or purpose of the novel. The story should advance in a continuous, well-balanced flow.

Setting and atmosphere. The setting and concomitant creation of atmosphere should be appropriate to the author's purpose and should be emphasized or deemphasized depending on the nature of the novel.

Style. An author's writing style may vary from the objectivity of writers like Hemingway to the subjectivity of Proust or Joyce. Regardless of its nature, the style should suit the material and theme, be smooth and dynamic, and not be so self-conscious that it intrudes on and detracts from the reader's enjoyment of the work.

Theme. Any theme is valid if the author is able to combine the above elements to make the central idea valid, believable, and important. The nature, complexity, and subtlety of themes should vary with the author's purpose and be appropriate for the intended audience.

Picture Books

In picture books and other books that rely heavily on illustrations to convey messages, the pictures should be clear, simple, and of suitable size, and they should interpret the story truthfully and be unified with the text. The medium used in the pictures (water colors, pen-and-ink drawings, line blocks) should be appropriate to the setting and the atmosphere created in the story.

Reference Books

Reference books and many other books of general nonfiction can be used effectively and efficiently if they contain the following: running heads (as in dictionaries), thumb indexing, extensive illustrations placed close to the related text, thorough indexes, cross-references, and pronunciations of difficult words. For multivolume sets, such as encyclopedias, the media specialist should also explore the revision policy as well as the nature and quality of supplements or yearbooks.

Textbooks

For many years the textbook was the main teaching tool. It still supplies a common body of knowledge for all students and in many ways can help to organize and facilitate instruction. Critics maintain, however, that the single-textbook concept stifles inquiry and critical thinking, deals with events superficially, does not allow for the individual student's needs and interests, and tends to lock the curriculum into a fixed sequence, and that the text is often poorly written. For these reasons the single text is increasingly being abandoned in favor of a multitextbook concept that uses several texts per course supplemented by a variety of other educational materials.

Textbooks are usually chosen by a selection committee. The committee should include at least one representative from the media center, and each of the basic criteria involving authority, scope, treatment, authenticity, and suitability must be vigorously applied. In addition, the following questions should be asked when a text is being considered:

Does the content of the textbook relate well to the syllabus of the course?

Are the reading and interest levels within the text suited to the students who will use it?

Is the material presented in a way to encourage further study and critical thinking?

Is the material interestingly presented?

Are illustrations used often and effectively?

Does the author present the material in a fair, unbiased manner?

If differing opinions exist, are all sides of a controversial question presented objectively?

In the area of social studies, is proper balance shown to the contributions of various racial, ethnic, and religious groups?

Are supplementary teaching aids available?

Are extensive multimedia bibliographies provided for further study?

Are such learning aids as a glossary, index, extensive table of contents, pronunciations, summaries, and lists of supplementary activities present?

Can the material be easily reorganized to accommodate the different needs of various teaching situations?

In what way, if any, can the material be updated?

Paperbacks

Many studies have been made that show how effective paperbacks can be to individualize and enrich instruction in the schools. These studies show that young people usually prefer a paperback over its hardcover counterpart. Although the distinction between categories in

paperbacks is now frequently blurred, paperbacks are usually classified as *mass market* or *quality*, the differences usually being price,
format, and distribution patterns. Mass-market paperbacks are generally less expensive, are presented in substantially different formats
than the original hardcover editions, and are available through magazine or paperback wholesalers. Quality paperbacks tend to be a little
higher in price, but they are often superior in format. They are available directly from publishers as well as from hardcover and paperback
book jobbers.

At one time the question in schools was: Should we use paperbacks?
The question now is: How do we use paperbacks? Here are some basic
uses: (1) to explore new areas of reader interest, (2) to supply a variety
of material to special students, (3) to provide multiple copies, (4) to
make available more books for the reluctant or slow reader, (5) to provide ephemeral material that has high but short-term appeal, (6) to
supply material that may rapidly become outdated, (7) to supply
material unavailable in any other format, (8) to supply branches with
collections of books through paperback book fairs, (9) to extend the
curriculum, (10) to provide individualized instruction.

Magazines and Newspapers

The habit of reading magazines grows during childhood, and by ado-
lescence magazines are usually preferred over all other kinds of reading.
Many reasons have been suggested for this: Magazines are easily accessible; their contents cater to a wide variety of interests; the use of
color and illustrations makes them attractive (they are, in a sense, the
adolescent version of the picture book); and their articles are short,
usually in easy-to-read language, and do not demand a great time commitment. Perhaps the most important reason, however, is that they
deal with current information and today's events, tastes, and interests.
In short, they are up-to-date and help keep their readers that way.

Newspaper reading also increases during the school years. In
childhood, first the comic-strip pages and next the sports sections are
important. As the child matures, the quality and quantity of newspaper reading expands. An increased emphasis in the curriculum on
current affairs and problems has added even greater importance to the
presence of extensive, well-rounded collections of newspapers and
magazines in the media center.

Magazines and newspapers purchased by schools should comply
with the standards of quality required of other media. The selections
should supply a variety of points of view and cater to the students'
varied interests. The newspapers in the collection should jointly reflect

local, state, and national coverage. Remember also that magazines and newspapers are excellent bait for catching the attention of reluctant readers and attracting them to the media center.

Whether a magazine or newspaper is indexed by one of the standard services, for example, *Reader's Guide*, or provides its own cumulative index, as does the *New York Times*, a selection criterion for magazines or newspapers that are to be used primarily for research. Many of the magazines popular for recreational reading are not found in the standard indexes. Availability in microform might also be considered before purchase. In any case, subscription lists should be reviewed thoroughly every year, and each title reevaluated at that time.

Pamphlets and Clippings

The vertical file in a library is the depository for pamphlets, clippings, pictures, student reports, and other ephemeral material. When well organized and kept current, it can be a valuable adjunct to the regular collection. Some of the purposes it can serve are:

To update the regular collection. Pamphlets and clippings often contain much more current information than do other media.

To supplement and extend material in the existing collection. A pamphlet might, for example, serve as a source of information on a specific subject for which the media center would not purchase more expensive sources.

To supply information and illustration on subjects not covered elsewhere or not treated elsewhere in similar depth.

To furnish a variety of points of view on a subject. This is of particular value with material on controversial subjects. Whereas a book usually reflects a single attitude, a series of clippings may reveal a great difference and range of opinion on the same subject.

Much of the material that is placed in the vertical file is either free or inexpensive. The major sources for clippings are magazines and newspapers, as well as discarded books. Pamphlets are available from a variety of sources. Media specialists should familiarize themselves with the many bibliographies of these free and inexpensive materials.

Two points to consider in pamphlet selection are: (1) because much of this material is free, it will have to be checked thoroughly for excessive or misleading advertising and for evidence of propagandizing; (2) the vertical file should be thoroughly and frequently weeded to dispose of materials that have outlived their usefulness.

Government Documents

Media centers often tend to overlook the wide and rich storehouse of materials available from the various government agencies at local, state, national, and international levels. The materials these sources issue are rather misleadingly called government documents. One tends to think of a government document solely as a published treaty, law, or the like. Instead, the scope of government documents is as wide as the interests and concerns of today's governments. The Government Printing Office in Washington, D.C., for example, is now officially known as the world's largest publisher. The pamphlets, books, maps, film, and phonograph records available from that office alone deal with such diverse subjects as child care, farming, Civil War battles, cooking, crime, and the national parks. Media centers should avail themselves of this large wealth of materials—much of it is free or inexpensive.

Motion Picture Films

The characteristics of motion present in so-called motion pictures is actually an optical illusion that exploits the eye's inability to distinguish adequately between images that are shown in quick succession. Because the eye retains an image for a fraction of a second after it is shown, this "retention of vision" causes a blending with the next image. If the images are closely related in sequence, the effect is one of movement. Sound films are shown at 24 images or frames per second, silent films, usually 16 frames per second. When films are projected at less than these speeds a disjointed or flickering effect occurs.

Motion pictures were first used in education following World War I. Since that time their potential has been thoroughly explored, and they have grown in use to the extent that today they are rated among the most powerful and effective presentational devices available to the educator. Like television, motion pictures appeal in a variety of ways to several senses simultaneously. Not only can they supply visual images in motion and in color; they also extend their dimension with sound.

On close examination, motion picture film has a dull and a glossy side. It is the dull side that contains the image and the sound track, if any.

Motion pictures can be classified by format and content. By format the basic classification involves the width of the film: 35mm and wider—used for commercial theatrical viewing; 16mm and 8mm—the two sizes used extensively in education. Sixteen millimeter is most useful if a large picture is required, but in an average classroom, 8mm gives satisfactory results in clarity and picture definition. In cost, size, and ease of transport, 8mm films and equipment have advantages over 16mm.

Sixteen-millimeter films can be either silent (silent films have sprocket holes on both sides of the film) or equipped with sound tracks. Sound films have sprocket holes on one side of the film and the sound track on the other. Sound is recorded on film in one of two ways: optically, through photographing the sound and converting it into bands of light and dark that can be reconverted with the use of a photoelectric cell, or magnetically, by attaching a continuous narrow strip of magnetic tape to the side of the film. The optical track is more common than the magnetic. Films in 16mm come in the regular reel-to-reel form that requires conventional threading of the machine, in cassettes that are self-threading and rewinding, and in closed-loop cartridges sometimes called repeating films because the beginning and end of the film are joined in the cartridge to form a continuous loop.

All of these variations (sound, either optical or magnetic, silent, reel-to-reel, cassette, cartridge) are also available in the 8mm field with even further diversifications. A few years ago standard or regular 8mm film was joined by a close relative: Super 8. This format has reduced-size sprocket holes and, therefore, has space on the film to accommodate larger pictures. Super 8 sound film's sprocket holes are on the opposite side from those of regular 8mm film. A slight mixing of film formats has taken place. For example, some longer 16mm films often now have accompanying shorter excerpts or brief related films on 8mm, for more intensive small-group or individual viewing. Unfortunately, the inability of the accompanying equipment to accommodate a wide diversity of film formats has produced great confusion and, as a result, buyer resistance, particularly to 8mm films and equipment. This lack of compatibility continues to be a major stumbling block to freer use of this medium by schools.

Films may also be classified by content. Traditionally they have, like books, been considered either educational (curriculum oriented) or recreational (entertainment oriented). Happily, this distinction is breaking down. Films can and should instruct and entertain at the same time. Classification by subject area—for example, science, history, geography—is often used. Other terms used in classifying films are animated films, travelogs, agency-sponsored films, training films, documentaries, and true-life dramas.

Because young people spend such a great deal of time before television and film screens, a movement to produce greater visual literacy among the young has grown in American education. People who use films with students should familiarize themselves with the techniques and capabilities of the medium and convey these to their students. When one is able to "think" with the eyes, the more one is able to appreciate the alternatives available to a director in filming a scene, the variety of effects produced by different types of film shots, the techniques and considerations used for cutting from one sequence to another, and other relationships that exist among the camera, the subject, and the viewer.

Perhaps better than any other medium, motion pictures convey the greatest sense of reality to an audience. The attention of the viewer is easily attained and identification possibilities are numerous. Through the medium of the realistic film, the audience can easily be taken to a distant country to study a foreign culture or transported back in time to witness important events of the past. In addition, film is also capable of conveying "unrealistic" motion. By filming at a very fast rate and then projecting at normal speeds, the effect of slow motion is produced and details perhaps otherwise undetectable become visible. On the other hand, through time-lapse photography—shooting pictures at a slower rate than usual, but projecting them at the normal speed—phenomena that ordinarily might take hours or days to take place can be shown in a matter of seconds. In the variation of time-lapse photography called the stop-motion effect, the cameraman shoots only a single picture at a time and the objects photographed are changed slightly for each picture so that an illusion of motion is produced in the final product. Other forms of animation are also used to produce unrealistic motion. Many projectors are now equipped with a "freeze frame," a mechanism that allows a single frame to remain on the screen without damaging the film.

Besides the advantages of wide range and of types of images that can be carried via motion picture film, there are other, more basic reasons for using it. Tests have shown repeatedly that material, particularly of a factual nature, presented through the motion picture medium is learned faster and retained longer than material presented through a more traditional medium. The skills necessary to absorb information from films are minimal—poor readers can grasp material presented in film far more readily than they can material in a printed format. Other assets of film are: New formats and equipment now make it possible for children to operate the machines and for a greater range in the size of the group viewing the film; details are easily presented on film; local production of films is fairly simple and not too costly; a wide variety of films at various levels and in various formats is available for purchase or rental.

There are some disadvantages to the medium of film. First, compared with other materials, films are more costly. This applies not only to purchasing but also to renting film. Potential purchasers should bear in mind that a film's time of usefulness will be limited (1) by the degree of recency in its content and (2) by the rate of its physical deterioration. Because single schools usually find it too costly to purchase long films, these films must be secured through other distribution centers, such as district- or countywide collection or rental libraries. This entails advance bookings—in some cases as much as six months—and sometimes planning that far ahead makes it impossible to ensure correct integration of the film into the curriculum. In addition, for economies in time and money, bookings are often made for only a two- or three-day period, but this limited time frequently is not sufficient for previewing, preparation for the presentation, audience viewing, and, if necessary, reviewing.

Another limitation placed on the use of film is that some teachers still consider films a form of entertainment—to be used as a "reward" for their students—rather than an important instructional aid. As a result, there has been more misuse of this medium in the classroom than of any other nonprint material. It is hoped that the emphasis on audiovisual materials in teacher training institutions and the development of in-service courses within school districts will change this situation.

Two additional limitations on the use of films involve projection conditions. First, many machines still require manual threading or other, rather complex procedures. Teachers often feel insecure in performing these operations and thus curtail their use of this medium. Second, showing most types of films to large groups still requires a darkened room, which decreases the opportunities for note taking and increases the possibility of behavioral problems.

The general criteria for evaluating educational materials may be used with films. Fortunately most films are available on a preview basis so that these criteria may be applied directly and not solely through reviewing sources. Preview records should be kept for future reference. Specific points to remember when selecting films are: (1) The content should be more effectively presented via film than is possible in another, less expensive format, (2) if the film is being considered for purchase, the cost must be weighed heavily against the number of subject areas in which it may be used, the length of time it will have value in the curriculum, and the number of showings anticipated per school year, and (3) the quality of the acting, the scenario, and the presentation techniques, as well as the nature of the photography, sound, and color, should be of acceptable standards or better.

Projected Still Pictures

Filmstrips

Of all the various formats available in projected audiovisual materials, certainly the filmstrip is the most popular and widely used. Basically, a filmstrip is a long strip of 35mm film on which a series of related still pictures called frames are arranged in a fixed order. The number of frames in a filmstrip can and does vary a great deal. A typical filmstrip, however, contains from 30 to 50 frames. Filmstrips are classified as either silent or sound. The silent filmstrips usually have either captions of explanatory text under the pictures or accompanying manuals that contain a printed running commentary. A sound filmstrip generally has packaged with it a phonograph record or audiotape, such as a sound cassette. One side of the phonograph records and tapes now packaged in these sets has an audible signal ("beep") to tell the operator to move to the next frame. The other side is used in equipment that moves the filmstrip along automatically on a special electronic nonaudible signal. Some manufacturers produce single cartridges that contain both filmstrip and sound tape. These can be easily dropped into a specially produced projector capable of accepting the single unit. Another manufacturer has developed a filmstrip with an optical sound track on the same film as the pictures. Here again, special equipment is required for its use.

The popularity of the filmstrip is due to several factors: The strips are comparatively inexpensive; there are thousands available on a wide range of subjects and at a variety of levels; and operation of filmstrip equipment is easy enough even for children. In addition, filmstrips are flexible and adaptable. They can be used with either large or small groups or by individuals. They are also compact and easily stored and have the added advantage of adjustable projection speed. Whole frames may be ignored or passed over quickly whereas others may be lingered over or returned to without great inconvenience.

The filmstrip does have some disadvantages of which media users should be aware. Two principal ones are that the filmstrip cannot show motion, and the pictures are locked into a fixed order, which makes changing the sequence difficult. One technical hazard is that with each showing the film is exposed to physical damage, such as scratching or ripping of sprocket holes; another is that for good projection, even though a daylight screen is used, the room must be partially darkened.

There are many aids available to help with the selection of filmstrips for a collection, including—in addition to those that cover many media—some dealing specifically with filmstrips, such as the National Information Center for Educational Media (NICEM) *Index to 35mm*

Filmstrips, and *Educators Guide to Free Filmstrips* (Educators Progress Service). Current reviews are featured in such standard reviewing media as *School Library Journal* (R. R. Bowker) and *Booklist* (ALA).

Specific criteria for evaluating filmstrips should start with these questions: Does the subject lend itself to the filmstrip format? If so, are the visuals sufficient in quantity and quality to convey the message adequately? On the technical side, the visuals should be clear, sharp, and interesting. They should show suitable variety in style (closeups—distance) and presentation (photos, charts, graphs). Captions on silent filmstrips should be legible, not too lengthy, and as with any running commentary, appropriate to the intended audience. Colors when used should be faithful to the original and be used for educational, not just for decorative, reasons. Recorded sound tracks should conform to good standards of aural presentation—high fidelity, clarity, lack of distortion, and good use of special effects. The sound and visual image should be well synchronized.

Slides

At one time the term "slide" applied exclusively to the larger $3\frac{1}{4} \times 4$-inch glass-mounted lantern slide. Although this size slide has declined in use enormously, it is still found to be valuable today, particularly in slides that delineate fine details on complex maps and diagrams. Generally speaking, most people now associate slides with the 2×2-inch cardboard-mounted slide made popular through home photography. Commercially produced slides of this variety are frequently mounted on sturdier material than cardboard, and for protection, many are completely covered with glass or a layer of clear plastic. These are more expensive, but they will withstand tough wear for longer periods.

Slides have basically the same advantages as filmstrips, but they may be used with more flexibility because they can be arranged in any sequence that will best suit the presentation; carousel trays make sequencing and projection simple. Slides may be produced locally and presentation may be varied to meet local and individual class needs. In many cases, such as recording a field trip, this simply means taking photographs in the usual way. For photographing diagrams, flat pictures, or parts of a book, a copy stand must be used, but this is a relatively simple procedure. Duplication of locally produced slides is possible through the use of the negatives, or of commercially produced slides (within copyright restrictions) through special equipment.

The disadvantages of slides are similar to those of filmstrips, with three additions. First, because each is a separate, small entity, sets of them can easily be disarranged, particularly when using a nonauto-matic projector that requires slides to be fed into the machine manu-ally. Second, most slides do not have the captions found on filmstrips; therefore, another medium, such as an accompanying manual, taped commentary, or teacher's remarks, is often needed to interpret the pic-ture. Last, slides are not subject to the same bibliographic control as are filmstrips. For example, there are no separate bibliographies of slides as there are of filmstrips, and many multimedia bibliographies ignore slides completely. The current reviewing media, as well, pay much less attention to slides than to other materials.

Criteria for filmstrips also apply to slides. With slides there should also be an evaluation of the strength of the mounting as well as the continuity and organization present within a set. A more specialized slide format is the stereoscopic slide reel in which two prints of the same picture are projected in a hand-held viewer simultaneously to give a three-dimensional effect. There are many reels available (par-ticularly those containing sight-seeing views of places). They are generally inexpensive and easily shown. However, only one student can use the viewer at a time.

Microforms

"Microform" is a generic term for media that carry printed informa-tion in a reduced size. There are two major divisions of microforms: (1) those reproduced on transparent film, (2) those reproduced on opaque cards. All microforms share the same basic advantages, which briefly are:

Space. Because of miniaturization, microforms have the highest storage density of any media. Entire libraries can now literally be stored in a few drawers of a card file, and in the case of magazine storage, microfilm takes about 5 percent of the space required to store a comparable number of issues in hard copy.

Completeness. The danger of mutilation and theft is minimal and files are therefore almost guaranteed to remain intact and complete.

Cost. Microforms are less expensive than their hardcover counter-part. For example, a volume of a periodical on microfilm costs less than the price of binding the same number of issues in hard copy.

Selection. Hundreds of thousands of books, periodicals, and news-papers are now available in microform, and in most cases it is the only form in which the material is available. Thus, when one of these items is under consideration for purchase, it is either a microform or nothing.

Convertibility. Microforms can be converted into paper copy with the use of a simple printing device. The process per page is inexpensive and takes only a few seconds.

There are also several disadvantages in using microforms in libraries, and ironically two of them involve factors already listed as advantages: cost and space. The initial cost of purchasing microform readers and reader-printers and the space required to house them in the library will reduce the savings from microform use in libraries whose microform collection is small. In addition to the cost disadvantages of purchasing and housing special hardware is the necessity either of teaching all would-be users how to use these machines or of facing a situation in which the library staff is responsible for threading and dismantling the machines each time they are used. Increased availability of microfilm cartridges will help in this area. However, using microforms is generally more time-consuming than using printed formats—not only is the reader's time expended in setting up the machine, but retrieval time is also slow. In the case of the microfilm spool, for example, a reader may have to run through an entire roll before finding the specific document that is being sought.

A certain amount of "reader resistance" to microforms has developed primarily because some microreaders produce difficult-to-read images, particularly around the edges, and because unless the microreader is portable, users generally must remain in one place to use the machine. Frequently after an initial exposure, youngsters have shown that they prefer paper copy. The disadvantages of microforms are greatly outweighed, however, by their many advantages and any library media center truly committed to developing broad-based collections should explore the tremendous wealth of material available in microform. Most library users are inclined to think of microfilm in terms of the open-spool, reel-to-reel format. This is certainly the oldest and most common format for microfilm. Although spools come in two sizes, 16mm and 35mm, the former is encountered primarily where microfilming of documents is done locally, for example, in a business concern where bills and receipts are photographed before they are destroyed. The spools distributed commercially from microfilm producers are usually 35mm and are generally about 100 feet long. Although spools are among the least expensive of microformats, they are the most difficult to use, and they expose the film to greater wear and chance of damage than do other microform formats.

The microfilm cartridge, or magazine, on the other hand, is the microformat that provides the advantages of the spool, yet permits self-threading and eliminates film damage from incorrect winding. While 16mm cartridges have been available for many years, libraries can convert existing 35mm collections to cartridge format simply by purchasing empty 35mm cartridges, into which spools can be snapped or threaded, and either cartridge readers or, as is possible with many machines, adapters for standard spool readers to allow automatic threading through cartridge use.

A third microformat, the aperture card, uses a standard (3¼ × 7⅞-inch) data-processing card with an open window into which is placed a microfilm chip, usually 35mm. Machine-readable information may be punched into the paper part of the card, while the microfilm part contains pertinent miniaturized documents. Through the use of a camera-processor (see Microform Equipment later in this chapter), a document can be photographed, processed, and mounted in an aperture card in less than a minute after exposure. Not only is speed of production an advantage, but also these cards can be updated easily and afford flexibility in sequencing the material on them. For these reasons many schools have placed student records on aperture cards, and libraries have used the format to store magazine articles, clippings, and other materials often found in the vertical file. Nova High School, Fort Lauderdale, Florida, for example, has built into its four resource centers a collection of magazine articles on local history, all on aperture cards. These cards are slightly more expensive to produce than other microforms and are not practical for use with documents over 24 pages in length. Because of these limitations, the basic use of aperture cards in all types of libraries has been to supplement the use of other microforms.

A microfiche (from the French word *fiche*, meaning index card) is microform that uses a transparent flat sheet of film containing reproductions in rows and columns of many pages of printed material. The standard microfiche is 4 × 6 inches and has a maximum capacity of what were originally 72 8½ × 11-inch pages. There are, however, a great variety of sizes and capacities within the microfiche format. Ultrafiche, or ultramicrofiche (UMF), allows an even greater reduction with a single fiche now able to carry more than 3,000 pages on a 4 × 6-inch sheet of film. Many variations of UMF are currently available. For example, Library Resources, Inc., developing their Micro-book Libraries, designed a 3 × 5-inch fiche capable of containing up to 1,000 page images in 50 columns and 50 rows. Microfiche is the least expensive way of publishing material, although to be economical it is not practical for documents of fewer than 24 pages. To give some indication of how inexpensive microfiche is, when bought in large quantities a single volume on microfiche, fully catalogued, averages about $1, or ⅓ of a cent per page.

Microforms are often available in either or both of two formats, positive or negative. In a positive image, the reader sees the type and photograph in the same relationship as the usual printed page, black print on a white background. In the negative image the relationship is reversed as in a photographic negative. The debate as to which is easier to read has never been resolved—perhaps it is a question of personal preference. Negative microfilm has been shown to be sturdier, however, and less prone to show scratches and dirt. On the other hand, reproduction of photographs on negative microforms appear unnatural and are often difficult to read. The question of positive versus negative becomes further complicated by the fact that most existing reader-printers reproduce solely in the form opposite to that of the film, that is, positive microfilm is printed in hard copy in the negative format and vice versa. Therefore, in addition to evaluating the relative importance of texts and photographs, the media specialist must also determine whether machine-reading or hard-copy printing will represent the greater use of the microform. There is now available a reader-printer that can give positive copy from either positive or negative film.

This dilemma also applies to the second major type of microforms, the opaque or micro-opaque card. The two major subdivisions in this group are microcards and microprints. The microcard is usually 3 × 5 inches and contains pages of print reduced in size and reproduced on an opaque card by a photographic process. The microprint is basically the same, except that it is larger (usually 6 × 9 inches), can contain more text, and is produced by a printing process. Most opaque microforms contain print on both sides. The trend in microform production seems now to be away from opaque card forms to those on transparent film. However, a great body of material is still available on microcards and microprints.

Whatever the types of microforms purchased for the school, the criteria for selection should be those used for other print media. Curriculum demands and requests from students and teachers will, of course, be extremely important. In the case of periodicals and newspapers in microform, other considerations will involve the availability of an index, excessive use of pictures, particularly colored ones (some color microfilm for periodicals like *National Geographic* is now available), and the amount of backlog available. Some of the major producers of microforms are Bell & Howell, Library Resources, Inc., Lost Cause Press, New York Times, 3M-IM Press, Reader Microprint Corp., NCR Microcards, ERIC, General Microfilm Co., and University Microfilms.

Because of spiraling costs associated with traditional publishing, microform publishing should be increasingly popular and useful, and a relatively inexpensive medium. Some developments that would be welcome in this area are inexpensive and more efficient hardware, standardization of format, particularly in the microfiche area, and development of inexpensive color microforms.

Transparencies

Both filmstrips and slides are forms of transparencies, but in the present context the term "transparency" refers to a single sheet or continuous role of clear acetate containing images that are enlarged through viewing with an overhead projector. Of all recent audiovisual innovations introduced into the school, certainly the overhead has received the widest adoption. Perhaps this is because it combines the advantages of an old and trusted teaching tool, the chalkboard, with the capability to project pictures. Transparencies may either be purchased commercially or prepared within the school. The simplest of the latter type is produced by writing on the acetate with a marking pen or grease pencil. Most single-sheet transparencies are $8\frac{1}{2} \times 11$ inches when mounted, but this size has been far from universally adopted. The illuminated surface or size of the overhead projector is usually 10×10 inches, and the actual size of the aperture in the transparency mounting is about 7×9 inches. Transparencies can be quite elaborate; a number of additional sheets, called overlays, can be placed on top of the original transparency to show complex relationships or progressive stages of development. The overlays are usually hinged to the mounting of the basic transparency. Many commercially produced transparencies come in sets, while others are sequenced and placed in binders. It is also possible to buy transparency masters that may be used locally to produce any desired number of actual transparencies.

A special process has been developed that makes it possible to simulate action on transparencies through the use of specially prepared film and an adapter attached to the overhead. Thus one is able to give the impression of pistons moving or electricity flowing without using machines with complex moving parts. Undoubtedly, transparencies with sound tracks on their mountings will be a future development.

Transparencies have many other advantages as well. The overhead is mechanically easy to handle and operate and supplies a large, clear image in a normally illuminated room—which allows note taking in comfort if desired. The overhead can be placed at the front of a class so that the user can face the audience, control attention, and observe student reactions. The transparency is always visible to the teacher, who is free to change it at will. The user also has control over the pacing and sequencing of the presentation. Transparencies are easy to return—which facilitates review of the material. Particularly through the use of overlays, complex subjects may be gradually and logically introduced. It is also important to note that many professionally produced transparencies are correlated for use with other media, chiefly textbooks. The use of the overhead is suited particularly to medium-size groups, such as a class in a classroom, as well as to large auditorium-size groups. Transparencies may be produced locally by a variety of methods. The simplest, as noted above, is produced by handwriting, and this is less time-consuming than writing on the chalkboard; more sophisticated methods include diazo, heat transfer, photography, and color lift. (See also Transparency Making in Chapter 10.)

The disadvantages of transparencies are few, but should be enumerated. First, their use is awkward, although certainly not impossible, for an individual viewer. The simulation of motion in locally produced transparencies is difficult to effect and involves added expense. Typical book or newspaper type is too small to be used in a transparency; a larger type—of the primary typewriter size, for example—is needed. Also, only paper with clay content can be used in locally producing transparencies by the color-lift process, and even then, the production of the transparency involves the destruction of the original print. A final disadvantage, of the professionally produced transparency, is lack of standardization in both size and packaging.

Commercially available transparencies are listed in dealers' catalogs and multimedia catalogs as well as in the NICEM *Index to Educational Overhead Transparencies*. Many manufacturers allow previewing privileges on sets of transparencies.

Specific criteria in choosing transparencies include quality of mounting, clarity and sharpness of picture, suitable definition of detail, use of color, omission of irrelevant material, ease of transparency identification by labeling and other devices, logical sequencing and organization if they are in sets, and durability of packaging.

Audio Materials

Audio learning materials make available a great variety of experiences through sound—drama, music, lectures, foreign languages, readings, actual occurrences, and recreations of events. They have been found to be particularly effective in curricular areas involving speech, language, and music. Programs to develop reading skills have also used with success such audio techniques as allowing children to follow the text of the book while listening to a recording of it.

Specific listening skills are needed to make maximum use of the medium. It is easy for a student to "tune out," wool-gather, or generally fail to pay attention while supposedly listening to a presentation.

It is often impossible to detect when this inattention sets in. The distraction level is also much higher for audio experiences than for those that involve both sight and sound. Sudden movements or extraneous noises can easily distract the listener. The material that can be presented solely through sound is also limited. For example, the text of a poem or the pronunciation of a foreign phrase are easily conveyed by this medium, but a description of a complex scientific process is not. However, because it lacks the specificity that visual materials present, audio experience often stimulates the imagination by allowing students to supply their own visual dimensions.

Four types of audio materials are generally used in media centers: (1) phonograph records, (2) tape recordings, (3) audiocards, and (4) radio broadcasts.

Phonograph Records

Phonograph records are known under a variety of names: phonodiscs, discs, audiodiscs, or, simply, recordings. Discs contain sound transcriptions and are manufactured in a variety of diameters and in formats designed to be played at different speeds. The most common format is the 12-inch, 33⅓rpm (revolutions per minute), lp (long-playing) record. The amount of recorded sound per side on this type of record varies from about ten minutes to over one-half hour. Other diameters for records are 7 inches (for "pop" singles), 10 inches (now not generally available), and 16 inches. The 16-inch record is used for radio station transcriptions. Other speeds are 16¾rpm (used in talking books), 45rpm (again chiefly for popular music), and 78rpm. (Seventy-eight revolutions per minute was the standard speed of shellac records, but recordings have not been manufactured for playing at this speed since the late 1940s when the plastic long-playing disc was developed). New recordings are now issued solely in some version of stereophonic sound. This means, basically, that each groove on the recording contains two or more separate sound channels.

Phonograph records have several advantages over tape recordings. Most people are familiar with them and know how to operate a record player. The material on a disc is easily retrieved and allows for flexibility in timing. No rewinds or advancing are necessary. The required material is available simply by placing the needle arm at the appropriate spot. Phonograph records are generally less expensive than tapes. Discs also have certain disadvantages: They are prone to damage, that is, they scratch easily and warp under certain conditions, and their sound quality deteriorates with frequent playing. These limitations can largely be avoided with care in handling and storage.

In the future, the use of the newly developed compact disc (CD) will eliminate these disadvantages. The CD player uses a small optical laser that never touches the surface of the disc to "read" audio information digitally encoded on the surface of the disc. These discs are 4.7 inches in diameter and carry up to one hour of recording per side.

Tapes

Basically, tape recording uses a magnetic tape, the nonshiny side of which is capable of carrying recorded sound. Like discs, tapes come in a variety of formats. The standard reel-to-reel tape recorder uses $1/4$-inch tape on reels 3, 5, or 7 inches in diameter. The speeds at which this tape is used for recording and playing back are $1\frac{7}{8}$, $3\frac{3}{4}$, and $7\frac{1}{2}$ips (inches per second). With slower speed there is usually a corresponding lessening of fidelity. Recording models vary from a single monaural to four-track stereo and in broadcasting, eight-track tape. The $1/4$-inch-wide tape is also available in cartridge form, with some in closed loop format to allow for continuous playback without rewinding.

The cassette tape has gained in popularity, overtaking reel-to-reel and cartridge tapes in usage figures. This tape is $1/8$-inch thick, enclosed in a container called a cassette, and played at $1\frac{7}{8}$ips. Like cartridges, cassettes are easily snapped into place in the player without threading. Cassettes vary in the amount of tape they contain. They are classified, therefore, by the amount of playing time each contains—from 10 to 120 minutes.

Unlike discs, tapes can serve as both a listening and recording medium. This is their basic advantage over conventional phonograph records. This element of participation has produced a variety of uses for tapes, particularly in language study. They are also less prone to damage and may be erased and used again and/or played back many times without changing the quality of the sound. While repairing tapes and rearranging material through splicing is easily accomplished on reel-to-reel tape, if a cassette or cartridge tape should break, it is extremely difficult to pry open either container and make the necessary repairs. In spite of fast-forward and rewind controls, a major drawback in tape use continues to be the difficulty of locating specific material recorded on the tapes.

Audiocards

An audiocard looks like a data-processing card, except that along its bottom edge it has a strip of magnetic tape containing up to 15 seconds of recorded sound. When the card is played in an audiocard player, the student sees what is printed on the card and hears the sound track. This device of presenting pictures and words simultaneously has been used successfully in teaching reading.

Radio Broadcasts

With the advent of television and the availability of great libraries of tapes and discs, the use of the radio in education has declined. It remains, however, a powerful device for presenting listening experiences, and a number of educational radio stations are still producing excellent broadcasts for the schools. With the advent of the inexpensive tape recorder, one great difficulty in radio broadcast utilization—how to synchronize the radio program with classroom activities—has been minimized. Programs can now be taped for listening at the class's convenience, when permission is granted.

Radio programs, along with many other audiovisual materials including commercially produced tapes and disc records, share one important limitation: They are agents of one-way communication that does not allow for an interchange of ideas with the listener. It is possible to talk back to a radio, but not possible to get an answer.

The general criteria for evaluating educational media apply to audio materials, but because distractions are often encountered in a listening situation, the selector must be especially aware of the quality of the performance as well as the quality of the recorded sound. The material must be appropriate, of suitable length, effectively presented, interesting, and, if possible, appealing to both the emotions and the intellect. Be sure to determine whether the content is best suited to a recorded form. For example, a tape recording of a play rehearsal has some distinct uses, but videotaping the same rehearsal might be more effective. In evaluating the technical quality, clear, distortion-free sound is important. Tapes and records should be made of durable material and clearly labeled to indicate titles, performers, times, and playback speed.

Television

Television is the most powerful communication medium yet invented. Virtually no aspect of American life has remained unchanged since the use of television became widespread. The field of education has conducted so many research studies with television that the conclusion is now obvious: Children learn through television as much as, if not more than, by conventional classroom presentations. Yet in spite of television's great potential as a teaching tool, its adoption by schools has been amazingly slow. In 1967, for example, a national survey conducted by Richard Mueller at Northern Illinois University showed that fewer than 20 percent of the schools questioned used television as part of the instructional program. Various reasons have been put forth to explain this condition: teacher apathy, fear and distrust of an eventual takeover by the medium, insufficient funds for receivers and broadcasting equipment, and a dearth of good programs.

To a novice the terminology connected with television can be imposing and at times confusing. Here is a brief glossary of terms with their abbreviations and meanings:

Very High Frequency (VHF). Refers to the broadcast frequencies between 30 and 300 megahertz received in a conventional television receiver on channels 2 through 13.

Ultra High Frequency (UHF). Involves the broadcast frequencies between 300 and 3000 megahertz over 70 possible UHF channels, that is, channels 14 through 83.

2500 Megahertz Instructional Fixed Service (2500 MH₃ ITFS). A series of 31 channels in the 2500 to 2690 megahertz or microwave range that has been set aside by the Federal Communications Commission (FCC) for educational broadcasting. Transmitters must be low-power and stationary, but repeater stations may relay signals. Each school's television receiver must be equipped with a special converter for this system.

Closed Circuit Television (CCTV). In this transmission system coaxial cable or microwave relays convey signals directly from broadcaster to receiver. The receiver must be linked directly to the transmitter to receive these signals.

Community Antenna Television (CATV). Also known as cable television, this is a closed-circuit system that distributes signals in a particular area and involves the use of a master antenna.

Open Circuit Television (OCTV). In this method of transmission, signals are conveyed through the atmosphere to the antenna of the viewers' receivers. The VHF and UHF channels, including commercial channels and the Public Broadcasting System (PBS) use this method.

Instructional Television (ITV). These programs originate in a single school system or often within a single school. They are developed to fulfill local needs and are usually transmitted through closed-circuit television.

Educational Television (ETV). These programs are broader in scope and in transmission areas than ITV. They are usually broadcast by an open-circuit, through-the-air system, although some are closed-circuit.

Videotape Recorder (VTR). A device that allows taping of both the visual and sound elements of an actual occurrence or another television program. The development of ½-inch videotape and inexpensive cameras has opened up the VTR field. Taping allows scheduling of programs for the convenience of teachers and students. Videotape is available in a variety of widths (from ¼ inch to 2 inches) and speeds. Care should be taken when making purchases because of the incompatibility of playback equipment with various kinds of tapes. The two basic formats at present are VHS and Beta, but within each there are a variety of features available, such as advance programmability (often as long as 14 days) with a specific number of programs that can be scheduled, various recording speeds, number of recording hours possible per cassette (usually up to 8 hours), tracking control, high-speed searching capabilities, freeze frame, digital counters with memory, and remote controls.

Videocassette. A fairly recent development in which the videotape is enclosed in a cartridge. The cassette may contain a commercially produced program or be blank for off-the-air taping. The videocassette is played back in conventional television sets via a special attachment. Off-air taping regulations are discussed in Chapter 10.

Television can do a great deal for education. It can bring the whole world, together with its best teachers and educational materials, into the classroom. Because it is such a high-intensity medium, it can shape attitudes as well as convey factual information. New courses can be offered and existing ones enriched. With the development of videorecorders and the possibility of instant playback, students (and teachers) have opportunities otherwise unavailable for self-evaluation.

Like motion pictures, television supplies a combination of visual and verbal stimuli. In addition it has several distinct advantages. It can reach a number of audiences simultaneously, and it can be both broadcast and received at the same time. Furthermore, no additional equipment, such as screens or separate speakers, are required, nor are special viewing conditions like darkened rooms necessary. It is also capable of supplying eyewitness news items. However, television programs are not able to provide for the great range of student differences; allow for audience reaction, or feedback; or check to see if the material is being understood.

The major networks will provide programming information on request. To find out what programs are scheduled, write the following network contacts:

Director of ABC Community Relations, ABC-TV, 1330 Avenue of the Americas, New York, NY 10019

Director of Educational and Community Services, CBS Broadcast Group, 51 W. 52 St., New York, NY 10019

Director, Corporate Information Services, NBC-TV, 30 Rockefeller Plaza, New York, NY 10020

Director of Program Information, PBS, 475 L'Enfant Plaza SW, Washington, DC 20024

In addition, consult local affiliates about upcoming, locally produced programs; local cable companies for their programming schedules; and *TV Guide* for any supplemental listings.

Program guides that include synopses and activities for television specials can be obtained by writing:

Cultural Information Service, 15 W. 24 St., New York, NY 10010

Prime Time School Television, 40 E. Huron, Chicago, IL 60611

Teachers Guides to Television, 699 Madison Ave., New York, NY 10021

WGBH, 125 Western Ave., Allston, MA 02134

WNET, 356 W. 58 St., New York, NY 10019

WQED, 482 Fifth Ave., Pittsburgh, PA 15213

Library media specialists can also purchase or rent videocassettes or films of television specials from many distributors. Write for their catalogs. Several are listed below:

ABC Wide World of Learning, Inc., 1330 Avenue of the Americas, New York, NY 10019

Agency for Instructional Television, Box A, Bloomington, IN 47402

Films Incorporated, 1144 Wilmette Ave., Wilmette, IL 60091

Films Incorporated, 440 Park Ave. S., New York, NY 10016

Learning Corporation of America, 1350 Avenue of the Americas, New York, NY 10019

PBS: The Public Television Library, Video Program Services, 475 L'Enfant Plaza SW, Washington, DC 20024

Perspective Films & Video, 65 E. Southwater Street, Chicago, IL 60601

Time-Life Video, 1230 Avenue of the Americas, New York, NY 10020

Criteria for television programs are similar to those for motion pictures. The program should show adequate planning and effective presentation. In the case of ETV and ITV programs, this involves cooperation between resource teachers and educators, performers and program production personnel. Each program should attempt to use the potential of the medium and not be simply a filmed lecture. The picture should be clear and undistorted, with details easily discernible, and when possible, it should be employed to clarify and add emphasis. Used with care and with wisdom, television can supply a fascinating new avenue to knowledge.

Art Reproductions

Like many public libraries, school media centers are now collecting mounted and framed art reproductions for home circulation to both faculty and students. Conventional collections continue to contain unmounted prints either singly or in portfolios. When purchasing art reproductions, check, if possible, the fidelity of the copy in terms of color and detail. The degree of size reduction, if any, will depend on intended use. The quality and durability of the frame and mounting are also important considerations.

Graphics

The word "graphics" is a broad term that refers to a whole group of materials with one characteristic in common—each visualizes information through combinations of words and drawings. Usually the data are presented in a summary or otherwise condensed form. Graphics include (1) graphs, (2) charts, tables, and diagrams, (3) cartoons, and (4) posters. Regardless of type, graphics share basic criteria for quality. The material should be presented clearly and simply—in an uncluttered way and with nonrelevant elements either deemphasized or omitted. The graphic should show that attention has been paid to such basic artistic principles as balance and harmony in spatial relationships and an overall unity of presentation. Lettering should be clear and legible and color, if used, should fulfill more than a decorative purpose. The graphic should have impact and demand attention. Last, it should not be awkward or unmanageable in size but it should be large enough for its intended use.

Graphs

A graph is a pictorial device used to present numerical data and their relationships. Statistics can suddenly become meaningful when presented in graph form. The material should be clear, interestingly organized, and capable of revealing comparisons easily. There are four major types of graphs. The *line* graph, the simplest and most popular type, presents data in a simple continuous line in relation to a horizontal and vertical grid. The *bar* graph is easiest to read; it represents relationships by the length of the bars. The *circle* or *pie* graph is used to show the relation of the parts to the whole. The *pictograph* or *picture* graph uses symbols rather than lines or bars to present the material. The pictograph, which has gained in popularity in recent times, had its origins in the way in which primitive tribes kept their records.

Charts, Tables, Diagrams

These terms are often used interchangeably, but charts and tables are, generally speaking, drawings that classify or otherwise analyze data. Some examples of charts are business charts, weather charts, and mariner's charts. Youngsters can draw their own charts to organize their school work or to trace progress in a particular school subject. Tables are used to list or tabulate data, usually figures. Common examples are airline and bus schedules and railroad timetables. Diagrams are graphics that show relationships, as in a process or device. They do not necessarily have to be realistic in representation. Diagrams include flow sheets or flow charts, used to represent a sequence of operations; time lines, to plot relationships in time and events; family trees, or genealogical diagrams; and flip charts that show sequences or steps on a series of sheets rather than in a single diagram.

Cartoons

A cartoon is a drawing or series of drawings that tells a story quickly. Cartoons may be used either to instruct or to entertain. Generally, they are so small that some sort of projection device, an opaque projector, for example, must be used for group viewing. Political and satirical cartoons rely heavily on symbols, which often must be explained to students before a cartoon can be understood.

Posters

Posters also tell short stories. Good posters relay a single specific message in a clear, dynamic manner. They have instant appeal and clarity of design and are large enough to be seen at a distance. Some sources of free or inexpensive posters are travel agencies, museums, art galleries, government offices, and industrial concerns.

Multimedia Kits and Educational Games

Many manufacturers package together different types of media dealing with the same subject. For example, a kit on a foreign country might contain items of realia, a portfolio of pictures, a film, slides, and perhaps filmstrips. Many schools have assembled their own kits, particularly in areas of local history, industry, and social conditions. Individual components of a kit or multimedia device should be evaluated separately as well as in relation to the rest of the material.

Educational games attempt to involve the learner in an educational situation while at the same time providing interest and amusement. Most games try to simulate a real-life situation. Thus, through projection and role-playing, the student undergoes experiences very similar to reality. Games have been developed around historical events, social problems, family situations, and political and economic questions. An imaginatively structured game that is accurate in detail can be an exciting way to produce active participation in the learning process.

Programmed Materials

Programmed instruction is a teaching method that breaks down the material to be learned into short, logical steps and presents each step in a separate discrete segment, or "frame." Students must respond by answering a question correctly before moving from one frame to the next. The student is also given immediate feedback on the degree of correctness in his response.

As recently as 1954, B. F. Skinner first proposed the idea that human beings could learn efficiently by the same methods that he utilized with his pigeons at Harvard University. The methods relied heavily on the reinforcement theory of learning, whereby after a correct answer is given, a reward is supplied to strengthen or reinforce the learning. Skinner's studies formed the theoretical basis for programmed instruction. Since that time a variety of commercially prepared programs have appeared in a number of different formats. When the program is presented in conventional book form, it is known as a programmed textbook. In this format each frame takes up part of a page and the correct answers are usually found by turning the page. Other programs involve various combinations of print and nonprint materials. Sometimes a program is housed in a mechanical device, a "teaching machine." Teaching machines vary in sophistication—from those operated manually by the student to complex, computer-based response systems. In general, programs—regardless of the method of presentation—are of three types: (1) *linear*, in which each student must work through every frame to complete the program, (2) *branching*— also known as *intrinsic* or *adaptive*—in which students may skip or bypass parts of the program after demonstrating mastery of the contents of those parts (when used in a programmed textbook, this technique is known as a scrambled text), and (3) *combination*, programs that are a mixture of the first two types.

Programs may be used in a variety of ways: (1) to teach new knowledge and skills completely independent of other presentational methods, (2) to enrich or supplement the present teaching program, (3) to complement regular teaching, (4) to review material, (5) to help absentees or poorer students catch up on regular classroom work. Proponents of programmed teaching suggest a number of reasons for using this medium in teaching. In summary, programs (1) allow educators to organize their material into logical, step-by-step presentations, (2) reduce teaching gaps and cheating, (3) offer flexible instructional possibilities for use by groups or by individuals, in classrooms, study carrels, or at home, (4) allow individualization of learning through self-pacing, (5) give teachers a concrete and immediate check on a student's progress, (6) force students to be active learners, (7) give students an immediate check on their progress, (8) reduce student error, (9) contain a "built-in" motivation, (10) free teachers for more professional tasks, (11) are often more efficient in realizing specific knowledge goals than are other forms of instruction, (12) are in some cases inexpensive, (13) are in many cases pretested and revised to ensure validity and reliability, and (14) can be nonverbal in scope.

Critics of programmed instruction use the following points to bring out the limitations of this method of instruction:

1. Programs lack intrinsic motivation. Motivation in its most effective form is a social phenomenon. Because the learner works in isolation, this form of motivation is missing.

2. The claim of individualized instruction in programs is a myth. Fundamentally, except for differences in pacing, students are learning the same thing—there is basically little provision for the child to develop or to express him- or herself creatively as an individual.

3. Programs compartmentalize knowledge in a way that makes cross-disciplinary approaches to subject matter difficult.

4. Basic principles and concepts are sometimes lost in programmed learning because knowledge is so fragmented into small steps that the broad aspects of a subject may be lost.

5. At present not all educational objectives can be programmed. Successful programs now appear to be limited to areas where mastery of specific information is the chief educational goal.

Perhaps the recent disillusionment in educational circles with programmed instruction came about because the medium was so patently misused in many situations. Instead of adapting programs to specific situations, integrating their use with other teaching methods and materials, and being willing to change traditional classroom organizational patterns concerning timetables and scheduling to accommodate this form of individualized instruction, many school systems began introducing programs before acquiring sufficient knowledge of the concept to implement its use efficiently and effectively.

Some school districts have hired programmers or trained their own personnel to construct programs that are custom-made for their own curriculum. This is a specialized, difficult, and expensive task and unfortunately one that is a luxury for most districts. Most rely on programs that are available for purchase. Recent developments in computer-assisted instruction (CAI) have created a new interest in the programming concept (see Chapter 9).

Several questions should be kept in mind before choosing commercially produced programs: Does the program (or part of it) contain the information you are trying to convey and is the approach to the knowledge compatible with your teaching goals? Is it logically constructed at a level suitable to your students? Is the material interestingly presented? Is it of suitable length to present the material effectively without inducing boredom? Is it linear or branching? If the former, will it hold the attention of the students using it and still accommodate their range of abilities and skills? Are the groups on which the program was pretested comparable to the ones that will be using it? Is there ample evidence that sufficient field tests have been made with the program to assure its quality? Will the administration of the program create the need for changes in the school's organizational pattern? Are those who will administer the program aware of these problems (for example, what to do with the students who finish first) and able, through preplanning, to cope with them?

Maps and Globes

Maps and globes are to-scale representations of a geographical area or areas. Both media involve sophisticated abstractions and their use therefore requires of students special skills related to the students' comprehension levels and ability to deal with symbols.

Maps and globes may sometimes be used together, but they differ basically in two qualities: dimension and accuracy. Whereas a globe is a three-dimensional model, usually of the world, most maps are flat or two-dimensional. No map can be considered as accurate as a globe. Even raised-surface topographical relief maps cannot usually convey the rounded quality of the total earth's surface, while flat maps of the earth may in fact distort the true nature of the earth's surface (this distortion varies from one projection to another). On the other hand, detail is difficult to portray on a globe, and only one-half of a globe can be seen at one time.

Globes can portray a variety of conditions—geographical, political, economic, or social—but if more than two relationships are shown on a single globe, there is a danger of confusion. Globes come in many sizes. A 16-inch diameter is usually the smallest suitable for group viewing. Larger globes are expensive and take up greater amounts of space (some inflatable models are now available, however). Many have raised surfaces to indicate physical features. Others, usually called slated globes, are constructed of materials that can be written on, but easily erased. Globes should be constructed of a durable material and, except in unusual cases, come in a flexible mounting—that is, one that the globe can be removed from and returned to easily. A popular form of mounting is the cradlemount with a gyro or horizon ring that allows for simulation of the earth's spinning.

Maps, like globes, can also portray a variety of relationships and, in comparison with globes, are much more flexible, versatile, and capable of conveying a greater variety of facts. Again, there is always the danger of overcrowding, of trying to convey too much material on a single map. In their zeal to provide accurate and complete information, cartographers can obscure the essentials through excess detail. This is particularly true on many historical maps that attempt in-depth coverage of great periods of time.

Maps vary in size according to the use for which they are intended. In addition to a degree of simplicity relative to use, a map's symbols should be easy to read, its scales and area markers should be plainly visible, and its colors and type size should be suitable to the contents. Additional considerations for maps are: (1) nature of the projection and its suitability to the material, (2) method of indicating the projection, (3) presence of an index, (4) up-to-dateness or, with historical maps, a cross-reference from old place names to those currently in use, (5) number of inserts and their value, (6) inclusion of parallels of latitude and meridians of longitude and their frequency, (7) accuracy of directions, boundaries, and areas, (8) storage facilities necessary (some maps can be folded, others must be stored flat), and (9) construction strength and glare-proof qualities.

Maps and globes are available from a variety of sources. In addition to commercial outlets, travel agencies, and transportation and petroleum companies, the U.S. government, as well as newspapers and periodicals, are fine sources that may be tapped.

Models, Dioramas, Mock-ups

A model is a recognizable, three-dimensional representation of an object that often involves a change in size relationship with the real thing. Through the use of models an object can be brought into a classroom in replica form that in real life would be too large or too small for convenient viewing. Also, cutaway models can show the inside of an object, for example, the interior of an internal-combustion engine or of human anatomy.

A diorama depicts a scene by using realistic replicas of objects in the foreground and a painted curved backdrop that gives the impression of depth. Thus the illusion of reality is created. Dioramas are often used to portray historical events or distant places.

A mock-up differs from an ordinary model in two ways: (1) it usually has moving parts, and (2) it is more abstract and less realistic than the model. Unnecessary details are either eliminated or abridged, and important elements are stressed.

In evaluating models, dioramas, and mock-ups, make sure that size relationships are made clear, that parts are suitably labeled, and that colors and composition of the materials help stress important features. The size of the model in relation to the nature of the group using it is also important, and finally, if the model can be taken apart, it should be easy to reassemble.

Opaque Pictures and Objects

Opaque projection is one of the oldest and simplest methods of showing materials to a group. It allows projection of still pictures of unique material without the preliminary photographic process necessary in the preparation of filmstrips and slides. Its chief asset is its versatility. Materials that may be projected include almost all kinds of printed matter—book pages, pictures, clippings, maps, and students' papers—as well as a wide variety of specimens and objects—such as leaves, rocks, coins, stamps, seashells, and fabrics. Time to prepare materials for projection is almost nil, and the enlarged projections can be easily traced onto a chalkboard for further classroom use. An additional advantage of the opaque projector is its ease of operation.

On the deficit side are several limitations. First, because this mode of projection relies on reflecting, or bouncing light off an object rather than having light pass through it, the source of light must be very strong and, more important, the room kept in total darkness. Second, for best results the projector is usually placed in front of the group; thus the teacher's back is to the audience, the view for students directly behind the projector may be restricted, and opening and closing some projectors results in sudden and distracting periods of intense glare for those close to the machine. Last, opaque projectors are often more bulky and cumbersome than other kinds of projection equipment.

Microslides

Microslides, or microscope slides, may be produced locally, but more frequently commercially prepared slides are purchased. Microslides can be projected by a microprojector so that a large group may see together what otherwise could be seen by one person using a microscope. The advantages of microprojectors are many: The need for each student to have a microscope is eliminated; the teacher can point out the important aspects of each slide to an entire class at once; time spent in instruction on the use of the microscope, focusing techniques, and such, is reduced or perhaps eliminated. Even slides showing living organisms can be projected in this way, but close care must be taken not to let heat generated from the light of the microprojector damage the slide material.

Realia

Realia are authentic materials or real objects and include such diverse articles as a leaf, a piece of cloth, an Indian arrowhead, or a frog preserved in formaldehyde. Bringing real objects into the educational process allows students direct, firsthand experiences. They are able, if necessary, to touch, smell, handle, taste, or manipulate the object. There is no language barrier to overcome, and the essential qualities of the material are conveyed much more accurately and clearly than through any type of reproduction.

The need for realia varies with the students' experiential level, availability of objects, and feasibility of incorporating the realia into a media center collection. Many real objects are too large, for example, or too expensive for inclusion. The media center staff should work with faculty, parents, and students to build a collection of objects, particularly those found in the everyday environment. Some examples: stamps; coins; butterflies, leaves, and other examples of flora and fauna; election posters, buttons, and related materials; fabrics; raw materials; and utensils.

Certain problems are inherent in the use of realia. Many objects are too small to be seen by a large group at once, others are too fragile or costly to be handled by students, and still others might create safety problems if not used with care. Nevertheless, the use of realia helps to bridge the gap between classroom teaching and real life and is also an excellent way to attract and hold the attention of students.

GENERAL CRITERIA FOR SELECTING
AUDIOVISUAL EQUIPMENT

Criteria for selecting audiovisual equipment vary considerably depending on the type of items being selected and the specific use for which each is intended. Some general criteria that may be applied regardless of the nature of the equipment under consideration follow. Specific lists on individual items (projectors, tape recorders) are given in the next section.

Safety

This consideration is of particular importance if the equipment is to be used by children. Make sure that there are no rough protruding edges, that the equipment is well balanced and does not topple easily, that dangerous moving parts (such as fan blades) are not exposed, and that electrical connections are suitably covered and grounded. Where applicable, simple and direct instructions for use should be included, preferably printed on the machine. It is also important to determine that no further hazards are produced during use—for example, a machine that generates excessive heat during operation can be a potential source of danger for youngsters.

Ease of Use

One frequent stumbling block to the use of audiovisual equipment is the complexity of the procedures necessary for its operation. For example, the bother of setting up a portable roller screen and threading a projector have been formidable deterrents to the use of the 16mm film. The use of permanently installed wall screens and self-threading projectors have helped change this particular situation.

Factors to be considered in determining ease of use are the number of steps necessary for operation, number of controls (switches, plugs) to be activated, accessibility and ease of use of these controls and any directions for their operation, and the manual dexterity needed. The length and nature of the formal instruction for successfully operating the machine are also important.

Performance

The piece of equipment must operate efficiently and consistently at a high level of performance. Depending on the type of equipment, this "high standard" involves such factors as the nature of the picture or image, fidelity of sound reproduction, presence of speed controls, amount of distracting noise or light produced, and quality of mechanical construction.

Size, Weight, Design

The physical properties of a piece of equipment often predetermine use levels. For example, lightness of weight and carrying ease are two essential characteristics of equipment intended for home circulation. Great bulk inhibits use; so do poor or inadequate cases or carrying devices. Not only should the design and exterior be attractive; it should also be capable of withstanding hard use.

Maintenance and Service

Equipment should be built sturdily enough to hold up under the tough wear of a school situation. Strongly built equipment requires fewer repairs, but if minor ones become necessary, these machines should be constructed so that the repairs can be made quickly and easily. Replacement parts should be available, and suitable warranties or guarantees should be issued at the time of purchase. Two additional items for consideration are (1) the amount of "on-the-spot" repair service available from the manufacturer or distributor as opposed to the time-consuming, costly process of sending an item back to the factory, and (2) the availability from the manufacturer of personnel to give in-service training in the operation of the equipment.

Compatibility

Each new piece of equipment under consideration must be seen in relation to the school's entire media inventory to determine whether the acquisition of this new equipment will provide a logical extension of the existing collection. Often only special materials can be used with a particular machine, making the dual investment in both equipment and materials prohibitive. If a new item does essentially the same job as a model already in the collection, perhaps a duplication of existing equipment might be advised over buying the new material and expending valuable in-service-training time in acquainting patrons with its operation. The specifications of each new piece of equipment should be checked to see if spare parts and repair operations are similar to those used with equipment already in the collection.

Versatility

The number and variety of uses that can be made of a piece of equipment should strongly influence selection, particularly when funds are limited. Often the same machine can be used effectively in a variety of teaching situations—for large-group and small-group instruction, at home and in the classroom, or with primary children and high school students. In other cases, the addition of simple adapters can change some pieces of equipment to accept other types of materials. For example, an attachment may be purchased to convert some filmstrip projector models into slide projectors or microfilm viewers into ones that also accept microfiche.

Availability of Software

There have been incidences of manufacturers marketing equipment for which there has not been a sufficient amount of compatible educational material issued to justify the initial equipment purchase. Promises of greater output often have not been met. As a result, many schools have inventories of expensive equipment and diminishing opportunities for using it. This was particularly true a few years ago with the rapid development of a variety of teaching machines without the necessary accompanying programs. The media selector should determine the nature and extent of the materials available suitable for the equipment under consideration. Occasionally, as in the case of Super 8mm sound film, for example, an initial delay in purchase of equipment until film production plans for the various systems were announced allowed extra time to weigh the merits of each before final acquisition plans were made.

Cost

The price of each prospective purchase must be evaluated in terms of the school's total equipment budget. Sometimes the purchase of expensive items will have to be postponed, or less expensive ones substituted, because of budgetary limitations. However, in the selection process the quality of the product should always be emphasized. Price lists can be consulted to find out costs of comparable equipment from other companies, but it should be stressed that when an item is priced higher than that of a competitor, superior performance standards could be the reason.

Need

Finally, all the above factors must be weighed against the answers to questions that probe the long-range usefulness of the acquisition: Is the purpose for which this equipment is being purchased worthy of the expense? What will be the consequences if the equipment is not acquired? Will the equipment be used often enough and by enough people to warrant purchase now?

SPECIFIC CRITERIA FOR SELECTING AUDIOVISUAL EQUIPMENT

Audio Equipment

Tape Recorders

Tape recorders are classified by two major types: reel-to-reel (which usually involves some form of manual threading) and cassette recorders. The latter type is more easily loaded and often less costly. Inexpensive playback equipment for cassettes has also become increasingly available.

The speed with which tape passes through the machine is measured in inches per second (ips), and it varies, with $1^7/_8$ips the standard for cassettes and reel-to-reel recorders usually handling speeds of $3\frac{3}{4}$ips and $7\frac{1}{2}$ips. Quarter- or four-track stereophonic tape is common for reel-to-reel machines, and most prerecorded tapes are in this format. As a rule, the faster the tape speed, the greater the fidelity of sound. The quality of the sound one settles for is an important evaluative criterion and depends primarily on the uses to be made of the machine. For voice reproduction only, inexpensive monophonic recorders and playbacks will usually suffice. Sound quality can be tested simply by recording and playing slow music through the machine. Other criteria include convenience and speed of rewinding, erasing or dubbing mechanisms, ease of threading and operating, type of microphone supplied (most are unidirectional, some are bidirectional or omnidirectional), presence of an automatic level control that adjusts the sound level being recorded, and the nature of the power source (AC current, battery, or both). Many tape recorders have a tape footage counter to aid in indexing tapes, several jacks for various kinds of input (radio, phonograph, microphone) and individual listening devices, a monitoring switch, and an automatic shutoff that stops the machine when no tape is going through. Both volume and tone controls should be present. Optional accessories that are often sold with tape recorders are earphones, a foot pedal (a help in transcribing from tape), a microphone stand and carrying case, and remote controls for connecting an automatic slide projector.

Record Players

Record players share many specific criteria with tape recorders, such as the necessity of having both tone and volume controls and the desirability of several jacks (often contained in a separate output box) to allow a number of listeners with headphones to tune in at the same time. Also, as in tape recorders, the quality of the sound reproduction required from your record player should correspond to the uses for which it is intended. Most record players can accommodate several formats—monaural, stereo, or both, at several speeds—measured as revolutions per minute (rpm): 16¾, 33⅓, 45, or 78rpm (a separate stylus should be provided for playing 78rpm records). The cartridge and stylus should be easy to replace and of a standard design. The tracking pressure (the pressure with which the stylus is forced into the groove) should not be too heavy, because this creates excessive record wear. Manual rather than automatic changers are recommended for schools. In some models the speakers can be separated from the machine and with others a microphone can be attached and the machine used as a public-address system.

Radios

Criteria for choosing radios include many of those used with other audio equipment. Particular attention should be paid to the quality of sound, whether AM, FM, or both are received, and the presence of jacks for taping or earphones.

Microform Equipment

Equipment associated with microforms falls into three broad categories: (1) readers, (2) reader-printers, and (3) equipment for local production of microforms.

Readers

No readers presently on the market will accept all microform formats, and the choice of a reader should be compatible with the kinds of microforms that are or will be collected. Also, since converting from one form to another generally requires special adapters, it is often less troublesome to have separate readers for each format.

In addition to the general criteria for choosing equipment (safety, flexibility, and so on), the following specific criteria should be followed in selecting microform readers:

1. Be aware of the important relationship between the reduction and magnification ratios of material. When this is 1:1, the material is reproduced on the reader screen at the same size as the original. However, sometimes for ease of reading a larger image will be needed, a ratio increase to 1:2, for example.

2. Carefully check the physical properties of the screen. Some readers have internal rear-view projection onto translucent screens while others have external projection onto opaque screens. In any case, the screen should be of adequate size. Ideally, it should accommodate the entire page, but if this is not possible, a scanning device should be present to easily move the image across the screen. Brightness and contrast should be uniform on all parts of the screen and at a level that promotes comfortable reading. The image should be clear and sharp, but without glare.

3. Carefully examine machine specifications to determine if it is possible to rotate the image (maps and charts are often published vertically rather than horizontally on the page); check the adequacy of the film-advance mechanism and see whether multiple-lens turrets are available to give a choice of several magnifications. The variety of readers is enormous; they come in many sizes, shapes, and weights— from large-screen, tentlike readers to small, hand-held microviewers. Unfortunately, few inexpensive, lightweight microform readers of superior quality are as yet on the market. Media center personnel should avail themselves of the many opportunities to check the quality of readers, reader-printers, and production equipment before purchase; reports from other users, demonstrations, manufacturer's specifications, and evaluations in the literature should be utilized.

Reader-Printers

Reader-printers are designed to perform the function of a microform reader as well as to produce hard copy from the microform. Most microprinters produce only negative prints from a positive microform or vice versa. Some machines, however, are capable of producing positive prints from positive forms.

Four basic printing methods are used in these machines: (1) photographic (similar to the darkroom developing process; this is a wet method), (2) electrolytic (another wet process using paper attached to foil), (3) electrostatic (can be either a wet or dry process, depending on the manufacturer; usually uses ordinary paper stock), (4) dry silver (a dry process using heat to effect the developing). Each method is usually associated with a particular manufacturer's line or lines. Specific criteria for the microform printer involve (1) print quality (type of print, size, legibility, contrast, permanence, cost) and (2) print mechanism (complexity, paper load, time required).

Equipment for Local Production of Microforms

There are two basic methods of creating microforms: The first, using magnetic tape from a computer, is rarely available to school library media centers; the second, much less rare, involves converting hard copy to master microfilm by photographing the material and processing or developing it. If aperture cards are used, a third step, mounting, is necessary.

The cameras used in microfilming are of two basic types: *planetary* (or flatbed) and *rotary* (or flow). The planetary camera is suspended above the material to be filmed and is manually operated. It is useful for filming books and large documents. The rotary camera films documents in sheet form by feeding them manually or by an automatic feeder through a slot in the front of the machine. Both types of cameras can produce either 16mm or 35mm film. Processors produce as an end product rolls of microfilm that may either be retained in the spool format or cut up and mounted. Some processors require the same darkroom facilities as the usual film-developing process. Because processors can be extremely expensive, school districts will often send their films to commercial processors. Mounting can be done through a simple hand-held device that both inserts the film and crops it to the desired size. Also available are many pieces of equipment that can perform more than one of the above steps successfully. Camera-processors are not uncommon, for example, and there is one that can photograph a document, process it, and produce a completed aperture card in less than a minute.

Motion Picture Projectors

Both 16mm and 8mm projectors share many criteria. The number of formats a machine can accept is important with both types. In the 16mm area this involves chiefly silent or sound film (an optical playback system is preferable to a magnetic one) and a cartridge or the usual reel-to-reel format. The 8mm field offers additional choices involving regular versus Super 8 film as well as different sized cartridges that range from the short continuous loop, single-concept film cartridges, to large ones that contain films of conventional length. The nature of the software to be used in a collection will dictate the types of projectors to be purchased.

If the machine must be threaded manually, this should be a simple operation to perform; if threading is automatic, manual dethreading should be possible during the showing. Some machines have a lower loop restorer. Other items to be checked are quality of sound and light output, steadiness of image, quality of framing device (to prevent parts of separate pictures appearing at the same time), amount of machine noise during operation, ease of focusing, and speed of the rewind process. The use of sprocket guards on some machines has cut the wear on film. Other machines are able to accept old or damaged film without causing the projector to malfunction. Additional controls found on some models allow for projecting still frames and a single-frame advance, while others have an automatic stop and shutoff switch. Remote controls are often available. Optional accessories may include a microphone, reel arm extension, rear-view projection mirror, zoom or wide-angle lenses, spare take-up reels, and a built-in screen.

Still Picture Projectors

Filmstrip, Slide, and Combination Filmstrip/Slide Projectors

Simplicity of use and built-in safeguards against misuse are two important criteria for evaluating filmstrip and slide projectors. With filmstrip projectors the film slot should be designed to prevent improper threading. Whether the machine is manually or automatically operated, the smoothness of the film feed into the projector is also important. The ease of use of the framing device, film take-up and rewind provisions, and safety features to prevent scratching of the film should also be checked.

In a slide-only projector the following should be determined: the number of slide sizes it accepts, amount of storage in slide carriers, whether a single slide can be used in a tray, provisions for skipping or holding slides, and in an automatic projector, the method for controlling the time interval between slides.

In both slide and filmstrip projectors investigate the number and nature of remote controls available; the amount of stray light, noise, and heat during projection; the brilliance and sharpness of the image; availability of lenses in various focal lengths; and hold controls for automatic machines. Such accessories as dust covers, projector stands, and extension cords are often available.

The ease of converting from slide to filmstrip projection should also be considered in combination machines. For individual filmstrip and slide viewers the power source (AC, battery, or both) and the size of the viewing screen are also important.

Opaque Projectors

Size, weight, and overall bulk have always been important evaluation points for opaque projectors. The size of the aperture and the maximum thickness of objects that can be projected should also be determined. The necessary amount of light should be produced without excessive heat or undue glare when the aperture is opened during operation. Some opaque projectors come equipped with built-in pointers to indicate particular parts of a picture as well as with additional lenses.

Overhead Projectors

The overhead projector has, for reasons chiefly involving ease of use and versatility, become one of the most frequently found pieces of AV equipment in today's schools. Before choosing an overhead, apply the general equipment criteria as well as the following points: The projection stage or aperture should be able to accommodate various sizes of transparent material for both vertical and horizontal projection (the standard stage size is 10 × 10 inches, and commercially produced transparencies are usually 7½ × 9½ inches). Some heat buildup in the stage is inevitable, but check, by operating the machine for about 30 minutes, to see if this buildup is so excessive that it melts grease markings or makes the stage difficult to touch.

The projector should be easily focused. For example, close-up projection on a small screen requires that the lens must be moved away from the transparency; this adjustment, as well as those necessary for tilting the head (preferable to tilting the entire machine) should be easily accomplished. Note that if a line drawn from the lens of the projector to the center of the screen does not form a right angle, a keystoned or wedge-shaped image will be projected. This distortion will be particularly noticeable if the projector is placed below and close to the screen. (Motion pictures are generally projected at a greater distance from the screen and keystoning is therefore not as great a problem with this medium). To minimize this effect, the top of the projection screen should be tilted toward the overhead projector. On some models additional lenses are available, such as wide lenses for use close to the screen and long lenses for auditoriums.

The image should be bright and consistently sharp and clear at both the center and the edges. Absence of glare and extraneous light is desirable—some models are equipped with glare shields. Most overheads are cooled by a blower controlled by some variation on a thermostatic control. The blower should be quiet and vibration-free. The machine should have an attachment to enable the use of blank rolls of transparent material, such as acetate.

The low maintenance cost is an established asset for the overhead. Few moving parts and simplicity of operation help reduce this cost. Related to overall ease of operation is the ease of changing the projection lamp (the average life of a lamp is usually about 75 hours); some machines offer, as an option, replacement attachments that involve only switching a knob or pressing a lever to make a change when a lamp burns out. Other maintenance features include convenience of fuse replacement, ease of cleaning, and simplicity of control switches. The outlet cord should be attached to the machine to prevent its loss. The standard length of the cord is 15 feet. On portable machines a storage space should be provided for the cord.

Many models have unusual features and accessories. For example, some machines are turned on or off simply by placing a transparency on the stage, others have attachments for slide projection. Now on the market are remote-controlled, automatic overhead projectors operated by a push-button switch similar to that on an automatic slide projector. Transparencies used in these machines are generally smaller than those used on conventional models. Overheads with sound attachments have also been developed and are currently being produced.

Television Receivers and Recorders

For use with groups, a television receiver should have a minimum screen size of 23 inches. Controls for brightness, contrast, and vertical and horizontal hold should be easily operated. The presence of jacks for a tape recorder, a videotape recorder, and/or headphones increases the versatility of the receiver. Other criteria concern loudspeaker size and quality of sound, whether both UHF and VHF are received, and whether the set may be easily adjusted for closed-circuit television. Criteria for videotape recorders (VTRs) are discussed earlier in this chapter.

SELECTION AIDS FOR EDUCATIONAL MATERIALS

Basic Selection Aids

Retrospective

Association for Childhood Education International. *Bibliography of Books for Children, 1980.* Washington, D.C.: ACEI, 1981.

Brown, Lucy Gregor. *Core Media Collection for Secondary Schools.* New York: R. R. Bowker, 1979.

———, and McDavid, Betty. *Core Media Collection for Elementary Schools.* New York: R. R. Bowker, 1978.

Carlsen, G. Robert. *Books and the Teen-age Reader: A Guide for Teachers, Librarians, and Parents.* New York: Harper (Bantam), 1980.

Child Study Children's Book Committee. *Children's Books of the Year.* Bank Street College of Education. Annual.

Children's Catalog, 14th ed. New York: H. W. Wilson, 1981.

Gillespie, John T., and Gilbert, Christine B. *Best Books for Children: Preschool through the Middle Grades,* 2nd ed. New York: R. R. Bowker, 1981.

Greene, Ellin, and Shoenfeld, Madalynne. *A Multimedia Approach to Children's Literature: A Selective List of Films, Filmstrips and Recordings Based on Children's Books,* 2nd ed. Chicago: American Library Association, 1977.

Haviland, Virginia. *The Best of Children's Books 1964–1978.* Washington, D.C.: Government Printing Office, 1981.

Huck, Charlotte S. *Children's Literature in the Elementary School.* New York: Holt, 1976.

Junior High School Library Catalog, 4th ed. New York: H. W. Wilson, 1980.

Library of Congress, Children's Literature Center. *Children's Books—[Year].* Washington, D.C.: Government Printing Office. Annual.

National Association of Independent Schools, Ad Hoc Library Committee. *Books for Secondary School Libraries,* 6th ed. New York: R. R. Bowker, 1981.

New York Public Library, Office of Children's Services. *Children's Books and Recordings.* New York: New York Public Library. Annual.

——. *Books for the Teen Age.* New York: New York Public Library. Annual.

Quimby, Harriet, and Weber, Rosemary. *Building a Children's Literature Collection.* Middletown, Conn.: Choice, 1978.

Senior High School Library Catalog, 12th ed. New York: H. W. Wilson, 1982.

Sutherland, Zena. *The Best in Children's Books: 1966–72.* Chicago: University of Chicago Press, 1973.

——. *The Best in Children's Books: 1973–78.* Chicago: University of Chicago Press, 1980.

——, et al. *Children and Books,* 6th ed. Glenview, Ill.: Scott Foresman, 1981.

Winkel, Lois. *The Elementary School Library Collection: A Guide to Books and Other Media,* 12th ed. Williamsport, Pa.: Bro-Dart Foundation, 1979.

Current

Booklist (semimonthly exc. monthly in August). American Library Association.

Bulletin of the Center for Children's Books (monthly exc. August). University of Chicago Press.

Choice (monthly exc. one July-August issue). American Library Association. For adult materials.

Curriculum Review (5 issues per year). Curriculum Review.

Horn Book (6 issues per year). Horn Book. Chiefly for elementary grades.

Library Journal (semimonthly exc. monthly in July and August). R. R. Bowker. For adult books.

Media and Methods (monthly). North American Publishing.

School Library Journal (monthly September through May). R. R. Bowker.

Voice of Youth Advocates (6 issues per year). VOYA, Inc. Chiefly for junior-senior high grades.

Additional Selection Aids by Type of Material

Books and Other Printed Materials

The Alan Review. Assembly on Literature for Adolescents. Urbana, Ill.: National Council of Teachers of English. 3 times a year.

American Association for the Advancement of Science. *Science Books and Films.* Washington, D.C.: American Association for the Advancement of Science. 4 times a year.

American Jewish Committee's Institute of Human Relations. *About 100 Books.* American Jewish Committee, 1977.

Association for Library Service to Children, ALA. *Let's Read Together.* Chicago: American Library Association, 1981.

Association for Library Service to Children, ALA. *Notable Children's Books.* Chicago: American Library Association. Annual.

———. *Notable Children's Books 1940–1970.* Chicago: American Library Association, 1977.

———. *Notable Children's Books 1971–1975.* Chicago: American Library Association, 1981.

Bader, Barbara. *American Picturebooks from Noah's Ark to the Beast Within.* Macmillan, 1976.

Baker, Augusta, and Greene, Ellin. *Storytelling: Art and Technique.* New York: R. R. Bowker, 1977.

Baskin, Barbara H., and Harris, Karen H. *Books for the Gifted Child.* New York: R. R. Bowker, 1980.

———. *Notes from a Different Drummer: A Guide to Juvenile Fiction Portraying the Handicapped.* New York: R. R. Bowker, 1977.

Bauer, Caroline Filler. *This Way to Books.* New York: H. W. Wilson, 1982.

Bernstein, Joanne E. *Books to Help Children Cope with Separation and Loss,* 2nd ed. New York: R. R. Bowker, 1983.

Bodart, Joni. *Booktalk!* New York: H. W. Wilson, 1980.

Books in Print. New York: R. R. Bowker. Annual. Nonevaluative.

Buttlar, Lois T., and Wynar, Lubomyr R. *Building Ethnic Collections: An Annotated Guide for School Media Centers and Public Libraries.* Littleton, Colo.: Libraries Unlimited, 1977.

Canadian Materials: An Annotated Critical Bibliography for Canadian

Schools and Libraries. Ottawa, Ont.: Canadian Library Association. 3 times a year.

Carr, Jo. *Beyond Fact: Nonfiction for Children and Young People.* Chicago: American Library Association, 1982.

Chadbourne, Sherry P. *Bibliography: An Overview and the Librarian's Role.* Urbana, Ill.: National Council of Teachers of English, 1976.

Children's Books in Print. New York: R. R. Bowker. Annual. Nonevaluative.

Cianciolo, Patricia Jean. *Picture Books for Children*, 2nd ed. Chicago: American Library Association, 1981.

Davis, Enid. *Liberty Cap.* Chicago: Academy Chicago Ltd., 1977.

Deason, Hilary. *AAAS Book List*, 3rd ed. Washington, D.C.: American Association for the Advancement of Science, 1970; suppl. 1978.

————. *AAAS Science Book List for Children*, 3rd ed. Washington, D.C.: American Association for the Advancement of Science, 1972.

Dickinson, A. T., Jr. *American Historical Fiction*, 3rd. ed. Metuchen, N.J.: Scarecrow, 1971.

Donelson, Kenneth L., and Nilsen, Allen Pace. *Literature for Today's Young Adults.* Glenview, Ill.: Scott Foresman, 1980.

Dreyer, Sharon Spredemann. *The Bookfinder: A Guide to Children's Literature about the Needs and Problems of Youth Aged 2-15.* 2 vols. Circle Pines, Minn.: American Guidance Service, vol. 1, 1977; vol. 2, 1981.

Duran, Daniel Flores. *Latino Materials: A Multimedia Guide for Children and Young Adults.* Santa Barbara, Calif.: ABC-Clio, 1979.

Fast, Elizabeth T. "Publishers' Catalogs: Puffery or Resource." *Wilson Library Bulletin* 51 (October 1976): 179.

Gillespie, John T. *More Juniorplots: A Guide for Teachers and Librarians.* New York: R. R. Bowker, 1977.

————, and Lembo, Diana. *Introducing Books: A Guide for the Middle Grades.* New York: R. R. Bowker, 1970.

————. *Juniorplots: A Book Talk Manual for Teachers and Librarians.* New York: R. R. Bowker, 1967.

Gillis, Ruth J. *Children's Books for Times of Stress: An Annotated Bibliography.* Bloomington: Indiana University Press, 1978.

Guide to Book Selection. Washington, D.C.: Reading Is Fundamental (RIF), 1976.

Hadlow, Ruth M. *Children's Books Too Good to Miss*, 7th ed. New York: University Press Books, 1980.

Haviland, Virginia. *Children's Books of International Interest*, 2nd ed. Chicago: American Library Association, 1978.

Harrah, Barbara K. *Sports Books for Children.* Metuchen, N.J.: Scarecrow, 1978.

Hearne, Betsy, and Kaye, Marilyn. *Celebrating Children's Books: Essays on Children's Literature.* New York: Lothrop, 1981.

Higgins, Judith H. *Energy: A Multimedia Guide for Children and Young Adults.* Santa Barbara, Calif.: ABC-Clio, 1979.

The High/Low Report (10 monthly issues). High/Low Report.

Iarusso, Marilyn Berg. *Stories: A List of Stories to Tell and to Read Aloud.* New York: New York Public Library, 1977.

Jacob, Gale Sypher. *Independent Reading Grades One through Three: An Annotated Bibliography with Reading Levels.* Williamsport, Pa.: Bro-Dart, 1975.

Johnson, Harry A. *Ethnic American Minorities: A Guide to Media and Materials.* New York: R. R. Bowker, 1976.

Large Type Books in Print, 5th ed. New York: R. R. Bowker, 1982. Nonevaluative.

Larrick, Nancy. *A Parent's Guide to Children's Reading.* Doubleday, 1975.

Lass-Windfin, Mary Jo. *Books on American Indians and Eskimos: A Selection Guide for Children and Young Adults.* Chicago: American Library Association, 1977.

Lenz, Millicent, and Mahood, Ramona, eds. *Young Adult Literature: Background and Criticism.* Chicago: American Library Association, 1980.

LiBretto, Ellen V., ed. *High/Low Handbook: Books, Materials, and Services for the Teenage Problem Reader.* New York: R. R. Bowker, 1981.

Libros en Espanol: An Annotated List of Children's Books in Spanish. New York: New York Public Library, 1977.

Lima, Carolyn W. *A to Zoo: Subject Access to Children's Picture Books.* New York: R. R. Bowker, 1982.

MacCann, Donnarau, and Richard, Olga. *The Child's First Books: A Critical Study of Pictures and Texts.* New York: H. W. Wilson, 1973.

MacDonald, Margaret Read. *The Storyteller's Sourcebook: A Subject, Title and Motif Index to Folklore Collections for Children.* Detroit: Gale, 1982.

Matthias, Margaret, and Thiessen, Diane. *Children's Mathematics Books: A Critical Bibliography.* Chicago: American Library Association, 1979.

Mary, Jill P., and Satterlie, Elizabeth L. "Finding Books That Help the Young to Understand Themselves and Others: Recent Professional Tools." *Top of the News*, Summer 1980, pp. 345–351.

Mills, Joyce White. *The Black World in Literature for Children.* Atlanta: Atlanta University Press. Annual.

Munat, Florence Howe. "A Checklist for High/Low Books for Young Adults." *School Library Journal*, April 1981, pp. 23–27.

National Council of Teachers of English. *Adventuring with Books: A Booklist for Pre-K-Grade 8.* Urbana, Ill.: NCTE, 1977.

——. *Books for You: A Booklist for Senior High Students.* Urbana, Ill.: NCTE, 1976.

——. *Your Reading: A Booklist for Junior High Students.* Urbana, Ill.: NCTE, 1975.

Pellowski, Anne. *The World of Storytelling*. New York: R. R. Bowker, 1977.

Quimby, Harriet. *Let's Read Together*, 4th ed. Chicago: Association for Library Service to Children, 1981.

Rosenberg, Judith K. *Young People's Literature in Series: Fiction*. Littleton, Colo.: Libraries Unlimited, 1972.

———. *Young People's Literature in Series: Non-fiction and Publishers' Series*. Littleton, Colo.: Libraries Unlimited, 1973.

———. *Young People's Literature in Series: Fiction, Non-Fiction and Publishers' Series, 1973–75*. Littleton, Colo.: Libraries Unlimited, 1977.

Sawyer, Ruth. *The Way of the Storyteller*. New York: Viking, 1962.

Shapiro, Lillian L. *Fiction for Youth: A Guide to Recommended Books*. New York: Neal-Schuman, 1981.

Spache, George D. *Good Reading for Poor Readers*. Garrard, 1978.

Spirt, Diana L. *Introducing More Books: A Guide for the Middle Grades*. New York: R. R. Bowker, 1978.

Stanford, Barbara Dodds, and Amen, Karenia. *Black Literature for High School Students*. Urbana, Ill.: National Council of Teachers of English, 1978.

Stensland, Anna Lee. *Literature by and about the American Indians: An Annotated Bibliography for Junior and Senior High School Students*. Urbana, Ill.: National Council of Teachers of English, 1973.

Subject Guide to Books in Print. New York: R. R. Bowker. Annual. Nonevaluative.

Subject Guide to Children's Books in Print. New York: R. R. Bowker. Annual. Nonevaluative.

Tway, Eileen. *Reading Ladders for Human Relations*, 6th ed. Urbana, Ill.: National Council of Teachers of English, 1981.

University Press Books for Secondary School Librarians. New York: American University Press Services. Annual.

Walker, Elisor. *Book Bait*, 3rd ed. Chicago: American Library Association, 1979.

———. *Doors to More Mature Reading*. Chicago: American Library Association, 1981.

Wall, Betty. *Children's Books: Awards and Prizes*. New York: Children's Book Council, 1979.

Withrow, Dorothy; Carey, Helen B.; and Hirzel, Bertha M. *Gateways to Readable Books*, 5th ed. New York: H. W. Wilson, 1975.

Young Adult Services Division, ALA. *Best Books for Young Adults*. Chicago: American Library Association. Annual.

Ziskind, Sylvia. *Telling Stories to Children*. New York: H. W. Wilson, 1976.

Reference Works

Bell, Marion V., and Swiden, Eleanor A. *Reference Books: A Brief Guide*, 8th ed. Baltimore: Enoch Pratt Free Library, 1978.

Committee of the Reference and Adult Services Division, ALA. *Reference Books for Small and Medium-sized Libraries*, 3rd ed. Chicago: American Library Association, 1982.

"Current Reference Books." Columns in *Wilson Library Bulletin.*

Deveny, Mary Alice. *Recommended Reference Books in Paperback.* Littleton, Colo.: Libraries Unlimited, 1981.

Kister, Kenneth F. "Recommended Reference Sources for School Media Centers." *School Library Journal*, December 1980, pp. 17–20.

Peterson, Carolyn Sue. *Reference Books for Elementary and Junior High School Libraries*, 2nd ed. Metuchen, N.J.: Scarecrow, 1975.

——, and Fenton, Ann D. *Reference Books for Children.* Metuchen, N.J.: Scarecrow, 1981.

Purchasing an Encyclopedia: 12 Points to Consider. Chicago: American Library Association, 1979.

"Reference and Subscription Books Review." Columns in *Booklist.*

Wynar, Christine Gehrt. *Guide to Reference Books for School Media Centers*, 2nd ed. Littleton, Colo.: Libraries Unlimited, 1981.

Textbooks

El-Hi Textbooks in Print. New York: R. R. Bowker. Annual. Nonevaluative.

EPIE Pro/Files. Stony Brook, N.Y. (Textbook series evaluation).

Paperbacks

Association for Childhood Education International. *Excellent Paperbacks for Children.* Washington, D.C.: ACEI, 1979.

Fader, Daniel. *The New Hooked on Books.* New York: Berkley, 1977.

Gillespie, John T. *Paperback Books for Young People.* Chicago: American Library Association, 1977.

Kliatt Paperback Book Guide (3 main issues and 5 interim suppl. per year). 425 Watertown St., Newton, MA 02158.

Paperbound Books in Print. New York: R. R. Bowker. Annual. Nonevaluative.

Magazines and Newspapers

Association for Childhood Education International. *Guide to Children's Magazines.* Washington, D.C.: ACEI, 1979.

Children's Magazine Guide: Subject Index to Children's Magazines (monthly and half-yearly cumulations). 7 North Pinkney St., Madison, WI 53705.

Dobler, Lavinia, and Fuller, Muriel, eds. *The Dobler World Directory of Youth Periodicals.* Citation, 1970.

Katz, Bill, and Katz, Linda Sternberg. *Magazines for Libraries*, 4th ed. New York: R. R. Bowker, 1982.

"Magazines as Information Sources: Patterns of Student Use." *School Media Quarterly*, Summer 1980, pp. 240–244, 249–250.

Richardson, Selma K. *Periodicals for School Media Programs*. Chicago: American Library Association, 1978.

Pamphlets and Free Materials

Association for Library Service to Children, Print and Poster Evaluation Committee. "Planning for a Print and Poster Collection in Children's Libraries." *Top of the News*, Spring 1981, pp. 283–287.

——. "Sources of Art Prints for Children's Collections." *Top of the News*, Winter 1981, pp. 198–201.

"Checklist" columns in *Library Journal* and *School Library Journal*.

"Edubits" column in *Instructor*.

Educators Guide to Free Guidance Material. Randolph, Wisc.: Educators Progress Service. Annual.

Educators Guide to Free Health, Physical Education and Recreation Materials. Randolph, Wisc.: Educators Progress Service. Annual.

Educators Guide to Free Science Materials. Randolph, Wisc.: Educators Progress Service. Annual.

Educators Guide to Free Social Studies Materials. Randolph, Wisc.: Educators Progress Service. Annual.

Educators Guide to Free Teaching Aids. Randolph, Wisc.: Educators Progress Service. Annual.

Educator's Index of Free Materials. Randolph, Wisc.: Educators Progress Service. Annual.

Educator's Sourcebook of Posters—Mostly Free: For Teachers and Librarians. Salem, Ore.: Dale E. Shaffer, 1981.

Elementary Teachers Guide to Free Curriculum Materials. Educators Progress Service. Annual.

Free! The Newsletter of Free Materials and Services (5 times a year). Dyad Services (London, Ont.).

The Free Stock Photography Directory. Allentown, Pa.: Infosource Business Publications, 1980.

George Peabody College for Teachers. *Free and Inexpensive Learning Materials*, 18th ed. Nashville, Tenn.: Incentive Publications, 1976.

Goodman, Leonard H. *Current Career and Occupational Literature*. New York: H. W. Wilson. Biennial.

Kouns, B. "Practical Librarian: Clipping and Sweet Talk for Free Information." *Library Journal*, April 15, 1979, p. 897.

"Marketplace" column in *Wilson Library Bulletin*.

"Materials Available" column in Children's Book Council's *Calendar*.

"Mediabag" column in *Media and Methods*.

Pepe, Thomas J. *Free and Inexpensive Educational Aids.* New York: Dover, 1966.

Smith, Adeline Mercer. *Free Materials for Librarians.* Jefferson, N.C.: McFarland and Co., 1980.

Sources: A Guide to Print and Nonprint Materials Available from Organizations, Industry, Government Agencies, and Specialized Publications. Neal-Schuman. 3 times a year.

Vertical File Index (monthly). Wilson.

Government Documents

Consumer Information Catalog. Pueblo, Colo.: Consumer Information Center. Free. Revised periodically.

"Government Documents" column in *Booklist.*

Leidy, Philip. *A Popular Guide to Government Publications.* New York: Columbia University Press, 1976.

Library of Congress Publications in Print. Washington, D.C.: Library of Congress. Frequent revisions.

Newsome, Walter L. *New Guide to Popular Government Publications for Libraries and Home Reference.* Littleton, Colo.: Libraries Unlimited. 1978.

Sachse, Gladys. *U.S. Government Publications for Small and Medium-sized Public Libraries: A Study Guide.* Chicago: American Library Association, 1982.

Selected List of U.S. Government Publications (monthly). Washington, D.C.: Supt. of Docs. Free.

Subject Bibliographies. Washington, D.C.: Supt. of Docs. Free series.

Wittig, Alice J. *U.S. Government Publications for the School Media Center.* Littleton, Colo.: Libraries Unlimited, 1979.

General Audiovisual Sources

Audiovisual Market Place 1983. New York: R. R. Bowker. Annual.

Boyle, Deirdre. *Expanding Media.* Phoenix, Ariz.: Oryx, 1977.

Dale, Doris Cruger. *Catalogs of Audiovisual Materials: A Guide to Government Sources.* EDRS, 1981.

Emmens, Carol A., ed. *An Audio-visual Guide to American Holidays.* Metuchen, N.J.: Scarecrow, 1978.

——. *Children's Media Market Place.* New York: Neal-Schuman, 1982.

Fast, Elizabeth T. "Media: The Language of the Young." *Top of the News*, Fall 1976, pp. 50–63.

Jonassen, David H. *Non-book Media: A Self-paced Instructional Handbook for Teachers and Library Media Personnel.* Hamden, Conn.: Shoe String, 1982.

Lundgaard, Harriet. *Epiegram: Materials* (monthly). Educational Products Information Exchange (New York).

Media Index K–12 (monthly). Media Index (Pleasantville, N.Y.).

Media Review Digest. Ann Arbor, Mich.: Pierian Press. Annual.

National Audio-Visual Association. *General A.V. Communications: Planning and Producing Your A-V Materials and Presentations.* A Bibliography. Fairfax, Va.: NAVA, 1981.

National Information Center for Educational Media. *Index to Black History and Studies.* NICEM. Nonevaluative. Revised periodically.

School Product News (monthly). School Product News.

Films

Association for Library Service to Children, ALA. *Notable Children's Films.* Chicago: ALSC. Annual.

Bennett, James R. "The Way I See It ... Free Film-guides as Propaganda Tools." *Educational Leadership*, December 1979, pp. 196–199.

Cohn, Emma. "Reviewing 16mm Films." *Top of the News*, Winter 1979, pp. 153–157.

Consortium of University Film Centers. *Educational Film Locator*, 2nd ed. New York: R. R. Bowker, 1980. Nonevaluative.

Educators Guide to Free Films. Randolph, Wisc.: Educators Progress Service. Annual.

Emmens, Carol. *Short Stories on Film.* Littleton, Colo.: Libraries Unlimited, 1978.

EFLA Evaluations (10 times per year). New York: Educational Film Library Association.

Frederick, Franz J. "Minitutorial on Screening Facilities." *School Media Quarterly*, Spring 1974, pp. 237–255.

Gaffney, Maureen, ed. *More Films Kids Like.* Chicago: American Library Association, 1977.

Jones, Emily. *Manual in Film Evaluation.* New York: Educational Film Library Association, 1967.

Landers Film Reviews (bimonthly, September through June). Landers Associates (Escondido, Calif.).

Limbacher, James L. *Feature Films on 8mm, 16mm, and Videotape*, 7th ed. New York: R. R. Bowker, 1982.

Miller, Hannah E. *Films in the Classroom: A Practical Guide.* Metuchen, N.J.: Scarecrow, 1979.

National Information Center for Educational Materials. *Index to 8mm Cartridges.* Los Angeles: NICEM. Nonevaluative. Revised periodically.

———. *Index to 16mm Educational Films.* Los Angeles: NICEM. Nonevaluative. Revised periodically.

New York Library Association. *Films for Children: A Selection List.* NYLA, 1977.

Parlato, Salvatore, J., Jr. *Films—Too Good for Words: A Directory of Non-narrated 16mm Films.* New York: R. R. Bowker, 1973.

Rice, Susan, ed. *Films Kids Like.* Chicago: American Library Association, 1973.

Sightlines (quarterly). New York: Educational Film Library Association.

Young Adult Services Division, Media Selection and Usage Committee. "A to Z: A Sampler of Animated Films." *Top of the News*, Winter 1981, pp. 202–206.

Young Adult Services Division, ALA. *Selected Films for Young Adults.* Chicago: YASD. Annual.

Filmstrips and Slides

Association of Library Service to Children, ALA. *Notable Children's Film-strips.* Annual.

DeLaurier, Nancy. *Slides Buyer's Guide.* University of Missouri at Kansas City, Dept. of Art and Art History, 1974.

Educators Guide to Free Filmstrips. Randolph, Wisc.: Educators Progress Service. Annual.

Freudenthal, Juan R. "The Slide as a Communication Tool." *School Media Quarterly*, Winter 1974, pp. 109–115.

National Information Center for Educational Materials. *Index to Educational Slide Sets.* Los Angeles: NICEM. Nonevaluative. Revised periodically.

———. *Index to 35mm Educational Filmstrips.* Los Angeles: NICEM. Nonevaluative. Revised periodically.

Ryan, Mach. "Preparing a Slide-tape Program: A Step-by-step Approach." *Audiovisual Instruction*, Pt. 1, September 1975; Pt. 2, November 1975.

Microfilms

Bahr, Alice Harrison. *Microfilms: The Librarian's View, 1978–79.* White Plains, N.Y.: Knowledge Industry Publications, 1978.

Buyer's Guide to Micrographic Equipment, Products and Services. Silver Spring, Md.: National Micrographics Association, 1980.

Folcarelli, Ralph J.; Tannenbaum, Arthur C.; and Ferragamo, Ralph C. *The Microform Connection: A Basic Guide for Libraries.* New York: R. R. Bowker, 1982.

Guide to Microfilms in Print. Westport, Conn.: Microfilm Review. Nonevaluative. Revised periodically.

Microfilm Marketplace: 1978–79. Westport, Conn.: Microfilm Review, 1978.

Saffady, William. *Micrographics.* Littleton, Colo.: Libraries Unlimited, 1978.

Transparencies

Green, Lee. *501 Ways to Use the Overhead Projector.* Littleton, Colo.: Libraries Unlimited, 1982.

National Audio-Visual Association. *Basic Tips in Producing and Using Overhead Transparencies.* Fairfax, Va.: NAVA, 1981.

National Information Center for Educational Materials. *Overhead Transparencies.* Los Angeles: NICEM. Nonevaluative. Revised periodically.

Phonograph Records and Tapes

Audio-Cassette Directory. Glendale, Calif.: Cassette Information Services, 1982.

The Audio-tape Collection: A Library Manual on Sources, Processing and Organization. Salem, Ohio: Dale E. Shaffer, 1973.

National Information Center for Educational Materials. *Index to Educational Audio Tapes.* Los Angeles: NICEM. Nonevaluative. Revised periodically.

———. *Index to Educational Records.* Los Angeles: NICEM. Nonevaluative. Revised periodically.

New York Library Association, Children's and Young Adults Services Section. *Recordings for Children.* New York: NYLA, 1981.

Schwann Record and Tape Guide. Boston: Schwann. Monthly. Also *Children's Recording Catalog.* Annual.

Television

Bahr, Alice Harrison. *Video in Libraries: A Status Report, 1979-80.* White Plains, N.Y.: Knowledge Industry Publications, 1980.

Burk, Leslie C., and Estives, Roberto, eds. *Video and Cable Guidelines.* Chicago: American Library Association, 1981.

Cherry, Susan Spaeth, ed. *Video Involvement for Libraries: A Current Awareness Package for Professionals.* Chicago: American Library Association, 1981.

Educators Guide to Free Audio and Video Materials. Randolph, Wisc.: Educators Progress Services. Annual.

Erbeck, Diane M. "Television and Children: A Pro/Con Reading List." *Top of the News,* Fall 1980, pp. 47-53.

Harwood, Dan. *Everything You Always Wanted to Know about Portable Videotape Recording.* Syosset, N.Y.: VTR Publishing Co., 1980.

Held, Jonathan. *Video and Cable: An Annotated Guide for Librarians.* Dallas: Dallas Public Library, 1981.

Malten, Leonard, and Greenfield, Allan. *The Complete Guide to Home Video.* New York: Harmony Books, 1981.

National Information Center for Educational Materials. *Index to Educational Videotapes.* Los Angeles: NICEM. Nonevaluative. Revised periodically.

The Video Source Book. National Video Clearing House, 1979.

The Video Tape/Disc Guide, 3 vols. Vol. 1, *Movies and Entertainment*; vol. 2, *Children's Programs*; vol. 3, *Sports and Recreation.* Syosset, N.Y.: National Video Clearing House, 1980.

Videologs, Inc. *Consumer's Handbook of Video Software.* Van Nostrand, 1981.

Winslow, Ken., ed. *The Video Programs' Index.* National Video Clearing House, 1981.

Kits, Games, and Programmed Learning

Bell, Irene Wood, and Wieckert, Jeanne E. *Basic Classroom Skills through Games.* Littleton, Colo.: Libraries Unlimited, 1980.

Gohring, Ralph J. "A Beginner's Guide to Resources in Gaming and Simulation." *Audiovisual Instruction*, May 1978, pp. 46–49.

Hendershot, Carl H. *Programmed Learning: A Bibliography of Programs and Presentation Devices*, 5th ed. Bay City, Mich.: Hendershot, 1982.

Horn, Robert. *Guide to Simulatory Games for Education and Training*, 4th ed. Beverly Hills, Calif.: Sage, 1980.

Moll, Jay K., and Hermann, Patricia. "Evaluation and Selection of Toys, Games and Puzzles: Manipulative Materials in Library Collections." *Top of the News*, November 1974, pp. 86–89.

SELECTION AIDS FOR EQUIPMENT

The Audio-visual Equipment Directory. Fairfax, Va.: National Audio-Visual Association. Annual.

Bensinger, Charles. *The Home Video Handbook.* Santa Barbara, Calif.: Video-Info Publishers, 1980.

Epiegram: Equipment (monthly, October through June). Stony Brook, N.Y.: Educational Products Information Exchange.

Hawken, William R. *Evaluation of Microfiche Readers: A Handbook for Librarians.* Washington, D.C.: Council on Library Resources, 1976.

Kubett, Harry. *Complete Handbook of Videocassette Recorders.* Blue Ridge Summit, Pa.: Tab Books, 1981.

Library Technology Reports (bimonthly). Chicago: American Library Association.

Rosenberg, Kenyon C., and Doskey, John S. *Media Equipment: A Guide and Dictionary.* Littleton, Colo.: Libraries Unlimited, 1976.

Shaver, Johnny M. "Selecting Initial Media Equipment for New Facilities." *School Media Quarterly*, Spring 1974, pp. 227–233.

9

COMPUTERS AND THE SCHOOL LIBRARY MEDIA CENTER

The ultimate impact of the computer on modern society has sometimes been compared to the effect brought about by the development of the machine during the Industrial Revolution. As one gave an extension to the human hand, the other is giving an extension to the human brain. Although we are less than half a century into the computer age, the changes already have been monumental in scope and have affected all aspects of life, including formal education. One of the most dramatic developments in computer equipment or hardware is the evolution of the microcomputer. Only a few years ago a computer with comparable capabilities would have filled several large rooms and cost millions of dollars. Today the equipment is often no larger than a regular television set and can cost as little as a few hundred dollars.

In this chapter we discuss some pertinent topics about computers: general background information, uses of the computer, information utilities, and considerations involved in purchasing equipment (hardware) or computer programs (software).

COMPUTERS AND THEIR OPERATIONS

There are basically three kinds of digital (the most common) computers, differentiated by size and capabilities, amount of memory, and price. They are main frames, minicomputers, and microcomputers. Regardless of size, these computers perform three major operations: input, storage and processing, and output.

Input

In the input stage, information and instruction are fed into the computer and translated into the only language it understands. This machine-readable language involves coding numbers, letters, and

238

other symbols by using binary digits (or bits) as the Morse code uses dots and dashes. In the case of binary digits, 0 and 1 are used like on-and-off electrical switches. By using the various combinations of 0s and 1s possible in groups of 8 bits (called a byte), 256 different bytes are possible, each standing for a different letter, number, or command. Most of the existing microcomputers use an 8-bit byte, but some newer, more expensive models are 16-bit machines that often allow for superior graphic capabilities and can perform many tasks simultaneously. Although the user might input regular words, somewhere within the computer these are converted to computer language.

Computers are usually classified as: (1) analog, those that deal directly with numbers representing measurable quantities like volts (in the same way a thermometer measures temperature), (2) digital, those that solve problems and perform other functions simply by organizing data in the form of binary digits (0 or 1) and performing arithmetic processes on this data, or (3) hybrid, a combination of the first two. When most people use the term *computer*, however, they are usually referring to the digital type.

Sets of input instructions are called programs. They are usually written in a "high-level" language, that is, a language closely resembling ordinary English, which might use such commands as "print" or "end," meaning to finish a program. Some of the common languages are PASCAL (simple and good for business programs), FORTRAN (short for FORmula TRANslating system, and used extensively by engineers and scientists), PLI (also used in business and science), COBOL (an acronym for Common Business Oriented Language, and good for business and data processing in libraries), LOGO (a fairly new language designed by MIT to teach children to program), and BASIC (short for Beginners All-purpose Symbolic Instruction Code). BASIC, developed in 1973, is the most popular computer language and the one "built in to" most microcomputers. However, there are many versions of BASIC (like dialects in a language), and its chief drawback is that it is not as concise as other computer languages and, therefore, requires more steps to create a program. Some computers allow for a change of language by changing circuit boards or feeding new programs on diskettes or tapes into the computer.

There are various kinds of input devices by which material can be sent to the main memory of the computer. The most basic is typing on a typewriterlike keyboard that is attached to the computer. Most keyboards also have visual display possibilities on a television monitor called a CRT (cathode ray tube) monitor or display unit. Other input devices are punched cards, magnetic tapes, magnetic discs, magnetic drums, and large-core storage units. In the microcomputer, the usual input devices are cassette tapes (slow but cheap) and diskettes, sometimes known as floppy discs or floppies. Each diskette is a magnetically treated, round plastic sheet encased in a stiff cardboard sleeve 5 ¼ inches in diameter (some versions are 8 inches in diameter). Diskettes are used on a disk drive, a device that either reads data on the diskette into the computer, or, as an output device, records information on the diskette. Disk drives are often built into the microcomputer but can be added separately. Each diskette holds the equivalent of 35 to 40 pages of print, or a maximum of 110,000 characters.

Storage and Processing

This operation is accomplished inside the computer by the Central Processing Unit (CPU). In main frames the CPU consists of three parts: (1) the main memory, (2) the control unit or section that selects and controls commands from the main memory (like a traffic policeman), and (3) the arithmetic logic unit (ALU), which manipulates the data (adds, subtracts). In microcomputers the CPU is made up of a single integrated circuit called a microprocessor with thousands of circuits on a single silicon chip. In spite of its complexity, the CPU is less than a few ounces in weight and no larger than one's thumbnail.

Regardless of the size of the computer, data is stored in the main memory until it is processed. Only information needed by the CPU is stored, but once this information has been processed, it is transferred to a separate unit for storage (auxiliary or peripheral) or sent to an output device. The memory contains many storage positions, called bytes, that number from a few thousand in microcomputers to millions of positions in main frames.

With microcomputers, memory capability is expressed in K denominations, each K being equal to 1,024. Thus, 16 K equals 16,384; this is equal to about eight double-spaced typewritten pages. In microcomputers there are two types of memory. ROM, which means "read only memory," is the permanent memory programmed at the factory; for example, a manufacturer could put the BASIC language interpreter into ROM. Random Access Memory (RAM) is the main memory in which programs and information are written and stored and from which they can be retrieved and changed. In terms of the tiny silicon chips found in memory, a ROM chip has all its circuits recorded by the manufacturer, whereas a RAM chip is essentially blank and can be programmed by whatever input device (keyboard, diskette, and so on) is being used. A RAM chip is usually volatile, that is, whatever is stored in it when the computer is turned off is lost. Therefore, if the data are to be saved, they must be stored via some output device while the computer is still in operation. In summary, the CPU does all the processing in the computer and sends signals to other parts of the computer to coordinate and direct all of the operations performed.

Output

The output equipment completes the communication cycle, "from user into computer and back to user." Output, like input, might be displayed on a CRT (cathode ray tube) screen or through the use of automatic typewriters and line printers that change the electrical data in main storage to readable print and supply what is called a printout. Other devices for storing output data are similar to their input counterparts, that is, data on keypunch cards, magnetic tapes, discs and drums, and, in the case of microcomputers, tape cassettes and diskettes. Some computers have audio capabilities that transmit output in the form of spoken words and phrases selected from human voice recordings.

COMPUTER USE IN SCHOOLS

This section is divided into two parts: general uses, and specific uses for the school library media center.

General Uses

The computer has five general uses in schools, concerning: computer literacy, programming, word processing, instruction implementation, and entertainment.

Promoting Computer Literacy

Today computer technology touches every aspect of our lives, from the checkout counter at the supermarket to the airline reservation desk, and in the same way that we must master information about other technologies, students must learn to understand and use computers. Some educators believe that in the near future a computer illiterate will be as helpless and educationally deprived as a printed-word illiterate. To be computer literate, students should be aware of: (1) what computers can and cannot do, (2) how they function, (3) basic principles of programming, (4) the basic vocabulary in the field, (5) computer-system components, (6) applications of computer technology, and (7) the impact of computers on society. To promote this new form of literacy, almost 50 percent of the nation's schools now have instructional computers and many have integrated courses in computer literacy into the curriculum.

Learning Programming

Learning to program is a useful skill for students to master. With the proliferation of microcomputers in the home and the desire to utilize their capabilities for personal computing, people have said that soon a knowledge of how to program will be as useful as knowing how to drive a car. Programming involves mastery of a "foreign" language (many doctoral programs now allow the substitution of proficiency in a computer language for a conventional one!), application of reasoning skills and logic to analyze a system, development of flow charts, writing the statements and commands, and, finally, translating these into programs using a computer language that, in turn, can be fed into the computer.

Teaching Word Processing

Word processing, or text editing, is a skill valuable not only to students in preparing written assignments, but also to teachers and media specialists for report writing. Word processing is like ordinary typing at a keyboard, but the results are shown on the display unit instead of on paper. There are several unique rewrite features to word processing that make it more efficient than typing. Some are:

1. Automatic return (word wrap). When you come to the end of a line, a broken word is automatically transferred to the next line.
2. Rearrangement of words or passages (block move). This allows for adding or subtracting pieces of text wherever you wish with an automatic expansion or contraction of the rest of the text to accommodate these changes.
3. Justification of margins. When a passage is completely typed, righthand margins can be made as neat and even as the left side, similar to a page in a book.
4. Search and replace. By typing a misspelled word followed by its correct spelling and utilizing the proper command, all misspellings of the word in the text will be corrected.
5. Typeovers. When unwanted letters or words are typed over, they automatically disappear.
6. Indexing. Many word processors now allow for generating key word indexes and footnotes as well as for automatic page numbering.

After suitable grammatical text and spelling corrections have been made and the material has been arranged in an attractive format, the text can be printed through the computer's printer or saved by using as output a cassette or diskette. Two newer developments in the offing involve feeding in as data a computerized dictionary to automatically correct spelling, and allowing a choice of type fonts within the text. There are many text-editing packages available at a variety of prices. Some of the most popular word processing software programs are Word Star (from IBM Personal Computer or Apple II), Select (from IBMPC, Apple II or III), Easy Writer II (from IBMPC) and Scriptset (from Radio Shack's TRS-80). It should be noted that some of these programs require adding a special operating system (cost starts at about $400) before they are operational.

Implementing Computer-Based Instruction

Computer use in education is not a new phenomenon, but when it was first tried in the late 1960s and early 1970s, the exorbitant cost of using expansive microcomputer time-sharing systems and the dearth of good programs caused widespread disillusionment. Now both of these conditions have changed radically and have given computer use in education a new lease on life. Computer-based instruction is actually divided into two functions: computer-assisted instruction (CAI) and computer-managed instruction (CMI).

Depending on the nature of the system, *computer-assisted instruction* can be used for more than simply supplying facts and asking questions about them. It can be involved in a variety of other functions, such as tutorial drill and practice, problem solving, and simulations. Contrary to popular opinion, programs need not be impersonal or dehumanizing. In fact, good CAI lessons are highly individualized, infinitely patient and tireless, yet demanding and challenging. Through the use of branching techniques in programs, the student is allowed to move at his or her own pace. The process is nonthreatening and usually enjoyed. Because today's students are so video-oriented, many educators find it easy to interest all sorts of students, even the most disaffected, in CAI.

Computer-managed instruction involves instructional support functions such as testing, record keeping, scheduling, and resource management. For examples, tests can be taken online at a terminal (or offline and the answers read into the computer). They can be marked electronically, saving teacher time and giving immediate feedback to the student with a remedial work prescription if necessary. This allows flexibility in test scheduling and provides for test security. Computer records can be kept to monitor student performance and attendance and to generate student records and progress reports. Using CMI can also facilitate grouping students for instruction by searching their academic records and can help produce achievement profiles. Microcomputers can be used for many "housekeeping" chores. Although many school systems use large computers for such functions as class scheduling, payroll, inventory, attendance, and grade reports, microcomputers can supplement or even supplant the large computer at the single-school or individual-classroom level.

Entertainment

Although computer games are intended to amuse and entertain, many serve educational purposes and teach strategy building and problem solving. Basically these games fall into three categories: fast-action games like Pac-Man where the only challenge is to visual/physical coordination, puzzle games involving mysteries or quests that require developing solutions to problems, and intellectual games that require amounts of time and intricate game plans to win; an example would be chess playing with the computer.

COMPUTER USE IN THE CENTER

Although computers are still not used widely in managing school district media programs, there have been a number of successful projects at both the district and multidistrict levels. Most of these involve ordering and cataloging, often through direct use of MARC tapes, contracting for OCLC services (see Chapter 10), or using a commercial system such as Baker and Taylor's Automated Buying System (BATAB). Others involve using terminals to establish contact and share services with networks. The Washington Library Network serves as a fine example of how a large multitype network can be used by schools (see Chapter 12), but even a single school equipped only with microcomputers can develop programs to automate library routines. Some areas in which projects have been developed are discussed in the following list.

1. Online catalogs. In 1981, by using a microcomputer and a hard-disc system (hard discs operate more quickly and can store much more information than diskettes) as the basic equipment, plus the guidance of the media specialist and expert programmers, a project called Computer Cat was developed for a small elementary school library media center in a suburb of Denver, Colorado. Access is multiple, including author, title, and sub-

ject. Printouts of bibliographies by subject or by other access points are possible, and updating and maintaining the catalog is simpler and more accurate than through the traditional system. Student acceptance has been excellent and upkeep costs are minimal, although initial cost for software and hardware is between $8,000 and $12,000. The software package alone is about $2,000 and is available through Colorado Computing Systems.

2. Circulation systems. Several enterprising library media specialists have devised circulation systems that also print overdue notices using only the center's microcomputer. One such program, called The Overdue Writer, is now available commercially for about $125 from the Library Software Co., Box 23897, Pleasant Hill, CA 94523.

3. Local databases. Often simple programs can be developed that allow for the storage of information of local interest, such as a field-trip directory, list of speakers or other resources available in the area, or directory of information and referral agencies. By computer these can be updated easily and made accessible from various access points, including subject, a union list of serial holdings of other libraries in the area might also be generated, which would show both location and extent of holdings.

4. Center instruction. When massive numbers of students are being tested in a media skills program (for example, after a series of orientation classes), answers can be fed into the computer to facilitate marking, generating printouts of scores and analyzing teaching effectiveness particularly as applied to various levels of student ability.

5. Scheduling. Microcomputers can be used effectively to control scheduling of classes and booking of equipment or various media formats like films. Equipment repair files can also be computerized. An examination of the cumulative booking files can be helpful in developing replacement lists or recommended acquisitions to offset a larger volume of use.

6. Inventory. Lists of equipment, books and other material, textbooks, equipment, parts, and supplies can easily be maintained by computer. Not only can it be used to produce current inventory listings, but, in the case of supplies and parts, it can print warnings of low inventory levels.

7. Vertical-file control. After the vertical-file authority list (which can also be used by patrons) has been computerized, staff can direct the computer to generate labels for pamphlets added to the file.

8. Student class schedules. Information on student borrowers, class schedules, home addresses, or borrower's number can easily be placed in the computer to identify and contact students. Teachers' schedules and class sizes can also be entered.

9. Statistics and accounts. Collection of statistics and production of circulation or other reports on usage are facilitated by the computer. Cumulative and comparative statistics are easily produced and, with the addition of simple graphics capabilities, can be presented in attractive, easily understood color pictorial formats. Even if budgets are centrally administered, the library media center can tabulate its own encumbrances and expenditures via computer and maintain an up-to-date accounting system that will be more current than are the periodic reports from a central office.

10. Reports and correspondence. Through the use of a word processor and a printer module, reports and letters can be written easily, labels generated, and lists produced.

These are only a sampling of the many uses currently being made of microcomputers in school library media centers. The extent of their use is often limited only by the imagination of the user. Remember, as well, that in every school and community there are many computer enthusiasts and both amateur and professional programmers who are often more than willing to help develop new computer applications within a center. When used with inventiveness and creativity, the computer can expand both the productivity and capabilities of the media center.

INFORMATION UTILITIES

As mentioned earlier, the advantages of participation in a computer network can include extended access to resources and availability of such services as cataloging, acquisitions and selection aid, and circulation for serials control. Communication between participating libraries can be almost instantaneous through the use of electric mail capabilities. Access to community bulletin boards and computer-based teleconferencing is also possible. Even in the absence of these forms of networking, the microcomputer, with minor equipment modification to allow for outside conversion, has access through the telephone to a wide variety of other data banks and information utilities. Through the addition of a telephone coupler known as a modem (short for modulator-simulator) or an acoustic coupler, one computer can talk to another via phone lines. Acoustic couplers can be used with any telephone; however, sometimes background noise will interfere with the signal. This can be avoided by installing a direct connect, which clips directly into a specific phone line but, of course, reduces the flexibility of the microcomputer by reducing the portability.

In many microcomputers a special software program costing between $50 and $100 is necessary to make the modem operate. Modems transmit information at different speeds measured in bauds, a baud being equal to one bit per second in a string of binary signals. Therefore, a 300-baud modem will send about 37 bytes or characters per second, which is fast enough for most users.

To make connection with another computer or information service, the searcher dials the desired phone number and places the telephone handset in position on top of the modem. Because making direct long-distance phone calls is expensive, two other communication networks are used by all major information utilities. They are TYMNET and TELENET, and, although they operate like and through the telephone system, they are considerably cheaper—only $5 to $8 per hour if one is calling from a city that is a local connecting station called a node. Otherwise it is necessary to dial long distance to a node city or use special In-Wats lines.

Accessing Databases

The large information utilities or databases available for access consist of a number of databases with which the utility can contract for distribution. A database is simply a structured collection of information on a particular subject in a format that can be stored, processed, and delivered electronically by a computer. Because leasing a single database could reach $1,000 to $50,000 per year, cost sharing through networks has produced great economies and access to information otherwise cost-prohibitive.

There are now over 600 databases in the United States and in excess of four million searches are conducted annually here and in Canada. Some databases originate from private companies (such as Magazine Index from Information Access Corporation), government agencies (Medlars from the National Library of Medicine), universities and colleges (NICEM lists from the University of Southern California), or professional organizations (MLA International Bibliography from the Modern Language Association).

Many databases have interesting origins. After spending months collecting data on the environment for a speech-writing assignment, a public relations man turned this source into, first, a conventional print bibliography and later to an online database, now with over 15,000 items, known as Envirotapes.

Probably the database best known to education is ERIC, from the government agency Educational Resources Information Center. ERIC is divided into 16 clearinghouses (for a list, see Chapter 13), each with a subject specialization (such as Career Education, Information Resources). Each clearinghouse collects, evaluates, abstracts, and indexes the publications and research reports in its subject area. From this activity several newsletters and reviewing journals are published and such bibliographies as *Research in Education* and *Current Index to Journals in Education*. All this bibliographic material is also available in a single bibliographic database of approximately 400,000 records for the years 1966 to the present. About 30,000 new records are added to the existing database every year. This description of the ERIC database points up the two chief advantages of using online searches: (1) a vast amount of information is made available that would be impossible to store in one library, and (2) far greater thoroughness and time savings result from online searches over those done manually.

Bibliographic databases are evaluated on their size, age and up-to-dateness, sources, subject scope, nature of subject headings (for example, popular vs. scientific terminology), and the nature of each unit record. Parts or fields of a record can include a document number (this identifies each document in the database), title, author, source and citation, document type, original language, index terms or identifiers, and an abstract. Good databases allow for a number of entry points per document (author, number, and so on) and to save precious computer time also allow for only selected points or fields of the record to be displayed on command, from just the document number to the entire bibliographic record including the abstract. Both online (done immediately at the terminal) and offline (done at the host computer on off hours) printing is possible, the latter being much cheaper because valuable time using both the database and the telecommunications system is saved. Offline, however, is much slower because mail delivery is involved. Per-hour charges for searching vary with each database, from a low of about $25 (for example, for ERIC) to more than $100, with the average between $60 and $90.

A recently developed database of specific interest to school library media specialists is the Children's Media Data Bank, which contains bibliographic information on well over 10,000 important media titles recommended in such catalogs as *The Elementary School Library Collection* (Bro Dart) and suitable for children preschool through elementary grades. Interest and reading levels as well as catalog information, price, and annotation are given. Searches can be accomplished by using such elements or combinations of elements as subjects, titles, and reading levels. MARC records for many thousands of journal titles are also included. The director of this project is Dr. Theodore Hines of the Library Science/Educational Technology Division of the University of North Carolina at Greensboro.

Searching databases is somewhat similar to doing reference work in that prior to the search one should try to determine the exact information needed and build a search strategy including the subject headings to be used. With database searching, most of the planning must be done in advance because online time is money. Special skills are also required because online searching is more complex. Because each database differs in use of subject headings and search methodology, a searcher must have a knowledge of the thesaurus (list of subject headings) for each database as well as the searching rules outlined in the user's manual. This specialized training can be secured from a number of sources: database producers, schools of library and information science, professional organizations, network organizations, and online user groups.

Kinds of Utilities

There are basically two kinds of data banks or utilities: those that are principally nonbibliographic, or suppliers of direct information, and those that are mainly bibliographic, that is, indicators of where information can be found.

Some nonbibliographic suppliers that might be of interest to schools are:

1. The Source (1616 Aderson Road, McLean, VA 22102). This subsidiary of the Reader's Digest Association, Inc., was originally designed for individual users, but many libraries now subscribe. It has a mixed bag of databases, including New York Times News Summary and Consumer Data Bank, stock information, subject searching for current stories in the news, financial reports on over 3,000 companies, computing capability, programming languages, and many CAI packages and games. An electronic mail or message-sending source to other Source subscribers is available. Initial hookup charges are $100, plus a user fee of approximately $6 to $26 per hour.

2. MICRONET, or Compuserve Information Services (5000 Arlington Centre Blvd., Columbus, OH 43220). This network offers information similar to that of the Source: electric mail, file editing, business programs, computing languages, and stock information. For current and historical data on over 40,000 topics, one can use their Micro Quote. Microcomputer programs are made available that can be transferred to your own computer and charged to a credit card. The hookup charges are $20 to $40; user fees range from $5 to $25 per hour.

3. EDUNET (Box 364, Princeton, NJ 02540). This consists of 15 different colleges and universities that share various computer resources, such as CAI modules, databases, teleconferencing simulation modules, and games. Rates available on request.

4. The New York Times Information Service (1719-A, Route 10, Parsippany, NJ 07054). This information bank is the most comprehensive source of news and general information presently available. Nine major newspapers and about 80 other publications from around the world are indexed, in addition to the *New York Times*. Because its coverage dates back to 1969 and includes such a wealth of political, social, financial, and biographical data, it can be useful in any curriculum area, but particularly in the social sciences. Unfortunately, the charges are somewhat high. The lowest training or setup charge is over $200 and the thesaurus and manual cost another $100. Connect time is between $80 and $110 per hour.

There are three major U.S. vendors of online bibliographic databases to libraries and other information centers:

1. DIALOG Information Retrieval Service (available through Lockheed Information Systems, 3460 Hillview Ave., Palo Alto, CA 94304). This is the oldest and largest system in operation. Begun in 1969 with only one database, it now contains over 100 databases representing well over 4 million records.

2. ORBIT (available through SDC Search Services System Development Corp., 2500 Colorado Ave., Santa Monica, CA 90406). This company first went public in 1973 with 3 databases; it now has over 30.

3. BRS (Bibliographic Retrieval Services, 702 Corporation Park, Scotia, NY 12302). The newest of the retrieval services, BRS was established in 1976 and now contains over 30 databases.

The choice of vendor for a library depends on several factors, the first being the databases offered. Some databases are offered exclusively by only one of these vendors. However, it should be pointed out that the seven most popular and widely used databases, including ERIC, are available through all three. The National Information Center for Educational Media (NICEM) bibliographies of nonprint educational media and the Magazine Index are available through Lockheed, but both Lockheed and BRS have Exceptional Child Education Abstracts and National Information Center for Special Education Materials databases. Other factors to consider are the treatment of each database (for example, retrospective coverage and updating conventions); system capabilities and protocol (for example, print options, ability to save searches, and nature of the command language); cost (for example, nature of contracts, volume discount, minimum use necessary, online and offline print charges); and customer service and support (for example, training available, manuals, and private file service).

At present only a few individual school library media centers offer online reference services, although many more have initiated these services for faculty and students at a districtwide level, often in cooperation with other local information agencies such as a public library system or a community college library. When more general-interest databases are developed that would help satisfy the reference needs of young people, it would seem that more of these information sources will be made available in schools.

BASIC CONSIDERATIONS IN SETTING UP A COMPUTER SYSTEM

When a school or a particular library media center enters the computer age, several factors must be considered before trying to determine what specific software or hardware should be purchased. First, one must determine the specific functions to be performed by the system. For example, it has been shown that computers can not only entertain and teach, but also keep records and do a variety of other chores. Once the major uses have been identified, choosing the amount and type of equipment to be purchased will become simpler. Peripheral uses and future application, as well as minimum requirements and preferred features, should also be factored in at this time. Do not begin comparing prices of equipment until there has been a firm determination of needs because, although budget is important, the overriding factor in the selection of a system must be adequacy.

Next, decisions should be made concerning who is primarily responsible for planning and implementing the project, chains of command, and delegation of responsibilities. Any specific constraints or restraints to the project should be noted. This would certainly involve such items as cost, space limitations, and need for suitable electrical wiring and outlets. There are also many managerial concerns that must be addressed: housing the equipment (for example, a special computer lab, classroom space, or in the library media center itself); storage, organization, and management of the software collection as well as hardware; supervision of the installation; and assurance of proper security. Problems involving maintenance of the collection must be noted.

With this position paper or tentative "game plan" in place, it is possible to proceed to the step of collecting detailed information, criteria, and uses of specific kinds of equipment and software packages, and beginning to make purchase choices. This information can be collected in a number of ways: through reading, visiting other computer installations, bringing in consultants, or inviting local vendors to furnish suggestions and quotations. The final decision on the vendors should also involve time of delivery, parts and maintenance, availability of service contracts, and in-service training opportunities as well as positive references from other customers.

Criteria for Selecting Computer Equipment

A number of factors should be considered when selecting computer equipment. They include:

1. *Availability of software.* In the long run probably the major investment will not be in the equipment but in the software it can accept. Unfortunately, these programs are expensive and difficult to develop; therefore, in the past their number and quality have been limited. Basically this software can be of two kinds: systems software that performs internal housekeeping chores and applications software that actually performs the task. The availability of all kinds of software to satisfy these needs is of paramount importance in selecting a system.

2. *Memory.* Not only should one check the size of the central processor memory but also the size to which it can be expanded and at what cost.

3. *Storage options.* In microcomputers this can be done on tape cassettes, floppy discs, hard discs, or videodiscs. Although cassettes are inexpensive, they are slow and inferior to disc storage, but even here the options for various kinds of disc storage must be considered, plus the limitations on how much disc storage can be added at what cost.

4. *Speed.* With larger computers particularly, the time necessary to run programs can be an important factor.

5. *Interfaces.* In the microcomputer this involves the potential to extend the basic functions of the computer by attaching such peripherals as printers or disc drives using the input/output ports on the machine. The more ports available, the greater the flexibility and opportunity for expansion. The limits of the power supply in individual models may also in turn limit the number of accessories possible. In large computers the total number of terminals that can be connected is important as well as limitations on remote location of these additional terminals. The number and quality of accessories that can be added to a computer are varied

and impressive. A few are light pens and joysticks (particularly important for learning-disabled students who cannot type), modems, time checks to check response delays, music synthesizers, speech synthesizers, and speech recognition boards, special disc or cassette interfaces, robots, graphic capabilities, and electric typewriter controls.

6. *Language used.* Many of the languages available for use on computers have been discussed earlier in this chapter. If you or your colleagues plan to write programs, the choice of the computer might rest on what language or languages it will use. With microcomputers, some version of BASIC is the usual offering, although many offer options in COBOL, FORTRAN, and PASCAL.

7. *Chip used.* This refers to the actual microprocessor housed in the computer. The most common chips are MDS 6502, 8 bit and Zilog Z 80A, 8 bit. The type of chip has importance for the buyer only when one is buying accessories because accessories are often limited to a particular chip-based machine.

8. *Display.* Some video display units are limited to 12 lines with only 32 characters per line, but 24 by 80 or 30 by 80 is, although more expensive, much more desirable. Clarity of resolution is determined by the number of pixels (an abbreviation of picture elements) the display has. The more pixels, the clearer the image. The availability of both upper- and lower-case letters might be important. Certainly color and graphic capabilities are to be considered.

9. *Keyboard.* A suitable keyboard is essential; usually keyboards most like those on electric typewriters are preferred over the membrane type or those with small and closely spaced keys.

10. *Printers.* Availability and quality of suitable printers are important criteria if printouts are required. Although the standard printout might be adequate for internal use, full-performance printers might be necessary for more formal professional presentations. In such cases, printers with interchangeable print wheels, or at least upper- and lower-case matrixes, would be important as well as many graphic possibilities. Print speed and print density (number of characters per inch) are additional factors.

11. *Compatibility and flexibility.* This involves the degree to which the equipment can be networked to additional terminals, disc drives, and other peripherals, and, indeed, to remote terminals and other computer systems.

12. *Service and maintenance.* A prospective buyer will want to determine the quality and speed of the repair and maintenance services available, as well as the nature and cost of service contracts.

13. *Documentation.* This refers to the guide manuals and other instructional devices supplied with the machine. Their thoroughness and clarity of presentation can help considerably in facilitating use. Many companies and dealers supply free training and instruction to groups to familiarize users with their products. It is estimated that no more than 15 hours of instruction and hands-on experience are necessary to provide a good grasp of microcomputers and their use.

14. *Other considerations.* Several more general criteria that could apply to other types of educational equipment, such as portability and weight, are discussed in Chapter 8.

Criteria for Selecting Computer Software

Because the software involved in computer-assistance instruction is essentially an automated form of programmed instructional material, basically the same evaluative criteria, such as logical construction, thorough instruction, adequate reinforcement, apply to both. (These are found in Chapter 8 and relate to programs involving instruction as well as drill and practice.) The expression "user friendly" is also often applied as a criterion for microcomputer programs. This means that a program stimulates users and guides them comfortably and with imagination from one step to the next.

It should be pointed out, however, that software is not interchangeable from one manufacturer's equipment to another's. Indeed, sometimes programs will not run on different models from the same manufacturer. In such cases, the programs are often available in a series of formats. Because of the high cost of programs, it is advisable, whenever possible, to schedule teacher previews of each program before purchase and to maintain files of these evaluations. Unfortunately, some manufacturers and distributors of software packages are reluctant to supply preview copies, primarily for fear of copyright infringements, but increasingly more are granting this privilege.

For software packages involving computer-managed instruction, that is, essentially information handling, the following additional criteria should be used:

1. Clarity of instruction and ease of use. The program should either be specifically formulated for a single operation (turnkey method) or clearly display user choices (menu method).

2. Storage capacity appropriate for amount of data to be handled.

3. Provision made for data security and privacy of records.

4. Fast input and retrieval time.

5. Various appropriate data handling formats available, for example, editing sorting.

6. Word processing capabilities present.

7. Ability to feed results into a centralized processing unit, either school or districtwide, available.

Sources of Information about Computers

The bibliography section that follows lists some basic readings on computers and their application in libraries. There are, of course, many other ways to increase one's awareness of computer development. Most colleges offer courses through their departments of computer science, education, or library science. Many introductory courses are also given through continuing education agencies in school districts or colleges. Professional associations will often sponsor workshops and institutes on the subject. Another valuable way of gaining practical experience is by joining one of the hundreds of local user groups that have sprung up across the country. These computer clubs offer an opportunity to learn firsthand about hardware and software and have specific questions answered. To locate one in your area, ask your computer dealer.

This section supplies directories of equipment and software manufacturers and distributors, plus lists of important software bibliographies and key periodicals in the field. One useful publication that covers many computer publications, user groups, funding sources, and the like is *The Classroom Computer News Directory of Educational Computer Resources* (Intentional Education, 341 Mount Auburn St., Watertown, MA 02172).

Microcomputer Manufacturers

The number of manufacturers of microcomputers seems to increase every day and even though many fall quickly by the economic wayside, even more spring up to take their place. Here is a sampling of the major manufacturers:

Apple Computer, Inc., 20525 Mariani, Cupertino, CA 95014

Atari, 100 Jericho Quadrangle, Suite 132, Jericho, NY 11753

Commodore Business Machines, 901 California Ave., Palo Alto, CA 94303

Computer Data Systems, 5460 Fairmont Dr., Wilmington, DE 19808

Cromemco, Inc., 280 Bernardo Ave., Mountain View, CA 94040

Digital Equipment Corporation, 146 Main St., Maynard, MA 01754

Dynabyte, 521 Cottonwood Dr., Milpitas, CA 95035

Exidy, 969 W. Maude Ave., Sunnyvale, CA 94086

The Heath Co., Benton Harbor, MI 49022

Hewlett-Packard, 11000 Wolfe Road, Cupertino, CA 95014

IBM Corp., Data Processing Div., Dept. 86R, 1133 Westchester Ave., White Plains, NY 10604

North Star, 2547 Ninth St., Berkeley, CA 94710

Ohio Scientific, 1333 S. Chillicothe Road, Aurora, OH 44202

Osborne and Associates, 630 Bancroft Ave., Berkeley, CA 94710

Radio Shack, Tandy Corp., 2617 W. Seventh St., Forth Worth, TX 76102

Texas Instruments, POB 225474, Dallas, TX 75265

Timex Sinclair, 1 Sinclair Plaza, Nashua, NH 03061

Vector Graphic Inc., 790 Hampshire Road, A&B, Westlake Village, CA 91361

Wang Laboratories, 1 Industrial Ave., Lowell, MA 01851

Software Manufacturers and Distributors

A large volume of software is available directly from equipment manufacturers. Much of this has been commissioned and produced expressly for their microcomputers. In addition, it has been estimated that there are about 5,000 other producers and distributors of software in the United States. The quality of the products varies widely. To supplement the above list, these are a few of the firms most active in creating new programs, distributing them, or both:

Bell & Howell Company, 1700 N. McCormick Road, Chicago, IL 60645

Charles Mann & Associates, Micro Software Div., 1926 S. Veteran Ave., Los Angeles, CA 90025

Computer Resource Center, Technical Education Research Centers, Inc., 8 Eliot St., Cambridge, MA 02138

Conduit, Box 388, Iowa City, IA 52244

Data Command, Box 548, Kankakee, IL 60901

Diversified Educational Enterprises, Inc., 725 Main St., Lafayette, Ind. 47901

Educational Activities, Inc., Box 392, Freeport, NY 11520

Educational Materials & Equipment, Box 17, Pelham, NY 10803

Edu-Ware Services, Inc., 22035 Burbank Blvd., Suite 223, Woodland Hills, CA 91367

Eye Gate Media, 146-01 Archer Ave., Jamaica, NY 11435

Gregg Division, McGraw-Hill Book Co., 1221 Ave. of the Americas, New York, NY 10020

JMH Software of Minnesota, 4850 Wellington Lane, Minneapolis, MN 55442

K-12 Micromedia, Box 17, Valley Cottage, NY 10980

Maine Software Library, Box 197, Standish, ME 04084 (rentals)

Math Software, 1233 Blackthorn Place, Deerfield, IL 60015

Micro Center, Box 6, Pleasantville, NY 10570

Micro Learningware, Box 2134, North Mankato, MN 56001

Microsoft Consumer Products, 10800 N.E. Eighth, Suite 507, Bellevue, WA 98004

Minnesota Educational Computing Consortium Instructional Services Div., 2520 Broadway Dr., St. Paul, MN 55113

J. L. Monnett Co., Box 545, Hammett Place, Braintree, MA 02184

Muse Software, 347 North Charles St., Baltimore, MD 21201

Opportunities for Learning, 8950 Lurline Ave., Chatsworth, CA 91311

Program Design, Inc., 11 Idar Court, Greenwich, CT 06830

Random House School Div., Dept. 985, Suite 291, Brandywine Road, Atlanta, GA 30341

Reston Publishing Co., 11480 Sunset Hills Road, Reston, VA 22090

Scholastic, Inc., 900 Sylvan Ave., Englewood Cliffs, NJ 07632

Science Research Associates, 155 N. Wacker Dr., Chicago, IL 60606

Software Exchange, 6 South St., Milford, NH 03055

Sterling Swift Publishing Co., 1600 Forview Road, Austin, TX 78704

Database Directories

Basic information on most databases can be found in the catalogs supplied by vendors. This information usually includes types of records (books, articles, reports, and so on), major subjects and dates covered, number of citations, searching costs, and updating procedures. If more detailed information is required, use:

Directory of On-Line Information Resources. Rockville, Md.: Updated frequently. CSG Press.

Landau, Ruth N., et al. *Directory of Online Databases.* Santa Monica, Calif.: Cuadra Associates, Inc. Published every six months with quarterly updates. Frequently cited under Cuadra.

Williams, Martha E., et al. *Computer-Readable Data Bases: A Directory and Data Sourcebook.* Washington, D.C.: American Society for Information Science. Revised frequently.

Software Directories

Many manufacturers of hardware issue catalogs of microcomputer programs suitable for their machines (for example, *Commodore Software Encyclopedia* is available from Commodore Business Machines), or they will be able to direct you to other sources. For example, all types of material available for the Apple II are listed in *The Blue Book* available from WIDL Video, 5245 W. Diversey, Chicago, IL 60639. Many of the periodicals listed below also review and list software and often print new programs. Beginning in 1981, *Booklist* began periodically reviewing microcomputer software programs (sometimes called "courseware"). This column looks at programs for the Apple II, PET, and TRS-80 microcomputers. A 1982 periodical, *Software Review*, is devoted exclusively to news and views on programs; available from Meckler Publishing, 520 Riverside Ave., Westport, CT 06880.

Some of the basic software directories are:

Chartrand, Marilyn, and Williams, Constance. *Educational Software Directory: A Subject Guide to Microcomputer Software.* Littleton, Colo.: Libraries Unlimited, 1982. This includes information on 900 programs, including those for creating programs for grades K–12.

A Directory of Educational Software. This directory, dated 1981, is now available only as ERIC document ED 196431.

EPIE Microcomputer Reports on Courseware/Hardware. The EPIE Institute has created a series of reports that review not only equipment but also computer programs available in such areas as mathematics, science, and language.

International Microcomputer Directory and *Minicomputer Software Directory, Inprint Software.* Annual. These directories are now available combined online as *International Software Directory* on DIALOG, which also offers the service of ordering much of the software listed.

Micro Software Report (library edition). Nolan Information Management Services, 21203A, Hawthorne Blvd., Suite 5323, Torrance, CA 90509. A guide to standard programs with library applications or those that are specifically library-oriented.

Van Diver, G., and Love, R. *Educator's Handbook and Software Directory*. Overland Park, Kan.: Vital Information, Inc., 1981. A general overview and handbook.

PERIODICALS ON COMPUTERS

Many of the periodicals listed below, like *Byte* and *InfoWorld*, plus approximately 30 others are indexed in the quarterly publication *Microcomputer Index* (issued by Microcomputer Information Services), also available online via DIALOG. The number of periodicals and newsletters on computers number in the hundreds. The following selective list is divided into three parts: general periodicals, periodicals for specific computer lines, and periodicals on computers in education and libraries.

General Periodicals

Byte (Box 590, Martinsville, NJ 08836). This is not for novices and is hardware-oriented.

InfoWorld (375 Cochitwuate Road, Box 880, Framingham, MA 01701). A weekly tabloid, technical and advanced.

Personal Computing (Box 2941, Boulder, CO 89321). Good general magazine for hobbyists and other nonexperts.

Popular Computing (Box 307, Martinsville, NJ 08836). Probably the best general magazine for the beginner.

Periodicals for Specific Computers (arranged by producer)
Apple

  Appleseed (Softside Publications, 6 South St., Milford, NH 03055)

  Compute (Compute, Box 5119, Greensboro, NC 27403). This is also useful for Commodore's Pet.

  Nibble (Nibble, Box 325, Lincoln, MA 01773)

  Softside: Apple (Softside)

Atari

A.N.A.L.O.G. (Analog, Box 23, Worcester, MA 01603)

IRIDIS (Iridis, Box 550, Goleta, CA 93017) (on cassette)

Softside: Atari (Softside)

Commodore (Pet)

Commodore Interface (Commodore Systems Div., 681 Moore Road, King of Prussia, PA 19406)

Cursor—Pet (Cursor, Goleta, CA 93017) (on cassette)

TRS-80 (Radio Shack)

CLOAD (Cload, Box 1267, Goleta, CA 93017) (on cassette)

Softside S-80 (Softside)

TRS-80 Monthly Newsletter (Computonics, Inc., Box 149, New York, NY 10956)

Periodicals on Computers in Education and Libraries

Access: Microcomputers in Libraries (Access, Box 764, Oakridge, OR 97463). This quarterly deals exclusively with microcomputer applications in a variety of libraries.

Classroom Computer News (Box 266, Cambridge, MA 02138). Issued bimonthly with useful articles on programs and their uses.

Computer Town, U.S.A. (Box E, Menlo Park, CA 94025). A free monthly bulletin.

The Computing Teacher (Dept. of Computers and Information Service, University of Oregon, Eugene, OR 97403). Issued nine times per year with articles ranging from practical to highly theoretical.

Educational Computer Magazine (Box 535, Cupertino, CA 95014). A bimonthly with many articles especially for school library media specialists.

DIRECTIONS FOR THE FUTURE

Combining television and computer technologies with existing communications networks gives promise of a dazzling array of information services that can be provided for schools, libraries, homes, and businesses. Two of the most touted are teletext and videotext. Teletext is a noninteractive (one-way) system linking the user and the information supplier through regular or cable television broadcast signals. Sequences of "pages" of information are transmitted to the user's television set, and to access them, a contents page (or pages) is consulted, appropriate selections are made via a hand-held keypad, and through the use of a special decoder, these pages are captured and stored for the use of the viewer. Teletext is much less expensive than videotext, is easily accessible, and requires little to update. For this reason it is now often used where current information is needed, for example, stock market reports, road and traffic conditions. However, because the entire database is continuously cycled, its size must be limited or lengthy delays occur in retrieving specific pages.

Videotext is more complex and sophisticated than teletext. This is an interactive (two-way) system that uses either cable television or telephone lines as the carrier of signals linking users and computer databases. These databases can contain all sorts of information, but basically there are five generic services involved: (1) information retrieval, (2) transactional services (like shopping or banking), (3) message referral, (4) computing uses, (5) monitoring (for building security, fire, and the like). Some of these services are already being offered for such pioneering videotext services as the Source described earlier. Users search for information by using special control panels and narrowing the search by starting with broad subjects and gradually making the subject more specific until the required information is found. Videotext databases are unlimited in the amount of information they can contain. However, because videotext is so electronically complex, it is still extremely expensive. As yet, the role of libraries and schools in the emerging videotext and teletext market is still to be defined.

An equally exciting and less remote development of recent years is the videodisc. Unfortunately, as with other electronic developments, different videodisc systems have been marketed and they are not compatible with each other. In the United States, there are basically two formats vying for supremacy. One system, developed by RCA, has already captured a great deal of the home entertainment market with its many full-length movies and television features. This is a capacitance or mechanical system involving a machine similar to a record player that is equipped with a diamond-tipped stylus and a turntable that rotates at 450 rpm. It accepts 12-inch discs (with jackets) and each side can hold about 60 minutes of playing time.

The other system, which seems better suited to educational and instructional purposes, was developed by MCA and Philips and involves an optical process whereby a lazer beam reads the pictures and sound from a disc rotating at 1,800 rpm. This beam is decoded by other components in the system. By pushing buttons on a keyboard, the user has random access to the 54,000 frames (or about 30 minutes of reel-time motion pictures) on each side of the disc. Other advantages are the capacity to freeze frames and supply slow motion, and the lack of wear on the discs.

The implications for school library media centers in videodisc technology are staggering. Some examples: films and television programs will become available in inexpensive disc formats, reducing the need for projection equipment, delays in loaning procedures, and even the central film library; books, articles, slide collections—even the card catalog—can be made available on videodiscs to patrons to peruse; and interactive instructional systems can be made available inexpensively. Indeed, many of these developments are underway, and videodiscs are available that cover the range of school subjects. However, the revolution in communications technology is only beginning to be felt by schools and libraries.

FOR FURTHER READING

Adams, John, and Adams, Robin. "Videotext and Teletext—New Roles for Libraries." *Wilson Library Bulletin* (November 1982), pp. 206–211.

Association for Educational Communications and Technology. *Educational Technology: A Glossary of Terms*. Washington, D.C.: AECT, 1979.

Barrette, Pierre. *The Microcomputer and the School Media Specialist*. Littleton, Colo.: Libraries Unlimited, 1981.

———. "Microcomputers in the School Media Program." *Catholic Library World* (October 1981).

Beiser, Karl. "Microcomputers Periodicals for Libraries." *American Libraries* (January 1983), pp. 43–48.

Bennett, Wilma E. *Checklist/Guide to Selecting a Small Computer*. E.D.R.S., 1980.

Chandor, Anthony. *Facts-on-File Dictionary of Microcomputers*. New York: Facts on File, 1981.

Chen, Ching-chih, and Bressler, Stacey E. *Microcomputers in Libraries*. New York: Neal-Schuman, 1982.

Cherry, Susan Spaeth. "Telereferences: The New TV Information Systems." *American Libraries* (February 1980), pp. 94–98.

Chirlian, Paul M. *Beginning Basic*. Beaverton, Ore.: Dilithium, 1979.

Clement, Frank. "Digital Made Simple." *Instructional Innovator* (March 1982), pp. 18–20.

Coan, James. *Basic BASIC: An Introduction to Computer Programming in BASIC Language*. Rochelle Park, N.J.: Hayden, 1978.

"Computer." Reprinted from the *World Book Encyclopedia*, 1981.

Costa, Betty. "An On-Line Catalog for an Elementary School Library Media Center." *School Library Media Quarterly* (Summer 1982), pp. 337–346.

Doeer, Christine. *Microcomputers and the 3 R's: A Guide for Teachers*. Rochelle Park, N.J.: Hayden, 1979.

Dowling, Karen, and Kirsch, Judy. "On-line Information Retrieval in a Local Education Agency." *School Media Quarterly* (Fall 1977).

Driver, Russell, and Driver, Mary Anne. "Automation in School Library Media Centers." *School Library Journal* (January 1982), pp. 21–25.

Dyer, Susan R., and Forcier, Richard C. "How to Pick Computer Software." *Instructional Innovator* (September 1982), pp. 38–40.

Falk, Howard. "Computer Software and Equipment Considerations." *School Library Journal* (November 1981), pp. 29–31.

Fenichel, Carol H., and Hogan, Thomas H. *On-Line Searching: A Primer.* Marlton, N.J.: Learned Information, 1981.

Franckowiak, Bernard. "Networks, Data Bases, and Media Programs: An Overview." *School Media Quarterly* (Fall 1977), pp. 15–20.

Frank, Mark. *Discovering Computers.* New York: Stonehenge Press and The American Museum of Natural History, 1981.

Frederick, Franz J. *Guide to Microcomputers.* Washington, D.C.: AECT, 1980.

Frenzel, Louis E. *Getting Acquainted with Microcomputers.* Indianapolis, Ind.: Howard W. Sams, 1979.

Goldberg, Albert L. "A Beginner's Guide to Microcomputer Resources." *Audio-Visual Instruction* (November 1979), pp. 22–23.

Gordon, Anita, and Karl Zinn. "Microcomputer Software Considerations." *School Library Journal* (August 1982), pp. 25–27.

Gutman Library, Harvard University Graduate School of Education. *Microcomputer Directory: Applications in Educational Settings.* Cambridge, Mass.: Harvard University, 1982.

Hall, Keith A. *Computer-Based Education: The Best of ERIC, June 1976–August 1980.* E.D.R.S., 1980.

Hedberg, Augustin. "Choosing the Best Computer For You." *Money* (November 1982), pp. 68–117.

Hines, Theodore C., Winkel, Lois, and Collins, Rosann. "The Children's Media Data Bank." *Top of the News* (Winter 1980), pp. 176–198.

———, and Brownrigg, Edwin Blake. "A Computer-Based Procedure for Increasing Information Access to Materials for School Library Media Programs." *School Media Quarterly* (Spring 1976), p. 245.

Hoffman, C. "The Computer in the High School Library." *Catholic Library World* (July–August 1978), pp. 10–11.

Human Resources Research Organization (HumRRO). *Academic Computing Directory.* Alexandria, Va.: HumRRO, 1980.

International Microcomputer Dictionary. Berkeley, Calif.: SYBEX, 1981.

Kent, Allen. "The On-Line Revolution in Libraries, 1969–." *American Libraries* (June 1979), pp. 339–342.

Kiechel, Walter. "Everything You Always Wanted to Know May Soon Be On-Line." *Fortune*, May 5, 1980, pp. 226–234.

Lipson, Shelley. *It's Basic: The ABC's of Computer Programming* (for children). New York: Holt, 1982.

Lopez, Antonio M. J. "Microcomputers: Tools of the Present and Future." *School Media Quarterly* (Spring 1981), pp. 164–167.

Lundeen, Gerald. "The Role of Microcomputers in Libraries." *Wilson Library Bulletin* (November 1980), pp. 178–185.

"Machine of the Year—The Computer Moves In." *Time*, January 3, 1983, pp. 14–39.

Mandell, Phyllis Levy. "Computer Literacy, Languages, and Careers" (bibliography of audiovisual programs). *School Library Journal* (April 1982), pp. 19–22.

Martin, Susan K. *Library Networks 1981-82.* White Plains, N.Y.: Knowledge Industry, 1981.

Milner, Stuart D. "How to Make the Right Decisions About Microcomputers." *Instructional Innovator* (September 1980), pp. 12–19.

Moody, Robert. *First Book of Microcomputers.* Rochelle Park, N.J.: Hayden, 1979.

Moskowitz, Mickey. "Developing a Microcomputer Program to Evaluate Library Instruction." *School Library Media Quarterly* (Summer 1982), pp. 351–356.

Myers, Darlene. *Computer Science Recourses: A Guide to Professional Literature.* White Plains, N.Y.: Knowledge Industry, 1981.

National Council of Teachers of Mathematics. *Guidelines for Evaluating Computerized Instructional Materials.* Reston, Va.: NCTM, nd.

Nevison, John M. *Little Book of Basic Style.* Reading, Mass.: Addison-Wesley, 1980.

Nicklin, R. C., and Tashner, John. "Micros in the Library Media Center?" *School Media Quarterly* (Spring 1981), pp. 168–181.

Osborne, Adam. *An Introduction to Microcomputers: The Beginner's Book.* Berkeley, Calif.: Osborne and Associates, 1982.

The Professional Librarian's Reader in Library Automation and Technology. White Plains, N.Y.: Knowledge Industry, 1980.

Rorvig, Mark E. *Microcomputers and Libraries: A Guide to Technology, Products and Applications.* White Plains, N.Y.: Knowledge Industry, 1981.

Sanders, William H. "Going Digital." *Instructional Innovator* (March 1982), pp. 14–16.

Simpson, George A. "Microcomputers in Library Automation." Princeton, N.J.: ERIC, ED 174 217.

Skapura, Robert. "The Overdue Writer: A Program Long Overdue." *School Library Media Quarterly* (Summer 1982), pp. 347–350.

Sneed, Charles. "The Videodisc Revolution: What's Ahead for Libraries." *Wilson Library Bulletin* (November 1980), pp. 186–189.

Thomason, Nevada. "Microcomputers and Automation in the School Library Media Center." *School Library Media Quarterly* (Summer 1982), pp. 312–319.

Truett, Carol. "How Well Do Media Specialists Meet the Challenge of the Computer." *Instructional Innovator* (February 1982), pp. 14–16.

Twaddle, Dan R. "School Media Services and Automation." *School Media Quarterly* (Summer 1979), pp. 257–268, 273–276.

"Understanding the Utilities." *American Libraries* (May 1980), pp. 262–278.

Willis, Jerry. *Peanut Butter and Jelly Guide to Computers.* Beaverton, Ore.: Dilithium, 1978.

———, and Miller, Merl. *Computers for Everybody.* Beaverton, Ore.: Dilithium, 1981.

Wisconsin Library Bulletin, May–June 1977. Entire issue on automation and school library media centers.

Zosel, Gary. "Computers and the Media Center: A Principal's Perception." *The Computing Teacher* (March 1982).

10

ACQUISITION AND ORGANIZATION

Staff functions and program activities depend not only on the resources of the center but also on the organizational patterns that the center adopts. The main goals of this managerial function are to acquire resources and make them available as quickly and efficiently as possible. An efficient processing system is a prerequisite for achieving these goals. Many individual school library media centers rely on commercial processing as an important adjunct to organization.

This chapter deals with the general rules that apply to acquisition in school library media centers, with emphasis on the minimally staffed center in an individual school building. The system of bidding is explained, and technical services, such as purchasing, processing, and cataloging, are covered along with local production of educational materials.

When a budget is approved by a board of education, final decisions about expenditures must be made. If the funds are allocated as requested, the procedure is generally predetermined. If budget requests have been reduced, the media specialist must design a priority system for expenditures. Since reductions affect the entire instructional program, the media specialist should discuss these problems with the principal, department heads, or grade-level coordinators. Once these preliminaries are completed, the specialist is ready to proceed to the two fundamental steps in the acquisition process—bidding and purchasing.

BIDDING

The federal government as well as many state education departments and school systems require competitive formal bidding for purchase of materials, supplies, or equipment in excess of specified amounts; the amounts vary from state to state—in some, for example, the cutoff figure is \$1,000. These agencies may require a less formalized bidding process for amounts that fall below a specified minimum, for example, \$300. State law, city ordinance, school board resolution, or administrative order are some of the regulations that mandate competitive bidding for all types of purchases, including materials and equipment.

The aim of bidding in expending public funds is to get the best goods and services at the lowest possible cost; the bid serves as a guard against favoritism to a vendor as well as a device for conserving public funds. The formal bid should protect the school and media center by the inclusion of penalty provisions and cancellation clauses for substandard or delinquent service on the vendor's part. It is also designed to give the supplier or vendor an opportunity to be considered by a larger buying audience, that is, an entire state. In practice, however, each media specialist with experience in competitive bidding realizes that bidding raises many problems: the negotiation of the contract through a fiscal agency (usually at the school district level, but sometimes through state or federal agencies); the possibility of poor service from the vendor; the accuracy of the billing. Vendors, on the other hand, have often encountered problems in dealing with some schools because of delayed payment, lack of partial payment on merchandise received, and seasonal ordering. Both find that unless the school media center works closely with the business office or school purchasing agency, the lack of coordination complicates the process.

Formal Bidding

The term "formal bidding" usually refers to a system in which sealed bids from vendors for certain items are publicly opened on a given date that has been advertised locally. Firms that meet certain qualifications and have given satisfactory service in the past are invited to enter a bid. Some nonstandard or monopoly items for which there are too few firms to compete may be excepted from the bid requirements—for example, a specialized type of equipment or a specific encyclopedia.

Another type of formal bidding is the state contract method by which firms negotiate a contract for a period of time with a state education department. As an alternative to local competitive bidding, school library media centers may be able to use state contracts. A list of dealers who have a contract with a state education department is generally available from the local district business office. As a typical example of a state that requires formal bidding, the New York State

Education Department expects all items to be placed on bid unless they represent either or both of the following categories: (1) an annual total expenditure for one item or type of item within a school district of less than $1,000, (2) a monopoly item (that is, an item available at a fixed price from only one source).

Informal Bidding

The term "informal bidding" suggests a less formalized bidding method and usually means that the bid need not be advertised. As few as two or three firms may be asked, even by telephone, for a bid price on the item or items needed. This system is widely used when the expenditure for an item falls between the minimum and maximum figures required for informal and formal bidding, for example, $100 and $1,000.

If neither the competitive bid nor the state contract bid method is used, the school library media center and local business office should agree on a standard bidding practice and set up guidelines. Whatever the procedure, the bidding should (1) provide satisfactory service to the media center, (2) guarantee fiscal integrity to the business office, and (3) grant realistic specifications on items for the vendors. The following guidelines should be written into the bids:

Specifications. A detailed description of the item, for example, for binding, saddle-stitching might be requested, or for 16mm projectors, a freeze-frame device might be stipulated.

Ordering frequency. A schedule for anticipated ordering, such as large orders in the fall and spring with regular school year biweekly orders.

Time of delivery. A time schedule for delivery expectations, for example, a 50 percent fulfillment of order within 60 days with a 90–120 day period for completion of order.

Substitutions and changes by suppliers. A definition of what substitutions and changes will be acceptable, such as revisions of older titles or newer models of equipment, but not a different filmstrip on the same subject.

Quality and condition of merchandise. A list of unacceptable conditions, such as transparencies that differ in definition or color from the samples; prints that are damaged in transit.

Policy on service and returns. A two-part statement on the expectations of (1) the service desired—a first-time service visit to install and put in working condition sophisticated equipment such as dial access, and (2) the conditions under which materials may be returned, for example, books with missing pages.

Invoices and packing slips. A notice that lists the number and disposition of the shipping and billing statements, such as sending duplicate copies of invoices to the media center and guaranteeing the arrival of shipments, with enclosed slips listing the material or equipment delivered.

Bid security. A statement that requires a bond or stipulates penalties in case of default of the agreement. For example, a school may ask a vendor (1) to secure a bond before the school will entertain a bid in excess of $8,000, for instance, for 16mm projectors, or (2) to deduct a percentage of the final payment if all material or equipment has not been received at the agreed-on delivery termination period.

Discounts. A list by type of material or equipment of the acceptable range of discounts, for example, 10–20 percent for technical or scientific print titles, 33–40 percent for trade print titles, 10 percent off list price for new model equipment, or larger discounts for quantity orders.

Full and partial payments. An agreement to reimburse the vendor within a reasonable time period for both orders delivered in full and in partial shipments, such as guaranteed payment by school within 30–60 days of completion of either type of order fulfillment.

Exhibit and exhibition merchandise. A written contract form that stipulates such things as the time period between receipt and return of goods; the condition of the materials; the kind and amount of materials and necessary display items; the method and length of payment if the materials are to be sold, the legal responsibility for the consignment, insurance coverage, and so on.

Services of an area representative. A statement that explains the expectation of ready local help from a distant company's field representatives, such as the availability of a sales or service person from a national producer of transparencies or manufacturer of photoduplication equipment to adjust claims or advise on use.

Cancellation clause. An enforceable statement that notes the conditions under which either the vendor or school may cancel an order, for example, if the vendor is not reimbursed after a reasonable period of time, if a delivery is delayed beyond a reasonable period of time, if the titles in an order are substituted for those originally specified, and so on.

Consignment privileges. A list of conditions under which materials may be delivered and sold or used under a deferred-payment agreement, such as paperbacks for sale in a media-center-operated store or at a materials fair may be purchased on consignment and paid for as they are sold; book clubs often use some form of this method. Time periods and accounting methods are important in the listing of consignment privileges.

Conditions of warranty. A statement that describes the circumstances under which materials or equipment may be repaired or exchanged, such as cassette player may be exchanged or a missing or malfunctioning part repaired free of charge within 90 days of purchase.

No standardized bid form that covers all these guidelines is presently in general use. The forms devised by governing bodies vary from one type for all merchandise to many different types, some of which may contain detailed specifications for a particular commodity. Some agreement among purchasing officials does exist, however, about the importance of the basis on which bids are evaluated; the least bid price in relation to the bidder's responsibility to the vendor. The lowest dollar amount bid price should not be the sole criterion, because the service and the speed with which it is given are also fundamental concerns in the acquisition of media. The responsibility of the bidder, whether manufacturer, producer, dealer, or agent, rests on many factors, including a sound financial condition, some experience in the work, good past performance. Whenever circumstances permit, the media specialist should consult with the school purchasing officer on these matters.

In dealing with the bidding process, the media specialist should also be aware of the following points:

1. Each item, from pamphlets to videotapes to newspapers, often requires a different vendor or purchasing method. For example, the materials may be produced privately or commercially, issued by governments, societies, universities, or others, or be available on exchange. These factors often serve to exempt school library media center materials from a bid requirement.
2. Some state laws and local school system regulations exempt library materials from a bid requirement.
3. The school district has certain requirements.
4. It is necessary to build a solid working relationship in which the school library media center's needs may be mutually understood and determined with the school district business office and in which the media specialist participates in the evaluation of the bids.

General Considerations in Relation to Vendors

Orders should be placed with reputable business concerns. Some procedures that can help media specialists avoid unsatisfactory service or fraudulent business practices are:

Examine and appraise items on deposit at educational media centers prior to ordering.

Utilize lists of sources in the professional literature.

Seek out other media specialists' recommendations.

Get information about local firms from the Better Business Bureau.

In addition, the media specialist should expect a vendor to fulfill the following criteria:

Maintain adequate physical facilities and a warehouse with a sizable inventory of items described in the state contract specifications or descriptions of the firm, in order to be able to fill a majority of orders from stock.

Have assets, capital, and a credit rating sufficient to handle potential business.

Offer a discount schedule that is competitive with other vendors' schedules, while still giving assurance of satisfactory service by allowing adequate overhead.

Have the staff and production and operating routines necessary to fulfill service requirements, including prompt reporting and follow-up on shipping orders.

Have a satisfactory record in fulfilling similar orders for others. This record should involve such considerations as accuracy of orders filled (such as specified edition or binding), percentage of orders filled (unfortunately an o.s. or out-of-stock report on an order often reflects the jobber's in-house stock rather than the publisher's), length of delivery time, nature of billing procedures, and quality of service when rectifying errors that have been made.

Materials may be ordered from their originating source—a publisher, producer, or manufacturer—or from wholesalers or jobbers. Many media specialists will order items in a variety of ways, depending on how the format is traditionally distributed. Some print-oriented wholesalers stock nonprint items in an effort to simplify the media center's acquisition problems. Wholesale distributors of some mix of print and nonprint items to a regional area are best identified through their advertisements in school media and library periodicals, particularly in notices in professional organization bulletins and newsletters. Two important sources for help in identifying suppliers and vendors for specific items are the *Audiovisual Market Place* (R. R. Bowker, annual), and *The Audio Visual Equipment Directory* (National Audio-Visual Association, annual). The first title includes a directory section that identifies under each company's name the print and nonprint items it handles. The second title lists types of equipment as well as vendors.

PURCHASING

Another part of the acquisitions process is the preparation of purchase orders, which lends itself to an organized, routine approach. A network of libraries or a school system with a central administrative unit can avail itself of the purchasing economies that result from the central coordination of orders, and the entire routine of purchasing may be handled by online computer processing.

The use of the computer in ordering not only frees the specialist from arduous clerical routines but also allows for printout reports in a variety of formats, such as by vendor, author, or purchase order. By adding additional information (subject headings, classification numbers), more uses can be made of the data, such as cataloging and the preparation of subject bibliographies, union lists, or book catalogs. Many automated districtwide ordering systems continue to employ the batch method, which uses the punched card as an input device. Others use more sophisticated equipment and input via magnetic tape or disc, but in single-school situations, microcomputers have also been employed to handle purchase orders through the use of locally produced programs on cassettes or floppy discs (see Chapter 9).

Other school systems have contracted with book jobbers to use their automated acquisition system for book selection as well as the generation of purchase orders and accounting documents. In such a situation, the library media specialist selects material from the jobber's lists and encodes ordering information on special forms that can be read by an optical scanner.

Where the ordering is not centralized, the ordering system should be designed by the media specialist in the individual school and approved by the school business office. Two considerations are important: The procedures should eliminate unnecessary duplication and they should use simple standardized order forms. Frequency of ordering varies from school to school. To simplify bookkeeping procedures, many business offices prefer fewer and larger orders to a multitude containing only a few items each. Infrequent—once-or-twice-a-year ordering—however, can result in a lack of up-to-dateness in collections, an inability to react to new curricular needs, and the risk of nonfulfillment of orders because an item has gone out of stock or out of print.

The school fiscal year is sometimes calculated from September 1 through August 31, and because in decentralized library media programs, professional personnel are not available to check orders or the like during the summer months, district business offices will often not allow ordering after a specified date (sometimes April 15) to ensure delivery and confirmation of payment before the end of the school year. To make certain that all of the budgeted funds will be expended in a given year, library media specialists will sometimes append supplementary lists of materials (usually books) in order of purchase priority. These can then be substituted for items not available until all the funds have been spent. Before leaving for summer vacation, the library media specialist usually prepares several orders to be charged to the next year's budget. At a minimum, these are orders for magazine and newspaper subscriptions, supplies, new books, and audiovisual materials. Although it is sometimes difficult, one must exercise restraint in order to ensure adequate funding for the rest of the school year.

Request Records

The following steps for maintaining request records may be used by any media center. Request cards, available commercially from library supply houses or produced locally, contain appropriate spaces for order information. The cards may also be easily adapted to supply other needed data. They may be used early in the selection process by teachers, administrators, students, and community members, as needed in the particular situation, to note their requests for materials. The library media center personnel can also use them when checking selection aids.

Items that should be included on request cards are: (1) author (or counterpart), (2) title, (3) format, (4) publisher (or producer), (5) publication date, (6) edition, (7) number of copies wanted, (8) department making recommendation, (9) individual making recommendation, and (10) authority (review media, date, and page). Space might also be provided for the International Standard Book Number (ISBN), a numeric device that, through coding, identifies a specific book by country of origin, publisher, and title. Increasingly, book jobbers and other vendors are utilizing this code for ordering purposes and using the conventional bibliographic information for verification purposes only. The back of the card could be used for a brief content note. When the item is received and a "New Additions to the School Library Media Center" or other bibliography is being prepared; the annotation will already have been written.

Because acquisition is a continuous process, the center's patrons should be regularly reminded to turn in their request cards to the media center. This cumulative file, often called a consideration file, can be kept by subject, grade level, or larger curriculum division in order to apportion funds equitably. When the appropriate fund for purchase of the item is assigned, the card may be filed in a separate "awaiting-purchase" file, or two or more files of cards may be kept, one for immediate purchase, the other for future acquisition when funds are available. Usually these awaiting-purchase files will serve more efficiently if they are subdivided by media format, because they will frequently be sent to vendors who specialize in one type of media, for example, academic games.

Before a purchase order is instituted, a clerk should carefully check the card against the center's card catalog, shelf list, or on-order files to determine whether the center already owns or has ordered the item. The accuracy of the basic information posted on the cards should also be checked against indexes and catalogs, such as *Books in Print*, NICEM indexes, *Booklist*, *Library Journal*, or *School Library Journal*. Once the card from the purchase files has been appropriately checked, a multiple-copy requisition form may be typed for each item. Cards for items not received after an order is completed (usually because of out-of-print status) are kept in another file known as the "desiderata" file, which should be checked periodically. If an item is still in demand, an alternate method of acquisition could be tried (for example, use of out-of-print dealers, purchase of a facsimile copy, or interlibrary loan).

ORDER PROCESSING

This section deals with order-processing methods and several steps of physical preparation of material (other than classification and cataloging, discussed later in this chapter) that are required to make the item usable in the school library media center.

Single-School Ordering and Processing

When the media center in the individual school is responsible for taking care of its own technical services, it must develop its own appropriate ordering and processing procedures.

Ordering

The information from the request card that should be transferred to the order card is: author, title, publisher, date of publication, edition, price, number of copies, and ISBN when necessary. Additional information includes date ordered, name of vendor, and name and address of school.

A minimum of two copies per item (original and duplicate) should be provided—for the business office and the library media center. To supply greater flexibility and usefulness, a form with multicopy duplicates is recommended. The following example illustrates how a six-copy color-coded order form could be used.

1st copy (white original)—for vendor

2nd copy (blue)—duplicate for vendor

3rd copy (yellow)—for school business office

4th copy (pink)—for media center use

5th copy (green)—for media center use

6th copy (beige, on index card stock)—punched for shelf list

The set of requisition forms is divided into two sections. The first section, including the original copy, goes to the school business office; the second section, including the sixth copy (on the index card stock) is kept by the media center—for example, in an on-order file, arranged by vendor, awaiting the arrival of the item.

The school's standard purchase order—which contains all the pertinent information, such as vendor, address, total price (if not a bid price, the list price is usually given), special instructions, and the legend, "as per attached forms"—should be attached to the first three copies and then sent to the school business office for official authorization and mailing to the vendor.

For efficient follow-through in the ordering procedure, the school business office should retain the third copy of each requisition form for its office files and send the original and a duplicate to the vendor with instructions to return the duplicate with the item ordered. The working arrangement should also allow the media specialist to telephone or wire for rush orders as needed on assurance to the vendor of an immediate confirmation purchase order. The media specialist should carefully check the center's expenditure records for the balances in each budget account, as well as the records that are kept in the school business office, before using this system of confirmation-purchase-order ordering.

Processing Preparations

When materials are received in the media center, they should be opened, checked, and prepared for processing. A clerk or student aide may check the items and the enclosed packing slip against the three copies of the requisitions in the center's on-order file. These slips, together with any processing element (Library of Congress catalog cards or processing kits from commercial producers), should be put with the item as it is checked in and placed on the processing assembly line. The status of the shipment should be noted by date on the media center's copy of the purchase order. These copies should be filed by vendor or purchase order number, whichever is used in the business office, to give the media specialist a quick-access file that corresponds to the accounts for the center at the business office.

On receipt of the items, there should be three (or four if the vendor returns a copy) requisition slips that may be used in various ways. For example, one of the slips may be returned as a notification to the requesting patron; the index-card-stock copy may be used as an inventory "by-format" card to supplement the inventory use of the shelf list card filed by subject or class; a third slip may be sent to department heads or grade-level teachers to provide a supplementary catalog of items especially useful for given areas; the fourth slip may be filed temporarily in the card catalog by title or author, whichever is more useful.

Because of the special characteristics of some of the media that are acquired by a center (microfilm that can be a monopoly item, film rentals, paperbacks, and so on), the media specialist should strive for the best possible working relationship with the business office in order to streamline ordering procedures, eliminate unnecessary paperwork, and guarantee the speedy receipt of media. One of the ways to ensure the last, as well as the goodwill of suppliers, is to arrange for prompt payment of invoices for partial shipments of an order. There are several ways to circumvent regulations that an order must be completed before any invoices on a partial shipment can be paid. A simple one requires only that the business office issue a confirming purchase order to cover invoices for the material received.

The media center should receive a copy of the vendor's invoice, from either the vendor or the business office, so that a running statement of the media center account funds can be kept in the center. In this way the media specialist will be able at any time to determine the encumbrances against the account balances. The media specialist should also check regularly with the school business office to verify these amounts.

Magazine Acquisition

To secure a maximum discount for library media centers and ensure continuity of coverage, magazines are usually ordered through a special magazine agency. Some of the better known national agencies are:

Ebsco Subscription Service
Box 1943
Birmingham, AL 35201

F. W. Faxon Co.
15 South West Park
Westwood, MA 02098

McGregor Agency
Mount Morris, IL 61054

Moore-Cottrell Subscription Agency
North Cohacton, NY 14868

Turner Subscription Agency
235 Park Ave. S.
New York, NY 10003

Many other reputable regional agencies could be added, and by dealing locally, complaints or problems might be more expeditiously handled. Members of local school library media associations or personnel from the state school library media agency will be able to help in choosing a suitable magazine jobber. These agencies will usually supply the necessary order forms. If using your own form, be sure to include the following data: (1) name and address of school library media center to which the magazine should be addressed, (2) name and address to which bill should be sent, (3) name of magazine and length of subscription (usually one year), (4) number of copies wanted, (5) whether it is a new subscription or a renewal, (6) date of issue that will begin the subscription, for example, "Begin all subscriptions with the September issue unless otherwise noted." Most magazine agencies will supply prospective customers with copies of catalogs that give recommendations of purchases for various types of libraries, indication of where the magazine is indexed, frequency of publication, and discount information. Some magazines (free ones, for example) and most newspapers cannot be ordered through magazine agencies but must be ordered separately. Evaluative criteria, tips on handling, and specific selection aids for magazines and other educational media are given in Chapter 8.

When magazines are received, they are "checked in" at a special magazine file in which there are cards arranged in alphabetical order for all the magazines to which the center subscribes. Commercial library supply houses can supply record cards to record daily, weekly, or monthly periodicals, as well as index cabinets or book units to store these cards. In addition to the name of magazine and space for checking when an issue is received, this check-in card sometimes has entries for other kinds of information, such as where the periodical is indexed and subscription expiration date. This file should be accessible to all patrons, but it is also advisable to prepare lists of the school library media center's magazine holdings that can be distributed within the school and placed close to the periodical indexes and magazine or microfilm storage facilities.

After a new issue of a periodical is checked in, it is stamped with the center's ownership marks, placed in a single-issue magazine binder, and put on the magazine rack or other suitable display unit. The superseded issue is retired to storage. Current issues of magazines should be displayed in transparent protective covers on shelves or racks. A checking record for daily newspapers is usually unnecessary unless the media center's holdings are extensive. Weekly newspapers are processed like magazines.

Monopoly Items and Standing Orders

Some materials such as encyclopedias are available from only one source—in the case of encyclopedias it is the publisher—and therefore cannot be ordered through a jobber. They are sometimes referred to as monopoly items and often include materials for which no library discount is given. If such an item is inadvertently ordered from the jobber, an "Order Directly from Publisher" report will probably appear on a future invoice.

Although library media specialists will ordinarily evaluate each item individually, occasionally, as in the case of encyclopedia yearbooks or other annuals, the center will automatically want future volumes. To save the inconvenience of constant reordering, an arrangement known as "standing orders" can be made whereby the jobber or publisher will automatically ship specified series or continuations to the center.

Pamphlet and Other Vertical File-Materials

Because much of the material for the vertical file is either free or inexpensive, acquisition of this material is best done at the single-school level rather than involving the business office in a multitude of small transactions. If possible, the library media center should have petty cash funds available so that checks or money orders can accompany requests. If these funds are not available through the central office, perhaps monies raised through book fairs, Parent-Teacher Association functions, or similar activities could be earmarked for this purpose. To facilitate the acquisition of pamphlets, most media centers develop a form letter (known as a begging letter) or postcard requesting the material. For free materials, space should be left in the letter for the address, an indication of where the material was listed (such as *Ver-*

tical File Index), title(s) or subject of the material requested, and number of copies needed. The letter should also contain the address to which the material should be sent and a sincere "thank you" for their generosity and help. Letters involving transmittal of money should also contain a statement, "Enclosed please find a check (money order) for. . . ."

When the material has been received and screened for suitability (see specific criteria and selection aids for pamphlets and clippings in Chapter 8), ownership marks and date of receipt should be stamped on the material. (This will be of value for future weeding of the file.) Because these items—usually referred to generically as ephemeral material—do not warrant the expenditure of time and money for cataloging, they are housed in file cabinets, usually in hanging file folders (clippings and pictures might also be placed in manila envelopes for safekeeping), and arranged alphabetically by subject. The subject lists used to organize these holdings should correspond to the one used for other materials (such as *Sears List of Subject Headings*). To direct patrons to this ephemeral material, subject cards should be inserted in the card catalog indicating where these additional items on the subject may be found. For example, the text on the card would read "BIRDS—Additional material will be found under this subject in the Vertical File."

There are several fine books on the administration of ephemeral materials. Three are:

Gould, Geraldine N. *How to Organize and Maintain the Library Picture/Pamphlet File*. Dobbs Ferry, N.Y.: Oceana, 1968.

Hill, Donna. *The Picture File: A Manual and Curriculum-Related Subject List*. Syracuse, N.Y.: Gaylord, 1979.

Miller, Shirley, *The Vertical File and Its Satellites*. Littleton, Colo.: Libraries Unlimited, 1979.

Microforms

Before ordering microforms for the first time, be sure to read the company catalogs thoroughly (see Chapter 8 under Microforms) to familiarize yourself with ordering procedures. In addition to billing address, the order form usually asks for title, volume or years for newspapers or periodicals format (35mm, 16mm), whether index is to be provided, negative or positive print required, and, if needed, the type of carriage. Because a microform is not intended to take the place of the "hard" copy of a periodical, the media specialist should verify that the paper copy has also been received. Microforms are checked in and catalogued in the same manner as other materials. That is, a regular magazine record card is filled out and filed for each periodical or newspaper in microform. On it is placed an indication of the center's holdings and the microform format. With books in microforms, regular cataloging procedures are followed. A description of the microform is given as a note on the catalog card. The cards are filed in the card catalog.

Government Documents

One of the easiest ways to stretch the center's acquisition budget is to investigate and utilize the wide variety of materials available from government agencies. Some are free; others are generally inexpensive when compared with their commercial counterparts. The range of subject matter is as wide as the types of formats and depth of coverage. The Government Printing Office (GPO) is the major publisher of U.S. government documents. They are distributed by the Superintendent of Documents, or SuDocs. The full address is Superintendent of Documents, U.S. Government Printing Office, Washington, DC 20402. The many bibliographies of government documents (some are described in Chapter 8) detail the instructions for ordering. The basic information needed is title, date, and stock number. Payment can be made in a variety of ways, for example, by check, money order, or the use of a deposit account or MasterCard and Visa. In addition to the mail-order service, there are more than 20 GPO bookstores located in major cities throughout the country, each stocking about 1,500 of the more popular titles. Two other important sources are The Consumer Information Center, Pueblo, CO 81009, and the Library of Congress, Washington, DC 20540.

Centralized Ordering and Processing

Processing at the single-school level has been unsatisfactory in several respects, not the least of which is the time factor, and experience indicates that some form of centralized processing or use of commercial sources should be established to relieve the individual school of this responsibility.

Much has been written about the advantages of central or commercial processing. In summary, the advantages are:

Personnel in the school library media center are freed to supply increased services to patrons.

Substantial savings in time, labor, and money are produced through larger discounts from jobbers, utilizing clerks for routine jobs, and reducing duplication of effort.

A large-scale, systematized work flow produces greater efficiency and reduces processing time.

There is uniformity in cataloging and classification.

Business routines are centralized and simplified.

Union catalogs to facilitate interlibrary loan and prevent unnecessary duplication of expensive materials can be prepared easily.

Some of the larger school systems have developed processing centers that rely heavily on data-processing equipment. It is still possible, however, to organize an effective operation even though automated devices are not available. For example, following are the steps by which materials are ordered and processed manually within a centralized unit:

1. A staff member makes out a six-copy, color-coded multiple-order slip, removes one copy for filing at the school, and sends the remaining five-part form to the centralized processing center.

2. At the processing center, the first copy of the five-part form is interfiled by publisher or distributor with orders from other schools.

3. The slips are arranged by title and sent to the respective vendors.

4. The second copy of the order slip is used to check the authority file to determine if a master set of catalog cards exists in the center. If so, a set of cards is reproduced and pockets and spine labels are printed. If a master set is not available, the center orders sets of catalog cards from such outlets as the Library of Congress.

5. The three remaining copies of the order form are placed with these materials until the arrival of the order. If cards are not available, the copies of the order form are held until the material is received. When it is delivered, the purchase price is entered on the three remaining copies of the order form.

6. One copy is sent to the center's accounting office, another is attached to the invoice, and the third is placed with the material and eventually sent back with the processed material to the school.

7. Media without catalog cards are sent to the catalog section and cataloged before the remaining steps in the process are taken, such as spine lettering and pasting in of pockets.

8. New master sets of cards are sent to the authority file, where they are filed by title.

9. When the material arrives in the school, media center personnel complete the processing routine by checking for errors and adding necessary information to the shelf-list card.

There are several alternative approaches to establishing a central processing center in each school district, and local conditions differ so considerably that in some cases efficiency and economy might suggest other solutions. Commercial cataloging is now available at reasonable prices through several companies. Although their major strength has been in the area of book processing, coverage for processing of nonbook materials is increasing. It is also possible for schools to contract with other outside agencies for their processing needs. A few states, North Carolina and Rhode Island, for example, have established statewide processing units. Some schools have reached agreements with public library systems, other school districts, or regional educational agencies to handle processing. A key factor is the availability of processing for audiovisual materials. Since many of these agencies do not offer this crucial service, some school districts have found it advisable to rely on the outside agency only for book processing and to create supplementary centers to process their nonprint media. Regardless of the pattern adopted, media should arrive at the school ready for use. In this way processing at the single-school level can be confined to those few educational materials produced within the school that cannot be handled by a central agency.

CLASSIFICATION AND CATALOGING

In organizing a collection a media specialist should keep accessibility and user convenience uppermost in mind. Materials on the same subject should be integrated and stored together if at all possible. Where physical conditions dictate housing parts of the collection by format, the same criteria involving accessibility should apply equally to all formats. Traffic flow, economical use of space, and user safety are factors of importance in deciding organizational patterns, but these patterns should be sufficiently flexible to allow for some modification.

Classification

Classification is the systematic arrangement of materials into groups according to some predetermined list of criteria. Of the number of classification schemes in existence, the one that has been almost universally adopted in media centers is the Dewey decimal classification (DDC), developed by Melvil Dewey after his careful study of several systems used to classify knowledge. Dewey began work on his system in 1872 while a student library assistant at Amherst College in Massachusetts. When it was published in 1876 it was greeted unenthusiastically by many librarians, but its growth in popularity paralleled the tremendous library expansion in the twentieth century. Its major rival is the Library of Congress (LC) classification system, which was developed in 1897 specifically for the recataloging of the Library of Congress's vast collection. The LC system uses both letters and numbers as location devices, and because of the complexity and the minuteness of its breakdown of subject matter, it has been adopted only for use with large or specialized collections. DDC, on the other hand, has many advantages for use in school media centers:

1. It brings materials on the same subject together in a logical and uniform sequence.

2. It is sufficiently simple to be understood by both staff and patrons without frequent referral to classification schedules.

3. Materials organized by this system can be found and retrieved quickly.

4. Because the system moves from large subject areas to more specialized ones through the addition of numbers, the degree of sophistication of the classification can vary with the size and nature of collections.

5. It is used in most libraries with which the students would be familiar.

6. Commercial cataloging sources as well as standard bibliographies and media-reviewing tools extensively utilize this classification system.

Some media centers use DDC for the print collection but have devised other classifying arrangements for nonprint items such as films, filmstrips, and phonograph records. The simplest and most common variation is to assign code names (such as F = film) and an accession number to the items and house each type of material separately, arranged by the numerical order in which they were acquired. There are obvious disadvantages to such a system: Materials on the same subject are not housed together (nor could they be without extensive reclassification); items are separated by format rather than content; if duplicate copies are added, their call numbers will vary and the possibilities of meaningful browsing are lessened because of the absolute dependence on the card catalog as a locating device. It is, therefore, recommended that DDC be used for classifying all types of media.

Cataloging

The card catalog is an index to the media center's collection and thus is the basic key to center resources. Its primary purpose is to indicate the materials that are in the collection and their location. It also provides bibliographic data and a description of content for each item. The single dictionary catalog, which contains all the catalog cards (author, title, subject) in one alphabet, is the most common type found in media centers, although many experiments with divided catalogs have brought an encouraging response from patrons. In some divided catalogs only the subject and subject-related cards are filed separately; in others all three types are dispersed in three distinct alphabets. Much of the traditional confusion in catalog use can be avoided with the divided catalog. Because locating nonprint materials is done primarily from the subject approach, the subject file has become the largest and most-used part of the catalog. A separate file that integrates subject cards for all the library holdings would seem advisable, to simplify and, in general, help in locating materials.

Of the several types of cards that may be in the catalog, the three basic types are: main entry (author, artist, composer, issuing agency), title (with many such nonbook materials as transparencies, the title frequently is also the main entry), and subject. Other types of cards are for added entries (joint authors, illustrators), analytical data (specific content), and cross-references. Some media centers have also experimented with a separate classified catalog with a single card for each item, arranged solely by call number. This differs from the shelf list in two respects: (1) It is for patron use, and (2) it integrates the cards of all materials with the same number, regardless of each item's location in the library. This special catalog gives the number and nature of the media center's entire holdings in particular subject areas and is helpful in acquainting patrons quickly with the center's collection.

In the past some media centers adopted a system of color-coding their catalog cards to identify various kinds of media. For example, a strip of red at the top of a card would indicate that the item was a filmstrip; green, a phonograph record, and so on. However, the number of distinctive colors is limited, and with the proliferation of kinds of material in media centers, various shades of each color have had to be used as designators, which often has only confused the patron. Color-coding is now being discouraged, principally because commercial processors and manufacturers of catalog cards and kits have not adopted it. Instead, they issue plain white cards that designate the medium after the title and, quite frequently, at the top left corner above the call number.

Prior to the time that libraries began using card catalogs, the printed (or often handwritten) book catalog was the usual format for listing a library's holdings. This method was abandoned because it was time-consuming and because it was difficult to keep the catalog up-to-date unless costly complete versions were issued frequently. The present increased application of computerized data processing in automating many library procedures has brought about a renewal of interest in the book catalog. As prices for computers become more reasonable, some school systems are able to purchase them or to contract for the use of computer time and services from commercial firms. A few schools have already converted the traditional card catalog into book format. The book catalog has many advantages. Once the initial catalog has been prepared, multiple copies can be produced inexpensively and placed in classrooms or other important locations, either inside or outside the school. In addition to providing greater accessibility, book catalogs are more compact, require no expensive cabinets, and are easier to read than cards in a card catalog. Another important advantage is the ease with which recataloging can be done in the book catalog in comparison to making similar changes in the card catalog. The single most important drawback to the book catalog is the initial expense of conversion.

Commercial Sources of Cataloging

In 1911, the Library of Congress began its system of printing catalog cards and offering them to libraries at a reasonable rate. Since then many commercial concerns have also developed and marketed cataloging services. Most use as the basis of their catalogs two Library of Congress products. The first is known as MARC tapes. In 1968, the Library of Congress began distributing their bibliographic or cataloging records on MAchine-Readable Cataloging (MARC) magnetic tapes. These now include books, maps, serials, and some audiovisual material such as films, transparencies, and filmstrips. Depending on the kind of service and format coverage, tapes are mailed out with frequency varying from weekly to monthly. For complete service, such as all MARC records, the annual cost is about $10,000 and the number of records received is over 250,000 per year.

The second service, which can also be included in the MARC database, is known as Cataloging in Publication (CIP) and was begun in 1971. Over 2,500 publishers have participated in the program. They submit galleys or advance publication data to the Library of Congress, whose catalogers determine the Dewey and LC classification numbers, LC card number, and basic cataloging information, including added entries and, in the case of childrens' books, a brief annotation. This information now appears in LC catalog card format on the verso of the title page in published books. Some large libraries that do their own cataloging use these entries for preliminary cataloging before the actual cards arrive.

Some commercial catalogers use CIP data to make catalog cards available on or before the actual publication date of the book. Space is provided for the customer to add the collation line. Because of the additional work this involves, it is an option that is perhaps not that valuable in school library media centers.

Using MARC tapes supplemented by in-house cataloging, many commercial producers of catalog cards now have holdings of over 1,000,000 titles. For the school library media center that does not have access to a centralized processing agency, the use of commercial cataloging (and processing if possible) has many advantages:

1. *Time.* The chief gain is in time saved by the library media staff to free them to supply more services to their patrons.

2. *Cost.* Weighing the cost of in-house cataloging, typing, and basic materials, the value of purchasing cards or kits is outstanding. Sets of cards or kits can be purchased for under a dollar, slightly more with full processing. It would be impossible for the single library media center or even an average-size school district to come close to this level of economy, even with the most efficient operation.

3. *Flexibility.* A number of options concerning specific cataloging requirements are available. As a basic choice, most offer: (1) LC classification with LC subject headings, (2) unabridged Dewey classification with LC subject headings, and (3) abridged Dewey classification with Sears subject headings (most frequently used by school library media centers). Other options include call-number formats and the possibility of ordering extra cards.

4. *Quality.* The copy is prepared by professional catalogers and, therefore, the quality should be uniformly high, certainly above the caliber that could be produced locally.

The salient disadvantage in using commercial processing is the need to adhere to cataloging decisions made outside the library media center. In some cases, for example, where subject headings have been specifically modified to fit particular curriculum requirements, it will be difficult to adjust to outside decisions. Therefore, when choosing a commercial cataloging firm, one must be particularly aware of the degree of individualization of service available. In evaluating these processing services, the following criteria will be helpful:

1. Types of materials cataloged—books, paperbacks, audiovisual material, out-of-print materials.

2. Services offered—full processing, partial, kits, or cards only.

3. Options allowed in cataloging—nature of specific requirements accommodated: classification systems, types of subject headings, flexibility in call-number choice, choice of alternate symbols (such as F or Fic, R or Ref, 921 or B), ease in changing these specifications when needed, and number of cards available.

4. Consistency in cataloging.

5. Quality of processing—plastic jackets, pockets, circulation cards, date-due slips, spine markings, installation of theft-detection devices, and binding for paperback books.

6. Clarity and readability of products.

7. Cost—in line with competition.

8. Ordering procedures—kinds of ordering information accepted, for example, ISBN, LC number, or regular bibliographic information (author, title, publisher), special forms needed for ordering, minimum order requirements.

9. Speed of delivery—most suppliers now guarantee that orders will be filled within one week of receiving, method of shipping (ordinary mail, UPS, first class), quality of packaging.

10. Method of payment—billing procedures, availability of prepaid purchase coupons or vouchers.

11. Order-fulfillment record—percentage of orders actually received, number of cards not received, back-ordering arrangements.

There are many sources of commercial cataloging services available. They are listed annually in *Library Journal*'s Buyer's Guide issue (also found in *School Library Journal*). The largest distributor is still the Library of Congress Cataloging Distribution Service, but for school library media centers, LC's product does not have the customized features available through commercial outlets. Some of the companies, however, supply cataloging and processing services only when the book is also purchased from them (for example, Baker & Taylor); others supply these services with or without book orders (Bro Dart); others only sell cataloging cards and kits (Catalog Card Corporation). Still others specialize in cataloging specific types of materials; for example, the Specialized Service and Supply Company in Cincinnati, Ohio, provides catalog kits for audiovisual materials exclusively.

Library of Congress Catalog Cards

Through its Cataloging Distribution Service, the Library of Congress distributes some 40 million catalog cards annually from a database that now represents over 7 million different bibliographic records. The actual printing of the cards is accomplished through an electronic printing service called CARDS (Card Automated Reproduction Demand Service), which uses laser, xerographic, and computer technology. Because cards are printed on demand and are automatically arranged and labeled by customer, the need for a large and costly inventory has been eliminated. Each individual card set consists of a multiple number of unit cards, enough to accommodate each of the suggested tracings found at the bottom of the card plus a shelf-list card. Adding the call number (LC and unabridged Dewey classification are given at the bottom of each card) and tracings are left to the individual library, allowing a free reign for any modifications needed. LC subject headings, not Sears, are used, but brief annotations are given for juvenile titles.

Details on how to open an account are supplied in a booklet, *Catalog Cards*, available from Customer Services Section, Cataloging Distribution Service, Library of Congress, Washington, DC 20541. For U.S. libraries, in brief, they are: file a new account application form (in brochure) and enter a maintenance deposit or agree to pay for services on receipt of a monthly bill. Each new subscriber receives a six-digit account number that must be used on orders or other correspondence. Customers use special card-order forms that are fed into an optical character reading and sorting system. Cards should be ordered by using the Library of Congress card number. This is usually found with other bibliographic information in most media selection sources as well as in the item itself. This number, unique to the piece of material it identifies, is assigned by the Library of Congress and consists of two digits, a hyphen, and one to six additional digits, for example, 75-44324. The first two digits indicate the year the number was issued, *not* the publication date. (This numbering system should not be confused with ISBN—a much more complex and detailed method of identifying books. This is administered in the United States by the R. R. Bowker Company, New York, which can supply further information on it.)

Cards can also be searched if detailed bibliographic data is supplied. For cards searched in this manner, an additional 60 cents is charged per set, which almost doubles the basic fee. Most orders are filled during the week following receipt of order.

The LC card services have a number of advantages for libraries, particularly large ones—reasonable prices, a large number of entries, detailed cataloging, flexibility in adapting tracings, and range of formats (for example, audiovisual materials, maps, documents, serial publications). But for small libraries, including the average school library media center, there are some grave drawbacks: the necessity to rework the material found on the unit card (for example, adapt the unabridged to abridged Dewey, convert LC subject headings to Sears), and type this information on the remaining cards. Another minus is the absence of further cataloging and processing services. The result has been that at present only secondary schools use LC card service with any degree of frequency.

OCLC and Other Major Online Bibliographic Utilities

The 1970s saw the growth of a number of online bibliographic utilities. *Online* in this case means that local terminals are hooked into the central processing unit of a computer and the user is able to interact with this computer. Most of these utilities focus on supplying cataloging information to member libraries. Each maintains a large bibliographic database or union catalog and also supplies, with varying degrees of access, additional services such as interlibrary loan, serials control, and acquisition subsystems. However, the supplying of cataloging information and accompanying catalog cards is the key service supplied by these organizations.

Many independent regional networks contract with these bibliographic utilities to supply services to their member libraries. Therefore, many local libraries utilize the services of these large utilities, but through the conduit of a regional network (for a discussion of these regional networks, see Chapter 12). At present the four largest utilities are: (1) RLIN, for Research Libraries Information Network (formerly known as BALLOTS); now owned and managed by the Research Library Group (RLG), it confines its activities to large academic libraries, (2) UTLAS, University of Toronto Library Automation System, national in scope but confined essentially to a Canadian market, (3) WLN, Washington Library Network, described at length in Chapter 12, and (4) OCLC, the largest and most used, formerly known as the Ohio College Library Center but now as the Online Computer Library Center, Inc.

At present about 30 percent of the total academic libraries in Canada and the United States, and 3 percent of the public libraries use a bibliographic utility. Only a few multidistrict school units or large centralized processing centers for schools are now using these utilities, although gradually the number is growing. Because almost 90 percent of these users is affiliated with OCLC, let us look more closely at how their cataloging system operates.

OCLC, a nonprofit organization located at 6565 Franz Road, Dublin, OH 43017, has about 3,500 member libraries, but indirectly serves over 6,000. Its online database contains over 9 million records of print and nonprint materials and is growing at the rate of approximately

25,000 records per week. Through original input cataloging, users contribute about 75 percent of the nonbibliographic records to the catalog; the rest comes from records generated at the national libraries (for example, Library of Congress MARC tapes). Users indicate that they have a 94 percent success rate in locating the item being searched.

Before going online, a library indicates its special cataloging needs. Subject headings, classification scheme, and call-number arrangement are just three of the areas where a personalized need may be indicated. Based on these surveys, a special computer program is built for each customer.

At the terminal, records can be retrieved through a variety of methods using various search keys: author (main or added entry), title, government document number, LC card number, ISSN, ISBN, or special OCLC numbers. When the user is satisfied that the record displayed on the terminal is the same as the data wanted in the catalog cards, the "Produce" and "Send" buttons are depressed. Shortly thereafter cards are printed to the user's specification and mailed to the requesting library with subject headings and call numbers in place. In a multilibrary district, cards can be sorted by OCLC and sent to individual school library media centers if requested.

Additional services that can be contracted for include the generation of accession lists, cumulative machine-readable tapes of cataloging archives, and printing capabilities for local production of spine, pocket, and book-card labels. Over 2½ million catalog cards are produced per week.

Most of the members are linked to the OCLC computer center by direct, private ("dedicated") telephone lines and specially designed cathode ray tube (CRT) terminals. Failing this direct connection, libraries can also access the computer through connection by telephone to TYMNET, a telecommunication carrier of computer data, or by direct dial. The latter two methods are more expensive if a great volume of transactions is expected. In addition to the expense involved in the hookups and ongoing telecommunication linkage charges, other costs involve initial equipment purchase and charges for database use for each catalog card produced. In short, this is not cost-effective for either a single school or a small school district. However, online cataloging can become a cost-effective reality for school library media centers through the development of multitype regional library cooperative networks or centralized processing centers.

Tips for the Do-It-Yourself Cataloger

When it is necessary to do original cataloging within the library media center, it should be done as simply and as quickly as possible. Here are some pointers:

1. Assemble basic tools to help you. Unless you catalog using the Library of Congress system, the three basic documents are:

Abridged Dewey Decimal Classification and Relative Index, 11th ed. New York: H. W. Wilson, 1979.

Barbara M. Westby, *Sears List of Subject Headings*, 12th ed. New York: H. W. Wilson, 1982.

Anglo-American Cataloging Rules, 2nd ed. Chicago: American Library Association, 1978.

The ALA tool, although the official cataloging code, can be somewhat forbidding in its detail. Some simpler manuals are:

Akers' Simple Library Cataloging by Arthur Curley and Jane Varlejs, 6th ed. Metuchen, N.J.: Scarecrow, 1977.

Commonsense Cataloging by Esther J. Piercy, revised by Rosalind Miller and Jane Terwillegar, 3rd ed. New York: H. W. Wilson, 1983.

Specifically to help with nonprint materials there is *Cataloging Audiovisual Materials: A Manual Based on AACR II* by Eugene Fliescher and Helen Goodman (Neal-Schuman, 1980). Very basic material is also covered in Mildred L. Nickel's *Steps to Service*, American Library Association, 1975.

2. Familiarize yourself with these tools, particularly with the basic structure of the Dewey decimal system and the methods of subdivision. The introduction to the abridged edition is helpful, as is the prefatory material in *Sears*.

3. Do not catalog in a vacuum. Use the resources within the existing collection and card catalog to help. For example, use commercially produced catalog cards as examples to follow concerning format. These are particularly helpful in cataloging AV materials. Not only will this promote consistency in format, but it will help solve problems involving the contents of the cards. Use the shelf list as a guide in assigning appropriate classification numbers. In this way you will be cataloging within a fixed framework and into an existing collection. Also, frequent referral to your copy of *Sears* (provided it has been marked properly and kept up-to-date) will be invaluable in assigning subject headings that are consistent with those already used.

4. Know the existing policies within the library media center concerning cataloging and classification. For example, the number of letters used from author's last name in the call number, the classification of biography (B, 921, and so on), use or nonuse of book numbers (Cuttering), special treatment of reference works or other materials.

5. Use blank 3 × 5-inch slips or cards as workslips. These are convenient to work and type from and approximate the same format as the actual catalog card.

Catalog Cards

Commercially produced catalog cards usually contain the following information:

Location device. Usually the call number, consisting of the Dewey decimal number and the first two or three letters of the main entry (in the case of biographies, the name of the person written about is used).

Main entry. In book materials, the author or person chiefly responsible for the content of the work; with nonprint media, frequently the title.

Title (and subtitle).

Medium identification. Film, filmstrip, and so on.

Additional main entry information. Coauthor, illustrator, or narrator, for example.

Imprint. Publisher, producer, manufacturer, and copyright date.

Collation. Description of the physical quality of the material, for example, number of pages or volumes, frames, sound or silent, length of running time, color or black and white. When applicable, a series note is included.

Annotation or contents summary. Optional.

Tracings. List of headings for which additional cards have been prepared, such as subject headings and other added entries.

When necessary, the above data can be modified to make a local catalog operation as simple and efficient as possible while still supplying the necessary information and points of access the patron will need. Some possible shortcuts are to include statements on illustrators, joint authors, translators, and series only if deemed necessary; to assign subject headings only to major topics; and to avoid analytics. Some pointers on preparing specific parts of the card are:

1. *Main entry.* Use the author's name as it appears on the title page (but check the card catalog for possible variations). Anthologies are entered under the editor, but translations are listed under the original author. Pseudonyms should be used (as Mark Twain). Corporate entries are arranged from the highest to the lowest appropriate level of the organization (such as U.S., Department of Agriculture; ALA, Young Adult Services Division); serial publications like almanacs and encyclopedias are entered under the title as main entry.

2. *Descriptive material.* Use the title as its appears on the title page. Always include imprint information (publisher and date) and number of pages (number of frames or other appropriate format information in the case of AV material), but the inclusion of other descriptive material should be weighed against usefulness.

3. *Classification and tracings.* After examining the dust jacket, table of contents, and preface, determine the principal subject of the work and, using *Sears* and *Dewey*, assign subject headings and classification number (check shelf list and catalog for integration with the main collection), assign additional subject headings when necessary (never more than four per title). Add additional tracings when necessary, such as an additional title card for a volume that contains two novels. If the subject of the book is also the title, for example, *Astronomy* or *Albert Einstein*, make only a subject card.

4. *Cross-references.* Check in *Sears* to make sure that proper "see" and "see also" cards exist for the subjects assigned if needed.

When the work slip has been completed, a basic unit card can be typed. After this has been checked, a full set of cards can be typed, including a title card, one for each of the tracings, and a shelf-list card.

Acquisitions Records and Shelf Lists

It is necessary to keep some sort of acquisitions record to indicate the status of the growth of the collection and the origin and cost of individual additions. In the past, school libraries often maintained a separate loose-leaf accession book in which was entered an account number, author, title, publisher, date, source, and library price. There was also a column labeled "remarks" in which the eventual disposition of the book (such as "missing" or "paid for") could be entered. This is currently considered a wasteful and time-consuming practice now replaced by using the shelf-list card. The shelf-list card is a unit card, that is, a duplicate of the author or main entry card. Instead of an alphabetical arrangement, these cards are organized in the shelf-list file in the order in which the material is shelved. On the card, using the space between the descriptive material and the tracings, access information can be typed. This usually consists of an accession number, source and date of acquisition, and price, in the following format:

83–0124   Bro Dart   6/83 $17.50

If an accession number is used, the first two digits represent the year and the rest of the number is the specific number for that item (for

example, the above item is the one hundred and twenty-fourth to be acquired in 1983). Smaller library media centers might wish simply to
use a copy number rather than an accession number, as in:

c.1   Bro Dart   6/83 $17.50

The accession or copy number should always be added to the library
material as well. In the case of books, it will be found on the upper
right-hand corner of the book pocket and card (for use in circulation
and inventory procedures) and sometimes in the book itself.

Processing

Ownership marks should be stamped on all library materials. With
books, this is usually done on the page after the title page, along the
edges, and on the book pocket. If the material has not been processed
commercially, a few additional steps are necessary. For example, when
kits are not used, a book pocket and card, each containing the call
number, author and title, accession number, and a pressure-sensitive
label with the call number on it should be prepared. With these, and a
date-due slip, the physical preparation of the material can be completed. Plastic covers are often used over dust jackets. They are attractive and also protect the binding. It has been estimated that these
covers double the shelf life of a book.

Many of these processing procedures are routine and, providing that
the steps are logically organized and flow easily, can often be handled
by students or other volunteers. The organization and delegation of
these routines, including acquiring and organizing library material,
should not be so time-consuming that they take the professional staff
away from the more essential aspects of the program.

LOCAL PRODUCTION OF MATERIALS

Although the range and variety of commercially prepared educational materials are extensive and increasing at a rapid rate, there will
always be a need in schools for educational materials that are useful
only in a specific local situation and are, therefore, not available for
purchase. For years either the chalkboard or the bulletin board was
used almost exclusively to meet this need. Today the school library
media center has become the headquarters for the production of a wide
variety of educational materials suitable for learning experiences
unique to a particular school. This section describes the major types of
local-production equipment and supplies found in many school library
media centers and their major uses. Specific equipment items, such as

tape recorders, that accept both commercially and locally prepared materials, are described in Chapter 8, as are the general criteria for selecting equipment. These criteria may also be applied to equipment for local production. Specific emphasis, however, should be placed on versatility—for example, many laminating machines can also be used to produce color-lift transparencies, and copiers will sometimes make both stencils and transparencies.

Mounting and Laminating Equipment

A number of techniques can be used for mounting flat pictures. The conventional method using rubber cement requires no special equipment, but the process is time-consuming and the results can vary considerably in quality. A faster and more professional-looking product can be obtained by using the dry-mount technique. Dry-mount tissue is very thin paper coated on each side with adhesive that becomes sticky when heat and pressure are applied. Although a common hand iron may be used, it is suggested for this purpose that a dry-mount press and tacking iron be part of the media center's basic equipment. Large maps or charts that require rolling and folding for convenient storage may also be mounted by this process by using a special backing cloth coated with adhesive on only one side. The center's dry-mount press should be big enough to handle the largest size material that it expects to mount and laminate.

Laminating, or affixing a transparent protective film to the face of a picture, can also be done in the dry-mount press. Several manufacturers produce special laminating film that can be used in their thermocopying machines. Also available are laminating acetates that may be applied by hand or with a cold-process laminating machine.

Duplicating and Thermocopying Machines

Multiple copies of printed material for use by teachers and students may be produced in a variety of ways, the simplest and most common being by spirit duplicator, or "ditto" machine. When one writes or draws on the master copy, a carbon impression is left on the underside from the attached dye sheet. Different colored dye sheets may be used. The dye is soluble in methyl alcohol—the "spirit"—placed in the drum of the machine. Although only a limited number of copies can be run from each master, the ease of preparation and operation has made this the most popular form of duplication.

Other copying machines should also be available, if not in the center, at least where they are easily accessible to media personnel. The mimeograph machine, which uses stencils and an inking process, is not as versatile as the spirit duplicator, but generally is capable of producing more and higher-quality copies per stencil. The gelatin hectographing process was once very popular, perhaps because it requires such a small initial investment—for hectograph ink or carbon papers, gelatin compound, and a shallow cookie pan. The uncertain quality of the product and the limited number of copies possible (between 15 and 50) has made hectographing less popular.

Dittos as well as single copies may also be reproduced on thermocopying machines. This process exposes and develops specially coated film or paper through heat generated by an infrared lamp in the machine. Thermocopiers can reproduce only certain types of materials: typewritten originals and carbons, mimeographed or printed material, and writing done with a soft lead pencil or with India ink. Ditto copies or writing done with most ballpoint, felt tip, or fountain pens cannot be reproduced by thermocopiers.

Other processes suitable for making a few copies at a time are electrostatic (xerography, electrofax), photocopy, and diazo. The diazo process is described in the next section.

Through their industrial arts classrooms or central printing facilities, many schools also have available to them more sophisticated equipment for producing printed materials, for example, printing machines that use either the letterpress method, which involves typesetting and preparation of plates, or the offset method.

Transparency-Making Equipment

Perhaps the most common locally produced transparencies are those handmade by drawing directly onto acetate sheets. Users of this technique should make sure that their drawing materials work well on acetate. Media center supplies should include a number of suitable felt pens and grease or wax pencils (with various size points), plus a supply of acetate and transparency mounts.

The diazo process (named after the diazo salt found on the acetate) is particularly suitable for the reproduction of colors, and—an added advantage—several copies of the same transparency can be produced easily. This process involves three steps: (1) producing a master on translucent paper (diazo masters are available commercially), (2) printing the image on the diazo acetate by exposing it and the master to an ultraviolet light source, and (3) developing the image on the acetate by placing it in a bath of ammonium hydroxide fumes. Equipment may be purchased that contains units for both exposing and developing the film. Ultraviolet light printers can also be bought separately and any large-mouthed glass container may be used as the developing unit (the so-called pickle jar method).

Many of the duplicating machines found in the school library media center or elsewhere in the school can also be used for transparency making. For example, many thermocopying machines and spirit duplicators will accept acetate sheets and produce translucent transparencies.

Laminating equipment (both hot and cold) as well as the dry-mount press can be used to transfer both black-and-white and color pictures onto transparency acetate. Regardless of the picture-transfer method used, the original must be printed on paper stock that is clay coated. It is also important to remember that the original is destroyed during the process of color lifting.

Photographic Equipment

Increasingly, both teachers and students are utilizing photographic equipment of all types to produce a variety of educational materials—from still photographs and slide presentations to motion pictures and videotapes. To accommodate these needs, the media center should have at least a basic inventory of photographic equipment that includes several still-picture cameras. Although fixed-focus and range-finder cameras are generally less expensive and perfectly adequate for long-range shooting, the reflex camera is more versatile and can easily be equipped with close-up lenses of photographing clearly at a distance of only a few inches. Copy stands with lighting attachments, light meters, and tripods are also important adjunct equipment. Many media centers now have darkroom facilities complete with equipment for developing and enlarging their own photographs.

Because of such innovations as cartridge loading and simplified focusing devices, very young children have become expert filmmakers. The further addition of the zoom lens permits a smooth and easy transition from one field of vision to another. Basic equipment for motion picture making involves an 8mm camera (preferably super 8), a 16mm camera, light meters, tripods, floodlights for special indoor filming, a film viewer, film splicer and scraper, rewinds, and extra reels. Videotaping equipment has also become much less expensive and sufficiently simple to operate that the purchase is feasible for individual schools. Two essential steps to take before purchasing a major piece of photographic equipment for the media center are: (1) get the advice of knowledgeable persons in the field and (2) request a demonstration at which some of the prospective users can be present.

Lettering and Display Equipment

Within the media center, there should be services—principally provided by media technicians—to help teachers and students produce posters, charts, dioramas, and other graphic material and to supply guidance and materials for bulletin boards, exhibits, and other forms of displays. Some of the skills involved in producing these instructional materials are specialized, but with the use of commercially produced aids and other simplifying techniques, locally produced materials can be both attractive and professional looking. There are, for example, many inexpensive ready-to-use lettering devices on the market. A few of these are three-dimensional letters (with or without pin backs), gummed punch-out letters, dry-transfer letters, rubber-stamp letters, and stencil lettering guides. The media center should contain not only a generous sampling of these but also a variety of other artist's supplies, including a wide selection of drawing pens, markers, and pencils, a supply of drawing paper and an illustrating board, spray-can paints, T-squares and other simple drafting instruments, and various cutting tools. Equipment should include a drawing board, primary (or bulletin) typewriter, and a paper cutter.

COPYRIGHT AND THE SCHOOL LIBRARY MEDIA CENTER

In recent years, producers and publishers of educational materials have become increasingly alarmed at what appear to be a flagrant disregard of existing copyright regulations, as well as either vagueness or absence of statements in the law, regarding the use of newer technologies, such as "off-air" taping of television programs. After many years of hearings and debates, Congress passed the Copyright Revision Act of 1976 (P.L. 94–553). Because the implications of this act are important for all libraries, professional personnel should acquaint themselves with at least the basic responsibilities and limitations imposed by this law.

Several excellent references are listed at the end of this chapter that can help guide one through the somewhat tortuous ramifications of the legislation. In regard to books and periodicals, the guidelines state that single copies for teachers can be made of: (1) a chapter from a book, (2) an article from a newspaper or periodical, (3) a short story, essay, or short poem, or (4) a pictorial work from a book, periodical, or newspaper. It should be remembered that these regulations apply only to works currently in copyright. The regulations for multiple copies for classroom use are much more stringent: (1) copying shall be for a specific course and not exceed one copy per student in that course, (2) the time between the decision to use the material and the actual use must be insufficient to receive permission to copy (the test of spontaneity), (3) an article must be fewer than 2,500 words; book excerpts fewer than 1,000 words; and a poem or excerpt from a poem no more than 250 words (the test of brevity), (4) no more than nine such multiple copying instances are allowed per course per term and this copying shall not create or replace existing anthologies, (5) no copying whatever is permitted from "consumable" works, for example, workbooks and standardized texts.

In short, the law prohibits copying that can act as a substitute for the purchase of materials. The law is equally strict in its delineation of circumstances that allow for the reproduction of phonograph records or tapes. In general this prohibits reproduction unless the copy is being used for archival purposes or the original is deteriorating and a replacement is not available at a fair price.

Unfortunately, this law seems to avoid the problem of the legality of off-air copying of television programs by nonprofit educational institutions. To rectify this, Congress appointed in 1979 a negotiating committee of users and producers that represented educational organizations, copyright proprietors, and industrial guilds and unions. Their guidelines first appeared in the *Congressional Record* of October 14, 1981, and in summary imposed the following limitations on recording off-air broadcast programs: (1) Retention of these copies shall not exceed 45 days after the original recording. This allows time either for purchasing a copy of the program or securing a license to retain the existing copy,* (2) copies may be used for instructional purposes for ten school days after the initial taping, (3) taping a program must be initiated by the request of a specific teacher and the program be shown no more than two times per class by that teacher (the second showing supposedly for review or reinforcement purposes), (4) tapes for other teachers can be made provided they meet the other guidelines (such as advance request and use within ten days), and (5) these guidelines do not apply to entertainment films that might be taped for use at lunchtime or for assembly programs.

At present these guidelines are simply a "gentleman's agreement" to ensure fair use and recompense for producers and owners of television programs. Like the regulations in the copyright act, they attempt to bring harmony to the often conflicting interests of proprietors and users. To achieve this balance requires the cooperation of both groups.

---

*Short- and long-term licenses are often available either directly from the broadcaster's headquarters or through the Television Licensing Center, 1144 Wilmette Ave., Wilmette, IL 60091. Most public broadcasting stations issue periodic lists of their offerings and regulations that apply to the taping and use of each.

FOR FURTHER READING

Akers, Susan. *Akers' Simple Library Cataloging*, 6th ed. Metuchen, N.J.: Scarecrow, 1977.

American Association of School Librarians. *Copyright, Media and the School Librarian: A Guide to Multimedia Copying in Schools.* Chicago: AASL, 1978.

American Library Association. *Librarian's Guide to the New Copyright Law.* Chicago: American Library Association, 1977.

———, Reference and Adult Services Division, Interlibrary Loan Committee. *Interlibrary Loan Codes, 1980/International Lending Principles and Guidelines, 1970.* Chicago: American Library Association, 1981.

Association for Educational Communications and Technology. *Copyright and Educational Media: A Guide to Fair Use and Permissions Procedures.* Washington, D.C.: AECT, 1977.

Association of American Publishers. *Explaining the New Copyright Law: A Guide to Legitimate Photocopying and Copyrighted Materials.* New York: AAP, 1977.

"At Last (Whew!); Off-Air Copying Guidelines." *Instructional Innovator* (September 1981), pp. 36–37.

Berman, Sanford. *Joy of Cataloging.* Phoenix, Ariz.: Oryx, 1981.

Bernhaudt, Frances Simonsen. *Introduction to Library Technical Services.* New York: H. W. Wilson, 1979.

Bullough, Robert V. *Creating Instructional Materials.* Columbus, Ohio: Merrill, 1974.

Carothers, Diane. *Self-Instructional Manual for Filing Catalog Cards.* Chicago: American Library Association, 1981.

Copyright, Media and the School Librarian; A Guide to Multimedia in Schools. Chicago: AASL, 1978.

Copyright Office, Library of Congress. "Copyright and the Librarian." Circular R21; also in *Information Hotline* (February 1978), pp. 17–21.

Corbin, John B. *A Technical Services Manual for Small Libraries.* Metuchen, N.J.: Scarecrow, 1971.

Cummins, Thompson. "Book Making." *Audio-Visual Instruction* (September 1979), pp. 32–35.

Dewey Decimal Classification and Relative Index, 11th abridged ed. New York: H. W. Wilson, 1979.

Gilkey, Richard. "Designing Student Production Facilities." *School Media Quarterly* (Spring 1974), pp. 256–259.

Gorman, Michael. *The Concise AACR2: Being a Rewritten and Simplified Version of Anglo-American Cataloging Rules*, 2nd ed. Chicago: American Library Association, 1981.

Hart, Thomas L. "Centralized Processing: Gain or Bane?" *School Media Quarterly* (Spring 1975), pp. 210–214.

Hill, Donna. *The Picture File: A Manual and Curriculum-Related Subject List.* Syracuse, N.Y.: Gaylord, 1979.

Johnson, Donald F. *Copyright Handbook*, 2nd ed. New York: R. R. Bowker, 1982.

Kemp, Gerrold E. *Planning and Producing Audio-Visual Material*, 3rd ed. New York: Crowell, 1975.

Kersten, Dorothy B. *Subject Headings for Church or Synagogue Libraries.* Bryn Mawr, Pa.: Church and Synagogue Library Association, 1978.

Laybourne, Kit, and Cianciolo, Pauline, eds. *Doing the Media: A Portfolio of Activities, Ideas, and Resources.* Chicago: American Library Association, 1979.

Mether, Calvin E., and Bullard, John R. *Audio-Visual Fundamentals: Basic Equipment Operation and Simple Materials Production.* Dubuque, Iowa: Wm. C. Brown, 1979.

Miller, Jerome K. *Applying the New Copyright Law: A Guide for Educators and Librarians.* Chicago: American Library Association, 1979.

———. "Copyright Considerations in the Duplication, Performance, and Transmission of Television Programs in Educational Institutions." *School Library Media Quarterly* (Summer 1982), pp. 357–370.

Miller, Shirley. *The Vertical File and Its Satellites: A Handbook of Acquisitions, Processing and Organization.* Littleton, Colo.: Libraries Unlimited, 1979.

Minor, Ed, and Frye, Harvey. *Techniques for Producing Visual Instructional Media.* New York: McGraw-Hill, 1977.

National Audio-Visual Association. *Finding Answers to Copyright Questions: Guide to Publications on Copyright.* Fairfax, Va.: NAVA, 1982.

The New Copyright Law—Questions Teachers and Librarians Ask. Chicago: American Library Association, 1978.

Olson, Nancy B. *Cataloging of Audio-Visual Materials: A Manual Based on AACR2.* Mankato, Minn.: Minnesota Scholarly Press, 1980.

Piercy, Esther. *Commonsense Cataloging.* New York: H. W. Wilson, 1983.

Rogers, Jo Ann V. "Mainstreaming Media Center Materials: Adopting 'AACR2.' " *School Library Journal* (April 1981), pp. 33–35.

———. "Nonprint Cataloging: A Call for Standardization." *American Libraries* (January 1979), pp. 46–48.

———. *Nonprint Cataloging for Multimedia Collections: A Guide Based on AACR2.* Littleton, Colo.: Libraries Unlimited, 1982.

Satterthwaite, Les. *Graphics: Skills, Media and Materials.* Dubuque, Iowa: Kendall/Hunt, 1979.

Schroeder, Don, and Lore, Gary. *Audio-Visual Equipment and Materials: A Basic Repair and Reference Manual.* Metuchen, N.J.: Scarecrow, 1979.

Taylor, Mary M., ed. *School Library and Media Center Acquisitions Policies and Procedures.* Phoenix, Ariz.: Oryx, 1982.

Waltzer, Margaret Allen. *Using Vertical Files and Government Documents in Schools.* M. A. Waltzer, 1980.

11

MANAGERIAL CONCERNS

This chapter covers some of the practical aspects of administering the school library media center, such as circulation techniques, maintaining the collection, inventory, record keeping, and conducting a successful book fair.

CIRCULATION

The chief aim of any circulation system is to facilitate the use of materials and ensure the accessibility of these materials to the users of the media center. Major criteria in evaluating a circulation system are ease of use, absence of friction-causing elements, economy, and efficiency. Supplementary considerations involve the desirability of formalizing registration procedures and issuing borrowers' identification cards, the simplicity of charging and discharging routines, the handling of overdues, the flexibility of the system in accommodating such preferred items as reserve books or vertical-file materials, and the ease of collecting circulation statistics. Some media centers, particularly at the secondary level, have experimented successfully with various mechanical, photographic, and electronic circulation devices. The initial cost of renting or purchasing the requisite equipment may be offset by greater efficiency and savings in staff time, particularly in situations of heavy circulation flow. The major drawback to these systems is that they require issuing user identification cards or plates. If these are kept on file in the center, an extra step—locating the card—is involved in the circulation procedure; if issued directly to the borrower, the cards are frequently lost, misplaced, or forgotten.

Most media centers use some variation of the Newark (N.J.) Circulation System. The essential elements are a book card (similar cards are used for other types of materials and equipment) and a date-due slip. The routines in the Newark System are so simple and so easily learned that its day-to-day operation can be handled by clerical or volunteer help. The user is asked to sign his or her name and homeroom number on the first vacant line of the book card. The due date is stamped next to the user's name on the book card and on the date-due slip. Some centers use a prestamped date-due card that replaces the book card in the book pocket. Book cards are placed in the circulation file until the material is returned and discharged. They are usually filed under due date by call number (or alphabetically by author in the case of fiction). Materials may be renewed easily by duplicating the initial procedure: the book card is retrieved from the circulation file and the borrower again signs name and homeroom number (or writes "R" under the first signature), and a new due date is stamped on the card and slip.

Simple variations of this system may be used for materials that do not have book cards. For example, cards should be made out for each magazine title to be circulated. To check out a magazine, the borrower writes his or her name and homeroom number and the date of the magazine on the card. The due date is then stamped on the card. Some centers also stamp the due date on a slip pasted in the magazine or attach a date-due slip to the back cover with a paper clip. When the magazine is returned, the borrower's name is crossed off the card.

Vertical-file materials may be checked out by having the borrower write his or her name and homeroom number and the number of items checked out and their subject headings on a book card marked "Vertical File." The material is placed in a protective envelope to which a date-due slip is attached. The discharging procedure is the same as that with magazines.

When a patron requests material that is currently in circulation, a reserve slip is made out giving call number, main entry, title, and the name and homeroom number of person making the request. The circulation file is then checked, and a flagging device (usually a metal clip or a transparent, color-coded book-card cover) is placed on the card for the title desired. When the item is returned, the reserve slip is located and placed in the material with the book card, and the prospective borrower is notified.

Length of loan periods and the number of items that may be checked out by an individual borrower should be as flexible and liberal as possible. While some curtailment might be necessary when collections are small and demand is heavy, when the collection reaches numerical adequacy, restrictive loan policies should be dropped and replaced with others that more closely match users' needs. A few media centers have been bold enough to adopt a loan period that can be as long as the school year if the material is not wanted by another patron. In these cases, instead of the due date, the checkout date is stamped in the material. Other centers allow items in the general collection to circulate for a semester. Extended loan periods are particularly important for students engaged in long-range independent study projects. Most centers, however, use loan periods of two to four weeks. To facilitate filing in the circulation file and also to give borrowers an easy way of remembering due dates, some centers have adopted a "fixed" date for returning materials. For example, all materials checked out in a particular week are due on a specified Monday two or three weeks later. Thus, Monday (or the first school day after, in case of holidays or vacations) becomes the day each week on which loaned materials are due back in the center.

Although no specific limits should be placed on the number or type of items that may be borrowed from the center, some reasonable and temporary restraints may have to be imposed, as necessitated by demand and curriculum requirements. For example, when duplicate copies of heavily used reference books are not owned in the center, a system of overnight loans might have to be used. The same problem can arise with media placed on reserve by teachers, current issues of periodicals, or pieces of equipment scheduled for use during the school day. Many of these situations can be avoided through judicious duplication of titles and extensive preplanning with the faculty. In unavoidable cases, restricted loans should be applied as sparingly as possible and always with the needs of users in mind.

In library jargon, "snag" refers to a situation in which the original book card for a returned item cannot be found. If, after a thorough check of the circulation file, the original card is still missing, duplicate copies of the book on the shelves and cards in the file that represent other circulating duplicate copies should be checked. If the correct original card still cannot be located, a book card marked "DUP" should be typed and the card number, main entry, and title should be added to the list of other materials for which duplicate book cards have been made. Should the original card appear, the replacement card should be destroyed and crossed off the duplicate card list.

Handling problems related to overdues has plagued librarians since library materials first began to circulate. It often seems that an inordinate amount of time and effort is spent in this area. One traditional recourse has been to impose fines, on the theory that students who lack feelings of obligation toward others will develop them when their (or their parents') finances are tapped. Many centers have abandoned the collection of fines, however, chiefly because they find it does not work—students are often quite willing to pay the small amount as a form of "rent" to keep the material they want. Perhaps more important, fines represent a negative or punitive measure that contradicts the attempt in schools to build attitudes of responsibility and citizenship. Opponents also point out that collecting fines is very time-consuming and that excessively repressive regulations create hostility and can lead to increased theft and mutilation of material. Still other centers compromise and levy fines only on material that is placed on a highly restricted loan schedule, such as overnight books, when the absence of the material from the center can produce great inconvenience for other users.

Regardless of whether fines are collected, other procedures are often adopted to remind students (and sometimes faculty) that the material they have on loan should be returned or renewed. The most widely accepted method is sending overdue notices to homerooms. These notices may be purchased commercially or printed in the school. Some centers use multicopy overdue notices so that, if necessary, second and third notices can be sent out without filling in new forms. In the case of material on which a reserve has been placed, the overdue notice should be sent out as soon as the item is due. For other materials, the preceding week's overdues should be removed from the current circulation file approximately once per week on a regular schedule. Overdue notices are then written and the cards returned to a special file marked "first notice." If within another week (or longer, depending on center policy) the material has not been returned, a second notice is sent out, and so on. Other techniques are sometimes used, such as setting aside certain days during the school year to have overdue or unused materials returned (in centers where fines are collected these are sometimes called "Amnesty Days"). In a few severe cases it is necessary to take stronger measures—such as sending notices to parents. However, before anything like this is resorted to, a professional staff member should contact the student and inform him or her personally of the items that are still due and the consequences that might occur.

When a student is directly responsible for the loss of an item or damage to it, some form of reimbursement should be made to the media center. However, because some accidents are unavoidable and some losses are not the fault of the borrower, adjustments might have to be made in order not to inflict unfair penalties. These decisions, as well as decisions involving delinquent borrowers, should be made only by the center's professional staff.

AV Material and Equipment

If possible, it is advisable to have circulation materials affixed to all media so that the same circulation procedures can be used as with books. With large items like films, photographs, records, and kits, this is usually not a problem, but individual filmstrips and cassettes may have to be placed in containers (available from library supply houses) to which pockets or some item can be fixed. Such a system also helps to promote the integrated shelving of all instructional materials. Sometimes school library media center libraries use different colored book cards for nonprint media so that these cards can be easily identified in the circulation file.

If affixing pocket, card, and date-due slips to each piece of audiovisual material proves too difficult, these items could be circulated in the same way that magazines are: That is, a book card can be made out for each piece of material and kept on file at the circulation desk. Borrowers bring the material to be checked out to the desk and fill in the appropriate card with name, homeroom number, and due date.

The circulation of equipment also poses problems. If space permits, in small and medium-size schools, the delivery of equipment to the classroom should emanate from the library media center. Requests should be made on sign-up sheets at least one day in advance, although advance bookings for at least two weeks ahead should be possible. Sign-up sheets should have space for: (1) period of time material is needed, (2) teacher's name, (3) room, (4) equipment needed, and (5) pickup time. Student AV squads or aides can be used to facilitate delivery and return, but in elementary or very small schools teachers might be made responsible for getting their own equipment. Book cards can also be used for circulating equipment. Through in-service training, teachers as well as student helpers should become familiar with operating basic equipment.

In larger schools AV equipment is often assigned to a teaching station or cluster of classrooms. In these cases it is still necessary to formulate some circulation policies to prevent conflicts or abuse of privileges. When equipment is decentralized and control is remote, it is often difficult to maintain an accurate inventory of equipment in good operating condition or to determine when booking conflicts might occur. Therefore, a small backup collection should still be maintained at the center.

Theft-Detection Devices

Recent sharp increases in theft of materials in many school library media centers have compelled the staff to examine the effectiveness of the security measures they have adopted to prevent these losses.

Sometimes a rearrangement of the collection and facilities, like placing the charging desk close to the exit, can help. Converting two entry-ways into one entrance and one exit might help control security. Some centers have instituted book checks at exits and either hire additional personnel or use present staff members to supervise them. Others use such methods as placing sections of the collection, particularly expensive or sought-after items, on reserve.

At one time a 3–4 percent annual loss rate was considered high, but now this seems average. If the loss is so great that the center is losing thousands of dollars per year, the installation of a theft-detection system should be considered. Most of these devices involve a system of sensitizing-desensitizing library materials by placing an adhesive or tag on the material that can be activated or deactivated by an electronic device. If the material is not desensitized through the checkout system, an alarm sounds if anyone tries to remove this material from the center. At present the three most popular systems are 3M Tattle Tape Book Detection System, Checkpoint Mark II/Check, and Gaylord/Magnavox. These and others are described in the November 1976 *Library Technology Reports* (Chicago: American Library Association, 1976).

Prospective buyers should be aware of the hidden costs in each system. Not only is there an initial cost price, but often charges involved in installation, leasing, and a service contract. As well, sensitizing each piece involves money for both materials and staff time. For example, commercial processors now charge between 30 and 40 cents per item to install theft-detection devices on items ordered and processed through them. Other considerations involve the effectiveness of the system, the false-alarm rate (with some systems, keys, jewelry, magnets, and such can activate the system), the ability to accommodate audiovisual materials, and the amount of inconvenience the system produces for both patrons and staff.

INVENTORY AND WEEDING PROCEDURES

An accurate inventory will reveal an exact account of the resources at hand. It is useful for many reasons: to indicate missing or lost materials, to reveal numerical strengths and weaknesses in the collection, to identify materials in need of repair, to serve as a vital part of the process of weeding the collection.

Precautions must be taken, however, to ensure that the inventory does not unduly disrupt the center's normal services. Closing the center for inventory, as is frequently done during the last week of school, can deprive students of center use at a time they need it most. Two possible alternatives are: (1) scheduling inventory at a time school is not in session (to facilitate performing this and other "housekeeping" chores, many districts have placed at least part of the media center's staff on an eleven-, rather than the conventional ten-month contract), and (2) making inventory taking a continuous process by drawing up a staggered schedule that covers the entire collection once per year, but in a piecemeal fashion. Inventory procedures are sufficiently simple that they can usually be handled by clerical personnel or well-trained student assistants.

The steps in taking inventory are:

1. Arrange the material to be inventoried in correct order.
2. Assign two people to work on the inventory—one to check the shelf list, the other to examine the item to see that the book card, pocket, and shelf list information is identical. The physical condition of the material is also checked at this time.
3. Remove from the shelf material that needs repair. If there are any discrepancies in the information on the book card, shelf list, and so on, the item should either be set aside or, in the case of books, turned down on the shelf for later checking.
4. If an item is missing, place a clip or some other tagging device on the shelf list card and, in the case of duplicate copies, a lightly penciled mark next to the missing accession or copy number.
5. Check the missing item in other sources, such as circulation files, bindery records, reserve collections, materials in the workroom for repair, and display cases. If the item is located, remove the clip and erase the shelf list marking.
6. Prepare inventory records giving a numerical count of the items in the collection and those that are missing.
7. Write a notification on the shelf list, such as "missing 9/83" if the item has still not been located after a suitable waiting period. Later, decisions concerning replacement will have to be made.

Weeding

The term "weeding" means in library terms what it does in gardening: to eliminate the unsuitable or unwanted. Three types of material should be weeded: (1) the out-of-date and no longer authentic; this condition occurs very frequently with science material, but no single subject is immune; (2) the worn-out or badly damaged; sometimes repairs can be made—for example, books can be rebound—but costs should be weighed carefully against the price of a replacement or of adding a different title; and (3) the unpopular or unused. These titles are perhaps the most difficult to throw out because in some cases it is an admission that an inappropriate purchase has been made; in other cases, however, it simply means that tastes and interests have shifted. Nevertheless, it is useless to have collections clogged with deadwood that obscures media that do attract youngsters. It is recommended that 4–5 percent of a collection should be weeded each year. This, of course, applies only to collections that have been in existence for a few years.

MAINTAINING THE COLLECTION

Preventive maintenance can ensure longer life for library materials. Items needing repair are usually identified at the charging desk or through inventory. In any case they should be removed from the shelves as soon as damage has been detected. In some cases, such as torn pages or wobbly spines, repairs are fairly easily accomplished with the use of a suitable transparent nonbrittle tape or application of glue inside the end pages. Other repairs, like tipping in pages, require more expertise. Many supply houses distribute (often free of charge) repair manuals that explain these procedures, and sometimes they will send representatives to demonstrate techniques for groups of library media specialists. Unfortunately, crayon or ball-point pen markings are difficult to erase. In such cases, if the damage is widespread, discarding the book is probably necessary.

When the spine of a book is broken and signatures are loose or falling out, a decision concerning rebinding must be made. Because of the high cost of rebinding, this should be done only when the book is otherwise in excellent condition and has ample margins to accommodate resewing, and the cost of replacement is significantly higher than rebinding. Exceptions should be made for books that are still needed in the collection but out of print. Books are usually sent to the binder only once or twice a year, including one shipment over the summer months. The book cards removed from the books when they are sent out can serve as a bindery record. Before choosing a bindery, be sure to check out its reliability, speed of delivery, and quality and attractiveness of the final product.

Simple repairs to audiovisual material and equipment, like splicing tapes or films and changing bulbs on overhead projectors, can be done at the school level, but more serious repairs should be done either by a district center or by an outside commercial firm. Equipment should be checked regularly (ideally after each use) and there should also be a thorough annual check of each piece of equipment. The usual standard of quality (efficiency, reliability, repair time, cost) should be applied before contracting with an outside agency to do equipment repairs.

RECORDS AND REPORTS

Record keeping and preparation of school library media center reports serve several purposes. Internally, these functions reveal to the center staff otherwise hidden strengths and weaknesses in the program and thus indicate areas for possible change or improvement. Externally they can serve as a communication device to acquaint others with the scope and nature of the program, its needs and future plans, and recommendations for rectifying shortcomings.

Records

The maintenance of accurate records is an integral part of a media center's operation. It is an administrative detail that cuts across the areas of acquisition and organization. Each school media center will develop its own system, but certain records are essential. There are basically four kinds of records prepared and maintained in the media center: (1) financial, (2) organizational, (3) service, and (4) archival.

Financial Records

The originals of many school library media center financial records are kept in the school or district business office, with copies in the center. Examples of financial records are:

Budget requests, annual and special

Budget allocations

Current statements of expenditures

Shipment receipts and invoices

Requisitions and purchase orders, with notations on partial-order status and final disposition

Receipts of any monies collected or expended by the library outside of regular financial procedures

Petty cash funds

Organizational Records

The organizational records usually include as priority items the shelf list and any supplementary inventory system for nonprint materials and equipment.

The shelf list is a classified card file of all the holdings of a school library media center. The card contains full bibliographic information, the number of copies, and the list price of the item. In centers that keep collections housed separately by format, an additional card file, one of the order form slips (see the discussion on Processing in Chapter 10) for nonprint media arranged by format can be useful for inventory. In addition, a card file for the equipment handled by the media center is useful for both inventory and repair and maintenance records. The appropriate information about the equipment, including vendor, list price, model number, warranty conditions, date of purchase, and repairs, should be noted and the card pulled when the item is being repaired. Other records for material that is out of the center for other reasons, for example, binding, film exchange, or repair, should also be kept. Simply keeping the charge cards in separate files will suffice. Typical organizational records include:

Shelf list of materials and equipment

Inventory records

Quantitative record of current holdings

Card and book catalogs (duplicates to departments, grade levels, or resource areas)

Subject authority file, such as *Sears*

Want lists

Record of materials on order

Records of loans and gifts

Checklist of periodical holdings

Records of materials and equipment being repaired and serviced

Lesson plans, instructional programs, tests and assignments

Files of promotional materials, for example, successful displays, exhibits, and programs

Materials describing school library media center procedures

Manuals

It is suggested that a single all-inclusive manual be prepared. From this, individual parts can be excerpted or adapted to prepare more specialized manuals (for example, for volunteers or student helpers) as needed. A suggested table of contents for the basic manual is:

1. Introduction, Philosophy, and Objectives
2. Services and Activities

3. Size and Nature of Collection

4. Selection and Acquisitions Policies and Procedures

5. Floor Plan

6. Arrangement, Storage, and Maintenance of Materials

7. Circulation and Distribution Practices (reserves, charging, overdues, renewals)

8. Personnel and Work Responsibilities

9. Budget

10. Record Keeping, Reports, and Evaluation

11. Public Relations, Publicity, and Displays

More detailed information on manuals is given in Chapter 5.

Inventory Records

After a complete inventory is finished, fairly accurate figures should
be available for the center's holdings by format (that is, books,
filmstrips, microfiche, and so on). Using these figures as a base, a
separate record for each medium should be kept in a loose-leaf binder
to record changes caused by additions or deletions and a running tally
of items in the collection. A simple four-column page could be used
with these headings; (1) date, (2) number of items added, (3) number of
items withdrawn, and (4) current balance. This will supply a valuable
up-to-date inventory of the collection. Using these figures, monthly
summary statistics should be prepared on a page listing, in a column
at the left, each media type (books, filmstrips) with separate columns
across the page for the numbers on hand at the beginning of each
month of the school year (such as September 1 through June 1). In this
way it is possible to indicate with some accuracy the actual holdings of
the center at any time during the school year. These statistics are also
invaluable in preparing monthly or midyear reports.

   Inventory records should also be kept for audiovisual equipment. A
simple list of equipment on hand can be kept on 3 × 5-inch cards as
part of the shelf list. A card should be made for each type of equipment
(such as overhead projectors, 16mm projectors) with columns for
manufacturer's name, model number, serial number, and inventory
number. The latter is a number assigned by the center, usually in con-
secutive order by equipment type, to easily identify each piece of
equipment. This number is also stamped or painted on the equipment.
In addition to this running inventory, a separate record, again usually
in a loose-leaf binder, should be kept for each item of equipment in-

dicating at the top of the page the type, manufacturer, cost, date of purchase, model and serial number and leaving, in column style on the rest of the page, spaces for repair and inspection records.

Service Records

Service records include chiefly statistical data on attendance, circulation, number of classes taught. Some centers also keep records on such items as number of reference questions asked and number of bibliographies prepared by the staff. To prevent statistics collecting from becoming an end in itself, it should always be determined in advance whether the data produced serve a sufficiently worthwhile purpose to warrant the expenditure of time and effort in producing them. It is also necessary to check the reports required by district centers, state departments of education, or accrediting agencies to find out the type of statistics asked for and the form they should take. The use of sampling techniques should be explored. They often produce similar results with greater economy of time and effort. For example, instead of counting attendance or circulation every school day, records might be kept for only a randomly selected number of school days. Library supply houses are good sources of printed forms used in posting both daily and monthly circulation figures. Some modifications might have to be made in these forms, however, if figures are to be broken down by both Dewey classification and format.

Some examples of service records are:

Job description and analysis of the library staff

Records of circulation and use of materials and equipment

Attendance records

School library media center instruction records

Procedural manual for school library media center instruction

Circulation statistics are an important part of a media center's organizational record keeping. They are usually kept on a daily basis and cumulated weekly, monthly, and annually, and provide one of the common bases for evaluating service. Media circulation records can be used to evaluate how well the objectives of a media center are being met. For example, the material can be recorded by medium, subject class, grade level. Finer breakdowns by curriculum or recreation-related areas, for example "Weather" or "Science Fiction," may be obtained by including extra information about course work or interest area when the items are charged out. Records may be dispensed with experimentally in special instances, for example, when student participation and performance in library programs are used as a measure for accountability in place of circulation count.

Other records important to media center operation are the schedules for equipment usage, group use of facilities, and library teaching in the classroom and center. A compilation of these records will be an important part of the monthly and annual reports to the administration. They will also provide statistics for a graphic record—charts, graphs, and so on. In a small center, a large monthly wall calendar will sometimes serve well as a visual record.

Perhaps the overriding considerations for the individual school library media specialist with a small staff is to set up the simplest routines possible and to know precisely for what purpose any record is kept. A continuous reevaluation to bring each routine and its desired purpose more closely into line is vital.

Archival Records

The archival file contains a copy of each important document related to the history of the media center. Financial records, administrative announcements, policy statements, media center publications, and statistical data are organized (usually by school year) and stored to supply a written record of the center's history. In some media centers, this activity is expanded to include such material as minutes of faculty meetings, student publications, and newspaper clippings related to the school and its programs.

Reports

Many state departments of education annually distribute to school library media centers forms for reporting the center's activities. The information requested is generally statistical in nature and includes such data as attendance figures, number of faculty members, number of classes taught, media center hours, size of collection, number of new acquisitions, circulation statistics, personnel figures, and budget information.

Media center staff also usually prepare an annual report for distribution to administrators at various levels and to the school faculty that not only chronicles the year's activities in narrative form but also supplies guidelines for future growth. This annual report can also be used to trace and compare developments from year to year. It should cover four areas of information:

Program

This, the most important section of the report, is a summary of the activities and accomplishments of the center during the preceding year. Information on services supplied to students and teachers should be included, as well as details on such areas as the center's part in curriculum development, reading and study guidance (for example, bibliography preparation), special projects and programs (book fairs or assembly programs), and the center's work in promotion and publicity. If the school library media center sponsors special clubs or a student assistant group, include material on these.

Statistics

The raw material for this section may be obtained from figures, already collected, related to such areas as size of collection, attendance, center hours, circulation. When possible the data should be reduced to the most meaningful units. For example, in addition to yearly totals, daily average figures should also be expressed. In this area charts and graphs can be used to good advantage. This part of the report contains a financial summary on appropriations and gifts as well as expenditures.

Staff Report

This section covers the professional activities of the staff, including activities related to the growth of staff competencies, such as participation in professional associations, courses taken, attendance at workshops and conferences, publications.

Recommendations

This section presents a series of recommendations concerning the future of the center, based on the material in the preceding sections of the report. The recommendations should be stated in terms of achieving specific short- and long-term goals, rather than as simple statements of need. It should be indicated that action may not be possible on all of the proposals.

In addition, the center will periodically prepare other types of reports. Decision on the content and treatment of the material in these reports should bear on: (1) why the report is being prepared—its purpose, and (2) the people who will read the report—its audience. For example, a primarily "selling" report—one that is intended to exert influence on a decision involving the center—should be brief, to the point, without extraneous material, and should carry its message with maximum impact. The use of charts, graphs, or other visuals can help achieve the goal of this type of report.

MANAGING A BOOK FAIR

Traditionally, book fairs* have been held to introduce children to books, to stimulate reading, and to promote growth of home libraries. They are also a way of earning money to help some educational project in the school library media center. Because of the high cost of hardcover books, paperbacks are now almost exclusively sold at fairs. Paramount to a successful book fair is choosing a distributor that is reliable, has experience in book fairs, and has a large inventory (or will order copies especially for your fair).

There are basically two types of book fairs. In one type, a single copy of a title is displayed and the children order from this display. With this type of fair, much of the excitement of purchasing a title is lost and there is also a great deal of paperwork and accounting necessary, particularly if some of the titles later prove to be out of stock. However, this kind of fair requires the least supervision and space. In the other type, multiple copies of titles are supplied. Some distributors work from bookmobiles or portable cabinets. The following book-fair guide is geared to the conventional "in-house" fair, but it can be adapted for other formats.

Allow at least two months' preparation time to order books, prepare committees, and build interest. Fairs are usually held for two or three days. The length of time should be sufficient for each class to visit the fair at least once (20 to 30 minutes per class) plus free time for those who wish to come again. The fair should stay open an hour after school to allow visitors from other schools to attend and one evening to encourage family participation.

Find a space to hold the fair where books can be displayed and central control can be exerted over entrances, exits, and traffic flow. Suggested places are an all-purpose room, auditorium stage, part of a gymnasium, corridors, or a student commons. If the school library media center is used, conventional services will have to be curtailed and the consequences should be weighed against the resultant benefits.

Advance interest can be generated through publicity releases.

---

*This material is based partly on a chapter in the authors' *The Young Phenomenon* (Chicago: American Library Association, 1972).

display of posters, distribution of promotional pieces, contests (for example, designing book marks, posters, writing limericks). When specific titles are known to be in the fair, a mimeographed list of them under such headings as Scary Stories, Adventure, and so on, should be prepared and distributed. When the books arrive, arrange displays or representative titles in display cases around the school.

Many helpers will be needed; therefore, reliance on volunteer help, particularly parents, is essential. Some helpers can be used to set up the fair (allow at least one-half day for this). During the fair four to six adults will be needed at all times: two to handle the cash and the others to supervise displays, straighten and replenish stock, and help the professional staff give reading guidance.

Selection and Ordering of Books

There are several ways to select books for the fair. One method is to give the book jobber some basic information—number of students and range of their ages and interests—and allow the jobber to do the selecting. Several wholesalers operate solely on this principle and many have now refined their selection techniques so that a reasonably good selection is assured. Unfortunately, some tend to err on the side of "safe" titles like the classics and old standbys. Consequently, one whole segment of your reading public, the slow or reluctant reader, will find few appealing titles. A second method is to select only certain basic titles (for example, those you know will be used for class assignment or for which students have expressed a special interest) and allow the jobber to fill in the remaining titles. A third method is for the library media specialist to select and order all of the books, using standard selection guides. However, not all wholesalers will accept this type of order because they think that special orders on consignment are too time-consuming and unprofitable. Often a wholesaler with a large stock on hand will allow librarians to browse in the warehouse and order from the available stock. If the titles on hand are sufficiently varied and numerous, librarians using this selection method will have the satisfaction of a large variety to order from and also the security of knowing the exact titles that will be available at the fair. Whatever selection method is used, orders should be placed well in advance. A minimum of one month is necessary; six to eight weeks is better. It may be difficult at first to estimate the number of books needed. The ability to do this comes with time and experience.

On average, one to two books are sold per student (of course, many more than this should be ordered to ensure a range in choice, but usually a wholesaler expects no more than one-third of the original order returned). In more affluent communities, and where reading is more popular, the average sold may be as high as five or six books per student.

In making selections, keep all levels of interest and ability in mind and base choices on what they will enjoy reading. Although quality literature should be presented, do not hesitate to include some popular fare—"just-for-fun" materials such as cartoon books, television tie-ins, and books on sports and romance. Reference books such as English-language and foreign-language dictionaries, a thesaurus, and those titles that provide guidance material and self-help tips are also popular.

Setting Up the Book Fair

When the books arrive, check the invoice to make sure you have received all the books for which you are being billed.

Inventory control is essential. One effective method is to insert a small slip of paper with the price written on the exposed end into each book. Sheets of these slips with various denominations are easy to ditto and cut apart by scissors or paper cutter. These slips are then taken out of the book at the cash desk to provide a rough inventory control, as well as a count of how many books are sold on a given day or to a particular class or group.

Arrange the books in the fair to produce a natural flow of students from the entrance to the exit. One advantageous arrangement is a long row of tables in front of which students pass to make their selections and behind which are some adult helpers arranging and replenishing stock. The cash desk should be at the end of the line and close to the exit.

Books should be arranged by categories similar to those used on the lists distributed earlier. Signs placed in wire holders could be used to designate each category.

In the single-display-book type of fair, or when all copies but the last of a title have been sold, orders can be taken. The necessary order form should be mimeographed in advance of the fair and contain spaces for the student's name, homeroom number, homeroom teacher, author, title, and price of paperback. Such book orders are paid for and the order slips retained at the cash desk. After the fair an order for these out-of-stock titles is placed with the jobber.

Finally, an important element to be considered in setting up the fair is the creation of a gala atmosphere. Special programs can be held before or during the book fair. Such programs could involve bringing a visiting author or illustrator to the school for a presentation, scheduling special storytelling or booktalk sessions about books in the fair, or showing one or more films based on a book or books in the fair. Contests during the fair, such as guessing the total number of books sold, are also fun.

After the Fair

Determine the value of the books ordered and paid for by students. That amount should be set aside to pay future invoices when the books arrive, or to refund the money to students if the books cannot be delivered. Sort out the unsold books by price, determine their value in each of the price categories, and subtract these totals from those on the original jobber's invoice. The difference remaining is the amount owed the jobber for copies sold; the difference between the book fair's receipts and the amount due the jobber represents the profit. Although jobbers frequently give a 20 percent discount off list price for paperback fairs, the profit may be less due to losses sustained during the sale and the value of prizes that have been given away.

It is always advisable to keep both financial and anecdotal records of your fair. The latter should include notes on best-selling titles and categories, detailed accounts of mistakes and pitfalls to avoid in the future, descriptions of successful procedures, and any recommended changes for subsequent fairs.

FOR FURTHER READING

Abbott, Andrew D., Jr., and Salesi, Rosemary A. "Preserve Your Media Collection Today." *Audiovisual Instruction* (September 1979), pp. 29–31.

Altman, Ellen. "Collection Evaluation—What It Means: How It's Done." *The Unabashed Librarian*, no. 35 (1980), pp. 13–14.

Audiovisual Instruction. *Planning and Operating Media Centers*. Washington, D.C.: AECT, 1975.

Bahr, Alice Harrison. *Book Theft and Library Security Systems 1981-82*. White Plains, N.Y.: Knowledge Industry, 1981.

Beatty, LaMond F. *Instructional Materials Centers*. Englewood Cliffs, N.J.: Educational Technology Publications, 1981.

Bock, Dorothy Joleen. *The Learning Resources Center: A Planning Primer*. *Library Journal* (Special Report), 1977.

Brewer, Margaret, and Willis, Sharon. *The Elementary School Library*. Hamden, Conn.: Shoe String, 1970.

Brown, James W., and Norberg, K. *Administering Educational Media: Instructional Technology and Library Services*, 2nd ed. New York: McGraw-Hill, 1972.

Brown, James W., Norberg, K., and Srygley, Sara K. *Administering Educational Media*. New York: McGraw-Hill, 1972.

Bruemmer, Alice, ed. *Library Management in Review*. London, England: School Library Association, 1982.

Cabeceiras, James. *The Multimedia Library: Materials, Selections and Use*. New York: Academic Press, 1978.

Cunha, George M. *Conservation of Library Materials: A Manual and Bibliography on the Care, Repair and Restoration of Library Materials* (2 vols.). Metuchen, N.J.: Scarecrow, 1971–1972.

Dane, Chase. "Managing the School Media Center." In *Current Concepts in Library Management*. Littleton, Colo.: Libraries Unlimited, 1979.

Davies, Ruth Ann. *The School Library Media Program: Instructional Force for Excellence*, 3rd ed. New York: R. R. Bowker, 1979.

Deal, Paula N. "A Study of Centralized Processing for School Media Centers." *Drexel Library Quarterly* (April 1977), pp. 80–90.

Evans, G. Edward. *Management Techniques for Librarians*. New York: Academic Press, 1976.

Freeman, Patricia. *Pathfinder*. New York: Harper, 1975.

Glogan, Lillian, Krause, Edmund, and Wexler, Miriam. *Developing a Successful Elementary School Media Center*. Englewood Cliffs, N.J.: Parker, 1972.

Hicks, Warren B. *Managing the Building Level School Library Media Program* (School Media Centers: Focus on Trends and Issues, No. 7). Chicago: American Library Association, 1981.

Knight, Nancy H. "Library Security Systems Come of Age." *American Libraries* (April 1978), pp. 229–232.

———. "Theft Detection Systems for Libraries—A Survey." *Library Technology Reports*, no. 12:575–690 (November 1976).

Lancaster, Frederick Wilf. "Evaluation of the Collection." In *The Measurement and Evaluating of Library Science*. Washington, D.C.: Information Resources Press, 1977.

Nickel, Mildred L. *Steps to Service: A Handbook of Procedures for the School Library Media Center*. Chicago: American Library Association, 1975.

Powell, Jon T. "Hardware Media Equipment Management." *Media and Methods* (March/April/May issues, 1981), pp. 5, 18 (March); 6, 7 (April); 10, 11 (May).

Prostano, Emanuel T., and Prostano, Joyce S. *The School Library Media Center*, 3rd ed. Littleton, Colo.: Libraries Unlimited, 1982.

Provan, Jill, and Glogowski, Maryruth P., eds. *Management Media Directory: An Annotated Guide of Commercially Available Audiovisual Programs . . .* Detroit: Gale, 1982.

Saunders, Helen E. The *Modern School Library*, 2nd ed. Metuchen, N.J.: Scarecrow, 1975.

Schmid, William T. *Media Center Management: A Practical Guide*. New York: Hastings House, 1980.

Shaffer, Dale E. *Management Concepts for Improving Libraries: A Guide for the Professional Librarian.* Salem, Ohio: D. E. Shaffer, 1979.

Snow, Kathleen M., and Hauck, Philomena. *The Media Center in the Secondary School.* Toronto, Ont.: McClelland and Stewart, 1973.

Taggart, Dorothy T. *Management and Administration of the School Library Media Program.* Hamden, Conn.: Library Professional Publications, 1980.

Terry, Jack D., Jr., and Hotes, R. D., eds. *The Administration of Learning Resources Centers.* Lanham, Md.: University Press of America, 1977.

Vaughan, Anthony, ed. *Studies in Library Management.* Hamden, Conn.: Shoe String, 1982.

Wilson, Alexander. *The Planning Approach to Library Management.* London, England: Library Association, 1979.

Wittich, Walter A., and Schuller, Charles F. *Instructional Technology: Its Nature and Use*, 6th ed. New York: Harper, 1979.

12

NETWORKS AND NETWORKING

The concept of libraries' engaging in cooperative activities or contractual arrangements with other agencies to expand the availability of material and services and, in some cases, share these resources with others is not new. As an example, shortly after World War II, under the leadership of the Library of Congress, many research libraries in the United States formulated a cooperative acquisition scheme, known as the Farmington Plan, to ensure that at least one of the libraries would obtain a copy of major foreign publications. The catalog card manufacturing and distribution service begun at the Library of Congress in 1901 could also be called an early type of library networking.

Since the advent of sophisticated telecommunication structures and affordable computer technology, formalized library networks have become a reality throughout the country. Existing networks form a variety of organizational patterns and structures, but in general they comprise a number of libraries cooperatively organized within a formal arrangement to share some combination of materials, information, and services.

Although many school library media center specialists have developed local cooperative projects with other libraries, such as reciprocal borrowing privileges and joint book evaluation, in general they have been rather slow to realize the benefits that could be gained by participating in more formalized library networks. Realizing that school library media centers should supply a vital link in satisfying the informational needs of all citizens, the National Commission on Libraries and Information Science convened a task force in 1977 to study networking. Their report, *The Role of the School Library Media Program in Networking*, was issued in December 1978. As expected, it revealed that very few schools are incorporated into existing and projected state networks, and furthermore that neither school administration and staff nor the library community at large realize the importance or potential of the contributions to networking that can come from the schools.

BENEFITS

The Commission's report specifies how the informational needs of the school and its community can be satisfied by participating in a network. Most important, at the student level a network can supply access to books, journals, and other resources that are not contained in a typical school collection but are nevertheless within the student's level of comprehension. Networking will also bring within reach materials for the special student whose informational needs might otherwise remain unsatisfied. Some examples include enrichment materials for the gifted, basic materials for poorer students, books for the visually impaired, specialized career information, and a wide range of resources catering to extracurricular interests. For teachers, networking could supply a wealth of learning materials to individualize instruction. Access to professional material as well as such databases as ERIC (Educational Resources Information Center) will help both teachers and administrators to develop professionally and to analyze educational developments and trends more capably.

Parents and the general public can benefit from the opportunity to use these many resources. There could also be immense benefits for the school library media specialist. This might involve a cataloging and preprocessing service for both print and audiovisual materials, development of cooperative examination centers to facilitate effective media selection, production of union lists of holdings of nearby libraries, and an efficient system for interlibrary loans.

In brief, the advantages of networking to the entire school community are: (1) provides access to more resources, (2) eliminates need for owning peripheral items, (3) accommodates differential purchase of expensive, little-used equipment, (4) allows for individualization of instruction, (5) promotes access to differentiated human experience and consultants, and (6) assures better use of present holdings by opening up access to others.

CONTRIBUTIONS

It is often thought that school library media centers (due to the size and limitations of their collections) have little to contribute to the resources and services of other participating libraries. Actually there are several areas where valuable contributions can be made, relating primarily to the unusual and specialized nature of their collections. In many schools substantial collections contain audiovisual materials including filmstrips, transparencies, slides, educational records, and videotapes that are not usually found extensively in other libraries. Other kinds of educational resources housed in schools could also be of value if shared, for example, professional materials and tools, local history and community resource files, specialized career materials, ethnic and foreign-language collections, and materials geared to those with special learning problems. Even the regular collection of children's or young adult titles could be used in institutions teaching courses in these areas or in public libraries, particularly during the summer months.

Schools and school districts have often developed specialized services that could benefit others if shared. Some school districts, for example, have automated processing centers, locally produced computer-assisted instruction units, materials examination centers, and sophisticated laboratories for local production of materials. Others already have, through computer terminals, access to databases. These resources could be shared either directly through accommodating additional libraries or indirectly through sharing practical experiences and specialized expertise.

EXISTING NETWORKS AND FUNCTIONS

Theoretically all types of library functions are potential components in networking schemes. However, the large investment in equipment and communication expenditures involved in sharing some operations has limited somewhat the functions that have been successfully networked on a large scale. Functions that tend to be most suited for networking are: (1) cataloging, (2) acquisitions, (3) interlibrary loan, and (4) reference services. Maintenance of circulation records and serial check-in, however, appear at present to be most efficiently handled at a local level.

Among the largest and best-known library networks in the United States today are:

1. Amigos, 11300 N. Central Expressway, Dallas, TX 75243
2. Bibliographic Center for Research (BCR), Rocky Mountain Region, Inc., 1777 S. Bellaire, Suite G-150, Denver, CO 80222
3. California Library Authority for Systems and Services (CLASS), 1415 Koll Circle, Suite 101, San Jose, CA 95112
4. Illinois Library and Information Network (ILLINET), Illinois State Library, Centennial Building, Springfield, IL 62756

5. Indiana Cooperative Library Services Authority (INCOLSA), 1100 W. 42 St., Indianapolis, IN 46208

6. Michigan Library Consortium (MLC), 720 Science Library, Wayne State University, Detroit, MI 48202

7. Minnesota Interlibrary Telecommunication Exchange (MINITEX), University of Minnesota, 30 Wilson Library, Minneapolis, MN 55455

8. New England Library Information Network (NELINET), 385 Eliot St., Newton, MA 02164

9. OCLC, Inc., 1125 Kinnear Road, Columbus, Ohio 43212

10. OHIONET, 2929 Kenny Road, Suite 280, Columbus, Ohio 43221

11. PALINET, 3420 Walnut St., Philadelphia, PA 19104

12. Research Libraries Group, Inc. (RLG), Jordan Quadrangle, Stanford University, Stanford, CA 94305

13. Southeastern Library Network, Inc. (SOLINET), Suite 410, 615 Peachtree St., N.E., Atlanta, GA 30308

14. SUNY/OCLC, SUNY Plaza, Albany, NY 12246

15. University of Toronto Library Automation System (UTLAS), 130 St. George St., Toronto, Ontario, Canada M55 1A5

16. Washington Library Network (WLN), Washington State Library, Olympia, WA 98504

These networks are called "full-service" in that they engage in cooperative activities involving a number of library functions. However, most of these services involve, at the local level, implementing bibliographic utilities like OCLC, or acting as a broker for computer database services such as LOCKHEED DIALOG. At present the membership of many of these networks is almost exclusively academic, special, or public libraries; however, an increasing number (such as CLASS, UTLAS, and WLN) are working with school districts.

The Washington Library Network has served in many respects as a prototype for others and although still young (founded in 1977), it has an enviable record of achievement. Because of the demographics of Washington State, it is possible to supply isolated pockets of the population with library service only by implementing a consolidated, highly centralized administrative structure. This structure is administered through the Washington State Library, which helped with other agencies to spearhead the development of a plan for a statewide library network. Legislation was passed in 1976 that allowed, on a volunteer basis, for the participation of all types of libraries. The following year WLN was begun and since its inception has undergone many organizational changes. At present the network has two major components: a resource sharing network for libraries in the state of Washington, and a multistate computer service. The former is presently most used by school libraries because it involves participation in resource sharing and reference and referral services. Interlibrary loans are possible among schools, colleges, and public libraries. In many areas delivery systems have been set up and regional reference services established. Other areas of participation include using online databases and contributing to microfiche union catalogs.

In addition to the development of local cooperative efforts, state-level coordination has been made possible between the two separate agencies that supervise school and public libraries. The computer system offers a variety of more sophisticated services. In bibliographic service, it maintains an online union catalog that provides shared cataloging facilities (as its base it uses Library of Congress MARC—Machine Readable Cataloging—tapes), interlibrary loan support, and the production of a computer-output microform (COM) and microfiche union catalog of the holdings of the online participants in the system. This is known as the Washington Library Network Resource Directory. The system can also produce book or microfiche catalogs and new title lists for local libraries, on-demand bibliographies, and catalog cards and label sets. There are many other subsystems in place at present, including an acquisitions subsystem that allows for the ordering, claiming, and accounting functions in purchasing and receiving library materials. By the mid-1980s, WLN will have about three million records in its database, which can be searched by such approaches as author, title, subject, title keyword, LC card, ISBN, and ISSN.

In addition to this large, multipurpose network, there are also many specialized, locally based networks where school library media centers have been active. Because of their large number, regional nature, and limited function, it is impossible to list them here, but a letter of inquiry to a state school library agency should produce a list of the agencies within that state.

At present the status of networking is still very much a patchwork, segmented one with some geographical areas and some types of libraries (mainly academic) better served than others. School library media centers, as yet, have minimal participation in most important library networks.

Many agencies and organizations, such as the National Commission on Libraries and Information Science and the Council on Library Resources, have actively espoused a cohesive national information network. There are, unfortunately, many factors working against this.

Lacking are concerted leadership and the federal economic resources to develop and impose a nationwide plan on the existing superstructure. As well, networks traditionally grow from the bottom up and, therefore, often come into being in structures that sometimes overlap existing networks or, by the nature of the services offered, more often preclude membership for other types of libraries (for example, bibliographic databases developed and distributed by the National Library of Medicine would have little direct value in a public school situation). Therefore, although the goal of a national information network is admirable, much work lies ahead before it can be achieved. In the meantime, much can be done either to develop regional networks that include school library media centers or to facilitate the entry of these centers into existing networks.

PROBLEMS IN NETWORKING

Before outlining steps that should be taken in preparation for networking, it is prudent first to look at the obstacles to networking and how they can be removed.

Legal Considerations

Sometimes local school districts or state library supervisory units have regulations founded in law that prohibit or limit the implementation of networking concepts. The fragmentation of responsibility by type of library in state agencies and the structure of federal finance assistance programs also might exclude school library media centers from participation or funding in cooperative interlibrary efforts. Because there must be a legally sound base for each network, a thorough study of existing regulations and policies should be made before organizing a new network or gaining admission to an existing one. State and federal library agencies will be helpful in giving information and advice. In general, when reasonable expectations and logical goals are formulated, necessary changes to promote resource sharing can usually be made in guidelines and policies.

Financial Considerations

Participation in networks involves the expenditure of money, particularly at the start-up phase. To a great extent the effectiveness of a network depends on the quality of the communication links that connect the individual member to the central agency. This alone might involve a considerable expenditure for telephone hookups, terminals, and other communication facilities. Another initial cost involves educating the media staff operating the system. Although many of these expenses occur only once, there are also ongoing costs that must be considered. It must be recognized that networks are often at first not cost-effective, but in weighing various funding factors immediate large expenditures should be viewed against long-range benefits and operating costs.

Attitudinal Considerations

Probably the most potent problem that inhibits cooperation is attitude. The chief purpose behind networking is the improvement of service through resource sharing. This fact often causes problems because it signifies less exclusive control of materials, assuming responsibility for materials borrowed, making provisions for supplying materials and services to other libraries, and adhering to sets of procedures and technical standards that at first might be in conflict with existing policies. It is sometimes felt that networking will cause a drain on resources that will outweigh any benefits. Often people are fearful of change and loath to experiment with the new and untried. These biases can be overcome only through a concentrated informational program to acquaint people with the facts about networking and a realization that students have rights to materials and services outside the confines of the single library media center. Methods include workshops, visits to networking agencies, guest speakers, and dissemination of literature.

Planning Considerations

Once the other inhibiting factors have been overcome, the last to surmount is effective preparation. If a new network is planned, each of the libraries involved must be given representation in planning policies. Services to be offered must be determined carefully, needs must be prioritized, costs detailed, and phasing-in timetables developed. Although the degree of planning for a library entering an existing network is not as extensive, it must be equally meticulous. Failure to plan properly and consider all factors affected by participation in a networking plan, can produce unforeseen difficulties and perhaps abandonment of the project during implementation stages.

EVALUATING A NETWORK

The decision to participate in an existing network should be based on a careful system analysis of the existing structure and its relation to the conditions within the school or school district. Following are some factors to be considered.

Network Features and Services

Some services offered by networks are cataloging, information for both print and nonprint materials, reference services, access to databases, interlibrary loan modules, acquisition procedures, serial control, and circulation. The nature of the service for which access is now provided is important. Outputs from the services could involve catalog cards (and kits), microform catalogs, union lists of various sorts, and mediagraphies. Additional services might include examination centers, in-service education, provision of consultants, and maintenance of a clearinghouse. Two further factors to be examined are the nature and effectiveness of the communication linkage (telephone? terminal hookups?) and the type of delivery system (mail?) utilized.

Cost

Installation cost is an important factor. This could involve consolidation hookups, terminals, other equipment to be purchased or leased, and air conditioning for climatic control. There are upkeep costs as well. A careful examination of the fee structure and how it is determined is important. Perhaps agreement can be reached to share expenses with other agencies or to enter into subcontracts to lighten this cost load in a single agency. In addition to user fees, other ongoing outlays involve upkeep expenses such as service contracts and communications charges. The costs for participation in one network should be compared with those in other networks offering similar services. The possibility of linking with existing systems already in operation or eventual interfacing with other networks are two additional considerations. Last, the overall question: Is the price worth the number of functions and services supplied?

Legal Status

The question of legal status involves not only determining initial eligibility to join the network, but also finding out if there are regulations that might restrict participation in present or proposed activities of the network. These restrictions often occur because of the vagaries of public funding and the cumbersome limits of jurisdiction placed on some government agencies that regulate library networks.

Impact on the Existing Library Agency

Some determination must be made on how admission to the network will affect the existing structure in terms of size of staff, changing emphasis on professional vs. nonprofessional duties, amount of training necessary to function within the network, and who should receive this training. One must also consider how to mount a program to acquaint the patrons with these new services and how the impact of the services will affect the total instructional program.

Network Organization and Management

There are several questions that should be answered in this area; for example, is the governance of the network centralized or decentralized? Is it essentially governed by one institution or are many institutions permitted at least adversary status? What are the rights of individual members? Do individual members have a significant voice in determining policies and procedures? Is one type of library favored over another in governance? What is the present financial status of the network? Is it dependent on grants and subsidies rather than being self-sustaining? Does this financial base presage a healthy future? How effective is network quality control in its product and standards of delivery? What are the future projections concerning fees and other fiscal responsibilities of members as well as the quality and quantity of services? Last, the eventuality should also be faced—how difficult is it to terminate membership in this network?

IMPLEMENTING THE NETWORKING CONCEPT

If, after thorough study and evaluation, an existing network appears to offer the services required at a level of fiscal and contractual obligations within your reach, an extensive brief should be prepared addressing each of the evaluative criteria previously mentioned (cost, legal status, and so on). This brief should stress the local and long-range consequences and advantages of membership, and should contain any supporting documents available. The process then begins of presenting these data at the appropriate administrative levels. Presentations can be made more effective by inviting media personnel and administrators from districts already involved in networking as resource people, or perhaps a representative from the network itself or from the state level network coordinating unit.

Should no network exist in which membership appears feasible, perhaps a project could be started to create an informal network to meet local needs. Again, a plan of action is needed. First, learn about the types of localized networks in existence by contacting resource people and studying the literature. Through this study and an examination of your own needs, determine areas where networks would be possible. Next, meet with others who might also have an interest in networking, determine common concerns, and isolate a single area where a cooperative effort could be mounted. Some areas for consideration might be reference services, resource sharing, a community resource file, and union lists of periodicals, equipment, or audiovisual material. Devise a plan to establish regular communication links and implement the services. Once this informal structure is in place, additional services might be added and eventually a more formalized structure adopted with more libraries involved and a governing structure adopted; overhead costs could be offset by a modest registration fee.

Regardless of the size of the network, once it is in place continuous evaluation is necessary that compares expectations with reality, balances the drain on existing resources against the benefits of an enriched collection, and, as a bottom line, weighs the costs against the educational gains achieved.

Networking is one of the most rapidly expanding areas in the library field. Each year brings more innovative developments and greater expectations. It is a movement that is here to stay and will increasingly involve all informational agencies and libraries at every level. It should always be remembered, however, in an area where access to information is paramount, that networks must be seen as another means to this end and not an end in themselves.

FOR FURTHER READING

Aaron, Shirley L. *A Study of Combined School-Public Libraries*. Chicago: American Library Association, 1980.

American Association of School Librarians. *The Role of the School Media Program in Networks and Interlibrary Cooperation*. Chicago: A.A.S.L. Committee on Networking, 1979.

American Library Association, American Association of School Librarians, Committee on Networking-Interconnection of Learning Resources. *"Networking and the Schools: A Discussion by the American Association of School Librarians' Committee on Networking."* Wisconsin Library Bulletin (May 1975), 71:111–112.

Bender, David R. "Networking and School Library Media Programs." *School Library Journal* (November 1979), pp. 29–30.

Duchesne, R. M. *Overview of Library Networking in Canada*. Ottawa, Ont.: National Library of Canada, 1980.

Dyer, Esther R. *Cooperation in Library Services to Children*. Metuchen, N.J.: Scarecrow, 1978.

Fite, Alice. "Networking: An Old Word Goes Back to School." *American Libraries* (November 1978), pp. 603–604.

Fleming, Lois D. "Public and School Libraries: Partners in the 'Big' Picture." *School Media Quarterly* (Fall 1978), pp. 25–30.

Frankowiak, Bernard. "Networks, Data Bases, and Media Programs: An Overview." *School Media Quarterly*, 6, no. 1 (Fall 1977): 15–20.

———. *School Library Media Programs and the National Program for Library and Information Sciences.* Related Paper No. 7, NCLIS, 1974.

Knieval, Helen A. *Cooperative Services: A Guide to Policies and Procedures.* New York: Neal-Schuman, 1982.

Kolb, Audrey. "Development and Potential of a Multitype Library Network." *School Media Quarterly*, 6, no. 1 (Fall 1977): 21–27.

———, and Morse, Jo. "Initiating School Participation in Networking." *School Media Quarterly*, 6, no. 1 (Fall 1977): 52–59.

Markuson, Barbara. "Library Networking Planning: Problems to Consider, Decisions to Make." *Wisconsin Library Bulletin* (May-June 1975), pp. 98–102.

———, and Woolls, Blanche. *Networks for Networkers: Critical Issues in Library Development.* New York: Neal-Schuman, 1980.

Martin, Susan K. *Library Networks 1981-82.* White Plains, N.Y.: Knowledge Industry, 1981.

National Commission on Libraries and Information Science, Task Force on the Role of the School Library Media Program in the National Program. *The Role of the School Library Media Program in Networking.* Washington, D.C.: NCLIS, 1978.

Poole, Carl N. "How Can Schools Use Community Resources?" *Educational Leadership* (April 1975) pp. 444–446.

Woolard, Wilma Lee. *Combined School/Public Libraries: A Survey with Conclusions and Recommendations.* Metuchen, N.J.: Scarecrow, 1980.

13

BEYOND THE SINGLE SCHOOL LIBRARY MEDIA CENTER

Many concerns of the school library media specialist exist beyond the daily routines of the individual center. Some with immediate and future implications, such as networking, are discussed in previous chapters. This chapter treats three important areas of immediate and future interest: associations, highlighting a few that are especially important to the school library media specialist; some government agencies of value to the specialist based on the knowledge that the political process in general and legislation in particular are vital; and a list of key publications for the media specialist.

ASSOCIATIONS

Some associations exert a strong influence on the everyday workings of a school library media center. Although they exist on different geo-political levels, they should be known to the school library media specialist. One way to identify these associations is by subject specialty, another by geographic level. An attempt is made here to present associations that tend to integrate many of the disciplines incorporated in school library media centers.

There are some extremely active and influential associations on the international scene. One that has earned the respect of the multinational library community is the International Federation of Library Associations (IFLA). Another, especially for school library media specialists, is the International Association of School Librarians (IASL), established in the late 1960s by Jean Lowrie, a former ALA president, to conduct international meetings and share in the transfer of information across continents. Also prevalent are special-interest associations, such as the International Board of Books for Youth

(IBBY), which has played a significant role in its sphere since the end of World War II. The associations highlighted in this chapter, although national in scope, engage in extensive international cooperative ventures.

Three of the largest national associations, besides the American Library Association (ALA), that are vital in many ways to the development of school library media centers are the American Association of School Librarians (AASL), the American Society for Information Science (ASIS), and the Association for Educational Communications and Technology (AECT). The first and third associations deal with both library and media issues, and also with a recognition of and participation in the latest stage of technology—computerization. The second association devotes itself to this newer school library media center concern—computerization and information transfer. Each of these three is highlighted in the following list of associations. Both AASL and AECT have extensive state affiliations; ASIS has local college chapters for graduate student members.

A finely attuned communications procedure links the national associations and those of each state. In addition, there are at least two types of state organizations: (1) combined school library and media organizations, and (2) separate library and media organizations. The California Media and Library Educators Association (CMLEA) is an example of the first. Some states follow the second example in not combining their library and media organizations. For school library media specialists, this means that both state associations have to be considered for membership. The Florida Association of Media Educators (FAME) includes media, school library, and education personnel, as well as others, and illustrates another type of state organization, one that centers around the school itself. All three types include the strength of affiliation throughout the state, as well as the many functions that are generally performed. These may include committee work, annual conventions, regional meetings, creation of guidelines for evaluation, discussion of current issues and recurring problems, and publications, including a regular periodical. Some of the publications currently on sale through one of the state associations, The New York Library Association (NYLA), are *Municipal and Local Documents* (proceedings of a 1977 workshop), *Media and Money* (aids on writing news releases), and *The Library Lobbyist* (guide to legislative process and lobbying).

Fortunately, there are local school library media associations for many specialists. However, if there is none in the reader's area, perhaps one should be organized. Local associations lend the aid and comfort of like-minded individuals who work in school library media centers and share many of the same concerns. These associations can be small or large and still exert a strong force in the region. An example is the Long Island School Media Association (LISMA), a combined library and media organization that operates in Long Island, New York. This highly developed local group provides an annual media fair for its members and others, a regular newsletter (*LISMA, INK*), an information network of local members, an informal placement service that coordinates its efforts through a central bureau at Palmer School of Library and Information Science, C. W. Post College, Long Island University, and more. Local associations can provide support for the individual school library media specialist.

Media specialists should be aware of the many important associations that are available and, within individual constraints, each person should join and participate in as many as possible for the maximum effect, from local to state to national to international. The continuing development of school library media specialists and centers depends on the strength that individuals are willing to lend to this effort. A list of helpful associations follows, beginning with a highlight summary of three large national groups.

American Association of School Librarians (AASL), 50 East Huron Street, Chicago, IL 60611; 312-944-6780. AASL is a division of the American Library Association (ALA), whose primary objective is to promote and improve library service and librarianship. The priorities are access to information, legislation/funding, intellectual freedom, public awareness, and personnel resources. Some other divisions of ALA of interest to a school library media specialist are:

Association for Library Service to Children (ALSC)

Association of Specialized and Cooperative Library Agencies (ASCLA)

Library Administration and Management Association (LAMA)

Library and Information Technology Association (LITA)

Reference and Adult Services Division (RASD)

Resources and Technical Services Division (RTSD)

Young Adult Services Division (YASD)

One of the largest divisions of ALA, AASL is interested in improving and extending library media services for young people. It is also responsible for planning programs of study and service in grades K–12; evaluating, selecting, utilizing, and promoting an awareness of school library media centers; encouraging research in the field; integrating the activities of other ALA divisions that are pertinent to AASL concerns; interpreting school library media centers to other educational associations; stimulating professional growth; encouraging organizational participation among school library media specialists; conducting activities and projects; and so on. There are approximately 40 committees, among them:

AACD (curriculum development)—Liaison

AASA (administrators)—Liaison

AECT-AASL—Joint

Early Childhood Education

Evaluation of School Media Programs

Facilities, Media Center

Intellectual Freedom Representation and Information

Legislation

Library Skills Instruction

NASSP—Liaison

NCTE—Liaison

Networking—Interconnection of Learning Resources

School Library Media Services to Children with Special Needs

Standards Program and Implementation

Student Involvement in the Media Center Program

Video Communications

Vocational/Technical Materials Selection

There are also special committees, such as Publications Advisory; sections, such as Non-Public Schools and Supervisors; and a strong state-affiliate assembly. The members are generally directly involved with individual district and school library media centers, as well as with people who are interested in one of the many areas of the field. The association is actively engaged in publicizing and granting awards to exceptional school library media center programs and people across the nation. It holds an annual conference in addition to the one held annually in June/July by the parent organization, ALA. AASL held its second annual fall conference in Houston, Texas, in 1982, at which it featured the instructional application and evaluation of microcomputers and accompanying software.

Publications: *School Library Media Quarterly* (the official periodical for members and other interested persons). Some of the publications especially related to school library media centers available from the

ALA Publication Service are *Copyright, Media, and the School Librarian: A Guide to Multimedia Copying in Schools; Media Programs for Today and Tomorrow: A Selected Bibliography; Policies and Procedures for Selection of Instructional Materials;* and *School Media Personnel Certification Model.* A checklist of other available publications can be obtained from AASL.

American Society for Information Science (ASIS), 1010 16th Street N.W., Washington, DC 20036; 202-659-3644. Established in 1937, the society acts as a clearinghouse for information and discussion about information systems and technology, including design and management. It is also a center for publications, available from Knowledge Industry Publications (2 Corporate Park Drive, White Plains, NY 10064), and Microfiche Publications (440 Park Ave. S., New York, NY 10016). There are approximately 5,000 members—individuals, students, and institutions, as well as approximately 26 local groups and 21 student groups. Members are generally information scientists, specialists, administrators, librarians, and others who are interested in the many phases of the information-transfer process, such as storage, retrieval, and use. Many members are actively engaged in significant stages of this process, such as classifying, indexing, systems analyses. ASIS provides a forum for discussion and evaluation of the theory and practice that are involved in communications. It sponsors publications pertinent to its concerns, as well as a 24-hour "jobline," reproduction services through Microfiche Publications, and a central depository. In addition, it presents honors in the field.

ASIS has about 23 special-interest groups, such as Arts and Humanities, Community Information Services, Computerized Retrieval Services, Information Services to Education, which may be of interest to school library media specialists. Known before 1968 as the American Documentation Institute (ADI), the society is affiliated with AFIPS, ALA, ANSI, IFD, and NFAIS. It holds an annual convention, generally in October.

ASIS committees are:

Awards and Honors

Budget and Finance

Conferences and Meetings

Constitutions and Bylaws

Education

Executive

International Relations

Inter-Society-Cooperation

Marketing

Membership

Nominations

Professionalism

Public Affairs

Publications

Research

Standards

Publications: *Bulletin; Journal; Annual Review of Information Science & Technology; Annual Directory & Handbook; Annual Proceedings; Computer-Readable Bibliographic Data Bases*; and monographs, such as *Key Papers in the Design & Evaluation of Information Systems*, edited by Donald W. King.

Association for Educational Communications and Technology (AECT), 1126 16th Street N.W., Washington, DC 20036; 202-466-4780. A professional association established in 1923, AECT deals with matters pertaining to educational technology, including audiovisual materials and computers. Membership is approximately 6,000. There are 9 divisions, 10 national affiliates, 55 state affiliates, and many national task forces (committees). The members are generally instructional technologists, school library media specialists or media specialists, religious educators, government media specialists, and school or state department of education media program personnel. Some members are employed in museums, public libraries, and other information agencies. AECT serves as a clearinghouse for its members, especially through its task forces. It gathers information and prepares guidelines for standards and research, as well as summaries on topics of concern to the membership. It also provides information on regulations, laws, and pending legislation that has direct immediate application to the educational technology field.

The association maintains: (1) the Educational Communications and Technology Foundation (ECT), which gives financial aid to further the work of AECT, and (2) the AECT Archives at the University of Iowa. The annual conventions are usually held in the beginning of each year in combination with the National Audiovisual Association (NAVA), which is a trade organization of producers and distributors of audiovisual or educational technology materials and equipment. Some of the AECT divisions are:

American Student Media Association (ASMA)

Association for Media Educators in Religion (AMER)

Association for Multi-Image (AMI)

Association for Special Education Technology (ASET)

Division of Educational Media Management (DEMM)

Division of Information Systems and Computers (DISC)

Division of Instructional Development (DID)

Division of School Media Specialists (DSMS)

Division of Telecommunications (DOT)

Federal Educational Technology Association (FETA)

Health Education Media Association (HEMA)

IFPA—Film and Video Communicators

International Congress for Individualized Instruction (ICII)

Media Design and Production Division (MDPD)

Minorities in Media (MIM)

National Association of Regional Media Centers (NARMC)

Publications: *Instructional Innovator* (with membership); *Educational Communication and Technology: A Journal; Journal of Instructional Development*, and various other division publications. Some nonperiodic publications are: *The Definition of Educational Technology; Educational Technology: A Glossary of Terms; The Art of Multi-Image; Freedom to Learn* (filmstrip); *Media, the Learner, and Intellectual Freedom: A Handbook; The National Slide Collection on Learning Resources; Classroom Projects Using Photography; Guide to Microcomputers; Media in Instruction; Creating Slide/Tape Programs* (filmstrip).

Other Important Associations and Agencies

The Combined Book Exhibit (CBE), 12 Saw Mill River Road, Hawthorne, NY 10532; 212-884-3602 (a division of F. W. Faxon Company, Inc.). A professional organization of book, periodical, and AV producers, CBE gives school library media specialists and other educators an opportunity to examine materials personally, generally at conferences and conventions. It also produces special programs to enable makers and users of materials to meet and communicate.

Consortium of University Film Centers (CUFC), c/o Kent State University, AV Services, 330 Library, Kent, OH 44242; 216-672-3456. CUFC is a group of professional university film rental center administrators whose aim is to improve education with effective use of motion pictures; assist in education by making films more available; foster cooperative planning among university film centers; gather and communicate regarding procedures and newer developments in the field. CUFC is also responsible for publications such as *The Educational Film Locator*, 2nd ed. (New York: R. R. Bowker, 1980).

Educational Products Information Exchange (Institute) (EPIE), Box 620, Stony Brook, NY 11790; 516-246-8664. A nonprofit institute, EPIE engages primarily in the evaluation of materials and equipment. It also gives in-service workshops and provides consultation on evaluation. In-depth assessments are reported in *Epiegram Materials* and *Epiegram Equipment* (all October–June).

Educational Resources Information Center (ERIC), National Institute of Education, Program on Dissemination and Improvement of Practice, 1200 19th Street N.W., Washington, DC 20208; 202-254-5550. ERIC coordinates the 16 clearinghouses listed below. Overall, there are more than 180,000 unpublished or hard-to-find documents whose focus borders directly or indirectly on some area of education. The ERIC database can be searched manually or online. It supplies hard-copy or microfiche copies of materials on request. ERIC clearinghouses are:

Clearinghouse for Junior Colleges, University of California, 96 Powell Library Bldg., Los Angeles, CA 90024

Clearinghouse on Adult, Career and Vocational Education, 1960 Kenny Road, Ohio State University, Columbus, OH 43210

Clearinghouse on Counseling and Personnel Services (ERIC/CAPS), Room 2108, School of Education, University of Michigan, Ann Arbor, MI 48109

Clearinghouse on Educational Management (ERIC/CEM), Library, University of Oregon, Eugene, OR 97403

Clearinghouse on Elementary and Early Childhood Education, University of Illinois, College of Education, Urbana, IL 61801

Clearinghouse on Handicapped and Gifted Children (ERIC/EC), CEC Information Services, Council for Exceptional Children, 1920 Association Dr., Reston, VA 22091

Clearinghouse on Higher Education (ERIC/HE), George Washington University, One Dupont Circle, Suite 630, Washington, DC 20036

Clearinghouse on Information Resources (ERIC/IR), School of Education, Syracuse University, Syracuse, NY 13210

Clearinghouse on Languages and Linguistics (ERIC/CLL), Center for Applied Linguistics, 3520 Prospect St. N.W., Washington, DC 20007

Clearinghouse on Reading and Communication Skills (ERIC/RCS), National Council of Teachers of English, 1111 Kenyon Road, Urbana, IL 61801

Clearinghouse on Rural Education and Small Schools (ERIC/ CRESS), Box 3AP, New Mexico State University, Las Cruces, NM 88003

Clearinghouse on Science, Mathematics, and Environmental Education (ERIC/SMEAC), The Ohio State University, 1200 Chambers Road, Columbus, OH 43212

Clearinghouse on Social Studies/Social Science Education (ERIC/ CHESS), Social Science Education Consortium, Inc., 855 Broadway, Boulder, CO 80302

Clearinghouse on Teacher Education (ERIC/SP), One Dupont Circle, Suite 610, Washington, DC 20036

Clearinghouse on Tests, Measurements, and Evaluation (ERIC/TM), Educational Testing Service (ETS), Rosedale Road, Princeton, NJ 08541

Clearinghouse on Urban Education (ERIC/CUE), Box 40, Teachers College, Columbia University, New York, NY 10027

Document Reproduction Service (EDRS), Computer Microfilm International Corporation (CMIC), 3030 N. Fairfax Dr., Suite 200, Arlington, VA 22201

Processing and Reference Facility, ORI, Information Systems Div., 4833 Rugby Ave., Suite 303, Bethesda, MD 20014

Publications: *Resources in Education* (monthly), *Current Index to Journals in Education* (monthly, Oryx Press), *How to Use ERIC.*

Joint Council on Educational Telecommunications (JCET), 1126 16th St. N.W., Washington, DC 20036. JCET is a group of about 20 nonprofit organizations in education and communication that serves as a clearinghouse for information on regulations and current legislation in the field. It also seeks to disseminate information among the communities about needs and opportunities in the present and developing communications technologies. The consortium includes individual organizations that give it nationwide representation.

Library of Congress (LC), Washington, DC 20540. Originally designated as the research arm of Congress, LC has been accepted popularly as the National Library of the United States. LC has numerous materials and services of interest to school library media specialists. Some are interlibrary loans for materials; traveling exhibits of prints and photographs; catalog cards and MARC tape (computer) for most media; folk-life materials and services; copyright for most media; national library service for the blind and physically handicapped, which provides materials and equipment for eligible persons; the Center for the Book (1977), which tries to stimulate appreciation for the printed word; the Geography and Map Division, which includes over 3.5 million manuscript, topographical, and subject maps; photoduplication services; the National Referral Service, which refers people with questions to knowledgeable authorities, but does not provide technical or bibliographic information to any beyond its clientele (Congress); the Automated Systems Office, which plans for automation; and the like. Some LC publications are *Special Collections in the Library of Congress*, 1980; *The Best of Children's Books 1964-1978;* free catalogs of spoken and folk music recordings sold by the Library. Others are available from the LC Central Services Division, Washington, DC 20540.

National Audiovisual Center (NAC), National Archives and Records Service, General Services Administration, Washington, DC 20904. NAC is a central clearinghouse for AV materials produced by and for the federal government. It maintains a master file of audiovisual information and publishes catalogs and other materials, such as: *Directory of U.S. Government Audiovisual Personnel,* and *Catalog of U.S. Government Produced Audiovisual Materials* (free).

National Center for Audio Tapes (NCAT), Educational Media Center, Stadium Building, University of Colorado, Campus Box 379, Boulder, CO 80309. NCAT is a central source for educational tape recordings that are sold on a service basis to educational users. The depository receives tapes from various contributors, including colleges and universities and private and government sources. Catalogs of over 4,000 programs plus foreign offerings are available.

National Information Center for Educational Media (NICEM), University of Southern California, University Park, Los Angeles, CA 90007. NICEM is a central facility that collects, catalogs, and disseminates information about nonbook material. The large database can be searched manually or online. Additionally, NICEM maintains online a file of media producers and distributors. The center is well known for its indexes of AV material by type, such as films, recordings, filmstrips, and so on (see *Books in Print*). Copies of most of the indexes are also available on microfiche.

National Institute of Education (NIE), 609 Riviere Building, Washington, DC 20208. Created as a parallel agency to the U.S. Office of Education in 1972, NIE functions primarily in educational research and development. The aim is to promote educational equity and to improve educational practice. NIE has 17 regional laboratories and serves (largely through them) as an information dissemination clearinghouse.

Television Information Office (TIO), 745 Fifth Ave., New York, NY 10022. TIO is a nonprofit organization that was formed to share information between the television industry and its many publics. It provides current information on its offerings to anyone interested. TIO supports the semiannual *Teachers Guide to Television*, which offers study aids for utilizing commercial television in the classroom. Numerous publications are available from the above address.

FEDERAL AND STATE AGENCIES AND PROGRAMS

Direct financial support of libraries by the federal government is a comparatively recent phenomenon. The launching of Sputnik aroused the concern to generate and pass into law the National Defense Education Act of 1958, which provided funds for materials in teaching languages, mathematics, and science. In 1964, the Library Services and Construction Act (an expansion of the Library Services Act of 1956) was passed, and in 1965 the Higher Education Act, and the Elementary and Secondary Education Act (ESEA), which was to have the most profound effect on school library media centers.

In time, ESEA, with its many subprograms and satellite activities, became difficult to administer, and so, as part of President Reagan's policy to consolidate and return, where possible, responsibility for administering the nation's education system to the state and local levels, Congress passed the Education Consolidation and Improvement Act (ECIA) of 1981 (P.L. 97–35), which took effect July 1, 1982. This provides noncategorical block grants to the states in two sections: Chapter 1, which supersedes Title I of ESEA (the largest educational program at the federal level), and provides financial assistance to meet the special needs of disadvantaged children; and Chapter 2, which consolidates 42 other elementary and secondary education programs into block grants for three broad purposes—basic skills improvement, improvement of support services, and special projects. This area includes not only all of the other titles formerly found under ESEA, but also those, for example, authorized by the Alcohol and Drug Abuse Education Act, Career Education Incentive Act, and programs ranging from Aid for the Gifted and Talented and Arts in Education to metric education. State education agencies administer Chapter 2, although total state allotments are determined by the ratio of a state's school-age population to the nation's total. At least 80 percent of the total funds must be distributed to local agencies, but up to 20 percent can be retained at the state level. Local allocations must be adjusted to provide highest per-pupil allocations where education costs are higher than average. Usually this is a result of the economic needs of families. In FY 1982, about $2.6 billion was awarded under Title I (now Chapter 1). The distribution was about 7 percent to preschool and kindergarten children, 69 percent to those in grades one through six, and 24 percent to high school grades. An additional $440 million was distributed through Chapter 2.

Administration of ECIA is one of the responsibilities of the Office for Elementary and Secondary Education (OESE), which is part of the Department of Education. This department, although created only in June 1980, has already had a beleaguered history involving many threats of dismantling.

Other responsibilities of OESE include administering the services provided by the Indian Education Act of 1972, and, also as part of Chapter 2, continuing the Inexpensive Book Program. This involves supplying financial support (almost $6 million per year) on a contractual basis to Reading Is Fundamental, Inc. (RIF), a program that gives books to disadvantaged children and encourages them to read. This program also receives help from the private sector through money and the work of volunteers.

The other office of the Department of Education involved most directly with libraries and library services is the Office of Educational Research and Improvement (OERI). This office has three program components. The first is the National Institute of Education (NIE). ERIC is considered one of the most effective of the creations of NIE, even though at present only about 4 percent of its $135 million annual budget is paid by the department. The remainder of its financial support comes from nonfederal sources. The National Center for Education Statistics (NCES) is also part of this office. This component works closely with the Bureau of the Census to generate material useful in planning by school districts. The third component is the Center for Education Improvement (CEI), which includes the Library Programs Division, the agency responsible for distributing assistance (over $70 million annually) to college, university, and public libraries. The National Commission on Excellence in Education (NCEE), an independent advisory board that holds hearings nationally, reports directly to the secretary of this office.

There are three other offices in the Department of Education that administer legislation affecting school library media centers. The Office of Special Education and Rehabilitation Services administers programs authorized by the Education for All Handicapped Children Act of 1975 (P.L. 94–142) and other legislation designed to help the education of handicapped youth. In FY 1982, more than $1.2 billion was appropriated for these programs. The Office of Bilingual Education and Minority Languages Affairs (OBEMLA) assists state and local agencies to develop and strengthen programs that help children who have limited English proficiency and whose first language is not English. The Office for Vocational and Adult Education (OVAE), through its many services, assists states in training youths and adults for work.

Some other government-related agencies that are sources of information and/or funds related to libraries are the National Commission on Libraries and Information Science (NCLIS, a planning agency); the National Endowment for the Arts and the National Endowment for the Humanities (Washington, DC); and the National Science Foundation (Division of Information, Science, and Technology, Washington, DC).

State Education Agencies

With the increased decentralization of the nation's educational system from national to state level, plus the steady retrenchment of federal library assistance programs, the role of state educational agencies in the development and administration of local and district school library media programs has become one of increasing importance. The Division of Library Development and Services of the Maryland State Department of Education, in their publication *Criteria for Modern School Media Programs* (1971), listed succinctly what could be regarded as the basic responsibilities and functions of a state agency:

1. To formulate long-range plans for the development of school media programs, including cooperative planning for regional and state services.

2. To provide advisory and consultative services to local school systems, particularly in the areas of new media services and technology and school media facilities.

3. To develop standards and guidelines for the improvement of media programs.

4. To provide programs of in-service education on the concepts and utilization of media to administrators, supervisors, media personnel, and teachers.

5. To develop proposals for needed research in media services.

6. To collect, analyze, and disseminate information on the scope and quality of media programs in the state.

7. To assist in the determination of qualifications for certification of media personnel.

8. To administer federal funds available for media programs.

9. To provide for the effective coordination of media services with the critical educational concerns of the state and local school systems.

10. To develop coordinated plans and policies with other personnel and agencies that will strengthen library media services for all citizens.

11. To act as a clearinghouse for information on library services in the state, and to foster interlibrary loan and cooperative arrangements with school, public, academic, or other libraries.

Because of the diversity and importance of these functions, it is important that media personnel either individually or through a district office, establish and maintain contact with the appropriate state school library media center agency and use their services (see Appendix I for a list of state consultants and addresses to facilitate initial contacts). It should also be noted that many of the agencies supply documents that can be helpful in such areas as selection of materials and development of the center's instructional program.

School Library Media Centers and the Political Process

The library profession has often been accused of having more interest in communicating internally than with those who make the major decisions affecting its future. Fortunately, this reluctance to be involved in the legislative process through lobbying or application of other forms of political pressure is waning, and the age of the librarian activist is at hand. For the novice in this area, here are some pointers. Be sure to organize your activity well. Depending on the level of activity (local or statewide), this might involve setting up a steering committee or forming a communications network. Be sure to plan thoroughly by formally stating short- and long-range goals, devising a timetable, and preparing suitable data and supporting documents. Sometimes the development of legislation workshops can be of benefit if they cover topics such as an explanation of the legislative process, hints on how to establish a legislative network, and techniques on how to contact and communicate with key officials. Seek outside support and form alliances with other interested organizations such as local PTA groups, local or state educational organizations, and legislative groups like the League of Women Voters. Communicate your needs and position politely but effectively to the necessary in-dividuals—politicians, legislators, board members—who can act as change agents on your behalf. Before these encounters, whether by mail, telephone, or in person, prepare yourself to present your position succinctly, accurately, and in terms of how your suggestions will benefit students. Cover only one or two issues at a time, be concise, and suggest a specific course of action. With written contact, a form or mimeographed letter, although better than nothing, is a poor substitute for a handwritten or typewritten one. Do not ignore other forms of communication, such as letters to the editor, press releases, news conferences, interviews, handouts, buttons, community bulletin boards, and speaking engagements. The growing success rate of librarians in influencing the political process promises well for the future.

SCHOOL LIBRARY MEDIA SPECIALIST READING SHELF

At the end of each chapter in this book are suggestions for further reading, but each media specialist might wish to build a basic collection of books and materials to supplement this handbook. Several other works cover some of the same material, but many are now somewhat out-of-date. Two of the most recent recommended titles are J. Cabeceiras, *The Multimedia Library: Materials Selection and Use* (New York: Academic Press, 1978) and Emanual Prostano and Joyce Prostano, *The School Library Media Center* (Littleton, Colo.: Libraries Unlimited, 1982). A practical, serviceable, basic work is Mildred L. Nichol, *Steps to Service* (Chicago: American Library Association, 1975).

Any professional shelf should certainly contain the national standard, *Media Programs: District and School* (Chicago: American Library Association/Association for Educational Communications and Technology, 1975). In developing the center's program, the best work continues to be Ruth Ann Davies, *The School Library Media Program: Instructional Force for Excellence* 3rd ed. (New York: R. R. Bowker, 1979).

Three yearbooks cover various aspects of the world of libraries and media without too great overlapping (although purchase of any or all might be beyond a single school budget): *The ALA Yearbook* (Chicago: American Library Association), *The Bowker Annual of Library and Book Trade Information* (New York: R. R. Bowker), and *Educational Media Yearbook* (Littleton, Colo.: Libraries Unlimited).

Several periodicals also cover news items and trends in the world of libraries and educational media: *American Libraries, Library Journal,* and *Wilson Library Bulletin.* Periodicals geared specifically to school library media centers and work with children and young adults are *Educational Innovator, School Library Journal, School Library Media Quarterly,* and *Top of the News.*

To this basic list of books and periodicals, each person will certainly add other titles that have proved helpful and could be considered basic. Some candidates in the book category are:

Brown, J. W., and Lewis, R. B. *A.V. Instructional Technology: Manual for Independent Study.* New York: McGraw-Hill, 1977.

Brown, J. W.; Lewis, R. B.; and Harcleroad, F. F. *A.V. Instruction: Technology, Media & Methods,* 6th ed. New York: McGraw-Hill, 1983.

Brown, J. W.; Norberg, K. D.; and Srygley, S. K. *Administering Educational Media: Instructional Technology & Library Services,* 2nd ed. New York: McGraw-Hill, 1972.

Chisholm, Margaret, and Ely, Donald. *Instructional Design & the School Library Media Specialist.* Chicago: American Association of School Librarians, 1980.

——. *Media Personnel in Education: A Contemporary Approach.* Englewood Cliffs, N.J.: Prentice-Hall, 1976.

Dale, E. *Audiovisual Methods in Teaching.* Hinsdale, Ill.: Dryden, 1969.

Erickson, C. W. H. *Administering Instructional Media Programs.* New York: Macmillan, 1968.

Freeman, Patricia. *Pathfinder: An Operational Guide for the School Librarian.* New York: Harper, 1975.

Hug, William E. *Instructional Design and the Media Program.* Chicago: American Library Association, 1975.

Martin, Betty, and Carson, Ben. *The Principal's Handbook on the School Library Media Center.* Hamden, Conn.: Shoe String, 1981.

Martin, Betty, and Hatfield, Frances S. *The School District Library Media Director's Handbook.* Hamden, Conn.: Shoe String, 1981.

Martin, Betty, and Sargent, Linda. *The Teacher's Handbook on the School Library Media Center.* Hamden, Conn.: Shoe String, 1980.

Robotham, John S., and LaFleur, Lydia. *Library Programs: How to Select, Plan and Produce Them,* 2nd ed. Metuchen, N.J.: Scarecrow, 1981.

Saunders, Helen E. *The Modern School Library,* 2nd ed. by Nancy Polette. Metuchen, N.J.: Scarecrow, 1975.

Shapiro, Lillian L. *Serving Youth: Communication and Commitment in the High School Library.* New York: R. R. Bowker, 1975.

Taggart, Dorothy T. *Management and Administration of the School Library Media Program.* Hamden, Conn.: Library Professional Publications, 1980.

Wedgeworth, Robert, ed. *A.L.A. World Encyclopedia of Library and Information Services.* Chicago: American Library Association, 1980.

Wittich, Walter A., and Schuller, Charles F. *Instructional Technology: Its Nature and Use,* 6th ed. New York: Harper, 1979.

The practices that are discussed in this and the preceding chapters on managing a single school library media center point out the differences between the school library of the past and today's center. The conventional school library was adequate when information was transmitted in traditional ways. Now, however, our electronic environment makes it imperative that educators utilize new sources of information and teach the skills necessary to understand and interpret them.

It is interesting to speculate on what the scope and contents of a handbook similar to this one will be in the future. Whatever the future may bring in public education, it seems assured that school library media centers are destined to play an increasingly important role.

FOR FURTHER READING

American Association of School Librarians, Legislative Committee. "Simple Steps to Successful Legislation." *School Media Quarterly* (Winter 1977), pp. 85–94. Reprints available.

Barron, J. Roy. "How Representative Is Your Representative?" *Audiovisual Instruction* (May 1975), pp. 42–43.

Bender, David R. "Cooperative Planning for Media Program Development." *School Media Quarterly* (Winter 1975), pp. 115–120.

——. "State Educational Agencies: Roles and Functions." *School Library Journal* (December 1975), pp. 27–29.

Boss, Richard W. *Grant Money and How to Get It: A Handbook for Librarians.* New York: R. R. Bowker, 1980.

Conroy, Barbara. *Library Staff Development and Continuing Education: Principles and Practices.* Littleton, Colo.: Libraries Unlimited, 1978.

Correy, Emmett, O.S.F. *Grants for Libraries: A Guide to Public and Private Funding Programs and Proposal Writing Techniques.* Littleton, Colo.: Libraries Unlimited, 1982.

Cowley, John. *Personnel Management in Libraries.* Hamden, Conn.: Shoe String, 1982.

Fite, Alice E. "A Year of Celebration: A.A.S.L.'s 25th Anniversary." *School Media Quarterly* (Summer 1976), pp. 293–295.

Franco, John M. "Leadership Responsibilities of School Library Media Specialists in Instructional Programs." *Ohio Media Spectrum* (October 1977), pp. 18–20.

Johnson, Millard F., Jr. "After the Online Catalog: A Call for Active Librarianship." *American Libraries* (April 1982), pp. 235–239.

Josey, E. J. *Libraries in the Political Process*. Phoenix, Ariz.: Oryx, 1980.

Owens, Major R. "School Libraries and the Political Process." *School Library Journal* (September 1976), pp. 22–23.

"Perceptions of the Role of the School Media Specialist." *School Media Quarterly* (Spring 1981), pp. 152–163.

Pond, Patricia. "Development of a Professional School Library Association: American Association of School Librarians." *School Media Quarterly* (Fall 1976), pp. 12–18.

Professional Development and Educational Technology: Nineteen Eighty. Chicago: AECT, 1980.

"Professionalism and Ethical Behavior: Relationship to School Library Media Personnel," *School Media Quarterly* (Winter 1980), pp. 82–100.

Reeves, William J. *Librarians as Professionals: The Occupation's Impact on Library Work Arrangements*. Lexington, Mass.: Lexington Books, 1980.

Schlessinger, Bernard S., and Jensen, Patricia. "Continuing Education— General Considerations with Application to School Librarians." In *Excellence in School Media Programs*. Chicago: American Library Association, 1980, pp. 198–208.

U.S. Department of Education. *Annual Report: Fiscal Year 1982*. Washington, D.C.: Government Printing Office, 1983.

Walker, Sue. "Issues Alert." *School Media Quarterly* (Summer 1982), pp. 375–381.

APPENDIX I

Directory of State School Library Media Center Agencies

ALABAMA

W. Raymond Jones
Educational Specialist
Library Media Services
111 Coliseum Blvd.
Montgomery, AL 36193

ALASKA

B. J. Morse
School Library Coordinator
Alaska State Library
650 International Airport Road
Anchorage, AK 99502

ARIZONA

Mary Choncoff
Education Program Specialist
Dept. of Education
1535 W. Jefferson
Phoenix, AZ 85007

ARKANSAS

Betty J. Morgan
Educational Administrative
  Supervisor
State of Arkansas Dept. of
  Education
State Education Building
Little Rock, AR 72201

CALIFORNIA

John Church
Director, Resources Center
Dept. of Education
721 Capitol Mall
Sacramento, CA 95814

COLORADO

Anne Marie Falsone
Assistant Commissioner, Office of
  Library Services
Colorado State Library
1362 Lincoln St.
Denver, CO 80203

CONNECTICUT

Betty V. Billman
State Dept. of Education
165 Capitol Ave., Room 375
Hartford, CT 06106

DELAWARE

Richard L. Krueger
Supervisor, Library Media Services
Dept. of Public Instruction,
  Library Information Center
Box 1402, Townsend Bldg.
Dover, DE 19901

351

FLORIDA

Sandra W. Ulm
Administrator, School Library
  Media Services
State Dept. of Education
Knott Bldg.
Tallahassee, FL 32301

GEORGIA

O. Max Wilson
Director, Div. of Instructional
  Media Services
Georgia Dept. of Education
Office of Instructional Services
Twin Towers East
Atlanta, GA 30334

HAWAII

Patsy Izumo
Director
State of Hawaii, Dept. of Education
Multimedia Services Branch
641 18th Ave.
Honolulu, HI 96816

IDAHO

R. H. Leverett
State Dept. of Education
Len B. Jordan Office Bldg.
Boise, ID 83720

ILLINOIS

Marie Rose Sivak
Educational Consultant
Education Innovation and Support
Illinois State Board of Education
100 N. First St.
Springfield, IL 62777

INDIANA

Phyllis Land
Director
Div. of Federal Resources and
  School Improvement
Room 229, State House
Indianapolis, IN 46204

IOWA

Betty Jo Buckingham
Consultant, Educational Media
State Superintendent's Office, State
  Dept. of Education
State Office Bldg.
Des Moines, IA 50319

KANSAS

June Saine Level
Library Media Consultant
Educational Assistance Section,
  Kansas State Dept. of Education
110 E. Tenth St.
Topeka, KS 66612

KENTUCKY

Judy Cooper
Program Manager
School Media Services
1830 Capital Plaza Tower
Kentucky Dept. of Education
Frankfort, KY 40601

LOUISIANA

J. Kelly Nix
State Superintendent
State of Louisiana, Dept. of
  Education
Box 44064
Baton Rouge, LA 70804

MAINE

Dorothy A. Gregory
Maine State Library
Media Services, LMA Bldg.
State House Station 64
Augusta, ME 04333

MARYLAND

Paula Montgomery
Chief, School Media Services Branch
Maryland State Dept. of Education
200 W. Baltimore St.
Baltimore, MD 21201-2595

MASSACHUSETTS

Commonwealth of Massachusetts
Board of Library Commissioners
648 Beacon St.
Boston, MA 02215

MICHIGAN

Marlene Thayer
School Library/Media Services
Michigan Dept. of Education
State Library Services
Box 30007, 735 E. Michigan Ave.
Lansing, MI 48909

MINNESOTA

Mary S. Dalbotten
Specialist, Educational Media
Minnesota State Dept. of Education
Capitol Square Bldg., 550 Cedar St.
St. Paul, MN 55101

MISSISSIPPI

John Barlow
State Dept. of Education
Educational Media Services
Box 771
Jackson, MS 39205

MISSOURI

State of Missouri
Dept. of Elementary and Secondary
   Education
Box 480
Jefferson City, MO 65102

MONTANA

Sheila Cates
Specialist, Library Media
Office of Public Instruction
State Capitol
Helena, MT 59620

NEBRASKA

Nebraska Dept. of Education
Box 94987, 301 Centennial Mall S.
Lincoln, NE 68509-4987

NEVADA

William F. Arensdorf
Chairperson, Instructional Materials
   and Equipment
State Dept. of Education
Capitol Complex
Carson City, NV 89710

NEW HAMPSHIRE

Horace Roberts
Educational Consultant
Library and Learning Resources
   Program
New Hampshire State Dept. of
   Education
Concord, NH 03301

NEW JERSEY

Anne E. Voss
Coordinator, School and College
   Media Services
Library Development Bureau, State
   of New Jersey Dept. of Education
State Library, Box 1898
Trenton, NJ 08625

NEW MEXICO

Virginia Downing
Library/Media Specialist
Bureau of School Libraries and
   Learning Resources
State Dept. of Education
Santa Fe, NM 87503

NEW YORK

Robert Barron
Chief
The University of the State of
   New York
Bureau of School Library Media
   Programs
New York State Education Dept.
Albany, NY 12234

NORTH CAROLINA

Mary A. Holloway
Special Assistant
Educational Media Services
Dept. of Public Instruction,
    State of North Carolina
Raleigh, NC 27611

NORTH DAKOTA

Patricia Herbel
Coordinator of Curriculum and NDN
The State of North Dakota
Dept. of Public Instruction
Bismarck, ND 58505

OHIO

Theresa M. Fredericka
Library Media Consultant
Ohio Dept. of Education
65 S. Front St., Room 1005
Columbus, OH 43215

OKLAHOMA

Barbara Spriestersbach
Assistant Administrator
State Dept. of Education
2500 N. Lincoln Blvd.
Oklahoma City, OK 73105

OREGON

George Katagiri
Coordinator
Instructional Technology, Oregon
    Dept. of Education
700 Pringle Parkway S.E.
Salem, OR 97310

PENNSYLVANIA

Doris M. Epler
Director
Div. of School Library Media and
    Educational Resource Services
Pennsylvania Dept. of Education
Bureau of State Library
333 Market St., Box 911
Harrisburg, PA 17108

RHODE ISLAND

Arthur R. Pontarelli
Commissioner
State of Rhode Island and
    Providence Plantations
Dept. of Education
22 Hayes St.
Providence, RI 02908

SOUTH CAROLINA

Mary F. Griffin
Library/Media Consultant
State of South Carolina
Dept. of Education
Columbia, SC 29201

SOUTH DAKOTA

Ardis L. Ruark
Director
Dept. of Education and Cultural
    Affairs
Educational Resource Service
Div. of Elementary and Secondary
    Education
Kneip Bldg.
Pierre, SD 57501

TENNESSEE

Christine Brown
Director, School Library Resources
Tennessee Dept. of Education
Curriculum and Instructional
    Services
Cordell Hull Bldg.
Nashville, TN 37219

TEXAS

Mary Boyvey
Texas Education Agency
201 E. 11th St.
Austin, TX 78701

UTAH

Kenneth L. Neal
Media Coordinator
Curriculum and Instruction Div.,
    State Board of Education

250 E. Fifth S.
Salt Lake City, UT 84111

VERMONT

Jean D. Battey
School Library Media Coordinator
Div. of Federal Assistance
State of Vermont Dept. of Education
Montpelier, VT 05602

VIRGINIA

Mary Stuart Mason
Supervisor, School Libraries and
   Textbooks
Commonwealth of Virginia, Dept of
   Education
Box 6Q
Richmond, VA 23216

WASHINGTON

Jean Wieman
Director
Programs and Learning Resources
State Superintendent of Public
   Instruction
Olympia, WA 98504

WEST VIRGINIA

Carolyn R. Skidmore
Director, ECIA Chapter 2
State of West Virginia, Dept. of
   Education
Charleston, WV 23505

WISCONSIN

Dianne McAfee Hopkins
Director, Bureau of Instructional
   Media Programs
Div. for Library Services, The State
   of Wisconsin
Dept. of Public Instruction
125 S. Webster St., Box 7841
Madison, WI 53707

WYOMING

Jack Prince
Coordinator, Instructional
   Resources
The State of Wyoming, Dept. of
   Education
Hathaway Bldg.
Cheyenne, WY 82002

APPENDIX II

Directory of Associations and Agencies

Action for Children's Television
(ACT)
46 Austin St.
Newtonville, MA 02160

Agency for Instructional Television
(AIT)
Box A
Bloomington, IN 47402

American Association for Gifted
Children, Inc.
15 Gramercy Park
New York, NY 10003

American Association for the
Advancement of Science
1515 Massachusetts Ave. N.W.
Washington, DC 20005

American Association for Vocational
Instructional Materials (AAVIM)
120 Engineering Center
Athens, GA 30602

American Association of
Elementary-Kindergarten
Education
1201 16th St. N.W.
Washington, DC 20036

American Association of Museums
(AAM)
1055 Thomas Jefferson St. N.W.
Washington, DC 20007

American Association of School
Administrators (AASA)
1801 N. Moore St.
Arlington, VA 22209

American Council on Education
One Dupont Circle N.W.
Washington, DC 20036

The American Film Institute (AFI)
John F. Kennedy Center for the
Performing Arts
Washington, DC 20566

American Foundation for the Blind,
Inc. (AFB)
15 W. 16th St.
New York, NY 10011

American Institute of Graphic Arts
(AIGA)
1059 Third Ave.
New York, NY 10021

American Library Association
(ALA)
50 E. Huron St.
Chicago, IL 60611

ALA Divisions (all located at ALA headquarters in Chicago):

American Association of School Librarians (AASL)

Association for Library Service to Children (ALSC)

Committee on Instruction in the Use of Libraries (IULC)
c/o Andrew M. Hansen, Staff Liaison

Library and Information Technology Association (LITA)

Young Adult Services Division (YASD)

American Society for Information Science (ASIS)
1010 16th St. N.W.
Washington, DC 20036

American University Press Service, Inc.
One Park Ave.
New York, NY 10016

Anti-Defamation League (ADL) of B'nai B'rith
823 United Nations Plaza
New York, NY 10017

Association for Childhood Education International (ACEI)
3615 Wisconsin Ave. N.W.
Washington, DC 20016

Association for Educational Communications and Technology (AECT)
1201 16th St. N.W.
Washington, DC 20036

Association for Supervision and Curriculum Development (ASCD)
225 N. Washington St.
Alexandria, VA 22314

Association of American Publishers
One Park Ave.
New York, NY 10016

Association of Independent Video and Filmmakers (AIVF) and the Foundation for Independent Video and Film (FIVF)
625 Broadway
New York, NY 10012

Bank Street College of Education
610 W. 112th St.
New York, NY 10025

Bay Area Video Coalition (BAVC)
2940 16th St., Room 200
San Francisco, CA 94103

Broadcasting Foundation of America (BFA)
52 Vanderbilt Ave.
New York, NY 10017

Cable Television Information Center (CTIC)
1800 N. Kent St., Suite 1007
Arlington, VA 22209

Canadian Library Association
151 Sparks St.
Ottawa, Ont. K1P 5E3, Canada

Catholic Audiovisual Educators Association (CAVE)
5722 Woodmont Ave.
Pittsburgh, PA 15226

Catholic Library Association (CLA)
461 W. Lancaster Ave.
Haverford, PA 19041

Center for Architectural Research (CAR)
Rensselaer Polytechnic Institute
Troy, NY 12181

Child Study Association of America/
  Wel-Met Inc.
50 Madison Ave.
New York, NY 10010

Child Welfare League of America
67 Irving Place
New York, NY 10003

Children's Book Council (CBC)
67 Irving Place
New York, NY 10003

Children's Media Data Bank
  (CMDB)
Department of Library Science/
  Educational Technology
School of Education
University of North Carolina at
  Greensboro
Greensboro, NC 27412

Children's Television Workshop
  (CTW)
One Lincoln Plaza
New York, NY 10023

Church and Synagogue Library
  Association
Box 1130
Bryn Mawr, PA 19010

The Combined Book Exhibit (CBE)
12 Saw Mill River Road
Hawthorne, NY 10532

Consortium of University Film
  Centers (CUFC)
c/o Kent State University
Audio Visual Services
330 Library
Kent, OH 44242

Council for Exceptional Children
  (CEC)
1920 Association Dr.
Reston, VA 22091

Council of Chief State School
  Officers (CCSSO)
400 N. Capitol St. N.W.
Washington, DC 20001

Council on International
  Non-theatrical Events (CINE)
1201 16th St. N.W.
Washington, DC 20036

Council on Interracial Books for
  Children (CIBC)
1841 Broadway
New York, NY 10023

Council On Library Resources (CLR)
One Dupont Circle
Washington, DC 20036

Dial-an-Author
c/o Bantam Books
School and College Dept.
666 Fifth Ave.
New York, NY 10103

Educators Progress Service
Dept. A7C
Randolph, WI 53956

EPIE Institute (Educational
  Products Information Exchange)
Box 620
Stony Brook, NY 11790

ERIC (Educational Resources
  Information Center)
National Institute of Education
Program on Dissemination and
  Improvement of Practice
1200 19th St. N.W.
Washington, DC 20208

ERIC Clearinghouse on Elementary
  and Early Childhood Education
  (ERIC/EECE)
College of Education

University of Illinois
1310 S. Sixth St.
Champaign, IL 61820

ERIC Clearinghouse on
Handicapped and Gifted Children
(ERIC/EC)
CEC Information Services
Council for Exceptional Children
1920 Association Dr.
Reston, VA 22091

ERIC Clearinghouse on Reading and
Communication Skills (ERIC/RCS)
National Council of Teachers of
English
1111 Kenyon Road
Urbana, IL 61801

Eastman Kodak Co.
Rochester, NY 14650

Educational Facilities
Laboratories (EFL)
680 Fifth Ave.
New York, NY 10019

Educational Film Library
Association (EFLA)
43 W. 61st St.
New York, NY 10023

Freedom to Read Foundation
(FTRF)
50 E. Huron St.
Chicago, IL 60611

Great Plains National ITV Library
(GPN)
Box 80669
Lincoln, NE 68501

Information Center on Children's
Cultures
U.S. Committee for United Nations
Children's Fund (UNICEF)
331 E. 38th St.
New York, NY 10016

International Association of School
Librarianship (IASL)
School of Librarianship
Western Michigan University
Kalamazoo, MI 49008

International Friendship League,
Inc.
22 Batterymarch St.
Boston, MA 02109

International Reading Association
(IRA)
800 Barksdale Road, Box 8139
Newark, DE 19711

International Simulation and
Gaming Association
(ISAGA)
c/o Cathy S. Greenblat
Dept. of Sociology
Rutgers—The State University
New Brunswick, NJ 08903

Joint Council on Educational
Telecommunications (JCET)
1126 16th St. N.W.
Washington, DC 20036

Library of Congress
Washington, DC 20540

Media Center for Children
(MCC)
3 W. 29th St.
New York, NY 10001

Michigan Library Association
226 W. Washington
Lansing, MI 48933

Microform Review, Inc.
520 Riverside Ave.
Box 405, Saugatuck Station
Westport, CT 06880

Modern Language Association of
America (MLA)
62 Fifth Ave.
New York, NY 10011

National Association for the
Education of Young Children
1834 Connecticut Ave. N.W.
Washington, DC 20009

National Association of Elementary
School Principals (NAESP)
1801 N. Moore St.
Arlington, VA 22209

National Association of Secondary
School Principals (NASSP)
1904 Association Dr.
Reston, VA 22091

National Association of State
Boards of Education (NASBE)
444 N. Capitol St. N.W., Suite 526
Washington, DC 20001

National Audio-Visual Association
(NAVA)
3150 Spring St.
Fairfax, VA 22031

National Audiovisual Center (NAC)
National Archives and Records
Service
General Services Administration
Washington, DC 20409

National Center for Audio Tapes
(NCAT)
Educational Media Center
Stadium Bldg.
University of Colorado
Campus Box 379
Boulder, CO 80309

National Center for Education
Statistics (NCES)
Presidential Bldg.

400 Maryland Ave. S.W.
Washington, DC 20202

National Commission on Libraries
and Information Science (NCLIS)
1717 K St. N.W., Suite 601
Washington, DC 20036

National Council for the Social
Studies (NCSS)
3615 Wisconsin Ave. N.W.
Washington, DC 20016

National Council of Teachers of
English (NCTE)
1111 Kenyon Road
Urbana, IL 61801

National Council of Teachers of
Mathematics (NCTM)
1906 Association Dr.
Reston, VA 22091

National Council of the Churches of
Christ—Communication
Commission (NCC-CC)
475 Riverside Dr.
New York, NY 10115

National Education Association
(NEA)
1201 16th St. N.W.
Washington, DC 20036

National Information Center for
Educational Media (NICEM)
University of Southern California
University Park
Los Angeles, CA 90007

National Instructional Materials
Information System
University of Southern California
University Park-RAN
Los Angeles, CA 90007

National Library Services for the
Blind and Physically Handicapped
Library of Congress
Washington, DC 20542

National Micrographics Association
8719 Colesville Road
Silver Spring, MD 20910

National PTA
700 N. Rush St.
Chicago, IL 60611

National Radio Broadcasters
Association (NRBA)
1705 De Sales St. N.W., Suite 500
Washington, DC 20036

National School Supply and
Equipment Association (NSSEA)
1500 Wilson Blvd., Suite 609
Arlington, VA 22209

National Science Teachers
Association (NSTA)
1742 Connecticut Ave. N.W.
Washington, DC 20009

National Storytelling Resource
Center
Box 112
Jonesborough, TN 37659

National Video Clearinghouse, Inc.
Box 3, Dept. 09AN
Syosset, NY 11791

New Games Foundation
Box 7901
San Francisco, CA 94120

New York Library Association
15 Park Row, Suite 434
New York, NY 10038

New York Public Library
8 E. 40th St.
New York, NY 10016

New York Times Information
Bank (NYTIB)
1719A Rte. 10
Parsippany, NJ 07054

"Newsline" Education, USA
The Source Library Services
Dept. LLA6
1616 Anderson Road
McLean, VA 22102

OCLC, Inc.
6565 Frantz Road
Dublin, OH 43017

On-Line Audiovisual Catalogers,
Inc.
c/o David Hedrick, Treas.
Gettysburg College Library
Gettysburg, PA 17325

Outdoor Education Association
(OEA)
c/o Edward J. Ambry
143 Fox Hill Road
Denville, NJ 07834

Public Broadcasting Service (PBS)
475 L'Enfant Plaza S.W.
Washington, DC 20024

Puppeteers of America, Inc.
5 Cricklewood Path
Pasadena, CA 91107

Reading Is Fundamental, Inc.
Smithsonian Institution
2500 L'Enfant Plaza
Washington, DC 20560

Society of Motion Picture and
Television Engineers, Inc.
(SMPTE)
862 Scarsdale Ave.
Scarsdale, NY 10583

Superintendent of Documents
U.S. Government Printing Office
Washington, DC 20402

Television Information Office (TIO)
745 Fifth Ave.
New York, NY 10022

Toy Manufacturers of America
  (TMA)
200 Fifth Ave.
New York, NY 10010

Universal Serials and Book
  Exchange (USBE)

3335 V St. N.E.
Washington, DC 20018

Wisconsin Library Association
201 W. Mifflin St.
Madison, WI 53703

World Pen Pals (WPP)
1690 Como Ave.
St. Paul, MN 55108

Young Filmakers/Video Arts
  (YF/VA)
4 Rivington St.
New York, NY 10002

APPENDIX III

Directory of Selected Library Furniture and Supply Houses

Advance Products Co.
Central at Wabash
Wichita, KS 67214

American Desk Manufacturing Co.
Box 429
Temple, TX 76501

American Seating Co.
901 Broadway N.W.
Grand Rapids, MI 49504

Aurora Steel Products
580 S. Lake St.
Aurora, IL 60507

Brewster Corp.
50 River St.
Old Saybrook, CT 06475

Brodart
1609 Memorial Ave.
Williamsport, PA 17705

Buckstaff Co.
1127 S. Main St.
Oshkosh, WI 54901

Claridge Products & Equipment
Box 910
Harrison, AR 72601

Br.:
14736 Wicks Blvd.
San Leandro, CA 94577

1200 Carnegie St.
Rolling Meadows, IL 60008

Box 189, 503 Ogden Ave.
Mamaroneck, NY 10543

Dahle USA
26 Berkshire Road
Rte. 34
Sandy Hook, CT 06482

Demco
Box 7488
2120 Fordem Ave.
Madison, WI 53707

Br.:
Box 7767
5683 Fountain Way
Fresno, CA 93727

Fixtures Manufacturing Corp.
1642 Crystal St.
Kansas City, MO 64126

Fleetwood Furniture Co.
Box 58
Zeeland, MI 49464

Fordham Equipment &
  Publishing Co.
3308 Edson Ave.
Bronx, NY 10469

Foster Manufacturing Co.
414 N. 13th St.
Philadelphia, PA 19108

Gaylord Bros.
Box 4901
Syracuse, NY 13221

  Br.:
  Box 8489
  Stockton, CA 95208

Heller Co.
Library Div.
181 Wabash Ave.
Montpelier, OH 43543

Highsmith Co.
Box 25
Fort Atkinson, WI 53538

Howe Furniture Corp.
155 E. 56th St.
New York, NY 10022

Josten's Library Services
1301 Cliff Road
Burnsville, MN 55337

Kidde Merchandising Equipment
  Group
Box 328
100 Bidwell Road
South Windsor, CT 06074

Knipp & Co.
3401 S. Hanover St.
Baltimore, MD 21225

Kole Enterprises
Box 520152
Miami, FL 33152

Krueger
Box 8100
Green Bay, WI 54308

Larlin Corp.
Box 1523
Marietta, GA 30061

Library Bureau
801 Park Ave.
Herkimer, NY 13350

  Br.: Lee's Summit, MO
  64063

Luxor Corp.
2245 Delany Road
Waukegan, IL 60085

Herman Miller, Inc.
Zeeland, MI 49464

Monroe Co.
424 Church St.
Colfax, IA 50054

Multiplex Display Fixture Co.
1555 Larkin Williams Road
Fenton, MO 63026

Republic Steel
Industrial Products Div.
1038 Belden Ave. N.E.
Canton, OH 44705

Rockaway Metal Products
  Corp.
175 Roger Ave.
Inwood, NY 11696

Slater Co.
300 W. Hubbard St.
Chicago, IL 60610

Steelcase, Inc.
1120 36th St. S.E.
Grand Rapids, MI 49501

Texwood Furniture Corp.
Box 6280
3508 E. First St.
Austin, TX 78762

Thonet Industries
Box 1587
491 E. Princess St.
York, PA 17405

Tuohy Furniture Corp.
42 Saint Albans Place
Chatfield, MN 55923

Virco Manufacturing Corp.
15134 S. Vermont Ave.
Gardena, CA 90427

Vogel-Peterson Co.
Box C90
Rte. 83 & Madison
Elmhurst, IL 60126

Wallach & Associates, Inc.
1515 E. 23rd St.
Cleveland, OH 44114

Worden Co.
Box 915-C
199 E. 17th St.
Holland, MI 49423

APPENDIX IV
Key Documents

Library Bill of Rights
Official Interpretations of the Library Bill of Rights
School Library Bill of Rights
Librarians' Code of Ethics
AECT Code of Ethics
Freedom to Read Statement
Citizen's Request Form for Reevaluation of Learning Resource Center Materials

LIBRARY BILL OF RIGHTS

The American Library Association affirms that all libraries are forums for information and ideas, and that the following basic policies should guide their services.

1. Books and other library resources should be provided for the interest, information, and enlightenment of all people of the community the library serves. Materials should not be excluded because of the origin, background, or views of those contributing to their creation.

2. Libraries should provide materials and information presenting all points of view on current and historical issues. Materials should not be proscribed or removed because of partisan or doctrinal disapproval.

3. Libraries should challenge censorship in the fulfillment of their responsibility to provide information and enlightenment.

4. Libraries should cooperate with all persons and groups concerned with resisting abridgment of free expression and free access to ideas.

5. A person's right to use a library should not be denied or abridged because of origin, age, background, or views.

6. Libraries which make exhibit spaces and meeting rooms available to the public they serve should make such facilities available on an equitable basis, regardless of the beliefs or affiliations of individuals or groups requesting their use.

Adopted June 18, 1948. Amended February 2, 1961, June 27, 1967, and January 23, 1980, by the ALA Council.

OFFICIAL INTERPRETATIONS OF
THE LIBRARY BILL OF RIGHTS

*The following interpretation was approved unanimously Jan. 27 at the 1982
ALA Mid-winter meeting.*

Administrative Policies and Procedures Affecting Access to Library Resources and Services

The right of free access to information for all individuals is basic to all aspects of library service regardless of type of library. Article 5 of the LIBRARY BILL OF RIGHTS protects the rights of an individual to use a library regardless of origin, age, background, or views. The central thrust of the LIBRARY BILL OF RIGHTS is to protect and encourage the free flow of information and ideas. The American Library Association urges that all libraries set policies and procedures that reflect the basic tenets of the LIBRARY BILL OF RIGHTS.

Many libraries have adopted administrative policies and procedures regulating access to resources, services, and facilities, i.e., specific collections, reference services, interlibrary loan, programming, meeting rooms, exhibit space. Such policies and procedures governing the order and protection of library materials and facilities, and the planning of library programs and exhibits, could become a convenient means for removing or restricting access to controversial materials, limiting access to programs or exhibits, or for discriminating against specific groups of library patrons. Such abuse of administrative procedures and policies is in opposition to the LIBRARY BILL OF RIGHTS.

The American Library Association recommends that all libraries with rare or special collections formulate policies and procedures for such collections so as not to restrict access and use due to age or the nature of the patron interest in the materials. Restricted access to such collections is solely for the protection of the materials, and must in no way limit access to the information and ideas contained in the materials.

The "Model Interlibrary Loan Code for Regional, State, Local, or Other Special Groups of Libraries" of the American Library Association recommends that all library patrons be eligible for interlibrary loan, in accordance with Article 5 of the LIBRARY BILL OF RIGHTS and the statement FREE ACCESS TO LIBRARIES FOR MINORS. The Model Interlibrary Loan Code states the importance of considering the needs and interests of all users, including children and young adults. Borrowing libraries should provide the resources to meet the ordinary needs of all of their primary clientele, and any members of their clientele should be eligible for interlibrary loan. When libraries adhere to the Model Interlibrary Loan Code, access to information is protected.

Library administrative policies should examine all restrictions to resources or services associated with age, as all are violations of Article 5 of the LIBRARY BILL OF RIGHTS and the statement on restricted access to library materials. For example, privileges associated with library cards should be consistent for all library users, no matter what the age. Library policies in which certain patrons, usually minors, are denied library privileges available to other library patrons are not endorsed by the American Library Association, as they violate Article 5 of the LIBRARY BILL OF RIGHTS, as well as the statement on FREE ACCESS TO LIBRARIES FOR MINORS. It is parents and only parents who may restrict their children—and only their children—from access to library materials and services.

Reference service policies and procedures, such as library policies limiting the time spent on answering telephone reference questions, should provide for equitable service to all library patrons, regardless of age or type of question. These policies must apply to both adult and child patrons.

Policies governing the use of meeting rooms and exhibits should be examined to ensure that minors are not excluded from a program of interest to them based on age. Meeting rooms and exhibit spaces should also be available on an "equitable basis, regardless of the beliefs or affiliations of individuals or groups requesting their use," and should not be denied to anyone based solely on age.

Policies should reflect that a person's right to attend a library initiated program "should not be denied or abridged because of origin, age, background, or views," as stated in LIBRARY INITIATED PROGRAMS AS A RESOURCE, an Interpretation of the LIBRARY BILL OF RIGHTS.

SCHOOL LIBRARY BILL OF RIGHTS—
for School Library Media Center Programs

Approved by American Association of School Librarians Board of Directors, Atlantic City, 1969.

The American Association of School Librarians reaffirms its belief in the Library Bill of Rights of the American Library Association. Media personnel are concerned with generating understanding of American freedoms through the development of informed and responsible citizens. To this end the American Association of School Librarians asserts that the responsibility of the school library media center is:

To provide a comprehensive collection of instructional materials selected in compliance with basic written selection principles, and to provide maximum accessibility to these materials.

To provide materials that will support the curriculum, taking into consideration the individual's needs, and the varied interests, abilities, socio-economic backgrounds, and maturity levels of the students served.

To provide materials for teachers and students that will encourage growth in knowledge, and that will develop literary, cultural and aesthetic appreciation, and ethical standards.

To provide materials which reflect the ideas and beliefs of religious, social, political, historical, and ethnic groups and their contribution to the

American and world heritage and culture, thereby enabling students to develop an intellectual integrity in forming judgments.

To provide a written statement, approved by the local Boards of Education, of the procedures for meeting the challenge of censorship of materials in school library media centers.

To provide qualified professional personnel to serve teachers and students.

LIBRARIANS' CODE OF ETHICS

Introduction. Since 1939, the American Library Association has recognized the importance of codifying and making known to the public and the profession the principles which guide librarians in action. This latest revision of the CODE OF ETHICS reflects changes in the nature of the profession and in its social and institutional environment. It should be revised and augmented as necessary.

Librarians significantly influence or control the selection, organization, preservation, and dissemination of information. In a political system grounded in an informed citizenry, librarians are members of a profession explicitly committed to intellectual freedom and the freedom of access to information. We have a special obligation to ensure the free flow of information and ideas to present and future generations.

Librarians are dependent upon one another for the bibliographical resources that enable us to provide information services, and have obligations for maintaining the highest level of personal integrity and competence.

1. Librarians must provide the highest level of service through appropriate and usefully organized collections, fair and equitable circulation and service policies, and skillful, accurate, unbiased, and courteous responses to all requests for assistance.

2. Librarians must resist all efforts by groups or individuals to censor library materials.

3. Librarians must protect each user's right to privacy with respect to information sought or received, and materials consulted, borrowed, or acquired.

4. Librarians must adhere to the principles of due process and equality of opportunity in peer relationships and personnel actions.

5. Librarians must distinguish clearly in their actions and statements between their personal philosophies and attitudes and those of an institution or professional body.

6. Librarians must avoid situations in which personal interests might be served or financial benefits gained at the expense of library users, colleagues, or the employing institution.

Adopted by ALA Council, June 30, 1981.

AECT CODE OF ETHICS*

Preamble

1. The Code of Ethics contained here in shall be considered to be principles of ethics. These principles are intended to aid members individually and collectively in maintaining a high level of professional conduct.

2. The Professional Ethics Committee will build documentation of opinion (interpretive briefs or ramifications of intent) relating to specific ethical statements enumerated herein.

3. Opinions may be generated in response to specific cases brought before the Professional Ethics Committee.

4. Amplification and/or clarification of the ethical principles may be generated by the Committee in response to a request submitted by a member.

Section I. Commitment to the Individual

In fulfilling obligations to the individual, the members:

1. Shall encourage independent action in an individual's pursuit of learning and shall provide access to varying points of view.

2. Shall protect the individual rights of access to materials of varying points of view.

3. Shall guarantee to each individual the opportunity to participate in any appropriate program.

4. Shall conduct professional business so as to protect the privacy and maintain the personal integrity of the individual.

5. Shall follow sound professional procedures for evaluation and selection of materials and equipment.

6. Shall make reasonable effort to protect the individual from conditions harmful to health and safety.

7. Shall promote current and sound professional practices in the use of technology in education.

8. Shall in the design and selection of any educational program or media seek to avoid content that reinforces or promotes sexual, ethnic, racial, or religious stereotypes. Shall seek to encourage the development of programs and media that emphasize the diversity of our society as a multicultural community.

*Used with permission of the Association for Educational Communications and Technology.

Section II. Commitment to Society

In fulfilling obligations to society, the member:

1. Shall honestly represent the institution or organization with which that person is affiliated, and shall take adequate precautions to distinguish between personal and institutional or organizational views.
2. Shall represent accurately and truthfully the facts concerning educational matters in direct and indirect public expressions.
3. Shall not use institutional or Associational privileges for private gain.
4. Shall accept no gratitudes, gifts, or favors that might impair or appear to impair professional judgment, or offer any favor, service, or thing of value to obtain special advantage.
5. Shall engage in fair and equitable practices with those rendering service to the profession.

Section III. Commitment to the Profession

In fulfilling obligations to the profession, the member:

1. Shall accord just and equitable treatment to all members of the profession in terms of professional rights and responsibilities.
2. Shall not use coercive means to promise special treatment in order to influence professional decisions of colleagues.
3. Shall avoid commercial exploitation of that person's membership in the Association.
4. Shall strive continually to improve professional knowledge and skill and to make available to patrons and colleagues the benefit of that person's professional attainments.
5. Shall present honestly professional qualifications and the evaluations of colleagues.
6. Shall conduct professional business through proper channels.
7. Shall delegate assigned tasks only to qualified personnel. Qualified personnel are those who have appropriate training or credentials and/or who can demonstrate competency in performing the task.
8. Shall inform users of the stipulations and interpretations of the copyright law and other laws affecting the profession and encourage compliance.
9. Shall observe all laws relating to or affecting the profession; shall report, without hesitation, illegal or unethical conduct of fellow members of the profession to the AECT Professional Ethics Committee; shall participate in professional inquiry when requested by the Association.

FREEDOM TO READ STATEMENT

The freedom to read is essential to our democracy. It is under attack. Private groups and public authorities in various parts of the country are working to remove books from sale, to censor textbooks, to label "controversial" books, to distribute lists of "objectionable" books or authors, and to purge libraries. These actions apparently rise from a view that our national tradition of free expression is no longer valid; that censorship and repression are needed to avoid the subversion of politics and the corruption of morals. We, as citizens devoted to the use of books and as librarians and publishers responsible for disseminating them, wish to assert the public interest in the preservation of the freedom to read.

We are deeply concerned about these attempts at suppression. Most such attempts rest on a denial of the fundamental premise of democracy: that the ordinary citizen, by exercising his critical judgment, will accept the good and reject the bad. The censors, public and private, assume that they should determine what is good and what is bad for their fellow citizens.

We trust Americans to recognize propaganda, and to reject obscenity. We do not believe they need the help of censors to assist them in this task. We do not believe they are prepared to sacrifice their heritage of a free press in order to be "protected" against what others think may be bad for them. We believe they still favor free enterprise in ideas and expression.

We are aware, of course, that books are not alone in being subjected to efforts at suppression. We are aware that these efforts are related to a larger pattern of pressures being brought against education, the press, films, radio and television. The problem is not only one of actual censorship. The shadow of fear cast by these pressures leads, we suspect, to an even larger voluntary curtailment of expression by those who seek to avoid controversy.

Such pressure toward conformity is perhaps natural to a time of uneasy change and pervading fear. Especially when so many of our apprehensions are directed against an ideology, the expression of a dissident idea becomes a thing feared in itself, and we tend to move against it as against a hostile deed, with suppression.

And yet suppression is never more dangerous than in such a time of social tension. Freedom has given the United States the elasticity to endure strain. Freedom keeps open the path of novel and creative solutions, and enables change to come by choice. Every silencing of a heresy, every enforcement of an orthodoxy, diminishes the toughness and resilience of our society and leaves it the less able to deal with stress.

Now as always in our history, books are among our greatest instruments of freedom. They are almost the only means for making generally available ideas or manners of expression that can initially command only a small audience. They are the natural medium for the new idea and the untried voice from which come the original contributions to social growth. They are essential to the extended discussion which serious thought requires, and to the accumulation of knowledge and ideas into organized collections.

We believe that free communication is essential to the preservation of a free

society and a creative culture. We believe that these pressures towards conformity present the danger of limiting the range and variety of inquiry and expression on which our democracy and our culture depend. We believe that
every American community must jealously guard the freedom to publish and
to circulate, in order to preserve its own freedom to read. We believe that
publishers and librarians have a profound responsibility to give validity to
that freedom to read by making it possible for the readers to choose freely
from a variety of offerings.

The freedom to read is guaranteed by the Constitution. Those with faith in
free men and will stand firm on these constitutional guarantees of essential
rights and will exercise the responsibilities that accompany these rights.

We therefore affirm these propositions:

*1. It is in the public interest for publishers and librarians to make available
the widest diversity of views and expressions, including those which are un-
orthodox or unpopular with the majority.*

Creative thought is by definition new, and what is new is different. The
bearer of every new thought is a rebel until his idea is refined and tested.
Totalitarian systems attempt to maintain themselves in power by the ruthless
suppression of any concept which challenges the established orthodoxy. The
power of a democratic system to adapt to change is vastly strengthened by the
freedom of its citizens to choose widely from among conflicting opinions
offered freely to them. To stifle every nonconformist idea at birth would mark
the end of the democratic process. Furthermore, only through the constant
activity of weighing and selecting can the democratic mind attain the strength
demanded by times like these. We need to know not only what we believe but
why we believe it.

*2. Publishers and librarians do not need to endorse every idea or presentation
contained in the books they make available. It would conflict with the public interest for them to establish their own political, moral or aesthetic views as the
sole standard for determining what books should be published or circulated.*

Publishers and librarians serve the educational process by helping to make
available knowledge and ideas required for the growth of the mind and the increase of learning. They do not foster education by imposing as mentors the
patterns of their own thought. The people should have the freedom to read and
consider a broader range of ideas than those that may be held by any single
librarian or publisher or government or church. It is wrong that what one man
can read should be confined to what another thinks proper.

*3. It is contrary to the public interest for publishers or librarians to deter-
mine the acceptability of a book solely on the basis of the personal history or
political affiliations of the author.*

A book should be judged as a book. No art or literature can flourish if it is to
be measured by the political views or private lives of its creators. No society of
free men can flourish which draws up lists of writers to whom it will not listen,
whatever they may have to say.

4. The present laws dealing with obscenity should be vigorously enforced. Beyond that, there is no place in our society for extralegal efforts to coerce the taste of others, to confine adults to the reading matter deemed suitable for adolescents, or to inhibit the efforts of writers to achieve artistic expression.

To some, much of modern literature is shocking. But is not much of life itself shocking? We cut off literature at the source if we prevent serious artists from dealing with the stuff of life. Parents and teachers have a responsibility to prepare the young to meet the diversity of experiences in life to which they will be exposed, as they have a responsibility to help them learn to think critically for themselves. These are affirmative responsibilities, not to be discharged simply by preventing them from reading works for which they are not yet prepared. In these matters taste differs, and taste cannot be legislated; nor can machinery be devised which will suit the demands of one group without limiting the freedom of others. We deplore the catering to the immature, the retarded or the maladjusted taste. But those concerned with freedom have the responsibility of seeing to it that each individual book or publication, whatever its contents, price or method of distribution, is dealt with in accordance with due process of law.

5. It is not in the public interest to force a reader to accept with any book the prejudgment of a label characterizing the book or author as subversive or dangerous.

The idea of labeling presupposes the existence of individuals or groups with wisdom to determine by authority what is good or bad for the citizen. It presupposes that each individual must be directed in making up his mind about the ideas he examines. But Americans do not need others to do their thinking for them.

6. It is the responsibility of publishers and librarians, as guardians of the people's freedom to read, to contest encroachments upon that freedom by individuals or groups seeking to impose their own standards or tastes upon the community at large.

It is inevitable in the give and take of the democratic process that the political, the moral, or the aesthetic concepts of an individual or group will occasionally collide with those of another individual or group. In a free society each individual is free to determine for himself what he wishes to read, and each group is free to determine what it will recommend to its freely associated members. But no group has the right to take the law into its own hands, and to impose its own concept of politics or morality upon other members of a democratic society. Freedom is no freedom if it is accorded only to the accepted and the inoffensive.

7. It is the responsibility of publishers and librarians to give full meaning to the freedom to read by providing books that enrich the quality of thought and expression. By the exercise of this affirmative responsibility, bookmen can demonstrate that the answer to a bad book is a good one, the answer to a bad idea is a good one.

The freedom to read is of little consequence when expended on the trivial; it is frustrated when the reader cannot obtain matter fit for his purpose. What is needed is not only the absence of restraint, but the positive provision of opportunity for the people to read the best that has been thought and said. Books are the major channel by which the intellectual inheritance is handed down, and the principal means of its testing and growth. The defense of their freedom and integrity, and the enlargement of their service to society, requires of all bookmen the utmost of their faculties, and deserves of all citizens the fullest of their support.

We state these propositions neither lightly nor as easy generalizations. We here stake out a lofty claim for the value of books. We do so because we believe that they are good, possessed of enormous variety and usefulness, worthy of cherishing and keeping free. We realize that the application of these propositions may mean the dissemination of ideas and manners of expression that are repugnant to many persons. We do not state these propositions in the comfortable belief that what people read is unimportant. We believe rather that what people read is deeply important; that ideas can be dangerous; but that the suppression of ideas is fatal to a democratic society. Freedom itself is a dangerous way of life, but it is ours.

Adopted June 25, 1953, by the ALA Council.
Endorsed by:
AMERICAN LIBRARY ASSOCIATION *Council, June 25, 1953*
AMERICAN BOOK PUBLISHERS COUNCIL *Board of Directors, June 18, 1953*

Subsequently Endorsed by:
AMERICAN BOOKSELLERS ASSOCIATION *Board of Directors*
BOOK MANUFACTURERS' INSTITUTE *Board of Directors*
NATIONAL EDUCATION ASSOCIATION *Commission for the Defense of Democracy through Education*

CITIZEN'S REQUEST FORM FOR REEVALUATION OF LEARNING RESOURCE CENTER MATERIALS

Initiated by _____

  Telephone _____ Address _____

REPRESENTING
  Self _____ Organization or group _____
                                             (name)

  School _____

MATERIAL QUESTIONED
  BOOK: author _____ title _____

  _____ copyright date _____

  AV MATERIAL: kind of media _____
                                  (film, filmstrip, record, etc.)

  title _____

  OTHER MATERIAL: identify _____

Please respond to the following questions. If sufficient space is not provided, please use additional sheet of paper.
1. Have you seen or read this material in its entirety? _____
2. To what do you object? Please cite specific passages, pages, etc. _____
3. What do you believe is the main idea of this material? _____
4. What do you feel might result from use of this material? _____
5. What reviews of this material have you read? _____
6. For what other age group might this be suitable? _____
7. What action do you recommend that the school take on this material? _____
8. In its place, what material do you recommend that would provide adequate information on the subject? _____

_____   _____
Date   Signature

INDEX

Acoustics. *See* Environment in school library media center
Acquisitions, 266–282
  records, 293–294
Acts of Congress supporting libraries, 343–345
Agency cooperation, 56–57
American Association of School Librarians (AASL), 11, 13, 17, 28, 74, 115, 335
American Education, 70
American Library Association (ALA), 1, 4, 6, 7, 8, 20, 74, 115, 117, 128, 137, 164, 335
American Society for Information Science (ASIS), 337–339
Association for Educational Communications and Technology (AECT), 13, 17, 28, 115, 338–339
Associations influencing the media center, 333–345
Audiocards, 203–204
Audiovisuals
  equipment and standards, 11, 216–225
  material selection, 201–202, 306
  specialists, 101, 102–103, 104–108, 116

Best Books for Children, 167
Bibliographic tools, 159
Bibliographic utilities, 289–290
Bibliographies for selection aids, 168
Bidding, 266–272
Book clubs, 174
Book fairs, 316–319
Book selection, 184–188
The Booklist, 167, 195

Books for Elementary School Libraries, 167
Budgets, 68–97
  systems, 86–94
  see also Acquisitions

Canadian Library Association, 131
Canadian School Library Association, 11
Catalog Cards, 288
Cataloging, 282, 284–294
Cataloging Audiovisual Materials, 291
Censorship, 15–16, 177–179
Center for Education Improvement (CEI), 344
Certain, Charles C., 6–8
Certain reports, 6–9
Certification requirements, standards, 9–10, 115–117
Children, media center services to, 5; *see also* School library media center, services
CIP program, 285–287
Circulation, 302–307
Classification, 282–283
Clerks. *See* Nonprofessional staff
Clinton, DeWitt, 1
Clippings, 189
Collections, 1, 2, 3, 5, 6, 7, 16, 25–29, 75–76, 139–143; *see also* Acquisitions; Managerial concerns; Media selection; Organizing collections, programs
Color in the media center. *See* Environment in school library media center
Combined Book Exhibit, 339

Community and the media center,
    55-56, 76, 157
Computer use, 238-262
Consortium of University Film Centers,
    339-340
Converting to a media center, 29-30
Cooperative Study of Secondary School
    Standards, 8
Coordinators, 101-102, 106-108, 119-
    120, 124
Copyright concerns, 298-299
Cost-allocation methods, 85-86
Criteria for media selection, 182-237
Curriculum. *See* School library media
    center, curriculum

Dalton Plan, 6
Dana, John Cotton, 4
Databases, 323; *see also* Computer use
Department of Audiovisual Instruction
    (DAVI), NEA, 11, 13; *see also* Asso-
    ciation for Educational Communica-
    tions and Technology (AECT)
"Development of Secondary School
    Libraries" (Greenman), 4
Dewey, John, 6
Dewey, Melvil, and classification sys-
    tem, 2, 3, 283, 285
Director, media center, 101-102
Douglas, Mary P., 8
Draper, Andrew S., 3

Education
    Department of, office of, 69-70, 120,
        345
    growth of public, 6-12
    U.S. Bureau of, 2
Education Consolidation and Improve-
    ment Act (ECIA), 343
Educational materials, selecting, 182-215
Educational Products Information
    Exchange (EPIE), 340
Educational Resources Information
    Center (ERIC), 340-341
Educators Guide to Free Filmstrips, 195
Electricity. *See* Environment in school
    library media center
Elementary and Secondary Education
    Act (ESEA), 11-12, 343
Elementary School Library, The, 8
Elementary School Library Standards.
    See Certain reports
Elementary School Media Programs, 20
Ellsworth, Ralph, 166

English Journal, 167
Environment in school library media
    center, 144-150
Equipment, 294-298; *see also* School
    library media center, equipment
Evaluative Criteria, 8

Facilities, 135-154
Facts on File, 70
Faculty and the specialist, 158
Federal agencies, 343-345
Film selection, services, 153-154,
    190-193
*Financial Accounting . . . for Local and
    State School Systems*, 78, 79
Footage. *See* Space requirements
Franklin, Ben, 1
Functions of the media center, 19-30
Funding, 69-71
Furnishings, 150-153

Games, educational, 209-210
Gardiner, Jewel, 8
Government document acquisition and
    selection, 190, 280
Graphics selection, 208-209

Hall, M. E., 5
Higher Education Act, 343

Implementation of the White House
    Conference Resolutions, Ad Hoc
    Committee on, 15
*Index to Educational Overhead Trans-
    parencies*, 201
Index to 35mm Filmstrips, 194-195
Information for the 80's, 15
Instruction in the media center. *See*
    School library media center, instruc-
    tion
Instructional materials, 143-144
Instructional TV, 74
*Instrument for Self-Evaluating an Edu-
    cational Media Program in School
    Systems, An*, 28
Intellectual freedom documents, 164
Intellectual Freedom Newsletter, 164,
    172
Inventory, 307-309, 312-313

Job descriptions, staff, 110–115
Johnson, B. Lamar, 8
Joint Council on Educational Telecommunications (JCET), 341

Knapp School Libraries Project, 12, 74

Languages, computer. *See* Computer use
Laws and the library, 1–17
Learning theories, 12–13
Librarianship
   certification, 9–10
   training, 10
Libraries
   public, 2, 5
   school, development of, 1–17
The Library in General Education, 8
The Library in the School (Fargo), 8
Library Journal, 2, 4, 5, 287
Library of Congress and systems, 283, 287–289, 322, 341–342
Library Services and Construction Act, 343
Lighting. *See* Environment in school library media center
Listening areas, 138–139
Logasa, Hannah, 8

Magazine acquisition and selection, 188–189, 276–278
Maintenance of collection and equipment, 144, 309–310
Managerial concerns, 304–319
Mann, Horace, 1
Manuals and guides, staff, 128
Maps and globes, 212–213
MARC database, 285, 286
Materials, local production of, 294–298
Media Programs: District and School, 13, 14, 28, 115
Media selection, 156–179, 182–237
Meeting Information Needs of the 80's, 131
Microcomputers. *See* Computer use
Microform acquisition and selection, 196–200, 279–280
Microslides, 215
Models, 214
Monopoly items, 278
Motion picture selection. *See* Film selection, services
Multimedia kits, 209–210

National Audiovisual Center (NAC), 342
National Center for Audio Tapes (NCAT), 342
National Center for Education Statistics, 16, 344
National Commission on Excellence in Education (NCEE), 344–345
National Commission on Libraries and Information Science (NCLIS), 14, 15, 131
National Council of Teachers of English, 6
National Defense Education Act (NDEA), 11, 74, 343
National Education Association (NEA), 4, 6, 7, 8, 11, 105
National Endowment for the Humanities, 74
National Information Center for Educational Media (NICEM), 194, 201, 342–343
National Institute of Education (NIE), 343, 344
National Newspaper Index database, 70
Networking, 322–331
Newark (N.J.) Circulation System, 302–303
Newspaper selection, 188–189
New York State, as model for library legislation, 1–5
New York Times database
Nonprofessional staff, 104–105, 106–108, 109–110

Opaque projection, 214–215
Ordering. *See* Acquisitions
Organizing collections, programs, 282–299, 160–163

Pamphlets, and acquisition of, 189, 278–279
Paraprofessionals, 103–104, 108–109
Periodicals, computer, 259–260
Personnel. *See* Staff in the school library media center
Phonograph selection, 202–203
Planning a center, 136
A Planning Guide for the High School Library, 8
Planning Programming Budgeting System (PPBS), 69, 86, 94, 96
Policy statement, 163–165
Politics and the school library media center, 346–347

Processing, 274–276, 280–282, 294
Professional staff, 101–103
Programmed materials, 210–212
Programs
  city, district, system, 122–124
  computer. *See* Computer use
  federal, state, 120–121
  see also School library media center,
    programs
*Public Libraries in the United States of
  America*, 2
Public relations, 51–57
*Public School Library Statistics for
  1958-59*, 10–11
Publications of associations, 336–337,
  338, 339
Publicizing the school library media
  center, 48–49
Purchasing, 272–274

Radio in broadcasts, media centers,
  153–154, 204
Reader's Guide, 35, 189
Reading areas, 138–139
Reading shelf, 347–349
Realia, 215
Records and reports, 310–316
Recruitment, staff, 117–119
*Report of the Task Force on the Role of
  the School Library Media Program
  in Networking*, 14–15, 322
Resources of the school library media
  center. *See* School library media
  center, resources
Reviewing tools, 159

*School Libraries for Today and Tomor-
  row*, 8
The School Library (Ellsworth), 166
School Library Journal, 167, 195, 287
School library media center
  attendance, 49–51
  budget, 68–97
  and community, 55–56, 76, 157
  curriculum, 33–34, 76, 78, 158–159
  emergence of, 12–17
  equipment, 25–29, 139–143, 144
  evaluating, 57–63
  facilities, 135–154
  functions, 19–30
  hours of service, 49–51
  instruction, 33–63
  media selection, 156–179, 182–237

  programs, 33–63, 160–163
  public relations, 51–57
  publicity, 48–49
  resources, 25–29
  services, 20–25
  staff, 100–131
  standards, 74–75
  students, 34–47, 53–54, 157–158
  tasks, 105–110
*School Library Personnel Task Analysis
  Survey*, 105
"Score Card for School Libraries," 7–8
The Secondary School Library, 8
Selection aids, 166–177
Senior High School Library Catalog, 167
*Services of Secondary School Media
  Centers, Evaluation and Develop-
  ment* (Gaver), 20
Shelf lists, 293–294
Skinner, B. F., 12
Slide selection, 195–196
Space requirements, 137–138
Specialists, school library media center,
  101–103, 104–108, 116–117
  offices, 142
Staff evaluation, selection, 117–127
Staff in the school library media center,
  100–131
*Standard Library Organization and
  Equipment for Secondary Schools.
  See* Certain reports
Standards for School Library Programs,
  115
Standards for School Media Programs,
  13
*Standards of Library Service for Cana-
  dian Schools*, 11
Standards of Media Selection, 165–166
Standing orders, 278
State agencies, 345–346
Storage areas, 142–143
Students in the school library media
  center, 34–47, 53, 54, 157–158
Supervision. *See* Staff evaluation

Tape selection, 203
Task Analysis Survey Instrument,
  105–110
Taxes for libraries, 2, 3
Technicians. *See* Nonprofessional staff
Television in the media center, 153–154,
  204–205
Television Information Office, 343
Theft-detection devices, 306–307
Thorndike, E. L., 12

Title II, 11–12
Towards a National Program for Library and Information Services, 14
Transparency selection, 200–201

User activities, 21–25

Vendors. *See* Bidding
Vertical files, 303

Viewing areas, 138–139
Volunteers. *See* Nonprofessional staff

Weeding, 307–309
White House Conference on Library and Information Science, 15
Winnetka Plan, 6
Wofford, Azile, 8
Word processing. *See* Computer use